THE JOURNAL

OF

NEGRO HISTORY

CARTER G. WOODSON
EDITOR

VOLUME I

ISBN: 978-1-63923-844-6

Printed: March 2023

Published and Distributed By:
Lushena Books
607 Country Club Drive, Unit E
Bensenville, IL 60106
www.lushenabks.com

ISBN: 978-1-63923-844-6

CONTENTS OF VOLUME I

VOL. I., No. 4.   OCTOBER, 1916.

THE JOURNAL

OF

NEGRO HISTORY

VOL. I—JANUARY, 1916—No. 1

THE NEGROES OF CINCINNATI PRIOR TO THE CIVIL WAR

The study of the history of the Negroes of Cincinnati is unusually important for the reason that from no other annals do we get such striking evidence that the colored people generally thrive when encouraged by their white neighbors. This story is otherwise significant when we consider the fact that about a fourth of the persons of color settling in the State of Ohio during the first half of the last century made their homes in this city. Situated on a north bend of the Ohio where commerce breaks bulk, Cincinnati rapidly developed, attracting both foreigners and Americans, among whom were not a few Negroes. Exactly how many persons of color were in this city during the first decade of the nineteenth century is not yet known. It has been said that there were no Negroes in Hamilton County in 1800.[1] It is evident, too, that the real exodus of free Negroes and fugitives from the South to the Northwest Territory did not begin prior to 1815, although their attention had been earlier directed to this section as a more desirable place for colonization than the shores of Africa.[2] As the reaction following the era of good feeling toward the Negroes during the revolutionary period had not reached its climax free per-

[1] Quillin, "The Color Line in Ohio," 18.
[2] "Tyrannical Libertymen," 10–11; Locke, "Antislavery," 31–32; Branagan, "Serious Remonstrance," 18.

sons of color had been content to remain in the South.[3] The
unexpected immigration of these Negroes into this section
and the last bold effort made to drive them out marked
epochs in their history in this city. The history of these
people prior to the Civil War, therefore, falls into three
periods, one of toleration from 1800 to 1826, one of persecution from 1826 to 1841, and one of amelioration from 1841
to 1861.

In the beginning the Negroes were not a live issue in
Cincinnati. The question of their settlement in that community was debated but resulted in great diversity of opinion rather than a fixedness of judgment among the citizens.
The question came up in the Constitutional Convention of
1802 and provoked some discussion, but reaching no decision, the convention simply left the Negroes out of the
pale of the newly organized body politic, discriminating
against them together with Indians and foreigners, by in-
corporating the word white into the fundamental law.[4] The
legislature to which the disposition of this question was
left, however, took it up in 1804 to calm the fears of those
who had more seriously considered the so-called menace of
Negro immigration. This body enacted a law, providing
that no Negro or mulatto should be allowed to remain permanently in that State, unless he could furnish a certificate
of freedom issued by some court in the United States.
Negroes then living there had to be registered before the
following June, giving the names of their children. No man
could employ a Negro who could not show such a certificate.
Hiring a delinquent black or harboring or hindering the
capture of a runaway was punishable by a fine of $50 and
the owner of a fugitive thus illegally employed could recover
fifty cents a day for the services of his slave.[5]

As the fear of Negro immigration increased the law of
1804 was found to be inadequate. In 1807, therefore, the
legislature enacted another measure providing that no
Negro should be permitted to settle in Ohio unless he could

[3] Woodson, "The Education of the Negro Prior to 1861," 230–231.
[4] Constitution, Article I, Sections 2, 6.
[5] Laws of Ohio, II, 63.

within twenty days give a bond to the amount of $500, guaranteeing his good behavior and support. The fine for concealing a fugitive was raised from $50 to $100, one half of which should go to the informer. Negro evidence against the white man was prohibited.[6] This law together with that of 1830 making the Negro ineligible for service in the State militia, that of 1831 depriving persons of color of the privilege of serving upon juries, and that of 1838 prohibiting the education of colored children at the expense of the State, constituted what were known as the "Black Laws."[7]

Up to 1826, however, the Negroes of Cincinnati had not become a cause of much trouble. Very little mention of them is made in the records of this period. They were not wanted in this city but were tolerated as a negligible factor. D. B. Warden, a traveler through the West in 1819, observed that the blacks of Cincinnati were "good-humoured, garrulous, and profligate, generally disinclined to laborious occupations, and prone to the performance of light and menial drudgery." Here the traveler was taking effect for cause. "Some few," said he, "exercise the humbler trades, and some appear to have formed a correct conception of the objects and value of property, and are both industrious and economical. A large proportion of them are reputed, and perhaps correctly, to be habituated to petit larceny." But this had not become a grave offence, for he said that not more than one individual had been corporally punished by the courts since the settlement of the town.[8]

When, however, the South reached the conclusion that free Negroes were an evil, and Quakers and philanthropists began to direct these unfortunates to the Northwest Territory for colonization, a great commotion arose in Southern Ohio and especially in Cincinnati.[9] How rapid this movement was, may be best observed by noticing the statistics of

[6] Laws of Ohio, V, 53.
[7] Hickok, "The Negro in Ohio," 41, 42.
[8] Warden, "Statistical, Political and Historical Account of the United States of North America," 264.
[9] Quillin, "The Color Line in Ohio," 32.

this period. There were 337 Negroes in Ohio in 1800; 1,890 in 1810; 4,723 in 1820; 9,586 in 1830; 17,342 in 1840; and 25,279 in 1850.[10] Now Cincinnati had 410 Negroes in 1819;[11] 690 in 1826;[12] 2,255 in 1840;[13] and 3,237 in 1850.[14]

It was during the period between 1826 and 1840 that Cincinnati had to grapple with the problem of the immigrating Negroes and the poor whites from the uplands of Virginia and Kentucky. With some ill-informed persons the question was whether that section should be settled by white men or Negroes. The situation became more alarming when the Southern philanthropic minority sometimes afforded a man like a master of Pittsylvania County, Virginia, who settled 70 freedmen in Lawrence County, Ohio, in one day.[15] It became unusually acute in Cincinnati because of the close social and commercial relations between that city and the slave States. Early in the nineteenth century Cincinnati became a manufacturing center to which the South learned to look for supplies of machinery, implements, furniture, and food.[16] The business men prospering thereby were not advocates of slavery but rather than lose trade by acquiring the reputation of harboring fugitive slaves or frightening away whites by encouraging the immigration of Negroes, they began to assume the attitude of driving the latter from those parts.

From this time until the forties the Negroes were a real issue in Cincinnati. During the late twenties they not only had to suffer from the legal disabilities provided in the "Black Laws," but had to withstand the humiliation of a rigid social ostracism.[17] They were regarded as intruders and denounced as an idle, profligate and criminal class with

[10] The Census of the United States, from 1800 to 1850.

[11] Flint's Letters in Thwaite's "Early Western Travels," IX, 239.

[12] Cist, "Cincinnati in 1841," 37; *Cincinnati Daily Gazette*, Sept. 14, 1841.

[13] *Ibid.*

[14] United States Census, 1850.

[15] *Ohio State Journal*, May 3, 1827; *African Repository*, III, 254.

[16] Abdy, "Journal of a Tour in the United States," III, 62.

[17] Jay, "Miscellaneous Writings on Slavery," 27, 373, 385, 387; Minutes of the Convention of the Colored People of Ohio, 1849.

whom a self-respecting white man could not afford to associate. Their children were not permitted to attend the
public schools and few persons braved the inconveniences of
living under the stigma of teaching a "nigger school."
Negroes were not welcome in the white churches and when
they secured admission thereto they had to go to the "black
pew." Colored ministers were treated with very little consideration by the white clergy as they feared that they
might lose caste and be compelled to give up their churches.
The colored people made little or no effort to go to white
theaters or hotels and did not attempt to ride in public con-
veyances on equal footing with members of the other race.
Not even white and colored children dared to play together
to the extent that such was permitted in the South.[18]

This situation became more serious when it extended to
pursuits of labor. White laborers there, as in other Northern cities during this period, easily reached the position of
thinking that it was a disgrace to work with Negroes. This
prejudice was so much more inconvenient to the Negroes of
Cincinnati than elsewhere because of the fact that most of
the menial labor in that city was done by Germans and
Irishmen. Now, since the Negroes could not follow ordinary
menial occupations there was nothing left them but the
lowest form of "drudgery," for which employers often preferred colored women. It was, therefore, necessary in some
cases for the mother to earn the living for the family because
the father could get nothing to do. A colored man could not
serve as an ordinary drayman or porter without subjecting
his employer to a heavy penalty.[19]

The trades unions were then proscribing the employment
of colored mechanics. Many who had worked at skilled
labor were by this prejudice forced to do drudgery or find
employment in other cities. The president of a "mechanical
association" was publicly tried in 1830 by that organization
for the crime of assisting a colored youth to learn a trade.[20]

[18] Barber, "A Report on the Condition of the Colored People of Ohio,"
1840.
[19] Proceedings of the Ohio Antislavery Convention, 1835, 19.
[20] Ibid.

A young man of 'high character, who had at the cabinet-
making trade in Kentucky saved enough to purchase his
freedom, came to Cincinnati about this time, seeking employment. He finally found a position in a shop conducted
by an Englishman. On entering the establishment, however,
the workmen threw down their tools, declaring that the
Negro had to leave or that they would. The unfortunate
"intruder" was accordingly dismissed. He then entered
the employ of a slave holder, who at the close of the Negro's
two years of service at common labor discovered that the
black was a mechanic. The employer then procured work
for him as a rough carpenter. By dint of perseverance and
industry this Negro within a few years became a master
workman, employing at times six or eight men, but he never
received a single job of work from a native-born citizen
from a free State.[21]

The hardships of the Negroes of this city, however, had
just begun. The growth of a prejudiced public opinion led
not only to legal proscription and social ostracism but also
to open persecution. With the cries of the Southerners for
the return of fugitives and the request of white immigrants
for the exclusion of Negroes from that section, came the
demand to solve the problem by enforcing the "Black
Laws." Among certain indulgent officials these enactments
had been allowed to fall into desuetude. These very demands, however, brought forward friends as well as enemies
of the colored people. Their first clash was testing the
constitutionality of the law of 1807. When the question
came up before the Supreme Court, this measure was
upheld.[22] Encouraged by such support, the foes of the
Negroes forced an execution of the law. The courts at first
hesitated but finally took the position that the will of the
people should be obeyed. The Negroes asked for ninety
days to comply with the law and were given sixty. When
the allotted time had expired, however, many of them had
not given bonds as required. The only thing to do then was

[21] Proceedings of the Ohio Antislavery Convention, 1835, 19.
[22] *African Repository*, V, 185.

to force them to leave the city. The officials again hesitated but a mob quickly formed to relieve them of the work. This was the riot of 1829. Bands of ruffians held sway in the city for three days, as the police were unable or unwilling to restore order. Negroes were insulted on the streets, attacked in their homes, and even killed. About a thousand or twelve hundred of them found it advisable to leave for Canada West where they established the settlement known as Wilberforce.[23]

This upheaval, though unusually alarming, was not altogether a bad omen. It was due not only to the demands which the South was making upon the North and the fear of the loss of Southern trade, but also to the rise of the Abolition Societies, the growth of which such a riotous condition as this had materially fostered. In a word, it was the sequel of the struggle between the proslavery and the antislavery elements of the city. This was the time when the friends of the Negroes were doing most for them. Instead of frightening them away a group of respectable white men in that community were beginning to think that they should be trained to live there as useful citizens. Several schools and churches for them were established. The Negroes themselves provided for their own first school about 1820; but one Mr. Wing had sufficient courage to admit persons of color to his evening classes after their first efforts had failed. By 1834 many of the colored people were receiving systematic instruction.[24] To some enemies of these dependents it seemed that the tide was about to turn in favor of the despised cause. Negroes began to raise sums adequate to their elementary education and the students of Lane Seminary supplemented these efforts by establishing a colored mission school which offered more advanced courses and lectures on scientific subjects twice a week. These students, however, soon found themselves far in advance of public

[23] *African Repository*, V, 185.
[24] For a lengthy account of these efforts see Woodson's ''The Education of the Negro Prior to 1861,'' 245, 328, 329; and Hickok, ''The Negro in Ohio,'' 83, 88.

opinion.[25]   They were censured by the faculty and to find a more congenial center for their operations they had to go to Oberlin in the Western Reserve where a larger number of persons had become interested in the cause of the despised and rejected of men.

During the years from 1833 to 1836 the situation in Cincinnati grew worse because of the still larger influx of Negroes driven from the South by intolerable conditions incident to the reaction against the race. To solve this problem various schemes were brought forth. Augustus Wattles tells us that he appeared in Cincinnati about this time and induced numbers of the Negroes to go to Mercer County, Ohio, where they took up 30,000 acres of land.[26] Others went to Indiana and purchased large tracts on the public domain.[27]   Such a method, however, seemed rather slow to the militant proslavery leaders who had learned not only to treat the Negroes as an evil but to denounce in the same manner the increasing number of abolitionists by whom it was said the Negroes were encouraged to immigrate into the State.

The spirit of the proslavery sympathizers was well exhibited in the upheaval which soon followed. This was the riot of July 30, 1836. It was an effort to destroy the abolition organ, *The Philanthropist,* edited by James G. Birney, a Southerner who had brought his slaves from Huntsville, Alabama, to Kentucky and freed them. The mob formed in the morning, went to the office of *The Philanthropist,* destroyed what printed matter they could find, threw the type into the street, and broke up the press. They then proceeded to the home of the printer, Mr. Pugh, but finding no questionable matter there, they left it undisturbed. The homes of James G. Birney, Mr. Donaldson and Dr. Colby were also threatened. The next homes to be attacked were those of Church Alley, the Negro quarter, but when two guns were fired upon the assailants they withdrew.

[25] Fairchild, ''Oberlin: Its Origin, Progress and Results.''
[26] Howe, ''Historical Collections of Ohio,'' 356.
[27] *The Southern Workman,* XXXVII, 169.

It was reported that one man was shot but this has never been proved. The mob hesitated some time before attacking these houses again, several of the rioters declaring that they did not care to endanger their lives. A second onset was made, but it was discovered that the Negroes had deserted the quarter. On finding the houses empty the assailants destroyed their contents.[28]

Yet undaunted by this persistent opposition the Negroes of Cincinnati achieved so much during the years between 1835 and 1840 that they deserved to be ranked among the most progressive people of the world.[29] Their friends endeavored to enable them through schools, churches and industries to embrace every opportunity to rise. These 2,255 Negroes accumulated, largely during this period, $209,000 worth of property, exclusive of personal effects and three churches valued at $19,000. Some of this wealth consisted of land purchased in Ohio and Indiana. Furthermore, in 1839 certain colored men of the city organized "The Iron Chest Company," a real estate firm, which built three brick buildings and rented them to white men. One man, who a few years prior to 1840 had thought it useless to accumulate wealth from which he might be driven away, had changed his mind and purchased $6,000 worth of real estate. Another Negro, who had paid $5,000 for himself and family, had bought a home worth $800 or $1,000. A freedman, who was a slave until he was twenty-four years old, then had two lots worth $10,000, paid a tax of $40 and had 320 acres of land in Mercer County. Another, who was worth only $3,000 in 1836, had seven houses in Cincinnati, 400 acres of land in Indiana, and another tract in the same county. He was worth $12,000 or $15,000. A woman who was a slave until she was thirty was then worth $2,000. She had also come into potential possession of two houses on which a white lawyer had given her a mortgage to secure the payment of $2,000 borrowed from this thrifty woman. Another Negro,

---

[28] For a full account see Howe, "Historical Collections of Ohio," 225–226.

[29] Barber, "Report on the Condition of the Colored People in Ohio," 1840, and *The Philanthropist*, July 14 and 21, 1840.

who was on the auction block in 1832, had spent $2,600 pur-
chasing himself and family and had bought two brick houses
worth $6,000 and 560 acres of land in Mercer County, said to
be worth $2,500.[30]

This unusual progress had been promoted by two forces,
the development of the steamboat as a factor in transportation and the rise of the Negro mechanic. Negroes employed
on vessels as servants to the travelling public amassed large
sums received in the form of "tips." Furthermore, the fortunate few, constituting the stewards of these vessels, could
by placing contracts for supplies and using business methods
realize handsome incomes. Many Negroes thus enriched
purchased real estate and went into business in Cincinnati.[31]
The other force, the rise of the Negro mechanic, was made
possible by overcoming much of the prejudice which had at
first been encountered. A great change in this respect had
taken place in Cincinnati by 1840. Many who had been
forced to work as menial laborers then had the opportunity
to show their usefulness to their families and to the community. Colored mechanics were then getting as much
skilled labor as they could do. It was not uncommon for
white artisans to solicit employment of colored men because
they had the reputation of being better paymasters than
master workmen of the more favored race.[32] White mechanics not only worked with colored men but often associated with them, patronized the same barber shop, and
went to the same places of amusement.[33]

In this prosperous condition the Negroes could help
themselves. Prior to this period they had been unable to
make any sacrifices for charity and education. Only $150
of the $1,000 raised for Negro education in 1835 was con-
tributed by persons of color. In 1839, however, the colored

[30] These facts are taken from A. D. Barber's "Report on the Condition
of the Colored People in Ohio" and from other articles contributed to *The
Philanthropist* in July, 1840.

[31] In this case I have taken the statements of Negroes who were employed
in this capacity.

[32] *The Philanthropist*, July 14 and 24, 1840; and May 26, 1841.

[33] Hickok, "The Negro in Ohio," 89.

people raised $889.30 for this purpose, and thanks to their economic progress, this task was not so difficult as that of raising the $150 in 1835. They were then spending considerable amounts for evening and writing schools, attended by seventy-five persons, chiefly adults. In 1840 Reverend Mr. Denham and Mr. Goodwin had in their schools sixty-five pupils each paying $3 per quarter, and Miss Merrill a school of forty-seven pupils paying the same tuition. In all, the colored people were paying these teachers about $1,300 a year. The only help the Negroes were then receiving was that from the Ladies' Anti-Slavery Society, which employed one Miss Seymour at a salary of $300 a year to instruct fifty-four pupils. Moreover, the colored people were giving liberally to objects of charity. Some Negroes burned out in 1839 were promptly relieved by members of their own race. A white family in distress was befriended by a colored woman. The Negroes contributed also to the support of missionaries in Jamaica and during the years from 1836 to 1840 assisted twenty-five emancipated slaves on their way from Cincinnati to Mercer County, Ohio.[34]

During this period they had made progress in other than material things. Their improvement in religion and morals was remarkable. They then had four flourishing Sabbath Schools with 310 regular attendants, one Baptist and two Methodist churches with a membership of 800, a "Total Abstinence Temperance Society" for adults numbering 450, and a "Sabbath School or Youth's Society" of 180 members. A few of these violated their pledges, but when we consider the fact that one fourth of the entire colored population belonged to temperance organizations while less than one tenth of the whites were thus connected, we must admit that this was no mean achievement. Among the Negroes public sentiment was then such that no colored man could openly sell intoxicating drinks. This growing temperance was exhibited, too, in the decreasing fondness for dress and finery. There was less tendency to strive merely to get a fine suit of clothes and exhibit one's self on the streets.

[34] *The Philanthropist*, July 14 and 21, 1840.

Places of vice were not so much frequented and barber
shops which on Sundays formerly became a rendezvous for
the idle and the garrulous were with few exceptions closed
by 1840. This influence of the religious organizations
reached also beyond the limits of Cincinnati. A theological
student from the State of New York said after spending
some time in New Orleans, that the influence of the elevation
of the colored people of Cincinnati was felt all the way down
the river. Travelers often spoke of the difference in the
appearance of barbers and waiters on the boats.[35]

It was in fact a brighter day for the colored people. In
1840 an observer said that they had improved faster than
any other people in the city. The *Cincinnati Gazette* after
characterizing certain Negroes as being imprudent and
vicious, said of others: "Many of these are peaceable and
industrious, raising respectable families and acquiring property."[36] Mr. James H. Perkins, a respectable citizen of the
city, asserted that the day school which the colored children
attended had shown by examination that it was as good as
any other in the city. He said further: "There is no question,
I presume, that the colored population of Cincinnati, oppressed as it has been by our state laws as well as by prejudice, has risen more rapidly than almost any other people in
any part of the world."[37] Within three or four years their
property had more than doubled; their schools had become
firmly established, and their churches and Sunday Schools
had grown as rapidly as any other religious institutions in
the city. Trusting to good conduct and character, they had
risen to a prosperous position in the eyes of those whose
prejudices would "allow them to look through the skin to
the soul."[38]

The colored people had had too many enemies in Cincinnati, however, to expect that they had overcome all opposition. The prejudice of certain labor groups against the

[35] *The Philanthropist*, July 21, 1840.
[36] *The Cincinnati Daily Gazette*, September 14, 1841.
[37] *The Philanthropist*, July 21, 1840.
[38] *Ibid.*

Negroes increased in proportion to the prosperity of the latter. That they had been able to do as well as they had was due to the lack of strength on the part of the labor organizations then forming to counteract the sentiment of fair play for the Negroes. Their labor competed directly with that of the whites and began again to excite "jealousy and heart burning."[39] The Germans, who were generally toiling up from poverty, seemed to exhibit less prejudice; but the unfortunate Irish bore it grievously that even a few Negroes should outstrip some of their race in the economic struggle.

In 1841 there followed several clashes which aggravated the situation. In the month of June one Burnett referred to as "a mischievous and swaggering Englattle grounning a cake shop," had harbored a runaway slutrol . Then a man named McCalla, his reputed master, came with an officer to reclaim the fugitive, Burnett and his family resisted them. The Burnetts were committed to answer for this infraction of the law and finally were adequately punished. The pro-slavery mob which had gathered undertook to destroy their home but the officials prevented them. Besides, early in August according to a report, a German citizen defending his blackberry patch near the city was attacked by two Negroes and stabbed so severely that he died. Then about three weeks thereafter, according to another rumor, a very respectable lady was insultingly accosted by two colored men, and when she began to flee two others rudely thrust themselves before her on the sidewalk. But in this case, as in most others growing out of rumors, no one could ever say who the lady or her so-called assailants were. At the same time, too, the situation was further aggravated by an almost sudden influx of irresponsible Negroes from various parts, increasing the number of those engaged in noisy frolics which had become a nuisance to certain white neighbors.[40]

Accordingly, on Tuesday, the twenty-ninth of August,

[39] *The Cincinnati Daily Gezette,* September 14, 1841.

[40] A detailed account of these clashes is given in *The Cincinnati Daily Gazette,* September 14, 1841.

there broke out on the corner of Sixth and Broadway a
quarrel in which two or three persons were wounded. On
the following night the fracas was renewed. A group of
ruffians attacked the Dumas Hotel, a colored establishment,
on McCallister Street, demanding the surrender of a Negro,
who, they believed, was concealed there. As the Negroes of
the neighborhood came to the assistance of their friends in
the hotel the mob had to withdraw. On Thursday night
there took place another clash between a group of young
men and boys and a few Negroes who seriously wounded
one or two of the former. On Friday evening the mob in-
cited to riotous acts by an influx of white ruffians, seemingly from the steamboats and the Kentucky side of the
river, gathering, assembled in Fifth Street Market without
being molested the police, armed themselves and marched
to Broadway and Sixth Street, shouting and swearing. They
attacked a colored confectionery store near by, demolishing
its doors and windows. James W. Piatt, an influential
citizen, and the mayor then addressed the disorderly persons, vainly exhorting them to peace and obedience to the
law. Moved by passionate entreaties to execute their poorly
prepared plan, the assailants advanced and attacked the
Negroes with stones. The blacks, however, had not been
idle. They had secured sufficient guns and ammunition to fire
into the mob such a volley that it had to fall back. The ag-
gressors rallied again, however, only to be in like manner
repulsed. Men were wounded on both sides and carried off
and reported dead. The Negroes advanced courageously, and
according to a reporter, fired down the street into the mass
of ruffians, causing a hasty retreat. This mêlée continued
until about one o'clock when a part of the mob secured an
iron six pounder, hauled it to the place of combat against the
exhortations of the powerless mayor, and fired on the Negroes. With this unusual advantage the blacks were forced
to retreat, many of them going to the hills. About two
o'clock the mayor of the city brought out a portion of the
"military" which succeeded in holding the mob at bay.[41]

41 *The Cincinnati Daily Gazette*, September, 1841.

On the next day the colored people in the district under fire were surrounded by sentinels and put under martial law. Indignation meetings of law-abiding citizens were held on Saturday to pass resolutions, denouncing abolitionists and mobs and making an appeal to the people and the civil authorities to uphold the law. The Negroes also held a meeting and respectfully assured the mayor and citizens that they would use every effort to conduct themselves orderly and expressed their readiness to give bond according to the law of 1807 or leave the city quietly within a specified time. But these steps availed little when the police winked at this violence. The rioters boldly occupied the streets without arrest and continued their work until Sunday. The mayor, sheriff and marshal went to the battle ground about three o'clock but the mob still had control. The officers could not even remove those Negroes who complied with the law of leaving. The authorities finally hit upon the scheme of decreasing the excitement by inducing about 300 colored men to go to jail for security after they had been assured that their wives and children would be protected. The Negroes consented and were accordingly committed, but the cowardly element again attacked these helpless dependents like savages. At the same time other rioters stormed the office of *The Philanthropist* and broke up the press. The mob continued its work until it dispersed from mere exhaustion. The Governor finally came to the city and issued a proclamation setting forth the gravity of the situation. The citizens and civil authorities rallied to his support and strong patrols prevented further disorder.[42]

It is impossible to say exactly how many were killed and wounded on either side. It is probable that several were killed and twenty or thirty variously wounded, though but few dangerously. Forty of the mob were arrested and imprisoned. Exactly what was done with all of them is not yet known. It seems that few, if any of them, however, were severely punished. The Negroes who had been committed

[42] A very interesting account of this riot is given in Howe's ''Historical Collections of Ohio,'' pages 226–228.

for safe keeping were thereafter disposed of in various ways. Some were discharged on certificates of nativity, others gave bond for their support and good behavior, a few were dismissed as non-residents, a number of them were discharged by a justice of the Court of Common Pleas, and the rest were held indefinitely.[43]

This upheaval had two important results. The enemies of the Negroes were convinced that there were sufficient law-abiding citizens to secure to the refugees protection from mob violence; and because of these riots their sympathizers became more attached to the objects of their philanthropy. Abolitionists, Free Soilers and Whigs fearlessly attacked the laws which kept the Negroes under legal and economic disabilities. Petitions praying that these measures be repealed were sent to the legislature. The pro-slavery element of the State, however, was equally militant. The legislators, therefore, had to consider such questions as extradition and immigration, State aid and colonization, the employment of colored men in the militia service, the extension of the elective franchise, and the admission of colored children to the public schools.[44] Most of these "Black Laws" remained until after the war, but in 1848 they were so modified as to give the Negroes legal standing in courts and to provide for their children such education as a school tax on the property of colored persons would allow[45] and further changed in 1849[46] so as to make the provision for education more effective.

The question of repealing the other oppressive laws came up in the Convention of 1850. It seemed that the cause of the Negroes had made much progress in that a larger num-

[43] It was discovered that not a few of the mob came from Kentucky. About eleven o'clock on Saturday night a bonfire was lighted on that side of the river and loud shouts were sent up as if triumph had been achieved. "In some cases," says a reporter, "the directors were boys who suggested the point of attack, put the vote, declared the result and led the way."—Cin. Daily Gaz. Sept. 14, 1841.

[44] Hickok, "The Negro in Ohio," 90 et seq.

[45] Laws of Ohio, XL, 81.

[46] Ibid., LIII, 118.

ber had begun to speak for them. But practically all of the members of the convention who stood for the Negroes were from the Western Reserve. After much heated discussion the colored people were by a large majority of votes still left under the disabilities of being disqualified to sit on juries, unable to obtain a legal residence so as to enter a charitable institution supported by the State, and denied admission to public schools established for white children.[47]

The greatest problem of the Negroes, however, was one of education. There were more persons interested in furnishing them facilities of education than in repealing the prohibitive measures, feeling that the other matters would adjust themselves after giving them adequate training. But it required some time and effort yet before much could be effected in Cincinnati because of the sympathizers with the South. The mere passing of the law of 1849 did not prove to be altogether a victory. Complying with the provisions of this act the Negroes elected trustees, organized a system, and employed teachers, relying on the money allotted them by the law on the basis of a per capita division of the school fund received by the board of education. So great was the prejudice of people of the city that the school officials refused to turn over the required funds on the grounds that the colored trustees were not electors and, therefore, could not be office-holders, qualified to receive and disburse funds. Under the leadership of John I. Gaines, therefore, the trustees called an indignation meeting and raised sufficient money to employ Flamen Ball, an attorney, to secure a writ of mandamus. The case was contested by the city officials, even in the Supreme Court, which decided against the officious whites.[48]

This decision did not solve the whole problem in Cincinnati. The amount raised was small and even had it been adequate to employ teachers, they were handicapped by another decision that no portion of it could be used for

[47] The Convention Debates.
[48] Special Report of the United States Commissioner of Education, 1871, page 372.

building schoolhouses. After a short period of accomplishing practically nothing the law was amended in 1853[49] so as to transfer the control of such schools to the managers of the white system. This was taken as a reflection on the blacks of the city and tended to make them refuse to cooperate with the white board. On account of the failure of this body to act effectively prior to 1856, the people of color were again given power to elect their own trustees.[50]

During this contest certain Negroes of Cincinnati were endeavoring to make good their claim to equal rights in the public schools. Acting upon this contention a colored man sent his son to a public school which, on account of his presence, became a center of unusual excitement. Isabella Newhall, the teacher, to whom he went, immediately complained to the board of education, requesting that he be expelled because of his color. After "due deliberation" the board of education decided by a vote of 15 to 10 that the colored pupil would have to withdraw. Thereupon two members of that body, residing in the district of the timorous teacher, resigned.[51]

Many Negroes belonging to the mulatto class, however, were more successful in getting into the white schools. In 1849 certain parents complained that children of color were being admitted to the public schools, and in fact there were in one of them two daughters of a white father and a mulatto mother. On complaining about this to the principal of the school in question, the indignant patrons were asked to point out the undesirable pupils. "They could not; for," says Sir Charles Lyell, "the two girls were not only among the best pupils, but better looking and less dark than many of the other pupils."[52]

Thereafter, however, much progress in the education of the colored people among themselves was noted. By 1844

[49] Laws of Ohio.
[50] Ibid., LIII, 118.
[51] The New York Tribune, February 19, 1855.
[52] Lyell, "A Second Visit to the United States of North America," II, 295, 296.

they had six schools of their own and before the war two well-supported public schools.[53] Among their teachers were such useful persons as Mrs. M. J. Corbin, Miss Lucy Black-burn, Miss Anne Ryall, Miss Virginia C. Tilley, Miss Martha E. Anderson, William H. Parham, William R. Casey, John G. Mitchell and Peter H. Clark.[54] The pupils were showing their appreciation by regular attendance, excellent deport-ment, and progress in the acquisition of knowledge. Speak-ing of these Negroes in 1855, John P. Foote said that they shared with the white citizens that respect for education and the diffusion of knowledge, which has been one of their ''char-acteristics,'' and that they had, therefore, been more gen-erally intelligent than free persons of color not only in other parts of this country but in all other parts of the world.[55] It was in appreciation of the worth of this class to the com-munity that in 1844[56] Nicholas Longworth helped them to establish an orphan asylum and in 1858 built for them a comfortable school building, leasing it with a privilege of purchasing it within four years.[57] They met these require-ments within the stipulated time and in 1859 secured through other agencies the construction of another building in the western portion of the city.

The most successful of these schools, however, was the Gilmore High School, a private institution founded by an English clergyman. This institution offered instruction in the fundamentals and in some vocational studies. It was supported liberally by the benevolent element of the white people and patronized and appreciated by the Negroes as the first and only institution, offering them the opportunity for thorough training. It became popular throughout the country, attracting Negroes from as far South as New Or-

[53] The Weekly Herald and Philanthropist, June 26, 1844, August 6, 1844, and January 1, 1845.

[54] The Cincinnati Directory of 1860.

[55] Foote, ''The Schools of Cincinnati,'' 92.

[56] The Weekly Herald and Philanthropist, August 23, 1844.

[57] Special Report of the United States Commissioner of Education, 372.

leans.[58] Rich Southern planters found it convenient to have their mulatto children educated in this high school.[59]

The work of these schools was substantially supplemented by that of the colored churches. They directed their attention not only to moral and religious welfare of the colored people but also to their mental development. Through their well-attended Sunday-schools these institutions furnished many Negroes of all classes the facilities of elementary education. Such opportunities were offered at the Baker Street Baptist Church, the Third Street Baptist Church, the Colored Christian Church, the New Street Methodist Church, and the African Methodist Church. Among the preachers then promoting this cause were John Warren, Rufus Conrad, Henry Simpson, and Wallace Shelton. Many of the old citizens of Cincinnati often refer with pride to the valuable services rendered by these leaders.

In things economic the Negroes were exceptionally prosperous after the forties. Cincinnati had then become a noted pork-packing and manufacturing center. The increasing canal and river traffic and finally the rise of the railroad system tended to make it thrive more than ever. Many colored men grew up with the city. A Negro had in the East End on Calvert Street a large cooperage establishment which made barrels for the packers. Knight and Bell were successful contractors noted for their skill and integrity and employed by the best white people of the city. Robert Harlan made considerable money buying and selling race horses. Thompson Cooley had a successful pickling establishment. On Broadway A. V. Thompson, a colored tailor, conducted a thriving business. J. Pressley and Thomas Ball were the well-known photographers of the city, established in a handsomely furnished modern gallery which was patronized by some of the wealthiest people. Samuel T. Wilcox, who owed his success to his position as a steward on an Ohio River line, thereafter went into the grocery business and built up

---

[58] Simmons, ''Men of Mark,'' 490.

[59] A white slaveholder, a graduate of Amherst, taught in this school. See *Weekly Herald and Philanthropist*, June 26, 1844.

such a large trade among the aristocratic families that he accumulated $59,000 worth of property by 1859.[60]

A more useful Negro had for years been toiling upward in this city. This man was Henry Boyd, a Kentucky freedman, who had helped to overcome the prejudice against colored mechanics in that city by exhibiting the highest efficiency. He patented a corded bed which became very popular, especially in the Southwest. With this article he built up a creditable manufacturing business, employing from 18 to 25 white and colored men.[61] He was, therefore, known as one of the desirable men of the city. Two things, however, seemingly interfered with his business. In the first place, certain white men, who became jealous of his success, burned him out and the insurance companies refused to carry him any longer. Moreover, having to do chiefly with white men he was charged by his people with favoring the miscegenation of races. Whether or not this was well founded is not yet known, but his children and grandchildren did marry whites and were lost in the so-called superior race.

A much more interesting Negro appeared in Cincinnati, however, in 1847. This was Robert Gordon, formerly the slave of a rich yachtsman of Richmond, Virginia. His master turned over to him a coal yard which he handled so faithfully that his owner gave him all of the slack resulting from the handling of the coal. This he sold to the local manufacturers and blacksmiths of the city, accumulating thereby in the course of time thousands of dollars. He purchased himself in 1846 and set out for free soil. He went first to Philadelphia and then to Newburyport, but finding that these places did not suit him, he proceeded to Cincinnati. He arrived there with $15,000, some of which he immediately invested in the coal business in which he had already achieved

[60] These facts were obtained from oral statements of Negroes who were living in Cincinnati at this time; from M. R. Delany's ''The Condition of the Colored People in the United States''; from A. D. Barber's ''Report on the Condition of the Colored People in Ohio,'' 1840; and from various Cincinnati Directories.

[61] Delany, ''The Condition of the Colored People in the United States,'' 92.

marked success. He employed bookkeepers, had his own wagons, built his own docks on the river, and bought coal by barges.[62]

Unwilling to see this Negro do so well, the white coal dealers endeavored to force him out of the business by lowering the price to the extent that he could not afford to sell. They did not know of his acumen and the large amount of capital at his disposal. He sent to the coal yards of his competitors mulattoes who could pass for white, using them to fill his current orders from his foes' supplies that he might save his own coal for the convenient day. In the course of a few months the river and all the canals by which coal was brought to Cincinnati froze up and remained so until spring. Gordon was then able to dispose of his coal at a higher price than it had ever been sold in that city. This so increased his wealth and added to his reputation that no one thereafter thought of opposing him.

Gordon continued in the coal business until 1865 when he retired. During the Civil War he invested his money in United States bonds. When these bonds were called in, he invested in real estate on Walnut Hills, which he held until his death in 1884. This estate descended to his daughter Virginia Ann Gordon who married George H. Jackson, a descendant of slaves in the Custis family of Arlington, Virginia. Mr. Jackson is now a resident of Chicago and is managing this estate.[63] Having lived through the antebellum and subsequent periods, Mr. Jackson has been made to wonder whether the Negroes of Cincinnati are doing as well to-day as Gordon and his colaborers were. This question requires some attention, but an inquiry as to exactly what forces have operated to impede the progress of a work so auspiciously begun would lead us beyond the limits set for this dissertation.

C. G. WOODSON

[62] The Cincinnati Directory for 1860.

[63] For the leading facts concerning the life of Robert Gordon I have depended on the statements of his children and acquaintances and on the various directories and documents giving evidence concerning the business men of Cincinnati.

THE STORY OF MARIA LOUISE MOORE AND FANNIE M. RICHARDS[1]

The State of Virginia has been the home of distinguished persons of both sexes of the white and colored races. A dissertation on the noted colored women of Virginia would find a small circle of readers but would, nevertheless, contain interesting accounts of some of the most important achievements of the people of that State. The story of Maria Louise Moore-Richards would be a large chapter of such a narrative. She was born of white and Negro parentage in Fredericksburg, Virginia, in 1800. Her father was Edwin Moore, a Scotchman of Edinburgh. Her mother was a free woman of color, born in Toronto when it was called York. Exactly how they came to Fredericksburg is not known. It seems, however, that they had been well established in that city when Maria Louise Moore was born.

This woman was fortunate in coming into the world at that time. So general had been the efforts for the elevation of the colored people that free Negroes had many of the privileges later given only to white people. Virginia then and for a long time thereafter ranked among the commonwealths most liberal toward the Negro. The dissemination of information among them was not then restricted, private teaching of slaves was common, and progressive communities maintained colored schools.[1a] In Fredericksburg such opportunities were not rare. The parents of Maria Louise Moore fortunately associated with the free Negroes who constituted an industrial class with adequate means to provide for the thorough training of their children. Miss Moore, therefore, easily acquired the rudiments of education and attained some distinction as a student of history.

[1] For many of the facts set forth in this article the writer is indebted to Miss Fannie M. Richards, Robert A. Pelham, and C. G. Woodson.

[1a] Woodson, The Ed. of the Negro Prior to 1861, pp. 92, 217, 218.

In 1820 Miss Moore was married to Adolphe Richards, a native of the Island of Guadaloupe. He was a Latin of some Negro blood, had noble ancestry, and had led an honorable career. Educated in London and resident in Guadaloupe, he spoke both English and French fluently. Because of poor health in later years he was directed by his friends to the salubrious climate of Virginia. He settled at Fredericksburg, where he soon became captivated by the charms of the talented Maria Louise Moore. On learning of his marriage, his people and friends marveled that a man of his standing had married a colored woman or a Southern woman at all.

Adjusting himself to this new environment, Mr. Richards opened a shop for wood-turning, painting and glazing. It is highly probable that he learned these trades in the West Indies, but having adequate means to maintain himself, he had not depended on his mechanical skill. In Fredericksburg he had the respect and support of the best white people, passing as one of such well-to-do free Negroes as the Lees, the Cooks, the De Baptistes, who were contractors, and the Williamses, who were contractors and brickmakers. His success was in a large measure due to the good standing of the family of Mrs. Richards and to the wisdom with which she directed this West Indian in his new environment.

They had in all fourteen children, the training of whom was largely the work of the mother. All of them were well grounded in the rudiments of education and given a taste for higher things. In the course of time when the family grew larger the task of educating them grew more arduous. Some of them probably attended the school conducted by a Scotch-Irishman in the home of Richard De Baptiste. When the reaction against the teaching of Negroes effected the closing of the colored schools in Virginia, this one continued clandestinely for many years. Determined to have her children better educated, Mrs. Richards sent one of her sons to a school conducted by Mrs. Beecham, a remarkable English woman, assisted by her daughter. These women were bent on doing what they could to evade the law interpreted as prohibiting any one from either sitting or standing to teach a black to read. They, therefore, gathered the colored children around them while they lay prostrate on the couch to teach them. For further evasion they kept on hand splinters of wood which they had the children dip into a match preparation and use with a flint for ignition to make it appear that they were showing them how to make matches. When this scheme seemed impracticable, one of the boys was sent to Washington in the District of Columbia to attend the school maintained by John F. Cook, a successful educator and founder of the Fifteenth Street Presbyterian Church. This young man was then running the risk of expatriation, for Virginia had in 1838 passed a law, prohibiting the return to that State of those Negroes, who after the prohibition of their education had begun to attend schools in other parts.[2]

It was because of these conditions that in 1851 when her husband died Mrs. Richards sold out her property and set out to find a better home in Detroit, Michigan. Some of the best white people of Fredericksburg commended her for this step, saying that she was too respectable a woman to suffer such humiliation as the reaction had entailed upon

[2] The law was as follows:

Be it enacted by the General Assembly that if any free person of color, whether infant or adult, shall go or be sent or carried beyond the limits of this Commonwealth for the purpose of being educated, he or she shall be deemed to have emigrated from the State and it shall not be lawful for him or her to return to the same; and if any such person shall return within the limits of the State contrary to the provisions of this act, he or she being an infant shall be bound out as an apprentice until the age of 21 years, by the overseers of the poor of the county or corporation where he or she may be, and at the expiration of that period, shall be sent out of the State agreeably to the provisions of the laws now in force, or which may hereafter be enacted to prohibit the migration of free persons of color to this State; and if such person be an adult, he or she shall be sent in like manner out of the Commonwealth; and if any persons having been so sent off, shall hereafter return within the State, he or she so offending shall be dealt with and punished in the same manner as is or may be prescribed by law in relating to other persons of color returning to the State after having been sent therefrom. Acts of the General Assembly of Virginia, 1838, p. 76.

persons of her race.[3] She was followed by practically all of the best free Negroes of Fredericksburg. Among these were the Lees, the Cooks, the Williamses and the De Baptistes. A few years later this group attracted the Pelham family from Petersburg. They too had tired of seeing their rights gradually taken away and, therefore, transplanted themselves to Detroit.

[3] The following enactments of the Virginia General Assembly will give a better idea of the extent of this humiliation:

4. Be it further enacted that all meetings of free Negroes or mulattoes at any school house, church, meeting-house or other place for teaching them reading or writing, either in the day or night, under whatsoever pretext, shall be deemed and considered as an unlawful assembly; and any justice of the county or corporation, wherein such assemblage shall be, either from his own knowledge, or on the information of others, of such unlawful assemblage or meeting, shall issue his warrant directed to any sworn officer or officers, authorizing him or them to enter the house or houses where such unlawful assemblage or meeting may be, for the purpose of apprehending or dispersing such free Negroes or mulattoes and to inflict corporal punishment on the offender or offenders at the discretion of any justice of the peace, not exceeding 20 lashes.

5. Be it further enacted that if any white person or persons assemble with free Negroes or mulattoes, at any school house, church, meeting-house, or other place for the purpose of instructing such free Negroes or mulattoes to read or write, such person or persons shall, on conviction thereof, be fined in a sum not exceeding fifty dollars, and moreover may be imprisoned at the discretion not exceeding two months.

6. Be it further enacted that if any white persons for pay or compensation, shall assemble with any slaves for the purpose of teaching and shall teach any slave to read or write, such persons or any white person or persons contracting with such teacher so to act, who shall offend as aforesaid, shall for each offence, be fined at the discretion of a jury in a sum not less than ten nor exceeding one hundred dollars, to be recovered on an information or indictment. Acts of the General Assembly of Virginia, 1831, p. 107.

I. Be it enacted by the General Assembly of Virginia that no slave, free Negro or mulatto, whether he shall have been ordained or licensed or otherwise, shall hereafter undertake to preach, exhort or conduct or hold any assembly or meeting, for religious or other purposes, either in the day time or at night; and any slave, free Negro or mulatto so offending shall for every such offence be punished with stripes at the discretion of any justice of the peace, not exceeding 39 lashes; and any person desiring so to do, shall have authority without any previous written precept or otherwise, to apprehend any such offender and carry him before such justice.

II. Any slave, free Negro or mulatto who shall hereafter attend any preaching, meeting or other assembly, held or pretended to be held for religious purposes, or other instruction, conducted by any slave, free Negro or mulatto preacher, ordained or otherwise; any slave who shall hereafter attend

The attitude of the people of Detroit toward immigrating Negroes had been reflected by the position the people of that section had taken from the time of the earliest settlements. Slavery was prohibited by the Ordinance of 1787. In 1807 there arose a case in which a woman was required to answer for the possession of two slaves. Her contention was that they were slaves on British territory at the time of the surrender of the post in 1796 and that Jay's Treaty assured them to her. Her contention was sustained.[4] A few days later a resident of Canada attempted under this ruling to secure the arrest and return of some mulatto and Indian slaves who had escaped from Canada. The court held that slavery did not exist in Michigan except in the case of slaves in the possession of the British settlers within the Northwest Territory July 11, 1796, and that there was no obligation to give up fugitives from a foreign jurisdiction. An effort was made to take the slaves by force but the agent of the owner was tarred and feathered.[4]

Generally speaking, Detroit adhered to this position.[4a]

any preaching in the night time although conducted by a white minister, without a written permission from his or her owner, overseer or master or agent of either of them, shall be punished by stripes at the discretion of any justice of the peace, not exceeding 39 lashes, and may for that purpose be apprehended by any person, without any written or other precept:

Provided, That nothing herein contained shall be so construed as to prevent the master or owner of slaves or any white person to whom any free Negro or mulatto is bound, or in whose employment, or on whose plantation or lot such free Negro or mulatto lives, from carrying or permitting any such slave, free Negro or mulatto, to go with him, her or them, or with any part of his, her, or their white family to any place of worship, conducted by a white minister in the night time: And provided also, That nothing in this or any former law, shall be construed as to prevent any ordained or licensed white minister of the gospel, or any layman licensed for that purpose by the denomination to which he may belong, from preaching or giving religious instruction to slaves, free Negroes and mulattoes in the day time; nor to deprive any masters or owners of slaves of the right to engage, or employ any free white person whom they think proper to give religious instruction to their salves; nor to prevent the assembling of slaves of any one owner or master together at any time for religious devotion. Acts of the General Assembly of Virginia, 1831–1832, pp. 20–21.

[4] Campbell, Political History of Michigan, 246.

[4a] Slavery did not immediately cease, however. The number of slaves in the vicinity of Detroit in 1773 were ninety-six; 127 in 1778; and 175 in 1783. Detroit had a colored population of 15 in 1805 and two years later a number

In 1827 there was passed an act providing for the registry of the names of all colored persons, requiring the possession of a certificate showing that they were free and a bond in the sum of $500 for their good behavior.[5] This law was obnoxious to the growing sentiment of freedom in Detroit and was not enforced until the Riot of 1833. This uprising was an attack on the Negroes because a courageous group of them had effected the rescue and escape of one Thornton Blackburn and his wife, who had been arrested by the sheriff as alleged fugitives from Kentucky.[6] The anti-slavery feeling considerably increased thereafter. The Detroit Anti-Slavery Society was formed in 1837, other societies to secure the relief and escape of slaves quickly followed and still another was organized to find employment and purchase homes for refugees.[7] This change of sentiment is further

had sufficiently increased for Governor Hull to organize a company of militia among them. The increase had been due to the coming of refugees from Canada. The Census of 1810 showed 17 slaves in Detroit; that of 1830 shows 32 in Michigan and an enumeration subsequent to 1836 shows that all were dead or manumitted. See Census of the United States.

[5] Laws of Michigan, 1827.

[6] This riot occurred on June 14, 1833. Thornton Blackburn and his wife, the alleged runaways from Kentucky, were lodged in jail pending the departure of a boat. A crowd of colored men and women, armed with clubs, stones and pistols, gathered in the vicinity of the jail. Upon the pretext of visiting Blackburn's wife a colored woman was admitted to the jail and by an exchange of clothing effected the escape of the prisoner who immediately crossed into Canada. Some time thereafter the sheriff attempted to take his other prisoner to the boat, but was knocked down and badly beaten. During the encounter the sheriff fired into the mob, but Blackburn was rescued and carried to Canada. This caused a great disturbance among the white people. They armed themselves and attacked the blacks wherever they could be found. The city council convened and undertook to dispose of the trouble by enforcing the law of 1827 requiring that colored people should stay off the streets at night. Utley, Byron and McCutcheon, ''Michigan as a Province and State,'' II, 347.

[7] Five years after the organization of the Detroit Anti-Slavery Society Henry Bibb, an ex-slave, came to the city and lectured for two years under the auspices of the Liberty Association, which was promoting the election of anti-slavery candidates. Public sentiment against slavery was becoming such that the Legislature of Michigan passed a law prohibiting the use of jails to detain fugitives. Frederick Douglass and John Brown found many friends of their cause in Detroit. Of the many organized efforts made to circumvent the law and assist fugitives one society purchased land and established homes for as many as 50 families between 1850 and 1872. Farmer, ''History of Detroit and Michigan,'' I, Chapter XLVIII.

evidenced by the fact that in 1850 it was necessary to call out the three companies of volunteers to quell an incipient riot occasioned by the arrest and attempt to return a runaway slave in accordance with the Fugitive Slave Law. Save the general troubles incident to the draft riots of the Northern cities of 1863,[8] Detroit maintained this benevolent attitude toward Negroes seeking refuge.

In this favorable community the Richards colony easily prospered. The Lees well established themselves in their Northern homes and soon won the respect of the community. Most of the members of the Williams family confined themselves to their trade of bricklaying and amassed considerable wealth. One of Mr. Williams's daughters married a well-to-do Waring living then at Wauseon, Ohio; another became the wife of one Chappée, who is now a stenographer in Detroit; and the third united in matrimony with James H. Cole, who became the head of a well-to-do family of Detroit. Then there were the Cooks descending from Lomax B. Cook, a broker of no little business ability. Will Marion Cook, the musician, belongs to this family. The De Baptistes, too, were among the first to get a foothold in this new environment and prospered materially from their experience and knowledge acquired in Fredericksburg as contractors.[8a] From this group came Richard De Baptiste, who in his day was the most noted colored Baptist preacher in the Northwest. The Pelhams were no less successful in establishing themselves in the economic world. They enjoyed a high reputation in the community and had the sympathy and cooperation of the influential white people in the

[8] The immediate cause of the riot in Detroit was the arrest, conviction, and imprisonment of a colored man called William Faulkner charged with committing an assault on a little girl. Feeling that the prisoner was guilty, bands of ruffians swept through the streets and mercilessly beat colored people. Seven years later it was discovered that Faulkner was innocent and to reimburse him for his losses and humiliation the same ruffians raised a handsome sum to set him up in business. See Farmer's History of Detroit and Michigan, Chapter XLVIII.

[8a] A study of the directories of Detroit shows that a considerable number of Negroes had entered the higher pursuits of labor. See especially the Detroit Directory for 1865.

city. Out of this family came Robert A. Pelham, for years editor of a weekly in Detroit, and from 1901 to the present time an employee of the Federal Government in Washington.[9]

The children of Mrs. Richards were in no sense inferior to the descendants of the other families. She lived to see her work bear fruit in the distinguished services they rendered and the desirable connections which they made after the Civil War. Her daughter Julia married Thomas F. Carey who, after conducting a business for some years in New York, moved to Toronto, where he died. From this union came the wife of D. Augustus Straker. Her daughter Evalina married Dr. Joseph Ferguson, who prior to 1861, lived in Richmond, Virginia, uniting the three occupations of leecher, cupper and barber. This led to his coming to Detroit to study medicine. He was graduated there and practiced for many years in that city. Before the Civil War her son John D. Richards was sent to Richmond to learn a trade. There he met and became the lifelong friend of Judge George L. Ruffin, who was then living in that city.[10]

The most prominent and the most useful person to emerge from this group of pioneering Negroes was her daughter Fannie M. Richards. She was born in Fredericksburg, Virginia, October 1, 1841. As her people left that State when she was quite young she did not see so much of the intolerable conditions as did the older members of the family. Miss Richards was successful in getting an early start in education. Desiring to have better training than what was then given to persons of color in Detroit, she went to Toronto. There she studied English, history, drawing and needlework. In later years she attended the Teachers Training School in Detroit. Her first thought was to take up teaching that she might do something to elevate her people. She, therefore, opened a private school in 1863, doing a higher grade of work than that then undertaken in the public schools. About 1862, however, a colored public

---

[9] Simmons, "Men of Mark," 356.

[10] In 1853 Judge Ruffin moved with his parents from Richmond to Boston, where he became judge of the Charleston District. Simmons, "Men of Mark," 469.

school had been opened by a white man named Whitbeck. Miss Richards began to think that she should have such a school herself.

Her story as to how she realized her ambition is very interesting. Going to her private school one morning, she saw a carpenter repairing a building. Upon inquiry she learned that it was to be opened as Colored School Number 2. She went immediately to William D. Wilkins, a member of the board of education, who, impressed with the personality of the young woman, escorted her to the office of superintendent of schools, Duane Dotty. After some discussion of the matter Miss Richards filed an application, assured that she would be notified to take the next examination. At the appointed time she presented herself along with several other applicants who hoped to obtain the position. Miss Richards ranked highest and was notified to report for duty the following September. Early one morning she proceeded to her private school in time to inform her forty pupils of the desirable change and conducted them in a body to their new home.

Miss Richards taught in this building until 1871, when by a liberal interpretation of the courts, the schools were mixed by ignoring race distinction wherever it occurred in the school laws of Michigan. She was then transferred to the Everett School where she remained until last June when she was retired on a pension after having served that system half a century. Although she taught very few colored children she said to a reporter several years ago:

"I have never been made to feel in any way that my race has been a handicap to me. Neither my pupils nor the teachers have ever shown prejudice; I do not doubt that it exists; I shall be in Heaven long before it has all disappeared, but I say it is with a colored teacher as it is with a white one. Her work is the only thing that counts. I have never been called before the board for a reprimand in all my years of teaching. The methods have changed a good deal since the time that I started in and it would be easy to lag behind, but I try not to. It means continual reading and study to keep up with the modern way of doing things, but I manage to do it, and when the time comes that I cannot do my work in a satisfactory manner I want the Board of Education to discharge me and get some one else.''

In testimony to these facts one of the daily papers of Detroit wrote her up in 1910, saying that she had kept her interest in modern pedagogic methods, maintained a high standard of scholarship in her school, and retained her sympathy with little children, who had rewarded her devotion to her work with their appreciation and love. To show how well she is loved by her pupils the writer was careful to state that these children as a gay group often surrounded her on her way to school, clinging to her hands, crowding about her as best they may, all chattering and pouring out accounts of their little doings. ''Frequently,'' says this writer, ''she is stopped on the street by grown men and women who long ago were her pupils and who have remembered her, though with the passing of the years, and the new classes of little ones who come to her every term, she has forgotten them.''[11]   Many have been accustomed to bring their children to the Everett School and speak of how glad they will be when these little ones will be under the care of their parents' former teacher.

Miss Richards estimates that in the years of school work, she has had in her room an average of fifty pupils a term, although sometimes the attendance overflowed to a much greater number. With eighty-eight terms of teaching to her credit, the number of pupils who owe part of their education to ''this gentle and cultured woman'' amounts well up into the tens of thousands, enough to populate a fair-sized city.

We can not close this article with a better testimonial than the following letter from one of her former pupils, the Honorable Charles T. Wilkins, a lawyer and an influential white citizen, who addressed her on the occasion of her retirement last June.

---

[11] This information was obtained from newspaper clippings in the possession of Miss Fannie M. Richards.

"*My dear Miss Richards:* The friendship of so long standing between your family and mine, and the high esteem in which, as an educator, a woman, and a Christian, you were always held by my father the late Colonel William D. Wilkins, lead me to take the liberty of writing to *congratulate* you upon the well-earned retirement from active work, which I have just learned from the press that you contemplate after so many years well spent in faithful service to our community. As a citizen and one who has always been most interested in the education of our youth, I wish to add my thanks to those which are felt, if not expressed by the many who know of your devotion to and success in leading the young in the way in which they should go.

"Though your active participation in this work is about to cease, may you long be spared as an example to those who follow you is the earnest hope of

"Yours very sincerely and respectfully,

(Signed) "Charles T. Wilkins"

W. B. Hartgrove

THE PASSING TRADITION AND THE AFRICAN CIVILIZATION

A close examination shows that what we know about the Negro both of the present and the past vitally affects our opinions concerning him. Men's beliefs concerning things are to a large extent determined by where they live and what has been handed down to them. We believe in a hell of roaring flames where in the fiercest of heat the souls of the wicked are subject to eternal burnings. This idea of hell was evolved in the deserts of the Arabian Peninsula where heat is one of the greatest forces of nature with which man has to contend. Among the native tribes of Northern Siberia dwelling in the regions of perpetual ice and snow, hell is a place filled with great chunks of ice upon which the souls of the wicked are placed and there subjected to eternal freezings. This idea of hell was evolved in the regions where man is in a continual battle with the cold.

The beliefs of Negroes concerning themselves have to a large extent been made for them. The reader no doubt will be interested to know that the prevailing notions concerning the inferiority of the Negro grew up to a large extent as the concomitant to Negro slavery in this country. The bringing of the first Negroes from Africa as slaves was justified on the grounds that they were heathen. It was not right, it was argued, for Christians to enslave Christians, but they could enslave heathen, who as a result would have an opportunity to become Christians. These Negro slaves did actually become Christians and as a result the colonists were forced to find other grounds to justify their continuation of the system. The next argument was that they were different from white people. Here we have a large part of the beginnings of the doctrine of the inferiority of the Negro.

When, about 1830, anti-slavery agitation arose in this

country, a new set of arguments were brought forward to justify slavery. First in importance were those taken from the Bible. Science also was called upon and brought forward a large number of facts to demonstrate that by nature the Negro was especially fitted to be a slave. It happened that about this time anthropology was being developed. Racial differences were some of the things which especially interested scientists in this field. The races were defined according to certain physical characteristics. These, it was asserted, determined the superiority or inferiority of races. The true Negro race, said the early anthropologists, had characteristics which especially indicated its inferiority. Through our geographies, histories and encyclopedias we have become familiar with representations of this so-called true Negro, whose chief characteristics were a black skin, woolly hair, protuberant lips and a receding forehead. Caricaturists seized upon these characteristics and popularized them in cartoons, in songs and in other ways. Thus it happened that the Negro, through the descriptions that he got of himself, has come largely to believe in his inherent inferiority and that to attain superiority he must become like the white man in color, in achievements and, in fact, along all lines.

In recent years it has been asked, "Why cannot the Negro attain superiority along lines of his own," that is, instead of simply patterning after what the white man has done, why cannot the Negro through music, art, history, and science, make his own special contributions to the progress of the world? This question has arisen because in the fields of science and history there have been brought forward a number of facts which prove this possibility. First of all, the leading scientists in the field of anthropology are telling us that while there are differences of races, there are no characteristics which per se indicate that one race is inferior or superior to another. The existing differences are differences in kind not in value. On the other hand, whatever superiority one race has attained over another has been largely due to environment.

A German writer in a discussion of the origin of African civilizations said some time ago ''What bold investigators, great pioneers, still find to tell us in civilizations nearer home, proves more and more clearly that we are ignorant of hoary Africa. Somewhat of its present perhaps, we know, but of its past little. Open an illustrated geography and compare the 'Type of the African Negro,' the bluish-black fellow of the protuberant lips, the flattened nose, the stupid expression and the short curly hair, with the tall bronze figures from Dark Africa with which we have of late become familiar, their almost fine-cut features, slightly arched nose, long hair, etc., and you have an example of the problems pressing for solution. In other respects, too, the genuine African of the interior bears no resemblance to the accepted Negro type as it figures on drug and cigar store signs, wearing a shabby stovepipe hat, plaid trousers, and a vari-colored coat. A stroll through the corridors of the Berlin Museum of Ethnology teaches that the real African need by no means resort to the rags and tatters of bygone European splendor. He has precious ornaments of his own, of ivory and plumes, fine plaited willow ware, weapons of superior workmanship. Justly can it be demanded 'What sort of civilization is this? Whence does it come?' ''

It is also pointed out that one of the most important contributions to the civilization of mankind was very probably made by the Negro race. This was the invention of the smelting of iron. The facts brought forward to support this view are: that no iron was smelted in Europe before 900 B. C.; that about 3,000 B. C., there began to appear on the Egyptian monuments pictures of Africans bringing iron from the South to Egypt; that at a time considerably later than this iron implements began to appear in Asia; that there is no iron ore in Egypt; and that in Negro Africa iron ore is abundant. In many places it is found on top of the ground and in some parts it can be melted by simply placing a piece of ore in the fire very much as you would a potato to be roasted.

Studies in the fields of ancient and medieval history are also showing that in the past there were in Negro Africa civilizations of probable indigenous origin which attained importance enough to be mentioned in the writings of the historians and poets of those periods. The seat of one of the highest of these civilizations was Ethiopia. Here the Negro nation attained the greatest fame. As early as 2,500 years before the birth of Christ the Ethiopians appeared to have had a considerable civilization. It was well known to the writers of the Bible and is referred to therein some forty-nine times. In Genesis we read of Cush, the eldest son of Ham. Cush is the Hebrew word for black and means the same as Ethiopia. One of the most famous sons of Cush was Nimrod, whom the Bible mentions as being "a mighty hunter before the Lord; whereof it is said, like Nimrod, a mighty hunter before the Lord." The Bible refers to Ethiopia as being far distant from Palestine. In the book of Isaiah we read "the land of the rustling of wings which is beyond the rivers of Ethiopia that sendeth ambassadors by the sea." The rivers of Ethiopia mentioned in Isaiah are the upper tributaries of the Nile, the Atbara, the Blue Nile and the Sobat.

The later capital of Ethiopia was Meroe. Recent excavations have shown Meroe to have been a city larger than Memphis. The Temple of Ammon, where kings were crowned, was one of the largest in the valley of the Nile. The great walls of cut stones were 15 feet thick and 30 feet high. Heaps of iron-slag and furnaces for smelting iron were discovered, and there were magnificent quays and landing places on the river side, for the export of iron. Excavations have also shown that for 150 years Egypt was a dependency of Ethiopia. The kings of the twenty-third and twenty-fourth Egyptian dynasties were really governors appointed by Ethiopian overlords, while the twenty-fifth dynasty was founded by the Ethiopian king, Sabako, in order to check Assyrian aggression. Palestine was enabled to hold out against Assyria by Ethiopian help. Sennacherib's attempt to capture Jerusalem and carry the Jews into captivity, was frustrated by the army of the Ethiopian king, Taharka. The nation and religion of Judah were thus preserved from being absorbed in heathen lands like the lost Ten Tribes. The Negro soldiers of the Sudan saved the Jewish religion.

The old Greek writers were well acquainted with Ethiopia. According to them in the most ancient times there existed to the South of Egypt a nation and a land designated as Ethiopia. This was the land where the people with the sunburnt faces dwelt. The Greek poet, Homer, mentions the Ethiopians as dwelling at the uttermost limits of the earth, where they enjoyed personal intercourse with the gods. In one place Homer said that Neptune, the god of the sea, ''had gone to feast with the Ethiopians who dwell afar off, the Ethiopians who are divided into two parts, the most distant of men, some at the setting of the sun, others at the rising.'' Herodotus, the Greek historian, described the Ethiopians as long lived and their country as extending to the Southern Sea.

The great fame of the Ethiopians is thus sketched by the eminent historian, Heeren, who in his historical researches says: ''In the earliest traditions of nearly all the more civilized nations of antiquity, the name of this distant people is found. The annals of the Egyptian priests were full of them; the nations of inner Asia, on the Euphrates and Tigris, have interwoven the fictions of the Ethiopians with their own traditions of the conquests and wars of their heroes; and, at a period equally remote, they glimmer in Greek mythology. When the Greeks scarcely knew Italy and Sicily by name, the Ethiopians were celebrated in the verses of their poets; they spoke of them as the 'remotest nation,' the 'most just of men,' the 'favorites of the gods.' The lofty inhabitants of Olympus journey to them and take part in their feasts; their sacrifices are the most agreeable of all that mortals can offer them. And when the faint gleam of tradition and fable gives way to the clear light of history, the luster of the Ethiopians is not diminished. They still continue the object of curiosity and admiration;

and the pens of cautious, clear-sighted historians often place them in the highest rank of knowledge and civilization.''

Of these facts most modern historians know but little and Negroes in general almost nothing. For example, how many have ever heard of Al-Bekri, the Arab writer, who in the eleventh century wrote a description of the Western Sudan of such importance that it gained him the title of ''The Historian of Negro Land?'' How much, by means of research, might be learned of the town of Ghana situate on the banks of the Niger, which the historian Al-Bekri described as a meeting place for commercial caravans from all parts of the world? This town, he said, contained schools and centers of learning. It was the resort of the learned, the rich, and the pious of all nations. Likewise, most of us have never heard perhaps of another Arab writer, Iben Khaldun, who in writing about the middle of the fourteenth century, of Melle, another of the kingdoms of the Sudan, reported that caravans from Egypt consisting of twelve thousand laden camels passed every year through one town on the eastern border of the empire on their way to the capital of the nation. The load of a camel was three hundred pounds. 12,000 camel loads amounted, therefore, to something like 1,600 tons of merchandise. At this time we are told that there was probably not a ship in any of the merchant navies of the world which could carry one hundred tons. 250 years later the average tonnage of the vessels of Spain was 300 tons and that of the English much less. The largest ship which Queen Elizabeth had in her navy, the *Great Mary,* had a capacity of a thousand tons; but it was considered an exception and the marvel of the age.

Another thing that is not generally known is the importance to which some of these Negro kingdoms of the Western Sudan attained during the middle ages and the first centuries of the modern era. In size and permanency they compared favorably with the most advanced nations of Europe. The kingdom of Melle of which the historian, Iben Khaldun, wrote, had an area of over 1,000 miles in extent and existed for 250 years. It was the first of the kingdoms of the Western Sudan to be received on equal terms with the contemporary white nations. The greatest of all the Sudan states was the kingdom of Songhay which, in its golden age, had an area almost equal to that of the United States and existed from about 750 A. D. to 1591. There is a record of the kings of Songhay in regular succession for almost 900 years. The length of the life of the Songhay empire coincides almost exactly with the life of Rome from its foundation as a republic to its downfall as an empire.

The greatest evidences of the high state of civilization which the Sudan had in the fourteenth and fifteenth centuries were the attention that was paid to education and the unusual amount of learning that existed there. The university of Sankore at Timbuctu was a very active center of learning. It was in correspondence with the universities of North Africa and Egypt. It was in touch with the universities of Spain. In the sixteenth century Timbuctu had a large learned class living at ease and busily occupied with the elucidation of intellectual and religious problems. The town swarmed with students. Law, literature, grammar, theology and the natural sciences were studied. The city of Melle had a regular school of science. One distinguished geographer is mentioned, and allusions to surgical science show that the old maxim of the Arabian schools, ''He who studies anatomy pleases God,'' was not forgotten. One of these writers mentions that his brother came from Jenne to Timbuctu to undergo an operation for cataract of the eyes at the hands of a celebrated surgeon there. It is said that the operation was wholly successful. The appearance of comets, so amazing to Europe of the Middle Ages and at the present time to the ignorant, was by these learned blacks noted calmly as a matter of scientific interest. Earthquakes and eclipses excited no great surprise.

The renowned writer of the Sudan was Abdurrahman Essadi. He was born in Timbuctu in 1596. He came of learned and distinguished ancestors. He is chief author of the history of Sudan. The book is said to be a wonderful document. The narrative deals mainly with the modern history of the Songhay Empire, and relates the rise of this black civilization through the fifteenth and sixteenth centuries and its decadence up to the middle of the seventeenth century. The noted traveller, Barth, was of the opinion that the book forms one of the most important additions that the present age has made to the history of mankind. The work is especially valuable for the unconscious light which it throws upon the life, manners, politics, and literature of the country. It presents a vivid picture of the character of the men with whom it deals. It is sometimes called the Epic of the Sudan.

From this brief sketch which I have given of the African in ancient and medieval times it is clear that Negroes should not despise the rock from which they were hewn. As a race they have a past which is full of interest. It is worthy of serious study. From it we can draw inspiration; for it appears that not all black men everywhere throughout the ages have been "hewers of wood and drawers of water." On the contrary, through long periods of time there were powerful black nations which have left the records of their achievements and of which we are just now beginning to learn a little. This little, however, which we have learned teaches us that the Negroes of today should work and strive. Along their own special line and in their own peculiar way they should endeavor to make contributions to civilization. Their achievements can be such that once more black will be dignified and the fame of Ethiopia again spread throughout the world.

Monroe N. Work

THE MIND OF THE AFRICAN NEGRO AS REFLECTED IN HIS PROVERBS

As a study of folk literature of different races offers one way of understanding their mental attitude toward life and its problems, the folk literature of the Negro will reveal to us his inherent moral and intellectual bias and the natural trend of his philosophy. Let us therefore examine some phases of this subject, paying particular attention to that part which relates especially to the proverbs. The sources of such literature are abundant. A little research in a well-equipped library brings one into a curious and informing mass of knowledge, ever increasing in bulk, in the French, German and English languages, as well as in many strange and highly inflected African tongues.

A cursory reading of this literature discloses at once that our general knowledge of Africa has been based in the past mainly on those external facts that strike the sense of sight, such as the physical appearance of the population, native dress and handiwork, musical instruments, implements of warfare, and customs peculiar to the social and religious life of the people. Only through the folk literature, however, can we get a glimpse of the working of the mind of the African Negro. Professor Henry Drummond, although he had traveled in Africa and had written at length about it, still exhibited a longing for this insight when he observed: "I have often wished that I could get inside of an African for an afternoon and just see how he looked at things." At that time much of the folk literature of that continent was not as now available. A deeper and more extensive reading of it at present strengthens our belief in the ancient saying "Out of Africa there is always something new," a rather disquieting thought, if we have reached the conclusion that native culture on that continent has never risen above the zero point.

A critical examination of the content of this folk literature will result in a division somewhat similar to that found
in the same type of literature of other races. Such a division discloses stories, poetry, riddles and proverbs. The
African folk literature is especially rich in proverbs. So
numerous are these proverbs that it has been said that there
is scarcely an object presented to the eye, scarcely an idea
excited in the mind, but it is accompanied by some sententious aphorism, founded on close observation of man and
animals and in many cases of a decidedly moral tendency.
Lord Bacon remarked many years ago that "the genius, wit
and spirit of a nation are discovered in its proverbs." Cer-
vantes in *Don Quixote* says "Methinks, Sancho, that there
is no proverb that is not true, because they are all judgments drawn from the same experience which is the mother
of all knowledge." If these sayings be true, then the proverbs of the African Negro should be examined in order to
see if they approach these observations.

For convenience of the reader an effort has been made to
arrange these sententious sayings under general subjects.
These selected by no means exhaust the mine of African
proverbial lore but are only a few nuggets that suggest the
Negro's power to infer and generalize and to express himself in a graphic and concise way relative to life as he observed and experienced it.[1]

Anger
    Anger does nobody good, but patience is the father of kindness.
Assistance
    Not to aid one in distress is to kill him in your heart.
Birth
    Birth does not differ from birth; as the free man was born so
    was the slave.

[1] Among the works which have been consulted in the preparation of this
article are the following:
    R. F. Burton, Wit and Wisdom from West Africa.
    S. W. Koelle, African Native Literature.
    A. B. Ellis, The Yoruba Speaking Peoples of the Slave Coast of West
Africa.
    Heli Chatelin, Folk Tales of Angola.

In the beginning our Lord created all. With him there is neither slave nor free man, but every one is free.

Boasting

Boasting is not courage.

He who boasts much cannot do much.

Much gesticulation does not prove courage.

Borrowing

Borrowing is easy but the day of payment is hard.

Chance

He who waits for chance may wait for a year.

Character

Wherever a man goes to dwell his character goes with him.

Every man's character is good in his own eyes.

Charity

Charity is the father of sacrifice.

Children

There is no wealth without children.

It is the duty of children to wait on elders, not elders on children.

Condemnation

You condemn on hearsay evidence alone, your sins increase.

Contempt

Men despise what they do not understand.

Covetousness

If thou seeketh to obtain by force what our Lord did not give thee, thou wilt not get it.

Danger of Beauty

He who marries a beauty, marries trouble.

Danger of Poverty

Beg help and you will meet with refusals; ask for alms and you will meet with misers.

Danger of Wealth

It is better to be poor and live long than rich and die young.

Disposition

A man's disposition is like a mark in a stone, no one can efface it.

Doing Good

If one does good, God will interpret it to him for good.

Duty to One's Self
>Do not repair another man's fence until you have seen to your own.

Effort
>You cannot kill game by looking at it.

Evil Doer
>The evil doer is ever anxious.

Experience
>We begin by being foolish and we become wise by experience.

Familiarity
>Familiarity induces contempt, but distance secures respect.

Faults
>Faults are like a hill, you stand on your own and you talk about those of other people.

Faults of the Rich
>If thou art poor do not make a rich man thy friend.
>If thou goest to a foreign country, do not alight at a rich man's house.

Favor of the Great
>To love the king is not bad, but a king who loves you is better.

Folly
>After a foolish action comes remorse.

Forethought
>A person prepared beforehand is better than after reflection.
>The day on which one starts is not the time to commence one's preparation.

Forgiveness
>He who forgives ends the quarrel.

Friends
>There are three friends in this world—courage, sense, and insight.

Friendship
>Hold a true friend with both of your hands.

Future
>Thou knowest the past but not the future.
>As to what is future, even a bird with a long neck can not see it, but God only.

Gossip
>Gossip is unbecoming an elder.

Gentleness

A matter dealt with gently is sure to prosper, but a matter dealt with violently causes vexation.

Hate

There is no medicine for hate.

Heart

It is the heart that carries one to heaven.

Heathen

He is a heathen who bears malice.

Hope

Hope is the pillar of the world.

Ignorance

Lack of knowledge is darker than night.

An ignorant man is always a slave.

Whoever works without knowledge works uselessly.

Immortality

Since thou hast no benefactor in this world, thy having one in the next world will be all the more pleasant.

Injury ·

He who injures another brings injury upon himself.

Laziness

Laziness lends assistance to fatigue.

A lazy man looks for light employment.

Love

One does not love another if one does not accept anything from him.

If you love the children of others, you will love your own even better.

Meekness

If one knows thee not or a blind man scolds thee, do not become angry.

Mother

Him whose mother is no more, distress carries off.

Necessity of effort

The sieve never sifts meal by itself.

Old Age

There are no charms or medicine against old age.

Opportunity

The dawn does not come twice to wake a man.

At the bottom of patience there is heaven.

Patience is the best of qualities; he who possesses it possesses all things.

People

Ordinary people are as common as grass, but good people are dearer than the eye.

Politeness

Bowing to a dwarf will not prevent your standing erect again.

"I have forgotten thy name" is better than "I know thee not."

Poverty

A poor man has no friends.

He who has no house has no word in society.

Riches

Property is the prop of life.

A wealthy man always has followers.

Sleep

Sleep has no favorites.

Strife

Strife begets a gentle child.

Sun

The sun is the king of torches.

Trade

Trade is not something imaginary or descriptive, but something real and profitable.

Truth

Lies, however numerous, will be caught by truth when it rises up.

The voice of truth is easily known.

Unselfishness

If you love yourself others will hate you, if you humble yourself others will love you.

Valor

Boasting at home is not valor; parade is not battle; when war comes the valiant will be known.

The fugitive never stops to pick the thorn from his foot.

Wisdom

A man may be born to wealth, but wisdom comes only with length of days.

A man with wisdom is better off than a stupid man with any amount of charms and superstition.

Know thyself better than he who speaks of thee.

Not to know is bad, not to wish to know is worse.

A counsellor who understands proverbs soon sets matters right.

PROVERBS BASED ON THE OBSERVATION OF ANIMALS

Butterfly

The butterfly that brushes against thorns will tear its wings.

Dog

If the dog is not at home, he barks not.

A heedless dog will not do for the chase.

A lurking dog does not lie in the hyena's lair.

Elephant

He who can not move an ant, and yet tries to move an elephant, shall find out his folly.

The elephant does not find his trunk heavy.

Were no elephant in the jungle, the buffalo would be a great animal.

Fly

If the fly flies, the frog goes not supperless to bed.

Fox

When the fox dies, fowls do not mourn.

Goat

When the goat goes abroad, the sheep must run.

Rat

When the rat laughs at the cat, there is a hole.

The rat has not power to call the cat to account.

The rat does not go to sleep in the cat's bed.

Wolf

He who goes with the wolf will learn to howl.

A. O. STAFFORD

WHAT THE NEGRO WAS THINKING DURING THE EIGHTEENTH CENTURY

ESSAY ON NEGRO SLAVERY[1]

No. I

Amidst the infinite variety of moral and political subjects, proper for public commendation, it is truly surprising, that one of the most important and affecting should be so generally neglected. An encroachment on the smallest civil or political privilege, shall fan the enthusiastic flames of liberty, till it shall extend over vast and distant regions, and violently agitate a whole continent. But the cause of humanity shall be basely violated, justice shall be wounded to the heart, and national honor deeply and lastingly polluted, and not a breath or murmur shall arise to disturb the prevailing quiescence or to rouse the feelings of indignation against such general, extensive, and complicated iniquity.—To what cause are we to impute this frigid silence— this torpid indifference—this cold inanimated conduct of the otherwise warm and generous Americans? Why do they remain inactive, amidst the groans of injured humanity, the shrill and distressing complaints of expiring justice and the keen remorse of polluted integrity?—Why do they not rise up to assert the cause of God and the world, to drive the fiend injustice into remote and distant regions, and to exterminate oppression from the face of the fair fields of America?

When the united colonies revolted from Great Britain, they did it upon this principle, "that all men are by nature and of right ought to be free."—After a long, successful, and glorious struggle for liberty, during which they manifested the firmest attachment to the rights of mankind, can they so soon forget the principles that then governed their determinations? Can Americans, after the noble contempt they expressed for tyrants, meanly descend to take up the scourge? Blush, ye revolted colonies, for having apostatized from your own principles.

Slavery, in whatever point of light it is considered, is repugnant to the feelings of nature, and inconsistent with the original

[1] "Othello," the author of these two essays, was identified as a Negro by Abbé Grégoire in his "De la litterature des Nègres."

rights of man. It ought therefore to be stigmatized for being unnatural; and detested for being unjust. Tis an outrage to providence and an affront offered to divine Majesty, who has given to man his own peculiar image.—That the Americans after considering the subject in this light—after making the most manly of all possible exertions in defence of liberty—after publishing to the world the principle upon which they contended, viz.: "that all men are by nature and of right ought to be free," should still retain in subjection a numerous tribe of the human race merely for their own private use and emolument, is, of all things the strongest inconsistency, the deepest reflexion on our conduct, and the most abandoned apostasy that every took place, since the almighty fiat spoke into existence this habitable world. So flagitous a violation can never escape the notice of a just Creator whose vengeance may be now on the wing, to disseminate and hurl the arrows of destruction.

In what light can the people of Europe consider America after the strange inconsistency of her conduct? Will they not consider her as an abandoned and deceitful country? In the hour of calamity she petitioned heaven to be propitious to her cause. Her prayers were heard. Heaven pitied her distress, smiled on her virtuous exertions, and vanquished all her afflictions. The ungrateful creature forgets this timely assistance—no longer remembers her own sorrows—but basely commences oppression in her turn.—Beware America! pause—and consider the difference between the mild effulgence of approving providence and the angry countenance of incensed divinity!

The importation of slaves into America ought to be a subject of the deepest regret, to every benevolent and thinking mind.—And one of the greatest defects in the federal system, is the liberty it allows on this head. Venerable in every thing else, it is injudicious here; and it is to be much deplored, that a system of so much political perfection, should be stained with any thing that does an outrage to human nature. As a door, however, is open to amendment, for the sake of distressed humanity, of injured national reputation, and the glory of doing so benevolent a thing, I hope some wise and virtuous patriot will advocate the measure, and introduce an alteration in that pernicious part of the government.—So far from encouraging the importation of slaves, and countenancing that vile traffic in human flesh; the members of the late continental convention[2] should have seized the happy opportunity of prohibiting for ever this cruel species of reprobated villainy.—That they did not do so, will for ever diminish the luster of their other proceedings, so highly extolled, and so justly distinguished for their intrinsic value.—Let us for a moment contrast the sentiments and actions of the Europeans on this subject, with those of our own countrymen. In France the warmest and most animated exertions are making, in order to introduce the entire abolition of the slave trade; and in England many of the first characters of the country advocate the same measure, with an enthusiastic philanthropy. The prime minister himself is at the head of that society; and nothing can equal the ardour of their endeavours, but the glorious goodness of the cause.[3]—Will the Americans allow the people of England to get the start of them in acts of humanity? Forbid it shame!

The practice of stealing, or bartering for human flesh is pregnant with the most glaring turpitude, and the blackest barbarity of disposition.—For can any one say, that this is doing as he would be done by? Will such a practice stand the scrutiny of this great rule of moral government? Who can without the complicated emotions of anger and impatience, suppose himself in the predicament of a slave? Who can bear the thoughts of his relatives being torn from him by a savage enemy; carried to distant regions of the habitable globe, never more to return; and treated there as the unhappy Africans are in this country? Who can support the reflexion of his father—his mother—his sister—or his wife—perhaps his children—being barbarously snatched away by a foreign invader, without the prospect of ever beholding them again? Who can reflect upon their being afterwards publicly exposed to sale—obliged to labor with unwearied assiduity—and because all things are not possible to be performed, by persons so unaccustomed to robust exercise, scourged with all the rage and anger of malignity, until their unhappy carcasses are covered with ghastly wounds and frightful contusions? Who can reflect on these things when applying the case to himself, without being chilled with horror, at

[2] The writer refers here to the Convention of 1787 which framed the Constitution of the United States.

[3] Here the writer has in mind the organization of the English Society for the Abolition of the Slave Trade and the support given the cause by Wilberforce, Pitt, Fox and Burke in England and by Brissot, Clavière and Montmorin in France.

circumstances so extremely shocking?—Yet hideous as this concise
and imperfect description is, of the sufferings sustained by many
of our slaves, it is nevertheless true; and so far from being exag-
gerated, falls infinitely short of a thousand circumstances of distress, which have been recounted by different writers on the subject, and which contribute to make their situation in this life, the
most absolutely wretched, and completely miserable, that can possibly be conceived.—In many places in America, the slaves are
treated with every circumstance of rigorous inhumanity, accumulated hardship, and enormous cruelty.—Yet when we take them
from Africa, we deprive them of a country which God hath given
them for their own; as free as we are, and as capable of enjoying
that blessing. Like pirates we go to commit devastation on the
coast of an innocent country, and among a people who never did
us wrong.

An insatiable, avaricious desire to accumulate riches, cooperat-
ing with a spirit of luxury and injustice, seems to be the leading
cause of this peculiarly degrading and ignominious practice. Being
once accustomed to subsist without labour, we become soft and voluptuous; and rather than afterwards forego the gratification of our
habitual indolence and ease, we countenance the infamous violation,
and sacrifice at the shrine of cruelty, all the finer feelings of elevated humanity.

Considering things in this view, there surely can be nothing
more justly reprehensible or disgusting than the extravagant finery
of many country people's daughters. It hath not been at all uncommon to observe as much gauze, lace and other trappings, on
one of those country maidens as hath employed two or three of her
father's slaves, for twelve months afterwards, to raise tobacco to
pay for. Tis an ungrateful reflexion that all this frippery and
effected finery, can only be supported by the sweat of another person's brow, and consequently only by lawful rapine and injustice.
If these young females could devote as much time from their
amusements, as would be necessary for reflexion; or was there any
person of humanity at hand who could inculcate the indecency of
this kind of extravagance, I am persuaded that they have hearts
good enough to reject with disdain, the momentary pleasure of
making a figure, in behalf of the rational and lasting delight of
contributing by their forbearance to the happiness of many thousand individuals.

In Maryland where slaves are treated with as much lenity, as perhaps they are any where, their situation is to the last degree ineligible. They live in wretched cots, that scarcely secure them from the inclemency of the weather; sleep in the ashes or on straw, wear the coarsest clothing, and subsist on the most ordinary food that the country produces. In all things they are subject to their master's absolute command, and, of course, have no will of their own. Thus circumstanced, they are subject to great brutality, and are often treated with it. In particular instances, they may be better provided for in this state, but this suffices for a general description. But in the Carolinas and the island of Jamaica, the cruelties that have been wantonly exercised on those miserable creatures, are without a precedent in any other part of the world. If those who have written on the subject, may be believed, it is not uncommon there, to tie a slave up and whip him to death.

On all occasions impartiality in the distribution of justice should be observed. The little state of Rhode Island has been reprobated by other states, for refusing to enter into measures respecting a new general government; and so far it is admitted that she is culpable.[4] But if she is worthy of blame in this respect, she is entitled to the highest admiration for the philanthropy, justice, and humanity she hath displayed, respecting the subject I am treating on. She hath passed an act prohibiting the importation of slaves into that state, and forbidding her citizens to engage in the iniquitous traffic. So striking a proof of her strong attachment to the rights of humanity, will rescue her name from oblivion, and bid her live in the good opinion of distant and unborn generations.

Slavery, unquestionably, should be abolished, particularly in this country; because it is inconsistent with the declared principles of the American Revolution. The sooner, therefore, we set about it, the better. Either we should set our slaves at liberty, immediately, and colonize them in the western territory;[5] or we should immediately take measures for the gradual abolition of it, so that it may become a known, and fixed point, that ultimately, universal liberty, in these united states, shall triumph.—This is the least we can do in order to evince our sense of the irreparable outrages we have committed, to wipe off the odium we have incurred,

---

[4] Rhode Island had failed to ratify the Constitution of the United States.
[5] During the first forty years of the republic there was much talk about colonizing the Negroes in the West.

and to give mankind a confidence again in the justice, liberality, and honour of our national proceedings.

It would not be difficult to show, were it necessary, that America would soon become a richer and more happy country, provided the step was adopted. That corrosive anguish of persevering in anything improper, which now embitters the enjoyments of life, would vanish as the mist of a foggy morn doth before the rising sun; and we should find as great a disparity between our present situation, and that which would succeed to it, as subsists between a cloudy winter, and a radiant spring.—Besides, our lands would not be then cut down for the support of a numerous train of useless inhabitants—useless, I mean, to themselves, and effectually to us, by encouraging sloth and voluptuousness among our young farmers and planters, who might otherwise know how to take care of their money, as well as how to dissipate it.—In all other respects, I conceive them to be as valuable as we are—as capable of worthy purposes, and to possess the same dignity that we do, in the estimation of providence; although the value of their work apart, for which we are dependent on them, we generally consider them as good for nothing, and accordingly, treat them with greatest neglect.

But be it remembered, that this cause is the cause of heaven; and that the father of them as well as of us, will not fail, at a future settlement, to adjust the account between us, with a dreadful attention to justice.

OTHELLO

BALTIMORE, May 10, 1788.

—*American Museum*, IV, 412–415.

ESSAY ON NEGRO SLAVERY

No. II

Upon no better principle do we plunder the coasts of Africa, and bring away its wretched inhabitants as slaves than that, by which the greater fish swallows up the lesser. Superior power seems only to produce superior brutality; and that weakness and imbecility, which ought to engage our protection, and interest the feelings of social benevolence in behalf of the defenceless, seems only to provoke us to acts of illiberal outrage and unmanly violence.

The practice which has been followed by the English nation, since the establishment of the slave trade—I mean that of stirring up the natives of Africa, against each other, with a view of purchasing the prisoners mutually taken in battle, must strike the humane mind with sentiments of the deepest abhorrence, and confer on that people a reproach, as lasting as time itself. It is surprising that the eastern world did not unite, to discourage a custom so diabolical in its tendency, and to exterminate a species of oppression which humbles the dignity of all mankind. But this torpid inattention can only be accounted for, by adverting to the savage disposition of the times, which countenanced cruelties unheard of at this enlightened period. What rudeness of demeanor and brutality of manner, which had been introduced into Europe, by those swarms of barbarians, that overwhelmed it from the north, had hardly begun to dissipate before the enlivening sun of civilization, when this infernal practice first sprang up into existence. Before this distinguished era of refined barbarity, the sons of Africa were in possession of all the mild enjoyments of peace— all the pleasing delights of uninterrupted harmony—and all the diffusive blessings of profound tranquility. Boundless must be the punishment, which irritated providence will inflict on those whose wanton cruelty has prompted them to destroy this fair arrangement of nature—this flowery prospect of human felicity. Engulphed in the dark abyss of never ending misery, they shall in bitterness atone for the stab thus given to human nature; and in anguish unutterable expiate crimes, for which nothing less than eternal sufferings can make adequate retribution!—Equally iniquitous is the practice of robbing that country of its inhabitants; and equally tremendous will be the punishment. The voice of injured thousands, who have been violently torn from their native country, and carried to distant and inhospitable climes—the bitter lamentations of the wretched, helpless female—the cruel agonizing sensations of the husband, the father and the friend—will ascend to the throne of Omnipotence, and, from the elevated heights of heaven, cause him, with the whole force of almighty vengeance, to hurl the guilty perpetrators of those inhuman beings, down the steep precipice of inevitable ruin, into the bottomless gulph of final, irretrievable, and endless destruction!

Ye sons of America, forbear!—Consider the dire consequences, that will attend the prosecution, against which the all-powerful God of nature holds up his hands, and loudly proclaims, desist!

In the insolence of self-consequence, we are accustomed to esteem ourselves and the christian powers of Europe, the only civilized people on the globe; the rest without distinction, we presumptuously denominate barbarians. But, when the practices above mentioned, come to be deliberately considered—when added to these, we take a view of the proceedings of the English in the East Indies, under the direction of the late Lord Clive, and remember what happened in the streets of Bengal and Calcutta—when we likewise reflect on our American mode of driving, butchering and exterminating the poor defenceless Indians, the native and lawful proprietors of the soil—we shall acknowledge, if we possess the smallest degree of candor, that the appellation of barbarian does not belong to them alone. While we continue those practices the term christian will only be a burlesque expression, signifying no more than that it ironically denominates the rudest sect of barbarians that ever disgraced the hand of their Creator. We have the precepts of the gospel for the government of our moral deportment, in violation of which, those outrageous wrongs are committed; but they have no such meliorating influence among them, and only adhere to the simple dictates of reason, and natural religion, which they never violate.

Might not the inhabitants of Africa, with still greater justice on their side, than we have on ours, cross the Atlantic, seize our citizens, carry them into Africa, and make slaves of them, provided they were able to do it? But should this be really the case, every corner of the globe would reverberate with the sound of African oppression; so loud would be our complaint, and so "feeling our appeal" to the inhabitants of the world at large. We should represent them as a lawless, piratical set of unprincipled robbers, plunderers and villains, who basely prostituted the superior power and information, which God had given them for worthy purposes to the vilest of all ends. We should not hesitate to say that they made use of those advantages only to infringe upon every dictate of justice; to trample under foot every suggestion of principle, and to spurn, with contempt, every right of humanity.

The Algerines are reprobated all the world over, for their unlawful depredations; and stigmatized as pirates, for their unreasonable exactions from foreign nations. But, the Algerines are no greater pirates than the Americans; nor are they a race more destructive to the happiness to mankind. The depredations of the latter on the coast of Africa, and upon the Indians' Territory make the truth of this assertion manifest. The piratical depredations of the Algerines appear to be a judgment from heaven upon the nations, to punish their perfidy and atrocious violations of justice; and never did any people more justly merit the scourge than Americans, on whom it seems to fall with peculiar and reiterated violence. When they yoke our citizens to the plow, and compel them to labour in that degraded manner, they only retaliate on us for similar barbarities. For Algiers is a part of the same country, whose helpless inhabitants we are accustomed to carry away. But the English and Americans cautiously avoid engaging with a warlike people, whom they fear to attack in a manner so base and unworthy; whilst the Algerines, more generous and courageous plunderers, are not afraid to make war on brave and well-disciplined enemies, who are capable of making a gallant resistance.

Whoever examines into the conditions of the slaves in America will find them in a state of the most uncultivated rudeness. Not instructed in any kind of learning, they are grossly ignorant of all refinement, and have little else about them, belonging to the nature of civilized man, than mere form. They are strangers to almost every idea, that doth not relate to their labour or their food; and though naturally possessed of strong sagacity, and lively parts, are, in all respects, in a state of most deplorable brutality.—This is owing to the iron-hand of oppression, which ever crushes the bud of genius and binds up in chains every expansion of the human mind.—Such is their extreme ignorance that they are utterly unacquainted with the laws of the world—the injunctions of religion—their own natural rights, and the forms, ceremonies and privileges of marriage originally established by the Divinity. Accordingly they lived in open violation of the precepts of christianity and with as little formality or restrictions as the brutes of the field, unite for the purposes of procreation. Yet this is a civilized country and a most enlightened period of the world! The resplendent glory of the gospel is at hand, to conduct us in safety through the labyrinths of life. Science hath grown up to maturity, and is discovered to possess not only all the properties of solidity of strength, but likewise every ornament of elegance, and every embellishment of fancy. Philosophy hath here attained the most exalted height of elevation; and the art of government hath received such refinements among us, as hath equally astonished our friends, our enemies and ourselves. In fine, no annals are more brilliant than those of America; nor do any more luxuriantly abound with examples of exalted heroism, refined policy, and sympathetic humanity. Yet now the prospect begins to change; and all the splendor of this august assemblage, will soon be overcast by sudden and impenetrable clouds; and American greatness be obliterated and swallowed up by one enormity. Slavery diffuses the gloom, and casts around us the deepest shade of approaching darkness. No longer shall the united states of America be famed for liberty. Oppression pervades their bowels; and while they exhibit a fair exterior to the other parts of the world, they are nothing more than "painted sepulchres," containing within them nought but rottenness and corruption.

Ye voluptuous, ye opulent and great, who hold in subjection such numbers of your fellow-creatures, and suffer these things to happen—beware! Reflect on this lamentable change, that may, at a future period, take place against you. Arraigned before the almighty Sovereign of the universe, how will you answer the charge of such complicated enormity? The presence of these slaves, who have been lost, for want of your instruction, and by means of your oppression, shall make you dart deeper into the flames, to avoid their just reproaches, and seek out for an asylum, in the hidden corners of perdition.

Many persons of opulence in Virginia, and the Carolinas, treat their unhappy slaves with every circumstance of coolest neglect, and the most deliberate indifference. Surrounded with a numerous train of servants, to contribute to their personal ease, and wallowing in all the luxurious plenitude of riches, they neglect the wretched source, whence they draw this profusion. Many of their negroes, on distant estates, are left to the entire management of inhuman overseers, where they suffer for the want of that sustenance, which, at the proprietors seat of residence, is wastefully given to the dogs. It frequently happens, on these large estates, that they are not clothed, 'till winter is nearly expired; and then, the most valuable only are attended to; the young, and the labourworn, having no other allowance, in this respect, than the tattered garments, thrown off by the more fortunate. A single peck of corn a week, or the like measure of rice, is the ordinary quantity of provision for a hard working slave; to which a small quantity of meat is occasionally, tho' rarely, added. While those miserable degraded persons thus scantily subsist, all the produce of their unwearied toil, is taken away to satiate their rapacious master. He, devoted wretch! thoughtless of the sweat and toil with which his wearied, exhausted dependents procure what he extravagantly dissipates, not contented with the ordinary luxuries of life, is, perhaps, planning, at the time, some improvement on the voluptuous art. —Thus he sets up two carriages instead of one; maintains twenty servants, when a fourth part of that number are more than sufficient to discharge the business of personal attendance; makes every animal, proper for the purpose, bleed around him, in order to supply the gluttonous profusion of his table; and generally gives away what his slaves are pining for;—those very slaves, whose labour enables him to display this liberality!—No comment is necessary, to expose the peculiar folly, ingratitude, and infamy of such execrable conduct.

But the custom of neglecting those slaves, who have been worn out in our service, is unhappily found to prevail, not only among the more opulent but thro' the more extensive round of the middle and inferior ranks of life. No better reason can be given for this base inattention, than that they are no longer able to contribute to our emoluments. With singular dishonor, we forget the faithful instrument of past enjoyment, and when, by length of time, it becomes debilitated, it is, like a withered stalk, ungratefully thrown away.

Our slaves unquestionably have the strongest of all claims upon us, for protection and support; we having compelled them to involuntary servitude, and deprived them of every means of protecting or supporting themselves. The injustice of our conduct, and barbarity of our neglect, when this reflexion is allowed to predominate, becomes so glaringly conspicuous, as even to excite, against ourselves, the strongest emotion of detestation and abhorrence.

To whom are the wretched sons of Africa to apply for redress, if their cruel master treats them with unkindness? To whom will they resort for protection, if he is base enough to refuse it to them? The law is not their friend;—alas! too many statutes are enacted against them. The world is not their friend;—the iniquity is too general and extensive. No one who hath slaves of his own, will protect those of another, less the practice should be retorted. Thus when their masters abandon them, their situation is destitute and forlorn, and God is their only friend!

Let us imitate the conduct of a neighboring state, and immediately take measures, at least, for the gradual abolition of slavery.[6] Justice demands it of us, and we ought not to hesitate in obeying its inviolable mandates.—All the feelings of pity, compassion, affection, and benevolence—all the emotions of tenderness, humanity, philanthropy, and goodness—all the sentiments of mercy, probity, honour, and integrity, unite to solicit for their emancipation. Immortal will be the glory of accomplishing their liberation; and eternal the disgrace of keeping them in chains.

But, if the state of Pennsylvania is to be applauded for her conduct, that of South Carolina can never be too strongly execrated.[7] The legislature of that state, at no very remote period, brought in a bill for prohibiting the use of letters to their slaves, and forbidding them the privilege of being taught to read!—This was a deliberate attempt to enslave the minds of those unfortunate objects, whose persons they already held in arbitrary subjection:—Detestable deviation from the becoming rectitude of man.

One more peculiarly distressing circumstance remains to be recounted, before I take my final leave of the subject.—In the ordinary course of the business of the country, the punishment of relatives frequently happens on the same farm, and in view of each other:—The father often sees his beloved son—the son his venerable sire—the mother her much-loved daughter—the daughter her affectionate parent—the husband the wife of his bosom, and she the husband of her affection, cruelly bound up without delicacy or mercy, and punished with all extremity of incensed rage, and all the rigour of unrelenting severity, whilst these unfortunate wretches dare not even interpose in each other's behalf. Let us reverse the case and suppose it ours:—all is silent horror!

OTHELLO

MARYLAND, May 23, 1788.

—American Museum, IV, 509–512.

LETTER ON SLAVERY BY A NEGRO

I am one of that unfortunate race of men, who are distinguished from the rest of the human species, by a black skin and wooly hair—disadvantages of very little moment in themselves, but which prove

[6] The writer refers here to the acts of Pennsylvania, providing for the abolition of slavery.

[7] In 1740 South Carolina enacted a law prohibiting any one from teaching a slave to read or employing one in "any manner of writing." Georgia enacted the same law in 1770.

to us a source of greatest misery, because there are men, who will not be persuaded that it is possible for a human soul to be lodged within a sable body. The West Indian planters could not, if they thought us men, so wantonly spill our blood; nor could the natives of this land of liberty, deeming us of the same species with themselves, submit to be instrumental in enslaving us, or think us proper subjects of a sordid commerce. Yet, strong as the prejudices against us are, it will not, I hope on this side of the Atlantic, be considered as a crime, for a poor African not to confess himself a being of an inferior order to those, who happen to be of a different colour from himself; or be thought very presumptuous, in one who is but a negro, to offer to the happy subjects of this free government, some reflections upon the wretched condition of his countrymen. They will not, I trust, think worse of my brethren, for being discontented with so hard a lot as that of slavery; nor disown me for their fellow-creature, merely because I deeply feel the unmerited sufferings which my countrymen endure.

It is neither the vanity of being an author, nor a sudden and capricious gust of humanity, which has prompted this present design. It has long been conceived and long been the principal subject of my thoughts. Ever since an indulgent master rewarded my youthful services with freedom and supplied me at a very early age with the means of acquiring knowledge, I have laboured to understand the true principles, on which the liberties of mankind are founded, and to possess myself of the language of this country, in order to plead the cause of those who were once my fellow slaves, and if possible to make my freedom, in some degree, the instrument of their deliverance.

The first thing then, which seems necessary, in order to remove those prejudices, which are so unjustly entertained against us, is to prove that we are men—a truth which is difficult of proof, only because it is difficult to imagine, by what argument it can be combatted. Can it be contended that a difference of colour alone can constitute a difference of species?—if not in what single circumstance are we different from the rest of mankind? what variety is there in our organization? what inferiority of art in the fashoning of our bodies? what imperfection in the faculties of our minds?— Has not a negro eyes? has not a negro hands, organs, dimensions, senses, affections, passions?—fed with the same food; hurt with the same weapons; subject to the same diseases; healed by the same means; warmed and cooled by the same summer and winter as a white man? if you prick us, do we not bleed? if you poison us, do we not die? are we not exposed to all the same wants? do we not feel all the same sentiments—are we not capable of all the same exertions—and are we not entitled to all the same rights, as other men?

Yes—and it is said we are men, it is true; but that we are men, addicted to more and worse vices, than those of any other complexion; and such is the innate perverseness of our minds, that nature seems to have marked us out for slavery.—Such is the apology perpetually made for our masters, and the justification offered for that universal proscription, under which we labour.

But, I supplicate our enemies to be, though for the first time, just in their proceedings toward us, and to establish the fact before, they attempt to draw any conclusions from it. Nor let them imagine that this can be done, by merely asserting that such is our universal character. It is the character, I grant, that our inhuman masters have agreed to give us, and which they have so industriously and too successfully propagated, in order to palliate their own guilt, by blackening the helpless victims of it, and to disguise their own cruelty under the semblance of justice. Let the natural depravity of our character be proved—not by appealing to declamatory invectives, and interested representations, but by showing that a greater proportion of crimes have been committed by the wronged slaves of the plantation, than by the luxurous inhabitants of Europe, who are happily strangers to those aggravated provocations, by which our passions are every day irritated and incensed. Show us, that, of the multitude of negroes, who have within a few years transported themselves to this country,[8] and who are abandoned to themselves; who are corrupted by example, prompted by penury, and instigated by the memory of their wrongs to the commission of crime—shew us, I say (and the demonstration, if it be possible, cannot be difficult) that a greater proportion of these, than of white men have fallen under the animadversions of justice, and have been sacrificed to your laws. Though avarice may slander and insult our misery, and though poets heighten the horror of their fables, by representing us as monsters of vice—the fact is, that, if treated like other men, and admitted to a participation of their rights, we should differ from them in nothing, perhaps, but in our

---

[8] This letter was originally published in England, where the number of negroes had considerably increased after the war in America.

possessing stronger passions, nicer sensibility, and more enthusiastic virtue.

Before so harsh a decision was pronounced upon our nature, we might have expected—if sad experience had not taught us, to expect nothing but injustice from our adversaries—that some pains would have been taken, to ascertain, what our nature is; and that we should have been considered, as we are found in our native woods, and not as we now are—altered and perverted by an inhuman political institution. But, instead of this, we are examined, not by philosophers, but by interested traders: not as nature formed us, but as man has depraved us—and from such an inquiry, prosecuted under such circumstances, the perverseness of our dispositions is said to be established. Cruel that you are! you make us slaves; you implant in our minds all the vices, which are in some degree, inseparable from that condition; and you then impiously impute to nature, and to God, the origin of those vices, to which you alone have given birth; and punish in us the crimes, of which you are yourselves the authors.

The condition of the slave is in nothing more deplorable, than in its being so unfavorable to the practice of every virtue. The surest foundation of virtue is love of our fellow creatures; and that affection takes its birth, in the social relations of men to one another. But to a slave these are all denied. He never pays or receives the grateful duties of a son—he never knows or experiences the fond solicitude of a father—the tender names of husband, of brother, and of friend, are to him unknown. He has no country to defend and bleed for—he can relieve no sufferings—for he looks around in vain, to find a being more wretched than himself. He can indulge no generous sentiment—for he sees himself every hour treated with contempt and ridiculed, and distinguished from irrational brutes, by nothing but the severity of punishment. Would it be surprising, if a slave, labouring under all these disadvantages—oppressed, insulted, scorned, trampled on—should come at last to despise himself—to believe the calumnies of his oppressors—and to persuade himself, that it would be against his nature, to cherish any honourable sentiment or to attempt any virtuous action? Before you boast of your superiority over us, place some of your own colour (if you have the heart to do it) in the same situation with us; and see, whether they have such innate virtue, and such unconquerable vigour of mind, as to be capable of surmounting such multiplied difficulties, and of keeping their minds free from the infection of every vice, even under the oppressive yoke of such a servitude.

But, not satisfied with denying us that indulgence, to which the misery of our condition gives us so just a claim, our enemies have laid down other and stricter rules of morality, to judge our actions by, than those by which the conduct of all other men is tried. Habits, which in all human beings, except ourselves, are thought innocent, are, in us, deemed criminal—and actions, which are even laudable in white men, become enormous crimes in negroes. In proportion to our weakness, the strictness of censure is increased upon us; and as resources are withheld from us, our duties are multiplied. The terror of punishment is perpetually before our eyes; but we know not, how to avert it, what rules to act by, or what guides to follow. We have written laws, indeed, composed in a language we do not understand and never promulgated: but what avail written laws, when the supreme law, with us, is the capricious will of our overseers? To obey the dictates of our own hearts, and to yield to the strong propensities of nature, is often to incur severe punishment; and by emulating examples which we find applauded and revered among Europeans, we risk inflaming the wildest wrath of our inhuman tyrants.

To judge of the truth of these assertions, consult even those milder and subordinate rules for our conduct, the various codes of your West India laws—those laws which allow us to be men, whenever they consider us as victims of their vengeance, but treat us only like a species of living property, as often as we are to be the objects of their protection—those laws by which (it may be truly said) that we are bound to suffer, and be miserable under pain of death. To resent an injury, received from a white man, though of the lowest rank, and to dare to strike him, though upon the strongest and grossest provocation, is an enormous crime. To attempt to escape from the cruelties exercised upon us, by flight, is punished with mutilation, and sometimes with death. To take arms against masters, whose cruelties no submission can mitigate, no patience exhaust, and from whom no other means of deliverance are left, is the most atrocious of all crimes; and is punished by a gradual death, lengthened out by torments, so exquisite, that none, but those who have been long familiarized, with West Indian barbarity, can hear the bare recital of them without horror. And yet I learn from writers, whom the Europeans hold in the highest esteem, that treason is a crime, which cannot be committed by a slave against his master; that a slave stands in no civil relation towards his master, and owes him no allegiance; that master and slave are in a state of war; and if the slave take up arms for his deliverance, he acts not only justifiably, but in obedience to a natural duty, the duty of self-preservation. I read in authors whom I find venerated by our oppressors, that to deliver one's self and one's countrymen from tyranny, is an act of the sublimest heroism. I hear Europeans exalted, as the martyrs of public liberty, the saviours of their country, and the deliverers of mankind—I see other memories honoured with statues, and their names immortalized in poetry—and yet when a generous negro is animated by the same passion which ennobled them,—when he feels the wrongs of his countrymen as deeply, and attempts to avenge them as boldly—I see him treated by those same Europeans as the most execrable of mankind, and led out, amidst curses and insults to undergo a painful, gradual and ignominious death: And thus the same Briton, who applauds his own ancestors for attempting to throw off the easy yoke, imposed on them by the Romans, punishes us, as detested parricides, for seeking to get free from the cruelest of all tyrannies, and yielding to the irresistible eloquence of an African Galgacus or Boadicea.

Are then the reason and morality, for which Europeans so highly value themselves, of a nature so variable and fluctuating, as to change with the complexion of those, to whom they are applied? —Do rights of nature cease to be such, when a negro is to enjoy them?—Or does patriotism in the heart of an African, rankle into treason?

A FREE NEGRO
—American Museum, V, 77 et seq., 1789.

REMARKABLE SPEECH OF ADAHOONZOU, KING OF DAHOMEY, AN IN-
TERIOR NATION OF AFRICA, ON HEARING WHAT WAS PASSING
IN ENGLAND RESPECTING THE SLAVE TRADE.

I admire the reasoning of the white men; but with all their sense, it does not appear that they have thoroughly studied the nature of the blacks, whose disposition differs as much from that of the whites, as their colour. The same great Being formed both; and since it hath seemed convenient for him to distinguish mankind by opposite complexions, it is a fair conclusion to presume that there may be as a great a disagreement in the qualities of their minds; there is likewise a remarkable difference between the countries which we inhabit. You, Englishmen, for instance, as I have been informed, are surrounded by the ocean, and by this situation seem intended to hold communication with the whole world, which you do, by means of your ships; whilst we Dahomans, being placed on a large continent, and hemmed in amidst a variety of other people, of the same complexion, but speaking different languages, are obliged by the sharpness of our swords, to defend ourselves from their incursions, and punish the depredations they make on us. Such conduct in them is productive of incessant wars. Your countrymen, therefore, who alledge that we go to war for the purpose of supplying your ships with slaves, are grossly mistaken.

You think you can work a reformation as you call it, in the manners of the blacks; but you ought to consider the disproportion between the magnitude of the two countries; and then you will soon be convinced of the difficulties that must be surmounted, to change the system of such a vast country as this. We know you are a brave people, and that you might bring over a great many of the blacks to your opinions, by points of your bayonets; but to effect this, a great many must be put to death and numerous cruelties must be committed, which we do not find to have been the practice of the whites; besides, that this would militate against the very principle which is professed by those who wish to bring about a reformation.

In the name of my ancestors and myself, I aver, that no Dahoman ever embarked in war merely for the sake of procuring wherewithal to purchase your commodities. I, who have not been long master of this country, have without thinking of the market, killed many thousands, and I shall kill many thousands more. When policy or justice requires that men be put to death, neither silk, nor coral, nor brandy, nor cowries, can be accepted as substitutes for the blood that ought to be spilt for example sake: besides if white men chuse to remain at home, and no longer visit this country for the same purpose that has usually brought them thither, will black men cease to make war? I answer, by no means, and if there be no ships to receive their captives, what will become of them? I answer, for you, they will be put to death. Perhaps you may be asked, how will the blacks be punished with guns and powder? I reply by another question, had we not clubs, and bows, and arrows before we knew white men? Did not you see me make *custom*—annual ceremony—for Weebaigah, the third king of Dahomey? And did you not observe on the day such ceremony was performing, that I carried a bow in my hand, and a quiver filled with arrows on my back? These were the emblems of the times; when, with such weapons, that brave ancestor fought and conquered all his neighbors. God made war for all the world; and every kingdom, large or small, has practiced it, more or less, though perhaps in a manner unlike, and upon different principles. Did Weebaigah sell slaves? No; his prisoners were all killed to a man. What else could he have done with them? Was he to let them remain in this country to cut the throats of his subjects? This would have been wretched policy indeed; which, had it been adopted, the Dahoman name would have long ago been extinguished, instead of becoming as it is at this day, the terror of surrounding nations. What hurts me most is, that some of your people have maliciously misrepresented us in books, which never die; alledging that we sell our wives and children for the sake of procuring a few kegs of brandy. No! We are shamefully belied, and I hope you will contradict, from my mouth, the scandalous stories that have been propagated; and tell posterity that we have been abused. We do, indeed, sell to the white men a part of our prisoners, and we have a right to do so. Are not all prisoners at the disposal of the their captors? and are we to blame, if we send delinquents to a far country? I have been told you do the same. If you want no more slaves from us, why cannot you be ingenious and tell the plain truth; saying that the slaves you have already purchased are sufficient for the country for which you bought them; or that the artists who used to make fine things, are all dead, without having taught anybody to make more? But for a parcel of men, with long heads, to sit down in England, and frame laws for us, and pretend to dictate how we are to live, of whom they know nothing, never having been in a black man's country during the whole course of their lives, is to me somewhat extraordinary! No doubt they must have been biased by the report of some one, who has had to do with us; who, for want of a due knowledge of the treatment of slaves, found that they died on his hands, and that his money was lost; and seeing that others thrived by the traffic, he envious of their good luck, has vilified both black and white traders.

You have seen me kill many men at the customs; and you have often observed delinquents at Grigwhee, and others of my provinces tied, and sent up to me. I kill them, but do I ever insist on being paid for them? Some heads I order to be placed at my door, others to be strewed about the market place, that the people may stumble upon them, when they little expect such a sight. This gives a grandeur to my customs, far beyond the display of fine things which I buy; this makes my enemies fear me, and gives me such a name in the Bush.[3] Besides, if I neglect this indispensable duty, would my ancestors suffer me to live? would they not trouble me day and night, and say, that I sent no body to serve them? that I was only solicitous about my own name, and forgetful of my ancestors? White men are not acquainted with these circumstances; but I now tell you that you may hear and know, and inform your countrymen, why customs are made, and will be made, as long as black men continue to possess their country; the few that can be spared from this necessary celebration, we sell to the white men; and happy, no doubt, are such, when they find themselves on the Grigwhee, to be disposed of to the Europeans. "We shall still drink water," say they to themselves; "white men will not kill us; and we may even avoid punishment, by serving our new masters with fidelity."—*The New York Weekly Magazine*, II. 430, 1792.

[3] The country expression for the woods was "Bush."

LETTERS SHOWING THE RISE AND PROGRESS OF THE EARLY NEGRO CHURCHES OF GEORGIA AND THE WEST INDIES[1]

AN ACCOUNT OF SEVERAL BAPTIST CHURCHES, CONSISTING CHIEFLY OF NEGRO SLAVES: PARTICULARLY OF ONE AT KINGSTON, IN JAMAICA: AND ANOTHER AT SAVANNAH IN GEORGIA

A letter from the late Rev. Mr. Joseph Cook of the Euhaw, upper Indian Land, South Carolina, bearing date Sept. 15, 1790, "A poor negro, commonly called, among his own friends, Brother George, has been so highly favoured of God, as to plant the first Baptist Church in Savannah, and another in Jamaica:" This account produced an earnest desire to know the circumstances of both these societies. Hence letters were written to the Rev. Mr. Cook at the Euhaw; to Mr. Jonathan Clarke, at Savannah; to Mr. Wesley's people at Kingston; with a view to obtain information, in which particular regard was had to the *character* of this poor but successful minister of Christ. Satisfactory accounts have been received from each of these quarters, and a letter from brother George himself, containing an answer to more than fifty questions proposed in a letter to him: We presume to give an epitome of the whole to our friends, hoping that they will have the goodness to let a plain unlettered people convey their ideas in their own simple way.

Brother George's words are distinguished by inverted commas, and what is not so marked, is either matter compressed or information received from such persons to whom application has been made of it.

George Liele, called also George *Sharp* because his owner's name was Sharp, in a letter dated Kingston, Dec. 18, 1791, says, "I was born in Virginia, my father's name was Liele, and my mother's name Nancy; I can not ascertain much of them, as I went to several parts of America when young, and at length resided in New Georgia; but was informed both by white and black people, that my father was the only black person who knew the

[1] Most of these letters were written by two colored preachers, George Liele and Andrew Bryan.

Lord in a spiritual way in that country: I always had a natural
fear of God from my youth, and was often checked in conscience
with thoughts of death, which barred me from many sins and bad
company. I knew no other way at that time to hope for salvation but only in the performance of my good works.'' *About
two years before the late war,* ''the Rev. Mr. Matthew Moore,[2] one
Sabbath afternoon, as I stood with curiosity to hear him, he un-
folded all my dark views, opened my best behaviour and good
works to me which I thought I was to be saved by, and I was convinced that I was not in the way to heaven, but in the way to
hell. This state I laboured under for the space of five or six
months. The more I heard or read, the more I'' saw that I ''was
condemned as a sinner before God; till at length I was brought
to perceive that my life hung by a slender thread, and if it was
the will of God to cut me off at that time, I was sure I should be
found in hell, as sure as God was in Heaven. I saw my condemnation in my own heart, and I found no way wherein I could escape
the damnation of hell, only through the merits of my dying Lord
and Saviour Jesus Christ; which caused me to make intercession
with Christ, for the salvation of my poor immortal soul; and I
full well recollect, I requested of my Lord and Master to give me
a work, I did not care how mean it was, only to try and see how
good I would do it.'' When he became acquainted with the method
of salvation by our Lord Jesus Christ, he soon found relief, particularly at a time when he was earnestly engaged in prayer; yea,
he says, ''I felt such love and joy as my tongue was not able to express. After this I declared before the congregation of believers
the work which God had done for my soul, and the same minister,
the Rev. Matthew Moore, baptized me, and I continued in this
church about four years, till the vacuation'' of Savannah by the
British. When Mr. Liele was called by grace himself, he. was
desirous of promoting the felicity of others. One who was an eye-
witness of it, says, *That he began to discover his love to other
negroes, on the same plantation with himself, by reading hymns
among them, encouraging them to sing, and sometimes by explain-
ing the most striking parts of them.* His own account is this,
''Desiring to prove the sense I had of ''my obligations to God, I
endeavoured to instruct'' the people of ''my own color in the

[2] Mr. Moore was an ordained Baptist minister, of the county of Burke,
in Georgia; he died, it seems, some time since. EDITOR.

word of God: the white brethren seeing my endeavours, and that the word of the Lord seemed to be blessed, gave me a call at a quarterly meeting to preach before the congregation.'' Afterwards Mr. Moore took the sense of the church concerning brother Liele's abilities, when it appeared to be their unanimous opinion, ''that he was possessed of ministerial gifts,'' and according to the custom which obtains in some of the American churches, he was licensed as a probationer. He now exercised at different plantations, especially on those Lord's Day evenings when there was no service performed in the church to which he belonged; and preached ''about three years at Brunton land, and at Yama-craw,'' which last place is about half a mile from Savannah. Mr. Henry Sharp, his master, being a deacon of the church which called George Liele to the work of the ministry, some years before his death gave him his freedom, only he continued in the family till his master's exit. Mr. Sharp in the time of the war was an officer, and was at last killed in the king's service, by a ball which shot off his hand. The author of this account handled the bloody glove, which he wore when he received the fatal wound. Some persons were at this time dissatisfied with George's liberation, and threw him into prison, but by producing the proper papers he was released; his particular friend in this business was colonel Kirkland. ''At the vacuation of the country I was partly obliged to come to Jamaica, as an indented servant, for money I owed him, he promising to be my friend in this country. I was landed at Kingston, and by the colonel's recommendation to general Campbell, the governor of the Island, I was employed by him two years, and on leaving the island, he gave me a written certificate from under his own hand of my good behaviour. As soon as I had settled Col. Kirkland's demands on me, I had a certificate of my freedom from the vestry and governor, according to the act of this Island, both for myself and family. Governor Campbell left the Island. I began, about September 1784, to preach in Kingston, in a small private house, to a good smart congregation, and I formed the church with four brethren from America besides myself, and the preaching took very good effect with the poorer sort, especially the slaves. The people at first persecuted us both at meetings and baptisms, but, God be praised, they seldom interrupt us now. We have applied to the Honourable House of Assembly, with a petition of our distresses, being poor people, desiring to worship Almighty God according to the tenets of the Bible, and they have granted us liberty, and given us their sanction. Thanks be to God we have liberty to worship him as we please in the Kingdom. You ask about those who,'' in a judgment of charity, "have been converted to Christ. I think they are about four hundred and fifty. I have baptized four hundred in Jamaica. At Kingston I baptize in the sea, at Spanish Town in the river, and at convenient places in the country. We have nigh *three hundred and fifty members;* a few white people among them, one white brother of the first battalion of royals, from England, baptized by Rev. Thomas Davis. Several members have been dismissed to other churches, and twelve have died. I have sent enclosed" an account of "the conversion and death of some. A few of Mr. Wesley's people, after immersion, join us and continue with us. We have, together with well wishers and followers, in different parts of the country, about fifteen hundred people. We receive none into the church without a few lines from their owners of their good behaviour towards them and religion. The creoles of the country, after they are converted and baptized, as God enables them, prove very faithful. I have deacons and elders, a few; and teachers of small congregations in the town and country, where convenience suits them to come together; and I am pastor. I preach twice on the Lord's Day, in the forenoon and afternoon, and twice in the week, and have not been absent six Sabbath Days since I formed the church in this country. I receive nothing for my services; I preach, baptize, administer the Lord's Supper, and travel from one place to another to publish the gospel, and to settle church affairs, all freely. I have one of the chosen men, whom I baptized, a deacon of the church, and a native of this country, who keeps the regulations of church matters; and I promoted a *free school* for the instruction of the children, both free and slaves, and he is the schoolmaster.

"I cannot justly tell what is my age, as I have no account of the time of my birth, but I suppose I am about forty years old. I have a wife and four children. My wife was baptized by me in Savannah, at Brunton land, and I have every satisfaction in life from her. She is much the same age as myself. My eldest son is nineteen years, my next son seventeen, the third fourteen, and the last child, a girl of eleven years; they are all members of the church. My occupation is a farmer, but as the seasons in this part of the country, are uncertain, I also keep a team of horses, and waggons for the carrying goods from one place to another, which I attend to myself, with the assistance of my sons; and by this way of life have gained the good will of the public, who recommend me to business, and to some very principal work for government.

"I have a few books, some good old authors and sermons, and one large bible that was given to me by a gentleman; a good many of our members can read, and are all desirous to learn; they will be very thankful for a few books to read on Sundays and other days.

"The last accounts I had from Savannah were, that the Gospel had taken very great effect both there and in South Carolina. Brother Andrew Bryan, a black minister at Savannah, has TWO HUNDRED MEMBERS, in full fellowship and had certificates from their owners of ONE HUNDRED MORE, who had given in their experiences and were ready to be baptized. Also I received accounts from Nova Scotia of a black Baptist preacher, Brother David George, who was a member of the church at Savannah; he had the permission of the Governor to preach in three provinces; his members in full communion were then *sixty*, white and black, the Gospel spreading. Brother Amos is at Providence, he writes me that the Gospel has taken good effect, and is spreading greatly; he has about THREE HUNDRED MEMBERS. Brother Jessy Gaulsing, another black minister, preaches near Augusta, in South Carolina, at a place where I used to preach; he was a member of the church at Savannah, and has *sixty members;* and a great work is going on there.

"I agree to election, redemption, the fall of Adam, regeneration, and perseverance, knowing the promise is to all who endure, in grace, faith, and good works, to the end, shall be saved.

"There is no Baptist church in this country but ours. We have purchased a piece of land, at the east end of Kingston, containing three acres for the sum of 155 l.[3] currency, and on it have begun a meeting-house fifty-seven feet in length by thirty-seven in breadth. We have raised the brick wall eight feet high from the foundation, and intend to have a gallery. Several gentlemen, members of the house of assembly, and other gentlemen, have subscribed towards the building about 40 l. The chief part of our congregation are SLAVES, and their owners allow them, in common, but three or four

[3] 140 l. currency is 100 l. sterling.

bits per week[4] for allowance to feed themselves; and out of so small a sum we cannot expect any thing that can be of service from them; if we did it would soon bring a scandal upon religion; and the FREE PEOPLE in our society are but poor, but they are all willing, both free and slaves, to do what they can. As for my part, I am too much entangled with the affairs of the world to go on,'' as I would, ''with my design, in supporting the cause: this has, I acknowledge, been a great hindrance to the Gospel in one way; but as I have endeavored to set a good example'' of industry ''before the inhabitants of the land, it has given general satisfaction another way. . . . And, Rev. Sir, we think the Lord has put it in the power of the Baptist societies in England to help and assist us in completing this building, which we look upon will be the greatest undertaking ever was in this country for the bringing of souls from darkness into the light of the Gospel. . . . And as the Lord has put it into your heart to enquire after us, we place all our confidence in you, to make our circumstances known to the several Baptist churches in England; and we look upon you as our father, friend, and brother.

''Within the brick wall we have a shelter, in which we worship, until our building can be accomplished.

''Your . . . letter was read to the church two or three times, and did create a great deal of love and warmness throughout the whole congregation, who shouted for joy and comfort, to think that the Lord had been so gracious as to satisfy us in this country with the very same religion with . . . our beloved brethren in the old country, according to the scriptures; and that such a worthy . . . of London, should write in so loving a manner to such poor worms as we are. And I beg leave to say, That the whole congregation sang out that they would, through the assistance of God, remember you in their prayers. They altogether give their Christian love to you, and all the worthy professors of Jesus Christ in your church at London, and beg the prayers of your congregation, and the prayers of the churches in general, wherever it pleases you to make known our circumstances. I remain with the utmost love . . . Rev. Sir, your unworthy fellow-labourer, servant, and brother in Christ.

(Signed) GEORGE LIELE.

[4] A bit was seven-pence half penny currency, or about five pence half-penny sterling.

P. S. We have chosen twelve trustees, all of whom are members of our church, whose names are specified in the title; the title proved and recorded in the Secretary's office of this island.

I would have answered your letter much sooner, but am encumbered with business: the whole island under arms; several of our members and a deacon were obliged to be on duty; and I being trumpeter to the troop of horse in Kingston, am frequently called upon. And also by order of government I was employed in carrying all the cannon that could be found lying about this part of the country. This occasioned my long delay, which I beg you will excuse.—*Baptist Annual Register*, 1790–3, pages 332–337.

To the Rev. Mr. John Rippon.

Kingston in Jamaica, Nov. 26, 1791.

Reverend Sir,

The perusal of your letter of the 15th July last, gave me much pleasure—to find that you had interested yourself to serve the glorious cause Mr. Liele is engaged in. He has been for a considerable time past very zealous in the ministry; but his congregation being chiefly slaves, they had it not in their power to support him, therefore he has been obliged to do it from his own industry; this has taken a considerable part of his time and much of his attention from his labours in the ministry; however, I am led to believe that it has been of essential service to the cause of GOD, for his industry has set a good example to his flock, and has put it out of the power of enemies to religion to say, that he has been eating the bread of idleness, or lived upon the poor slaves. The idea that too much prevails here amongst the masters of slaves is, that if their minds are considerably enlightened by religion or otherwise, that it would be attended with the most dangerous consequences; and this has been the only cause why the Methodist ministers and Mr. Liele have not made a greater progress in the ministry amongst the slaves. Alas! how much is it to be lamented, that a full QUARTER OF A MILLION of poor souls should so long remain in a state of nature; and that masters should be so blind to their own interest as not to know the difference between obedience inforced by the lash of the whip and that which flows from religious principles. Although I much admire the *general doctrine* preached in the Methodist church, yet I by no means approve of their discipline set up by Mr. Wesley, that reverend man of God. I very early saw into the impropriety of ad-

mitting slaves into their societies *without permission of their owners,*
and told them the consequences that would attend it; but they rejected my advice; and it has not only prevented the increase of
their church, but has raised them many enemies. Mr. Liele has
very wisely acted a different part. He has, I believe, admitted no
slaves into society but those who had obtained permission from
their owners, by which he has made many friends; and I think the
Almighty is now opening a way for another church in the capital,
where the Methodists could not gain any ground: a short time will
determine it, of which I shall advise you.—I really have not time
to enter so fully on this subject as I wish, being very much engaged
in my own temporal affairs, and at present having no clerk.—The
love I bear to the cause of God, and the desire I have of being any
ways instrumental to the establishing of it in this land of darkness,
has led me to write this: but before I conclude, I have some very
interesting particulars to lay before you:—Mr. Liele has by the
aid of the congregation and the assistance of some few people,
raised the walls of a church ready to receive the roof, but has not
the means to lay it on and finish it; nor do I see any prospect of its
going further, without he receives the aid of some religious institution from home. One hundred and fifty pounds, I think, would
complete it; and if this sum could be raised, it would greatly serve
the cause of GOD, and might be the means of bringing many hundred souls, who are now in a state of darkness, to the knowledge
of our great Redeemer. If this could be raised the sooner the
better. Our family contributed towards the purchase of the Methodist chapel; nor shall our mite be wanting to forward this work if
it meets with any encouragement from home.—I am a stranger to
you, but you may know my character from Daniel Shea, Esq.; and
John Parker, Esq.; merchants in your city; or from Mr. Samuel
Yockney, tea-dealer, in Bedford Row.

Perhaps you may expect me to say something of Mr. Liele's character. He is a very industrious man—decent and humble in his
manners, and, I think, a good man. This is my opinion of him.
I love all Christians of every denomination, and remain, with respect and sincere regard,

Reverend Sir,

Your friend and servant,

(Signed) STEPHEN COOKE.

—*Baptist Annual Register,* 1790–1793, pages 338 and 339.

SKETCHES OF THE BLACK BAPTIST CHURCH AT SAVANNAH, IN
GEORGIA ; AND OF THEIR MINISTER ANDREW BRYAN, EX-
TRACTED FROM SEVERAL LETTERS

SAVANNAH, July 19, 1790, &c.

Dear Brother,

"With pleasure I receive your favor of the 20th ult. more particularly, as I trust the correspondence may be of use to Brother
Andrew's church; concerning the origin of which, I have taken
from him the following account.

"Our Brother *Andrew* was one of the black hearers of *George
Liele,*" of whom an account was given before; and was hopefully
converted by his preaching from chapter III. of St. John's Gospel,
and a clause of verse 7, *Ye must be born again;* prior to the departure of *George Liele* for Jamaica, he came up from Tybee River,
whore departing vessels frequently lay ready for sea, and baptized
our Brother *Andrew*, with a wench of the name *Hagar*, both belonging to *Jonathan Bryan*, Esq.; these were the last performances
of our Brother *George Liele* in this quarter. About eight or nine
months after his departure, *Andrew* began to exhort his black
hearers, with a few whites. Edward Davis, Esq.; indulged him
and his hearers to erect a rough building on his land at *Yamacraw*,
in the suburbs of Savannah for a place of worship, of which they
have been very artfully dispossessed. In this their beginning of
worship they had frequent interruptions from the whites; as it
was at a time that a number of blacks had absconded, and some
had been taken away by the British. This was a plausible excuse
for their wickedness in their interruptions. The whites grew more
and more inveterate; taking numbers of them before magistrates—
they were imprisoned and whipped. *Sampson,* a brother of *Andrew,* belonging to the same master, was converted about a year
after him, and continued with him in all their persecutions, and
does until now. These, with many others, were twice imprisoned,
and about *fifty* were severely whipped, particularly *Andrew, who
was cut and bled abundantly,*" while he was under their lashes;
Brother *Hambleton* says, he held up his hand, and told his perse-
cutors that he rejoiced not only to be whipped, but *would freely
suffer death for the cause of Jesus Christ.* "The chief justice
Henry Osborne, Esq.; *James Habersham,* Esq.;[1] and *David Mon-*

---

[1] The Rev. Mr. George Whitefield's intimate friend.

tague, Esq.; were their examinants, and released them. Their kind *master* also interceded for them; and was much affected and grieved at their punishment.'' Brother *Hambleton* was also an advocate for them; and further says, that at one of their examinations *George Walton,* Esq.; spoke freely in favour of the sufferers, saying, that such treatment would be condemned even among barbarians. ''The chief justice *Osborne* then gave them liberty to continue their worship between sunrising and sun set; and their indulgent *master* told the magistrate, that he would give them the liberty of his own *house or his barn,* at a place called Brampton, about three miles from town, and that they should not be interrupted in their worship. In consequence hereof, they made use of their masters *barn,* where they had a number of hearers, with little or no interruption, for about two years. During the time of worship at Brampton Brother Thomas Burton, an elderly baptist preacher, paid them a visit, examined and baptized about *eighteen* blacks: at another period while there they received a visit from our brother *Abraham Marshall,*[2] who examined and baptized about forty and gave them two certificates from under his hand;'' copies of which follow:

This is to *certify,* that upon examination into the experiences and characters of a number of *Ethiopians,* and adjacent to Savannah, it appears that God has brought them out of darkness into the light of the Gospel, and given them fellowship one with the other; believing it is the will of Christ, we have constituted them a church of Jesus Christ, to keep up his worship and ordinances.

(Signed) A. MARSHALL, V.D.M.

Jan. 19, 1788.

This is to certify, that the Ethiopian church of Jesus Christ at Savannah, have called their beloved *Andrew* to the work of the ministry. We have examined into his qualifications, and believing it to be the will of the great Head of the church, we have appointed him to preach the Gospel, and to administer the ordinances, as God in his providence may call.

(Signed) A. MARSHALL, V.D.M.

[2] The Editor of the Baptist Annual Register said that he had not the honor of a correspondence with this respectable minister but that his name stood thus in the Georgia Association of 1788. At ''Kioka, Abraham Marshall, 22 baptized, 230'' members in all.

Jan. 20, 1788.

"After the death of their master his son, Dr. *William Bryan,* generously continued them the use of the *barn* for worship, until the estate was divided among the family. Our Brother *Andrew,* by consent of parties, purchased his freedom, bought a lot at Yamacraw, and built a residence near the dwelling house which their master had given *Sampson* liberty to build on his lot; and which have ever been made use of for worship. But by the division of their master's estate, the lot whereon *Sampson* had built a house to live in, and which until this time continues to be used for worship, by *Andrew,* fell into the hands of an attorney, who married a daughter of the deceased Mr. Bryan, and receives no less than 12 l a year for it. *Sampson* serves as a clerk, but frequently exhorts in the absence of his brother who has his appointments in different places to worship.

"Brother *Andrew's* account of his number in full communion is TWO HUNDRED AND TWENTY-FIVE, and about THREE HUNDRED AND FIFTY have been received as converted followers, many of whom have not permission" from their owners "to be baptized.—The whole number is judged to be about five hundred and seventy-five, from the towns being taken to this present July. I have consulted brother *Hambleton,* who thinks they have need of a few Bibles, the Baptist Confession of Faith, and Catechism; Wilson on Baptism, some of Bunyan's works, or any other that your wisdom may think useful to an illerate people. They all join in prayers for you and yours and beg your intercession at the throne of grace for them, as well as for the small number of whites that dwell here; and among them I hope you will not forget your poor unworthy brother, and believe me, with sincere affections and brotherly love, your in the bonds of the Gospel,

(Signed) JONATHAN CLARKE[3]

Concerning the church at Savannah, the late Rev. Mr. Joseph Cook, of the Euhaw, upper Indian land, thus writes: "From the enclosed you will see how it became a church, and what they have suffered, which is extremely affecting, but they now begin to rise from obscurity and to appear great. I have some acquaintance with their pastor, and have heard him preach; his *gifts are small,* but he is *clear in the grand doctrines* of the Gospel.—I believe him

[3] The character of Mr. Jonathan Clarke, according to the writer, might be learned at May and Hill's, merchants, Church-row, Fenchurch-street.

to be *truly pious* and he has been the instrument of doing more good among the poor slaves than all the learned doctors in America.''

The friends of our adorable Redeemer will, no doubt, rejoice to find that this large body of Christians negroes, under the patronage of some of the most respectable persons in their city, ''have opened a subscription for the erecting of a place of worship in the city of Savannah, for the society of black people of the Baptist denomination—the property to be vested in the hands of seven or more persons in trust for the church and congregation.''

Their case[4] is sent to England, recommended by

> J. JOHNSON,[5] Minister of the Union Church.
> JOHN HAMILTON.
> EBENEZER HILLS.
> JOSEPH WATTS.
> D. MOSES VALLOTTON.
> JOHN MILLENE.
> ABRAHAM LEGGETT.

Since the preceding account has been in the press, and other letters have been received, of which the following is an extract.

KINGSTON, JAMAICA, May 18, 1792.

Rev. and Dear Sir,

In answer to yours I wrote December 18 last, and as I have not received a line from you since, I send this, not knowing but the other was miscarried. Mr. Green has called upon me, and very kindly offered his service to deliver a letter from me into your hands; he also advised me to send you a copy of our church covenant, which I have done: being a collection of some of the principal texts of scripture which we observe, both in America and this country, for the direction of our practice. It is read once a month here on sacrament meetings, that our members may examine if they live according to all those laws which they profess,

[4] It was committed to the care of the Editor of the Baptist Annual Register.

[5] The Rev. Mr. Johnson was well known in London; he sailed for America in the fall of 1790; and laboured in the *Orphan House* at Savannah, built by Mr. Whitefield, and assigned in trust to the countess of Huntingdon. On May 30, 1775, the orphan house building caught fire and was entirely consumed, except the two wings which still remained. Editor of the Baptist Annual Register.

covenanted and agreed to; by this means our church is kept in scriptural subjection. As I observe in my last the chiefest part of our society are poor illiterate slaves, some living on sugar estates, some on mountains, pens, and other settlements, that have no learning, no not to know so much as a letter in the book; but the reading this covenant once a month, when all are met together from the different parts of the island, keeps them in mind of the commandments of God. And by shewing the same to the gentlemen of the legislature, and the justices, and magistrates, when I applied for a sanction, it gave them general satisfaction; and wherever a negro servant is to be admitted, their owners, after the perusal of it, are better satisfied. We are this day raising the roof on the walls of our meeting house; the height of the walls from the foundation is seventeen feet. I have a right to praise God, and glorify him for the manifold blessings I have received, and do still receive from him. I have full liberty from *Spanish Town*, the capital of this country, to preach the Gospel throughout the Island: the Lord is blessing the work everywhere, and believers are added daily to the church. My tongue is not able to express the goodness of the Lord. As our meeting house is out of town "(about a mile and a half)," I have a steeple on it, to have a bell to give notice to our people and more particularly to the owners of slaves that are in our society, that they may know the hour on which we meet, and be satisfied that our servants return in due time; for which reason I shall be greatly obliged to you to send me out, as soon as possible, a bell that can be heard about two *miles* distance, with the price. I have one at present, but it is rather small. The slaves may then be permitted to come and return in due time, for at present we meet very irregular in respect to hours. I remain, with the utmost regards, love and esteem,

Rev. Sir, yours, &c.

GEORGE LIELE.

Copy of a Recommendatory Letter of Hannah Williams, a Negro Woman, in London. It is all in print, except the Part of it which now appears in Italics.

Kingston, Jamaica, we that are of the Baptist Religion, being separated from all churches, excepting they are of the same faith and order after Jesus Christ, according to the scriptures, do certify, that our beloved *Sister Hannah Williams, during the time she was a member of the Church at Savannah, until the evacuation, did walk as a* faithful, well-behaved Christian, and to recommend her to join any church of the same faith and order. Given under my hand this 21st day of *December,* in the year of our Lord, 1791.

GEORGE LIELE.

—Baptist Annual Register, 1790–1793, pages 339–344.

ACCOUNT OF THE NEGRO CHURCH AT SAVANNAH, AND OF TWO NEGRO MINISTERS.

SAVANNAH, Dec. 22, 1792.

Dear Brother Rippon,

By return of Capt. Parrot in the ship Hannah, opportunity offers to acknowledge receipt of your kind favour with two boxes of books agreeable to invoice, which were very thankfully acceptable to our Brother Andrew, as well as to myself, and were delivered agreeable to your request. Within a month past a few of our Christian friends providentially collected at my house, when it was thought necessary we should commence a subscription for the building of a Baptist Meeting-house in this city, as the corporation has given us a lot for that purpose. Mr. Ebenezer Hills and myself were appointed trustees, and we have subscribed £35. 6s. if we can get as much more, we intend to begin the work, please God to smile on our weak endeavours, and the place will be made sufficiently large to accommodate the black people: they have been frowned upon of late by some despisers of religion, who have endeavoured to suppress their meeting together on Thursday evening in the week which was their custom, but is now set aside; so that they only continue worship from the sun rise to sun set on Sabbath days.

I copied brother Andrew's last return of members for brother Silas Mercer, who was here since the association of Coosawhatchie, which is as follows: Return made to the Georgia Association,

Supposed to be two or three years past	250	
Baptized since (say 80 in this year 1792)	159	409
Excommunicated	˙8	
Dead	12	20
Total remaining Nov. 26, 1792		389

Brother Andrew lately brought me a letter from brother George Liele, of Jamaica, expressive of the great increase of his church in that island. Andrew is free only since the death of his old master, and purchased his freedom of one of their heirs at the rate of 50 l. He was born at Goose Creek, about 16 miles from Charleston, South Carolina; his mother was a slave, and died in the service of his old master: his father, a slave, yet living, but rendered infirm by age for ten years past. Andrew was married nine years since, which was about the time he and his wife were brought to the knowledge of their wretched state by nature: His wife is named Hannah and remains a slave to the heirs of his older master; they have no children; He was ordained by our Brother Marshall: he has no assistant preacher but his Brother Sampson, who continues a faithful slave, and occasionally exhorts. Some white ministers from the country preach in his church. Jesse Peter, another Negro (whose present master is Thomas Galphin), is now here, and has three or four places in the country where he attends preaching alternately; a number of white people admire him. While he is here, I propose to be informed more particularly of his situation, etc. Although a slave his master indulges him in his profession and gives him uncommon liberty. To return to Andrew, he has four deacons appointed, but not regularly introduced. He supports himself by his own labour. There are no white people that particularly belong to his church, but we have reason to hope that he has been instrumental in the conviction and converting of some whites. Amos, the other Negro minister, mentioned by Brother George, resides at one of the Bahama Islands, which is called New Providence, and is about four days sail towards the southeast. There is one white church at Ogeechee, and another at Effingham; each of these are about twenty miles from this, which are the nearest and only ones. Perhaps fifty of Andrew's church can read, but only three can write.

For the present, accept of the sincere love and kind respects of the Black Society, with Andrew's particular thanks. My ears have heard their petitions to the throne of grace for you particularly, which no doubt they will continue; and let me entreat your prayers for them, and for the connected societies of this State.

Your brother in the Lord Jesus,

JONATHAN CLARKE.

—*Baptist Annual Register*, 1790–1793, pages 540–541.

KINGSTON, Jamaica, Jan. 12, 1793.

Our Meeting-house is now covered in and the lower floor was completed the 24th of last month. We supposed we are indebted for lumber, lime, bricks, &c. between 4 and 500 l. I am not able to express the thanks I owe for your kind attention to me, and the cause of God. The Schoolmaster, together with the members of our church, return their sincere thanks for the books you have been pleased to send them, being so well adapted to the society, they have given great satisfaction.

I hope shortly to send you a full account of the number of people in our societies in different parts of this island. I have baptized near 500.

I have purchased a piece of land in Spanish Town, the capital of this Island, for a burying ground, with a house upon it, which serves for a Meeting-house. James Jones, Esq., one of the magistrates of this town, and Secretary of the Island, told me, that the Hon. William Mitchell, Esq., the Custos, had empowered him to grant me license to preach the Gospel, and they have given me liberty to make mention of their names in any congregation where we are interrupted. Mr. Jones has given permission for all his negroes to be taught the word of God. The gospel is taking great effect in this town. My brethren and sisters in general, most affectionately give their christian love to you, and all the dear lovers of Jesus Christ in your church at London, and beg that they, and all the other churches, will remember the poor Ethiopian Baptists of Jamaica in their prayers, I remain, dear Sir and brother, your unworthy fellow labourer in Christ.

GEORGE LIELE.

—*Baptist Annual Register*, 1790–1793, page 542.

KINGSTON, JAMAICA, April 12, 1793.

Rev. and Dear Sir,

I AM one of the poor, unworthy, helpless creatures born in this island, whom our glorious master Jesus Christ was graciously pleased to call from a state of darkness to the marvelous light of the gospel and since our Lord has bestowed his mercy on my soul, our beloved minister, by consent of the church, appointed me deacon, schoolmaster, and his principal helper.

We have great reason in this island to praise and glorify the Lord for his goodness and loving kindness in sending his blessed Gospel amongst us by our well-beloved minister, Brother Liele.

We were living in slavery to sin and satan, and the Lord hath redeemed our souls to a state of happiness to praise his glorious and
ever blessed name; and we hope to enjoy everlasting peace by the
promise of our Lord and master Jesus Christ. The blessed Gospel
is spreading wonderfully in this island; believers are daily coming
into the church and we hope, in a little time, to see Jamaica become
a Christian country.

I remain respectfully, Rev. and Dear Sir,
Your poor Brother in Christ,
THOMAS NICHOLS SWIGLE.

Mr. George Gibbs Bailey, of Bristol, now at Kingston, in Jamaica, writes thus, under date May 9, 1793. "I have inquired of
all those who I thought could give me an account of Mr. Liele's conduct without prejudice, and I can say with pleasure, what Pilate
said, I can *find no fault in this man.* The Baptist church abundantly thrives among the Negroes, more than any denomination in
Jamaica; but I am very sorry to say the Methodist church is declining greatly."

Another sensible Gentleman, of Kingston, in Jamaica, much attached to Mr. Wesley's interest, also says, "I will be very candid
with you and tell you that I think the Baptist church is the church
that will spread the Gospel among the poor Negroes and I hope
and trust, as there is reason to believe that your church will be preferred before all others by the Negroes, that those of you who are
in affluence will contribute and send out a minister and support
him," &c.—*Baptist Annual Register,* 1790–1793, pages 542–543.

FROM THE REV. ABRAHAM MARSHALL, WHO FORMED THE NEGRO
CHURCH AT SAVANNAH, TO MR. RIPPON.

KIOKA, GEORGIA, May 1, 1793.

Rev. and Dear Sir,

YOURS came safe to hand, and gave singular satisfaction.
Neither spreading plains, nor rolling oceans, can prevent us from
weeping with those that weep, and rejoicing with those that rejoice.
I have had it in contemplation for some time to open a correspondence with our dear friend on the other side of the flood, but my constant travelling has hitherto prevented; I am highly pleased that
you have opened the way. . . .

As to the Black Church in Savannah, of which you had a particular account by Mr. Clarke, I baptized forty-five of them in one day, assisted in the constitution of the church, and ordination of the minister. They have given repeated proofs, by their sufferings, of their zeal for the cause of God and religion; and, I believe, are found in the faith, and strict in discipline.

I am also intimately acquainted with Jessy Golfin; he lives thirty miles below me, in South Carolina, and twelve miles below Augusta; he is a negro servant to Mr. Golfin, who, to his praise be it spoken, treats him with respect. His countenance is grave, his voice charming, his delivery good, nor is he a novice in the mysteries of the kingdom.

From less than the least,

ABRAHAM MARSHALL.

—*Baptist Annual Register*, 1790–1793, page 545.

A LETTER FROM THE NEGRO BAPTIST CHURCH IN SAVANNAH, AD-
DRESSED TO THE REVEREND DOCTOR RIPPON

SAVANNAH-GEORGIA, U. S. A., Dec. 23, 1800.

My Dear and Reverend Brother,

After a long silence occasioned by various hindrances, I sit down to answer your inestimable favour by the late dear Mr. White, who I hope is rejoicing, far above the troubles and trials of this frail sinful state. All the books mentioned in your truly condescending and affectionate letter, came safe, and were distributed according to your humane directions. You can scarcely conceive, much less than I describe, the gratitude excited by so seasonably and precious a supply of the means of knowledge and grace, accompanied with benevolent proposals of further assistance. Deign, dear sir, to accept our united and sincere thanks for your great kindness to us, who have been so little accustomed to such attentions. Be assured that our prayers have ascended, and I trust will continue to ascend to God, for your health and happiness, and that you may be rendered a lasting ornament to our holy Religion, and a successful Minister of the Gospel.

With much pleasure, I inform you, dear sir, that I enjoy good health, and am strong in body, tho' sixty-three years old, and am blessed with a pious wife, whose freedom I have obtained, and an only daughter and child who is married to a free man, tho' she, and consequently, under our laws, her seven children, five sons and two daughters, are slaves. By a kind Providence I am well provided for, as to worldly comforts, (tho' I have had very little given me as a minister) having a house and lot in this city, besides the land on which several buildings stand, for which I receive a small rent, and a fifty-six acre tract of land, with all necessary buildings, four miles in the country, and eight slaves; for whose education and happiness, I am enabled thro' mercy to provide.

But what will be infinitely more interesting to my friend, and is so much more prized by myself, we enjoy the rights of conscience to a valuable extent, worshiping in our families and preaching three times every Lord's-day, baptizing frequently from ten to thirty at a time in the Savannah, and administering the sacred supper, not only without molestation, but in the presence, and with the approbation and encouragement of many of the white people. We are now about seven hundred in number, and the work of the Lord goes on prosperously.

An event which has had a happy influence on our affairs was the coming of Mr. Holcombe, late pastor of Euhaw Church, to this place at the call of the heads of the city, of all denominations, who have remained for the thirteen months he has been here among his constant hearers and his liberal supporters. His salary is 2000 a year. He has just had a baptistery, with convenient appendages, built in his place of worship, and has commenced baptizing.

Another dispensation of Providence has much strengthened our hands, and increased our means of information; Henry Francis, lately a slave to the widow of the late Colonel Leroy Hammond, of Augusta, has been purchased by a few humane gentlemen of this place, and liberated to exercise the handsome ministerial gifts he possesses amongst us, and teach our youth to read and write. He is a strong man about forty-nine years of age, whose mother was white and whose father was an Indian. His wife and only son are slaves.

Brother Francis has been in the ministry fifteen years, and will soon receive ordination, and will probably become the pastor of a branch of my large church, which is getting too unwieldy for one body. Should this event take place, and his charge receive constitution, it will take the rank and title of the 3rd Baptist Church in Savannah.

With the most sincere and ardent prayers to God for your temporal and eternal welfare, and with the most unfeigned gratitude, I remain, reverend and dear sir, your obliged servant in the gospel.

(Signed) ANDREW BRYAN.

P. S. I should be glad that my African friends could hear the above account of my affairs.—*The Baptist Annual Register*, 1798– 1801, page 366.

STATE OF THE NEGROES IN JAMAICA

KINGSTON, JAMAICA, 1st May, 1802.

Rev. and Dear Sir,

Since our blessed Lord has been pleased to permit me to have the rule of a church of believers, I have baptized one hundred and eleven: and I have a sanction from the Rev. Dr. Thomas Rees, rector of this town and parish, who is one of the ministers appointed by his Majesty to hold an ecclesiastical jurisdiction over the clergy in this island, confirmed by a law passed by the Legislative Body of this island, made and provided for that purpose.

Our church consists of people of colour and black people; some of free condition, but the greater part of them are slaves and natives from the different countries in Africa. Our number both in town and country is about five hundred brethren, and our rule is to baptize once in three months; to receive the Lord's supper the first Lord's-day in every month, after evening services is over; and we have meetings on Tuesday and Thursday evenings throughout the year. The whole body of our church is divided into several classes, which meet every Monday evening, to be examined by their Class-leaders, respecting their daily walk and conversation; and I am truly happy to acquaint you, that since the gospel has been preached in Kingston, there never was so great a prospect for the spread of the fame as there is now. Numbers and numbers of young people are flocking daily to join both our society and the Methodists, who have about four hundred. Religion so spreads in Kingston, that those who will not leave the Church of England to join the Dissenters, have formed themselves into evening societies: it is delightful to hear the people at the different places singing psalms, hymns, and spiritual songs; and to see a great number of them who lived in the sinful state of fornication (which is the common way of living in Jamaica), now married, having put away that deadly sin.

Our place of worship is so very much crowded, that numbers are obliged to stand out of doors: we are going to build a larger chapel as soon as possible. Our people being poor, and so many of them slaves, we are not able to go on so quick as we could without we should meet with such friends as love our Lord and Master Jesus Christ, to enable us in going on with so glorious an undertaking.

I preach, baptize, marry, attend funerals, and go through every work of the ministry without fee or reward; and I can boldly say, for these sixteen years since I began to teach and instruct the poor Ethiopians in this island, the word of God (though many and many times travelling night and day over rivers and mountains to inculcate the ever-blessed gospel), that I never was complimented with so much as a pair of shoes to my feet, or a hat to my head, or money or apparel, or any thing else as a recompense for my labour and my trouble, from any of my brethren or any other person:— my intention is to follow the example set before me by the holy apostle Saint Paul, to labour with my hands for the things I stand in need of to support myself and family, and to let the church of Christ be free from incumbrances.

We have five trustees to our chapel and burrying-ground, eight deacons, and six exhorters.

I had the pleasure of seeing Mr. V. of his Majesty's ship Cumberland, in this town, who has been at my house, and at our chapel, and has seen all my church-books and the manner in which I have conducted our society. He has lately sailed for England with Admiral Montagu; and when he sees you, he will be able to tell you of our proceedings better than I can write.

All my beloved brethren beg their christian love to you and all your dear brethren in the best bonds; and they also beg yourself and them will be pleased to remember the poor Ethiopian Baptists in their prayers, and be pleased also to accept the same from, Reverend and Dear Sir,

Your poor unworthy Brother, in the Lord Jesus Christ,

(Signed) T. N. S.

P. S. Brothers Baker, Gilbert, and others of the Africans, are going on wonderfully in the Lord's service, in the interior part of the country.

July 1, 1802).

—*Baptist Annual Register*, 1801–1802, pages 974–975.

LETTER TO DR. RIPPON

KINGSTON, JAMAICA, Oct. 9, 1802.

Rev. and Dear Sir,

I take the liberty to give you a further account of the spread of the Gospel among us.

On Saturday the 28th August last we laid our foundation stone for the building of the New Chapel; fifty-five feet in length, and twenty-nine and half feet in breath. The brethren assembled together at my house, and walked in procession to our place of worship, where a short discourse was delivered upon the subject, taken from Mat. XVI. 18. *Upon this rock I will build my Church, and the gates of Hell shall not prevail against.* As soon as divine service was over, we laid a stone in a pillar provided for that purpose, and on the stone was laid a small marble plate, and these words engraven thereon, St. John's Chapel was founded 28th August 1802, before a large and respectable congregation. The bricklayers have just raised the foundation above the surface of the earth. And as our Church consists chiefly of Slaves, and poor free people, we are not able to go on so fast as we could wish, for which reason we beg leave to call upon our Baptist friends in England, for their help and support of the Ethiopian Baptists, setting forward the glorious cause of our Lord and Master Jesus Christ, now in hand.

My last return of the Members in our Society on the 10th August last stood thus,   595

     Expelled 2
     Dismissed 26
     Dead 19   47

       Members in society 10th August 1802 548

Since which, we have had sixty-two more added to the Church, almost all young people, and natives of different countries in Africa, which make 610 in Society.

About two months ago, I paid my first visit to a part of our Church held at Clinton Mount, Coffee Plantation, in the parish of Saint Andrew, about 16 miles distance from Kingston, in the High Mountains, where we have a Chapel and 254 brethren. And when I was at breakfast with the Overseer, he said to me, I have no need of a book-keeper (meaning an assistant), I make no use of a whip, for when I am at home my work goes on regular, and when I visit the field I have no fault to find, for every thing is conducted as it ought to be. I observed myself that the brethren were very industrious, they have a plenty of provisions in their ground, and a plenty of live stock, and they, one and all together, live in unity, brotherly love, and in the bonds of peace.

Last Lords Day, the 3rd October, was our quarterly baptism, when we walked from our place of Worship at noon, to the water, the distance of about a half mile, where I baptised eighteen professing believers, before a numerous and large congregation of spectators, which make in all 254 baptised by me since our commencement.

I am truly happy in acquainting you, that a greater spread of the gospel is taking place at the west end of the island.—A fortnight ago, the Rev. Brother Moses Baker visited me, he is a man of colour, a native of America, one of our baptist brothers and a member of our church, he is employed by a Mr. Winn, (a gentleman down in the country who possesses large and extensive properties in this island), to instruct his negroes in the principles of the Christian religion; and Mr. Vaughan has employed him for that purpose, and both these gentlemen allow him a compensation Mr. Winn finds him in house room, lands, &c., &c., and by his instructing those slaves at Mr. Vaughan's properties, several miles from Mr. Winn's estate, a number of slaves belonging to different properties (no less than 20 sugar estates in number) are become converted souls.—Mr. Baker's errand to me was, that he wanted a person to assist him, he being sent for by a Mr. Hilton, a gentleman down in the parish of Westmoreland (50 miles distance from Mr. Baker's dwelling place), to instruct his and another gentlemen's slaves, on two large sugar estates, into the word of God, producing to me at the same time the letters and invitations he received. I gave him brother George Vineyard, one our exhorters, and old experienced professor (who has been called by grace upwards of eighteen years) to assist him; he also is a native of America, and this gentleman Mr. Hilton, has provided a House, and maintainance, a salary, and land for him to cultivate for his benefit upon his own estate, and brother Baker declared to me, that he has in the church there, fourteen hundred justified believers, and about three thousand followers, many under conviction for sin. The distance brother Baker is at from me is 136 miles, he has undergone a great deal of persecution and severe trials for the preaching of the gospel, but our Lord has delivered him safe out of all—Myself and brethren were at Mr. Liele's Chapel a few weeks ago at the funeral of one of his elders, he is well, and we were friendly together. All our brethren unite with me in giving their most christian love to you, and all the dear beloved brethren in your church in the best bonds, and beg, both yourself and them, will be pleased to remember the Ethiopian Baptists in their prayers, and I remain dear Sir, and brother,

Your poor unworthy brother, in the Lord Jesus Christ,

(Signed) THOMAS NICHOLAS SWIGLE.

P. S. These sugar estates, in the parish where Brother Baker resides, are very large and extensive; and they have three to four hundred slaves on each property.—*Baptist Annual Register*, 1800–1802, pages 1144–1146.

BOOK REVIEWS

The Haitian Revolution, 1791 to 1804. By T. G. STEWARD. Thomas Y. Crowell Company, New York, 1915. 292 pages. $1.25.

In the days when the internal dissensions of Haiti are again thrusting her into the limelight such a book as this of Mr. Steward assumes a peculiar importance. It combines the unusual advantage of being both very readable and at the same time historically dependable. At the outset the author gives a brief sketch of the early settlement of Haiti, followed by a short account of her development along commercial and racial lines up to the Revolution of 1791. The story of this upheaval, of course, forms the basis of the book and is indissolubly connected with the story of Toussaint L'Overture. To most Americans this hero is known only as the subject of Wendell Phillips's stirring eulogy. As delineated by Mr. Steward, he becomes a more human creature, who performs exploits, that are nothing short of marvelous. Other men who have seemed to many of us merely names—Rigaud, Le Clerc, Desalines, and the like, are also fully discussed.

Although most of the book is naturally concerned with the revolutionary period, the author brings his account up to date by giving a very brief resumé of the history of Haiti from 1804 to the present time. This history is marked by the frequent occurrence of assassinations and revolutions, but the reader will not allow himself to be affected by disgust or prejudice at these facts particularly when he is reminded, as Mr. Steward says, "that the political history of Haiti does not differ greatly from that of the majority of South American Republics, nor does it differ widely even from that of France."

The book lacks a topical index, somewhat to its own disadvantage, but it contains a map of Haiti, a rather confusing appendix, a list of the Presidents of Haiti from 1804 to 1906 and a list of the names and works of the more noted Haitian authors. The author does not give a complete bibliography. He simply mentions in the beginning the names of a few authorities consulted.

J. R. FAUSET.

The Negro in American History. By JOHN W. CROMWELL. The
American Negro Academy, Washington, D. C., 1914. 284
pages. $1.25 net.

In John W. Cromwell's book, "The Negro in American History," we have what is a very important work. The book is mainly biographical and topical. Some of the topics discussed are: "The Slave Code"; "Slave Insurrections"; "The Abolition of the Slave Trade"; "The Early Convention Movement"; "The Failure of Reconstruction"; "The Negro as a Soldier"; and "The Negro Church." These topics are independent of the chapters which are more particularly chronological in treatment.

In the appendices we have several topics succinctly treated. Among these are: "The Underground Railroad," "The Freedmen's Bureau," and, most important and wholly new, a list of soldiers of color who have received Congressional Medals of Honor, and the reasons for the bestowal.

The biographical sketches cover some twenty persons. Much of the information in these sketches is not new, as would be expected regarding such well-known persons as Frederick Douglass, John M. Langston, and Paul Laurence Dunbar. On the other hand, Mr. Cromwell has given us very valuable sketches of other important persons of whom much less is generally known. Among these are Sojourner Truth, Edward Wilmot Blyden, and Henry O. Tanner.

The book does not pretend to be the last word concerning the various topics and persons discussed. Indeed, some of the topics have had fuller treatment by the author in pamphlets and lectures. It is to be regretted that the author did not feel justified in giving a more extensive treatment, as the great store of his information would easily have permitted him to do.

The book is exceptionally well illustrated, but it lacks information regarding some of the illustrations. Not only are the readers of a book entitled to know the source of the illustrations but in the case of copies of paintings, and other works of art, the original artist is as much entitled to credit as an author whose work is quoted or appropriated to one's use.

Negro Culture In West Africa. By GEORGE W. ELLIS, K.C., F.R.
G.S. The Neale Publishing Co., New York, 1914. 290 pages.
$2.00 net.

This study by Mr. Ellis of the culture of West Africa as represented by the Vai tribe, is valuable both as a document and as a
scientific treatment of an important phase of the color problem. As
a document it is an additional and a convincing piece of evidence
of the ability of the Negro to treat scientifically so intricate a problem as the rise, development, and meaning of the social institutions
of a people. Easy, yet forceful in style; well documented with
footnotes and cross references; amply illustrated with twenty-seven
real representations of tools, weapons, musical instruments and
other pieces of handwork; containing, incidentally, a good bibliography of the subject; and finally, with its conclusions condensed in
the last four pages, it is a book excellent in plan and in execution.
The map, however, which has been selected for the book is over-
crowded and, therefore, practically useless.

As a scientific study, its value is suggested by the topics emphasized, viz., "Climate," "Institutions," "Foreign Influence,"
"Proverbs," "Folklore," and "Writing System." Referring to
the climate the author says: "In West Africa the body loses its
strength, the memory its retentiveness, and the will its energy.
These are the effects observed upon persons remaining in West
Africa only for a short time, and they form a part of the experience of almost every person who has lived on the West Coast.
White persons,—with beautiful skin, clear and soft, and with rosy
cheeks,—after they have been in West Africa for a while become
dark and tawny like the inhabitants of Southern Spain and Italy.
If we can detect these effects of the West African climate in only a
short time upon persons who come to the West Coast, what must
have been the effect of such a climate upon the Negroes who for
centuries have been exposed to its hardships?"

The moral life of the Vais appears to be the product of their
social institutions and their severe environment. These institutions
grow out of the necessities of government for the tribe under circumstances which suggest and enforce their superstitions and
beliefs. This is not so with respect to education. It seems that
the influence of the "Greegree Bush" (a school system) is now
considerably weakened by the Liberian institutions on the one hand,
the Mohammedan faith and customs on the other. So that now this

institution falls short of achieving its aims, and putting its principles into practice.

The study as a whole gives evidence of the author's eight years of travel and research, and can be read with profit by all friends of mankind.

WALTER DYSON.

The Education of the Negro Prior to 1861. By C. G. WOODSON, Ph.D., G. P. Putnam's Sons, New York, 1915. 460 pages. $2.00 net.

The very title of Dr. Woodson's book causes one who is interested in the race history to ask questions and think. There are comparatively few people who know anything about the efforts made to educate the Negro prior to 1861. Consequently, from the first page of the book to the last, the reader is continually acquiring facts concerning this most interesting and important phase of the Colored-American's history of which he has never heard before, and some of which seem too wonderful to be true. But it is not possible to doubt anything which is found in Dr. Woodson's book. One knows that every statement he reads concerning the education of the Negro prior to 1861 is true, for the author has taken pains to substantiate every fact that he presents.

It is difficult to imagine any phase of race history more fascinating and more thrilling than an account of the desperate and prolonged struggle between the forces which made for the mental and spiritual enlightenment of the slave and those which opposed these humane and Christian efforts with all the bitterness and strength at their command. The reasons assigned by those who favored the education of the slaves and the methods suggested together with the arguments used by those who were opposed to it and the laws enacted to prevent it furnish an illuminating study in human nature.

One is surprised to find that very early in the history of the colonies there were scholars and statesmen who did not hesitate to declare their belief in the intellectual possibilities of the Negro. These men agreed with George Buchanan that the Negro had talent for the fine arts and under favorable circumstances could achieve something worth while in literature, mathematics and philosophy. The high estimate placed upon the innate ability of the Negro may be attributed to the fact that early in the history of the country there was a goodly number of slaves who had managed to attain a certain intellectual proficiency in spite of the difficulties which had to be overcome. By 1791 a colored minister had so distinguished himself that he was called to the pastorate of the First Baptist Church (white) of Portsmouth, Va. Benjamin Banneker's proficiency in mathematics enabled him to make the first clock manufactured in the United States. As the author himself says "the instances of Negroes struggling to obtain an education read like the beautiful romances of a people in an heroic age."

Indeed the reaction which developed against allowing the slaves to pick up the few fragments of knowledge which they had been able to secure was due to some extent to the enthusiasm and eagerness with which they availed themselves of the opportunities afforded them and the salutary effect which the enlightenment had on their character. The account of the establishment of schools and churches for slaves who were transplanted to free soil is one of the most interesting chapters in the book. The struggle for the higher education shows that tremendous obstacles had been removed, before the race was allowed to secure the opportunity which it so earnestly desired. In the chapter on vocational training the effort made by colored people themselves to secure economic equality, and the determined opposition to it manifested by white mechanics are clearly and strongly set forth. In the appendix of the book one finds a number of interesting and valuable treatises, while the bibliography is of great assistance to any student of race history.

In addition to the fund of information which is secured by reading Dr. Woodson's book, a perusal of it can not help but increase one's respect for a race which under the most disheartening and discouraging circumstances strove so heroically and persistently to cultivate its mind and allowed nothing to turn it aside and conquer its will.

"The Education of the Negro Prior to 1861" is a work of profound historical research, full of interesting data on a most important phase of race life which has hitherto remained unexplored and neglected.

MARY CHURCH TERRELL.

NOTES

In the death of Booker T. Washington the field of history lost one of its greatest figures. He will be remembered mainly as an educational reformer, a man of vision, who had the will power to make his dreams come true. In the field of history, however, he accomplished sufficient to make his name immortal. His *"Up from Slavery"* is a long chapter of the story of a rising race; his *"Frederick Douglass"* is the interpretation of the life of a distinguished leader by a great citizen; and his *"Story of the Negro"* is one of the first successful efforts to give the Negro a larger place in history.

Doubleday, Page and Company will in the near future publish an extensive biography of Booker T. Washington.

During the Inauguration Week of Fisk University a number of Negro scholars held a conference to consider making a systematic study of Negro life. A committee was appointed to arrange for a larger meeting.

Dr. C. G. Woodson is now writing a volume to be entitled *"The Negro in the Northwest Territory."*

The Neale Publishing Company has brought out *"The Political History of Slavery in the United States,"* by J. Z. George.

"Lincoln and Episodes of the Civil War," by W. E. Doster, appears among the publications of the Putnams.

"Black and White in the South," is the title of a volume from the pen of M. S. Evans, appearing with the imprint of Longmans, Green and Company.

T. Fisher Unwin has brought out *"The Savage Man in Central Africa,"* by A. L. Cureau.

"Reconstruction in Georgia, Social, Political, 1865–1872," by C. Mildred Thompson, appears as a comprehensive volume in the Columbia University Studies in History, Economics, and Public Law.

THE JOURNAL

OF

NEGRO HISTORY

Vol. I—April, 1916—No. 2

THE HISTORIC BACKGROUND OF THE NEGRO PHYSICIAN

In a homogeneous society where there is no racial cleavage, only the selected members of the most favored class occupy the professional stations. The element representing the social status of the Negro would, therefore, furnish few members of the coveted callings. The element of race, however, complicates every feature of the social equation. In India we are told that the population is divided horizontally by caste and vertically by religion; but in America the race spirit serves both as horizontal and vertical separations. The Negro is segregated and shut in to himself in all social and semi-social relations of life. This isolation necessitates separate ministrative agencies from the lowest to the highest rounds of the ladder of service. During the days of slavery the interests of the master demanded that he should direct the general social and moral life of the slave, and should provide especially for his physical well-being. The sudden severance of this tie left the Negro wholly without intimate guidance and direction. The ignorant must be enlightened, the sick must be healed, and the poor must have the gospel preached to them. The situation and circumstances under which the race found itself demanded that its professional class, for the most part, should be men of their own blood and sympathies. The needed service could not be effectively performed by those who assumed and asserted racial arrogance, and bestowed their professional service as cold crumbs that fell from the master's table. The professional class who are to uplift and direct the lowly must not say, "So far shalt thou come, but not any farther," but rather, "Where I am, there ye shall be also."

There is no more pathetic chapter in the history of human struggle than the emergence of the smothered ambition of this race to meet the social exigencies involved in the professional needs of the masses. In an instant, in the twinkling of an eye, the plowhand was transformed into a priest, the barber into a bishop, the housemaid into a schoolmistress, the day-laborer into a lawyer, and the porter into a physician. These high places of intellectual and professional authority, into which they found themselves thrust by stress of social necessity, had to be operated with at least some semblance of conformity to the standards which had been established by the European through the traditions of the ages. The higher place in society occupied by the choicest members of the white race, and that too after long years of arduous preparation, had to be assumed by black men without personal or formal fitness. The stronger and more aggressive natures pushed themselves into these higher callings by sheer force of untutored energy and uncontrolled ambition.

An accurate study of the healing art as practiced by Negroes in Africa as well as its continuance after transplantation in America would form an investigation of great historical interest. This, however, is not the purpose of this paper. It is sufficient to note the fact that witchcraft and the control of disease through roots, herbs, charms and conjuration are universally practiced on the continent of Africa. Indeed, the medicine man has a standing and influence that is sometimes superior to that of kings and queens. The natives of Africa have discovered their own materia medica by actual practice and experience with the medicinal value of minerals and plants. It must be borne in mind that any pharmacopeia must rest upon the basis of practical experiment and experience. The science of medicine was developed by man in his groping to relieve pain and to curb disease, and was not handed down ready made from the skies. In this groping, the African, like the rest of the children of men, has been feeling after the right remedies, if haply he might find them.

It was inevitable that the prevailing practice of conjuration in Africa should be found among Negroes after they had been transferred to the new continent. The conjure man was well known in every slave community. He generally turned his art, however, to malevolent rather than benevolent uses; but this was not always the case. Not infrequently these medicine men gained such wide celebrity among their own race as to attract the attention of the whites. As early as 1792 a Negro by the name of Cesar[1]

[1] The Negro Cesar's Cure for Poison

Take the roots of plantane and wild hoarhound, fresh or dried, three ounces, boil them together in two quarts of water to one quart, and strain it; of this decoction let the patient take one third part, three mornings fasting, successively, from which, if he finds any relief, it must be continued until he is perfectly recovered. On the contrary, if he finds no alteration after the third dose, it is a sign that the patient has not been poisoned at all, or that it has been with such poison that Cesar's antidote will not remedy, so may leave off the decoction.

During the cure the patient must live on spare diet, and abstain from eating mutton, pork, butter, or any other fat or oily food.

N. B. The plantane or hoarhound will either of them cure alone, but they are most efficacious together.

In summer you may take one handful of the roots and of the branches of each, in place of three ounces of the roots each.

For drink during the cure let them take the following: Take of the roots of goldenrod, six ounces or in summer, two large handfuls of the roots and branches together, and boil them in two quarts of water to one quart, to which also may be added, a little hoarhound and sassafras; to this decoction after it is strained, add a glass of rum or brandy, and sweeten with sugar for ordinary drink.

Sometimes an inward fever attends such as are poisoned, for which he ordered the following: Take one pint of wood ashes and three pints of water, stir and mix well together, let them stand all night and strain or decant the lye off in the morning, of which ten ounces may be taken six mornings following, warmed or cold according to the weather.

These medicines have no sensible operation, though sometimes they work on the bowels, and give a gentle stool.

had gained such distinction for his curative knowledge of roots and herbs that the Assembly of South Carolina purchased his freedom and gave him an annuity of one hundred pounds.

That slaves not infrequently held high rank among their own race as professional men may be seen from the advertisements of colonial days. A runaway Negro named Simon was in 1740 advertised in *The Pennsylvania Gazette*[2] as being able to "bleed and draw teeth" and "pretending to be a great doctor among his people." Referring in 1797 to a fugitive slave of Charleston, South Carolina, *The City Gazette and Daily Advertiser*[3] said: "He passes for a Doctor among people of his color and it is supposed practices in that capacity about town." The contact of such practitioners with the white race was due to the fact that the profession of the barber was at one time united with that of the physician. The practice of phlebotomy was considered an essential part of the doctor's work. As the Negro early became a barber and the profession was united with that of the physician, it is natural to suppose that he too would assume the latter function. That phlebotomy was considered an essential part of the practice of the medi-

The symptoms attending such as are poisoned, are as follows: A pain of the breast, difficulty of breathing, a load at the pit of the stomach, an irregular pulse, burning and violent pains of the viscera above and below the navel, very restless at night, sometimes wandering pains over the whole body, a reaching inclination to vomit, profuse sweats (which prove always serviceable), slimy stools, both when costive and loose, the face of pale and yellow color, sometimes a pain and inflamation of the throat, the appetite is generally weak, and some cannot eat anything; those who have been long poisoned are generally very feeble and weak in their limbs, sometimes spit a great deal, the whole skin peels, and lastly the hair falls off.

Cesar's cure for the bite of a rattlesnake: Take of the roots of plantane or hoarhound (in summer roots and branches together), a sufficient quantity; bruise them in a mortar, and squeeze out the juice, of which give as soon as possible, one large spoonful; this generally will cure; but if he finds no relief in an hour after you may give another spoonful which never hath failed.

If the roots are dried they must be moistened with a little water.

To the wound may be applied a leaf of good tobacco, moistened with rum.
The Massachusetts Magazine, IV, 103–104 (1792).

[2] *The Pennsylvania Gazette*, Sept. 11, 1740.

[3] *The City Gazette and Daily Advertiser*, June 22, 1797.

cine is seen from the fact that it was practiced upon George Washington in his last illness. An instance of this sort of professional development among the Negroes appears in the case of the barber, Joseph Ferguson. Prior to 1861 he lived in Richmond, Virginia, uniting the three occupations of leecher, cupper, and barber. This led to his taking up the study of medicine in Michigan, where he graduated and practiced for many years.

The first regularly recognized Negro physician, of whom there is a complete record, was James Derham, of New Orleans. He was born in Philadelphia in 1762, where he was taught to read and write, and instructed in the principles of Christianity. When a boy he was transferred by his master to Dr. John Kearsley, Jr., who employed him occasionally to compound medicines, and to perform some of the more humble acts of attention to his patients. Upon the death of Dr. Kearsley, he became (after passing through several hands) the property of Dr. George West, surgeon to the Sixteenth British Regiment, under whom, during the Revolutionary War, he performed many of the menial duties of the medical profession. At the close of the war, he was sold by Dr. West to Dr. Robert Dove at New Orleans, who employed him as an assistant in his business, in which capacity he gained so much of his confidence and friendship, that he consented to liberate him, after two or three years, upon easy terms. From Dr. Derham's numerous opportunities of improving in medicine, he became so well acquainted with the healing art, as to commence practicing in New Orleans, under the patronage of his last master. He once did business to the amount of three thousand dollars a year. Benjamin Rush, who had the opportunity to meet him, said: "I have conversed with him upon most of the acute and epidemic diseases of the country where he lives and was pleased to find him perfectly acquainted with the modern simple mode of practice on those diseases. I expected to have suggested some new medicines to him; but he suggested many more to me. He is very modest and engaging in his manners. He speaks

French fluently and has some knowledge of the Spanish language."[4]

The most noted colored physician after the time of James Derham was Doctor James McCune Smith, a graduate of the University of Glasgow. He began the practice of medicine in New York about 1837, and soon distinguished himself as a physician and surgeon. He passed as a man of unusual merit not only among his own people but among the best elements of that metropolis. That he was appreciated by the leading white physicians of the city is evidenced by the fact that in 1852 he was nominated as one of the five men to draft a constitution for the "Statistic Institute" of which he became a leading member. For a number of years he held the position of physician to the colored orphan asylum, serving on the staff with a number of white doctors.

Living in a day when the Negro was the subject of much anthropological and physiological discussion, Doctor Smith could not resist participating in this controversy. There were at this time a number of persons who were resorting to science to prove the inferiority of the Negro. Given a hearing extending over several evenings, Doctor Smith ably discussed "The Comparative Anatomy of the Races" before an assembly of the most distinguished ladies and gentlemen of the city, triumphing over his antagonist. In 1846 he produced a valuable work entitled "The Influence of Climate on Longevity, with Special Reference to Insurance." This paper was written as a refutation of a disquisition of John C. Calhoun on the colored race. Among other things Doctor Smith said: "The reason why the proportion of mortality is not a measure of longevity, is the following: The proportion of mortality is a statement of how many persons die in a population; this, of course, does not state the age at which those persons die. If 1 in 45 die in Sweden, and 1 in 22 in Grenada, the age of the dead might be alike in both countries; here the greater mortality might actually accompany the greater longevity."[5]

4 The Columbian Gazette, II, 742–743.
5 Delany, "Condition of the Colored People," 111.

The first real impetus to bring Negroes in considerable numbers into the professional world came from the American Colonization Society, which in the early years flourished in the South as well as in the North. This organization hoped to return the free Negroes to Africa and undertook to prepare professional leaders of their race for the Liberian colony. ''To execute this scheme, leaders of the colonization movement endeavored to educate Negroes in mechanic arts, agriculture, science and Biblical literature. Exceptionally bright youths were to be given special training as catechists, teachers, preachers and physicians. Not much was said about what they were doing, but now and then appeared notices of Negroes who had been prepared privately in the South or publicly in the North for service in Liberia. Dr. William Taylor and Dr. Fleet were thus educated in the District of Columbia. In the same way John V. DeGrasse, of New York, and Thomas J. White, of Brooklyn, were allowed to complete the medical course at Bowdoin in 1849. In 1854 Dr. DeGrasse was admitted as a member of the Massachusetts Medical Society. In 1858 the Berkshire Medical School graduated two colored doctors who were gratuitously educated by the American Educational Society.''[6] Dr. A. T. Augusta studied medicine at the University of Toronto. He qualified by competitive examination and obtained the position of surgeon in the United States Army, being the first Negro to hold such a position. After the war he became one of the leading colored physicians in the District of Columbia. Prior to 1861 Negroes had taken courses at the Medical School of the University of New York; Caselton Medical School in Vermont; Berkshire Medical School in Pittsfield, Massachusetts; the Rush Medical School in Chicago; the Eclectic Medical School in Philadelphia; the Homeopathic College of Cleveland; and the Medical School of Harvard University.

The next colored physician of prominence was Martin R. Delany. Delany grew to manhood in Pittsburgh, where early in his career he began the study of medicine, but aban-

6 C. G. Woodson, ''The Education of the Negro Prior to 1861.''

doned it for pursuits in other parts. In 1849 he returned to that city and resumed his studies under Doctors Joseph P. Gazzan and Francis J. Lemoyne, who secured for him admission to the medical department of Harvard College after he had been refused by the University Pennsylvania, Jefferson College, and the medical colleges of Albany and Geneva, New York. After leaving Harvard, he, like Dr. Smith, became interested in the discussion of the superiority and inferiority of races, and traveled extensively through the West, lecturing with some success on the physiological aspect of these subjects. He then returned to Pittsburgh, where he became a practitioner and distinguished himself in treating the cholera during the epidemic of 1854. About this time his worth to the community was attested by his appointment as a member of the Subcommittee of Referees who furnished the Municipal Board of Charity with medical advice as to the needs of white and colored persons desiring aid. In 1856 he removed to Chatham, Canada, where he practiced medicine a number of years. Doctor Delany thereafter like William Wells Brown, an occasional physician, devoted most of his time to the uplift of his people, traveling in America, Africa and England. He became such a worker among his people that he was known as a leader rather than a physician. He served in the Civil War as a commissioned officer of the United States Army, ranking as major.

Up to this point the colored physician had appeared as an occasional or exceptional individual, but hardly as forming a professional class. Following the wake of the Civil War colleges and universities were planted in all parts of the South for the sake of preparing leaders for the newly emancipated race. Several medical schools were established in connection with these institutions. The rise of the Negro physician as a professional class may be dated from the establishment of these institutions. The School of Medicine of Howard University, Washington, D. C., and the Meharry Medical College at Nashville, Tennessee, proved to be the strongest of these institutions and to-day are supplying the Negro medical profession with a large number of its annual recruits.

Dr. Charles B. Purvis, who was graduated from the Medical College of Western Reserve University in Cleveland, Ohio, in 1865, is perhaps the oldest colored physician in the United States; and by general consent ranks as dean of the fraternity. He shared with Dr. A. T. Augusta the honor of being one of the few colored men to become surgeons in the United States Army. Shortly after graduation he was made assistant surgeon in the Freedmen's Hospital at Washington, D. C., with which institution he was connected during the entire period of his active professional life. The development and present position of the medical school at Howard University is due to Dr. Purvis more than to any other single individual. For several years he has been retired upon the Carnegie Foundation. Dr. George W. Hubbard, a distinguished white physician, dean of the Meharry Medical College, Nashville, Tennessee, has also been a great pioneer and promoter of the medical education of the Negro race.

At first, the Negro patient refused to put confidence in the physician of his own race, notwithstanding the closer intimacy of social contact. It was not until after he had demonstrated his competency to treat disease as well as his white competitor that he was able to win recognition among his own people. The colored physician is everywhere in open competition with the white practitioner, who never refuses to treat Negro patients, if allowed to assume the disdainful attitude of racial superiority. If the Negro doctor did not secure practically as good results in the treatment of disease as the white physician, he would soon find himself without patients.

According to the last census there were in the United States 3,077 Negro physicians and 478 Negro dentists. When we consider the professional needs of ten millions of Negroes, it will be seen that the quota is not over one fourth full. There is urgent need especially for an additional number of pharmacists and dentists. It must be said for the Negro physician that their membership more fully measures up to the full status of a professional class than that of any other profession among colored men. Every member of the profession must have a stated medical education based upon considerable academic preparation, sufficient to enable them to pass the rigid tests of State Boards in various parts of the country. The best regulated medical schools are now requiring at least two years of college training as a basis for entering upon the study of medicine. Under the stimulus of these higher standards the Negro medical profession will become more thoroughly equipped and proficient in the years to come.

These physicians maintain a national medical association which meets annually in different parts of the country and prepare and discuss papers bearing upon the various phases of their profession. There are under the control of Negro physicians a number of hospitals where are performed operations verging upon the limits of surgical skill. The profession has developed not a few physicians and surgeons whose ability has won recognition throughout their profession. A number of them have performed operations which have attracted wide attention and have contributed to leading journals discussions dealing with the various forms and phases of disease, as well as their medical and surgical treatment.

By reason of the stratum which the Negro occupies, the race is an easy prey to disease that affects the health of the whole nation. The germs of disease have no race prejudice. They do not even draw the line at social equality, but gnaw with equal avidity at the vitals of white and black alike, and pass with the greatest freedom of intercourse from the one to the other. One touch of disease makes the whole world kin, and also kind. The Negro physician comes into immediate contact with the masses of his race; he is the missionary of good health. His ministration is not only to his own race, but to the community and to the nation as a whole. The white plague seems to love the black victim. This disease must be stamped out by the nation through concerted action. The Negro physician is one of the most efficient agencies to render this national service. During the entire history of the race on this continent, there has been no more striking indication of its capacity for self-reclamation and of its ability to maintain a professional class on the basis of scientific efficiency than the rise and success of the Negro physician.

KELLY MILLER

THE NEGRO SOLDIER IN THE AMERICAN REVOLUTION

The facts as to the participation of Negroes in the American Revolution have received the attention of several writers. Yet not one of them has made a scientific presentation of the facts which they have discovered. These historians have failed to consider the bearing of the status of the free Negro during the colonial period, the meaning of the Revolution to the Negro, and what the service of the Negro soldiers first enlisted effected in changing the attitude of the people toward the blacks throughout the original thirteen colonies.

To a person who has lived in the nineteenth or twentieth century it would seem incredible that Negroes, the majority of whom were then slaves, should have been allowed to fight in the Continental Army. The layman here may forget that during the eighteenth century slavery was a patriarchal institution rather than the economic plantation system as it developed after the multiplication of mechanical appliances, which brought about the world-wide industrial revolution. During the eighteenth century a number of slaves brought closely into contact with their masters were gradually enlightened and later emancipated. Such freedmen, in the absence of any laws to the contrary, exercised political rights,[1] among which was that of bearing arms. Negroes served not only in the American Revolution, but in every war of consequence during the colonial period. There were masters who sent slaves to the front to do menial labor and to fight in the places of their owners. Then there were slaves who, finding it easier to take occasional chances with bullets than to bear the lash, ran away from their masters and served as privateers or enlisted as freemen.[2]

[1] Bancroft, "History of the United States," VIII, 110; MacMaster, "History of the United States."

[2] See "Documents" in this number.

The newspapers of the colonial period often mentioned these facts in their advertisements of fugitive slaves. In 1760 a master had considerable difficulty with a slave who escaped from New England into New Jersey, where he said he would enlist in the provincial service.[3] Advertising for his mulatto servant, who was brought up in Rhode Island, James Richardson of Stonington said that the fugitive had served as a soldier the previous summer.[4] A few free Negroes found their way into the colonial militia along with white soldiers. This passed, of course, not without some opposition, as in the case of Massachusetts. In 1656 that colony excluded Negroes and Indians from the militia, and according to Governor Bradstreet's report to the Board of Trade in 1680 and subsequent action taken by that colony in 1775 and 1776, it adhered to this policy.[5]

Favorable as this condition of Negroes during the colonial period seemed, the situation became still more desirable during the Revolution itself. This upheaval was social as well as political. Aristocracy was suddenly humiliated and the man in the common walks of life found himself in power, grappling with problems which he had long desired to solve. Sprung from the indentured servant poor white class, the new rulers had more sympathy for the man farthest down. The slaves, therefore, received more consideration. In the heat of the excitement of war the system lost almost all of its rigor, the slave codes in some cases falling into desuetude. The contest for liberty was in the mouths of some orators of the Revolution the cause of the blacks as well as that of the whites, and the natural rights of the former were openly discussed in urging the independence of the United States. When men like Laurens, Henry, Hamilton and Otis spoke for the rights of the American colonies, they were not silent on the duty of the American people toward their slaves.[6]

[3] The New York Gazette, Aug. 11, 1760.
[4] Supplement to the Boston Evening Post, May 23, 1763.
[5] Moore's "Slavery in Mass.," 243; Mass. Hist. Soc. Coll., VII, 336.
[6] Adams, "Works of John Adams," X, 315; Moore, "Notes on Slavery in Mass.," 71. Hamilton, Letter to Jay, March 14, 1779.

In 1774 a patriot in the Provincial Congress of Massachusetts spoke of the "propriety, that while we are attempting to free ourselves from slavery, our present embarrassments, and preserve ourselves from slavery, that we also take into consideration the state and circumstances of the Negro slaves in this province."[7]

When the Revolution came the Negro was actually in the army before the question of his enlistment could be raised by those who had not yet been won to the cause of universal freedom. Feeling the same patriotism which the white man experienced, the Negro bared his breast to the bullet and gave his life as a sacrifice for the liberty of his country. According to Bancroft, "the roll of the army of Cambridge had from its first formation borne the names of men of color." "Free Negroes," said he, "stood in the ranks by the side of white men. In the beginning of the war they had entered the provincial army; the first general order which was issued by Ward had required a return, among other things, of the complexion of the soldiers; and black men, like others, were retained in the service after the troops were adopted by the continent."[8]

Before the various officials had had time to decide whether or not the Negro should be enlisted, many had numbered themselves among the first to spill their blood in behalf of American liberty. Peter Salem had distinguished himself at Bunker Hill by killing Major Pitcairn,[9] a number of other Negroes under the command of Major Samuel Lawrence had heroically imperilled their lives and rescued him when he had advanced so far beyond his troops that he was about to be surrounded and taken prisoner,[10] and Salem Poor of Colonel Frye's regiment had acquitted himself with such honor in the battle of Charlestown that fourteen American officers commended him to the Continental Congress

[7] Moore, "Historical Notes on the Employment of Negroes in the American Revolution," 4.
[8] Bancroft, "History of the United States," VIII, 110.
[9] Washburn, "History of Leicester," 267.
[10] Washington, "The Story of the Negro," I, 315.

for his valor.[11]   But great as were the services rendered by these patriots of color, the increase in the number of blacks in the Continental Army gave rise to vexatious questions. There were those who, influenced by the theories which had made the Revolution possible, hailed with joy the advent of the Negro in the rôle of the defender of his country, which they believed owed him. freedom and opportunity. Some, having the idea that the Negro was a savage, too stupid to be employed in fighting the battles of freemen, seriously objected to his enlistment.   Others were fearful of the result from setting the example of employing an uncivilized people to fight the British, who would then have an excuse not only for enlisting Negroes[12] but also the Indians. A still larger number felt that the question of arming the slaves would simply reduce itself to one of deciding whether or not the colonies should permit the British to beat them playing their own game.[13]

In the beginning, however, those who believed the Negroes should be excluded from the army triumphed.   Massachusetts officially took a stand against the enlistment of slaves.   The Committee of Safety, of which John Hancock and Joseph Ward were members, reported in May, 1775, to the Provincial Congress the opinion that as the contest then between Great Britain and her colonies respected the liberties and privileges of the latter, that the admission of any persons but freemen as soldiers would be inconsistent with the principles supported and would reflect dishonor on the colony.[14]   They urged that no slaves be admitted into the army under any consideration whatever.   No action was taken.   This was not seemingly directed at the enlistment of free Negroes; but it must have had some effect, for in July of the same year, when Washington took command of the army at Cambridge, there were issued from his headquarters to recruiting officers instructions prohibiting the

[11] Manuscript, Massachusetts Archives, CLXXX, 241.

[12] Journals of the Continental Congress, 1775, pp. 221, 263; 1776, pp. 60, 874; 1779, pp. 386, 418.

[13] Ford, ''Washington's Writings,'' VIII, 371.

[14] Journal of the Provincial Congress of Massachusetts, 553.

enlistment of any Negro, any person not native of this country, unless such person had a wife and a family and was a settled resident.[15]

This matter became one of such concern that the officials of the Continental Army had to give it more serious consideration. Communications relative thereto directed to the Continental Congress provoked a debate in that body in September, 1775. On the occasion of drafting a letter to Washington, reported by a committee consisting of Lynch, Lee and Adams, to whom several of his communications had been referred, Rutledge, of South Carolina, moved that the commander-in-chief be instructed to discharge from the army all Negroes, whether slave or free.[16] It seems that Rutledge had the support of the Southern delegates, but failed to secure a majority vote in favor of this radical proposition.

The matter was not yet settled, however. On the eighth of the following month there was held a council of war consisting of Washington, Ward, Lee, Putnam, Thomas, Spencer, Heath, Sullivan, Greene and Gates, to consider the question whether or not it would be advisable to enlist Negroes in the new army or "whether there be any distinction between such as are slaves and those who are free." It was unanimously agreed to reject all slaves and by a large majority to refuse Negroes altogether.[17] Upon considering ten days later the question of devising a method of renovating the army, however, the question of enlisting Negroes came up again before a Committee of Conference. The leaders in this council were Benjamin Franklin, Benjamin Harrison, Thomas Lynch, the Deputy Governors of Connecticut and Rhode Island, and the Committee of Council of Massachusetts Bay. They were asked the question whether Negroes should be excluded from the new enlistment, especially such as were slaves. This council also agreed that Negroes should be rejected altogether.[18] Accordingly, the general

15 Moore, "Historical Notes," 5.
16 Ibid., 6.
17 Ibid., 6.
18 Ibid., 7.

orders from Washington, dated November 12, 1775, declared
that neither Negroes, boys unable to bear arms, nor old men
unfit to endure fatigues of the campaign should be enlisted.
    The men who had taken this position had acted blindly.
They had failed to consider the various complications which
might arise as a result of the refusal to admit Negroes to the
army. What would the Negroes think when they saw their
offering thrown away from the altar of their country?
Were the Revolutionary fathers so stupid as to think that
the British would adopt the same policy? They could not
have believed that the situation could be so easily cleared.
Before the Revolution was well on its way the delegates
from Georgia to the Continental Congress had already experienced certain fears as to the safety of Georgia and South
Carolina. They believed that if one thousand regular
troops should land in Georgia under a commander with adequate supplies and he should proclaim freedom to all loyal
Negroes, twenty thousand of them would join the British
in a fortnight. It was to them a matter of much concern
that the Negroes of these provinces had such a wonderful
art of communicating intelligence among themselves as to
convey information several hundred miles in a week or in a
fortnight.[19] The colonists, too, could not ignore the bold
attempt of Lord Dunmore, the dethroned governor of Virginia, who issued a proclamation of freedom to all slaves
who would fight for the king, endeavored to raise a black
regiment among them, and actually used a number of Negroes in the battle at Kemp's Landing, where they behaved
like well-seasoned soldiers, pursuing and capturing one of
the attacking companies.[20] Referring thereafter to Lord
Dunmore as an arch-traitor who should be instantly crushed,
George Washington said: "But that which renders the
measure indispensably necessary is the Negroes; if he gets
formidable numbers of them, will be tempted to join" him.
    Subsequent developments showed that these misgivings
were justified. In July, 1776, General Greene learned on

[19] Adams's Works, II, 428.
[20] Life and Correspondence of Joseph Reed, I, 135.

Long Island that the British were about to organize in that
vicinity a regiment of Negroes aggregating 200.[22] Taking
as a pretext the enrollment of Negroes in the Continental
Army, Sir Henry Clinton proclaimed from Philipsburgh in
1779 that all Negroes taken in arms or upon any military
duty should be purchased from the captors for the public
service, and that every Negro who would desert the ''Rebel
Standard'' should have full security to follow within the
British lines any occupation which he might think proper.[23]
In 1781 General Greene reported to Washington from North
Carolina that the British there had undertaken to embody
immediately two regiments of Negroes.[24] They were operating just as aggressively farther South. ''It has been
computed by good judges,'' says Ramsey, ''that between
the years 1775 and 1783 the State of South Carolina lost
25,000 Negroes,[25] that is, one fifth of all the slaves, and a
little more than half as many as its entire white population.
At the evacuation of Charleston 241 Negroes and their families were taken off to St. Lucia in one transport, the Scimi-
tar.''[26] Yet in Georgia it is believed that the loss of Ne-

[22] Force, American Archives, I, 486. Fifth Series.
[23] ''By his Excellency, Sir HENRY CLINTON, K.B., General and Commander-in-Chief of all His Majesty's Forces within the Colonies lying on the
Atlantic Ocean, from Nova Scotia to West Florida, inclusive, etc.

''PROCLAMATION

''Whereas, The Enemy have adopted a practice of enrolling NEGROES
among their troops: I do hereby give Notice, that all NEGROES taken in Arms,
or upon.any military Duty shall be purchased for the public service at a
stated price; the Money to be paid to the Captors.

''But I do most strictly forbid any Person to sell or claim Right over
any Negroe, the Property of a Rebel, who may take refuge with any part of
this Army: And I do promise to every Negroe who shall desert the Rebel
Standard full Security to follow within these Lines any occupation which he
may think proper.

''Given under my Hand at Head-Quarters,
Philipsburgh, the 30th day of June 1779.
H. CLINTON.
By his Excellency's Comman,
JOHN SMITH, Secretary.''

[24] The Journal of the Continental Congress, II, 26.
[25] Ramsay, ''The History of South Carolina'' [Edition, 1809], I, 474–475.
[26] The Gazette of the State of South Carolina, Nov. 22, 1784.

groes was much greater, probably three fourths or seven
eighths of all in the State. There the British were more
successful in organizing and making use of Negroes. One
third of the 600 men by whom Fort Cornwallis was garri-
soned at the siege of Augusta were Negroes. So effective
were some of these Negroes trained by the British in Georgia
that a corps of fugitive slaves calling themselves the "King
of England's Soldiers," so harassed the people on both
sides of the Savannah River, even after the Revolution,
that it was feared that a general insurrection of the slaves
there would follow as a result of this most dangerous and
best disciplined band of marauders that ever infested its
borders.[27]

The leaders of the Revolution, therefore, quickly receded
from their radical position of excluding Negroes from the
army. Informed that the free Negroes who had served in
the ranks in New England were sorely displeased at their
exclusion from the service, and fearing that they might join
the enemy, Washington departed, late in 1775, from the established policy of the staff and gave the recruiting officers
leave to accept such Negroes, promising to lay the matter
before the Continental Congress, which he did not doubt
would approve it.[28] Upon the receipt of this communication the matter was referred to a committee composed of
Wythe, Adams and Wilson, who recommended that free Negroes who had served faithfully in the army at Cambridge
might be reenlisted but no others.[29] In taking action on such
communications thereafter the Continental Congress followed the policy of leaving the matter to the various States,
which were then jealously mindful of their rights.

Sane leaders generally approved the enlistment of black
troops. General Thomas thought so well of the proposition
that he wrote John Adams in 1775, expressing his surprise
that any prejudice against it should exist.[30] Samuel Hop-

---

[27] Moore, "Historical Notes," 14.
[28] Sparks, "Washington's Works," III, 218.
[29] *Ibid.*
[30] Letter of General Thomas to John Adams, Oct. 24, 1775.

kins said in 1776 that something should be speedily done with respect to the slaves to prevent their turning against the Americans. He was of the opinion that the way to counteract the tendency of the Negroes to join the British was not to restrain them by force and severity but by public acts to set the slaves free and encourage them to labor and take arms in defense of the American cause.[31] Interested in favor of the Negroes both by "the dictates of humanity and true policy," Hamilton urged that slaves be given their freedom with the swords to secure their fidelity, animate their courage, and influence those remaining in bondage by opening a door to their emancipation.[32] General Greene emphatically urged that blacks be armed, believing that they would make good soldiers.[33] Thinking that the slaves might be put to a much better use than being given as a bounty to induce white men to enlist, James Madison suggested that the slaves be liberated and armed.[34] "It would certainly be consonant to the principles of liberty," said he, "which ought never to be lost sight of in a contest for liberty." John Laurens, of South Carolina, was among the first to see the wisdom of this plan, directed the attention of his co-workers to it, and when authorized by the Continental Congress, proceeded to his native State, wishing that he had the persuasive power of a Demosthenes to make his fellow citizens accept this proposition.[35] In 1779 Laurens said: "I would advance those who are unjustly deprived of the rights of mankind to a state which would be a proper gradation between abject slavery and perfect liberty, and besides I am persuaded that if I could obtain authority for the purpose, I would have a corps of such men trained, uniformly clad, equipped and ready in every respect to act at the opening of the next campaign."

All of the colonies thereafter tended to look more favor-

[31] Moore, Historical Notes, 4.

[32] Hamilton's "Works," I, 76–78.

[33] Moore, "Historical Notes," 13.

[34] Madison's Papers, 68.

[35] Letter of Hamilton to Jay, March 14, 1779; and Journals of the Continental Congress.

ably upon the enlistment of colored troops. Free Negroes
enlisted in Virginia and so many slaves deserted their masters for the army that the State enacted in 1777 a law providing that no Negro should be enlisted unless he had a
certificate of freedom.[36]   That commonwealth, however,
soon took another step toward greater recgonition of the
rights of the Negroes who desired to be free to help maintain the honor of the State.   With the promise of freedom
for military service many slaves were sent to the army as
substitutes for freemen.   The effort of inhuman masters to
force such Negroes back into slavery at the close of their
service at the front actuated the liberal legislators of that
commonwealth to pass the Act of Emancipaton, proclaiming
freedom to all Negroes who had thus enlisted and served
their term faithfully, and empowered them to sue *in forma
pauperis*, should they thereafter be unlawfully held in
bondage.[37]

In the course of time there arose an urgent need for the
Negro in the army.   The army reached the point when
almost all sorts of soldiers were acceptable.   In 1778 General Varnum induced General Washington to send certain
officers from Valley Forge to Rhode Island to enlist a battalion of Negroes to fill the depleted ranks of that State.[38]
Setting forth in the preamble that "history affords us frequent precedents of the wisest, freest and bravest nations
having liberated their slaves and enlisted them as soldiers to
fight in defense of their country," the Rhode Island Assembly resolved to raise a regiment of slaves, who were to be
freed upon their enlistment, their owners to be paid by the
State according to the valuation of a committee.   Further
light was thrown upon this action in the statement of Governor Cooke, who in reporting the action of the Assembly to
Washington boasted that liberty was given to every effective
slave to don the uniform and that upon his passing muster he

---

[36] Hening, Statutes at Large, IX, 280.
[37] *Ibid.*, XI, 308, 309.
[38] Rhode Island Colonial Records, VIII, 640, 641.

became absolutely free and entitled to all the wages, bounties and encouragements given to any other soldier.[39]

The State of New Hampshire enlisted Negroes and gave to those who served three years the same bounty offered others. This bounty was turned over to their masters as the price of the slaves in return for which their owners issued bills of sale and certificates of freedom.[40] In this way slavery practically passed out in New Hampshire. This affair did not proceed so smoothly as this in Massachusetts. In 1778 that legislature had a committee report in favor of raising a regiment of mulattoes and Negroes. This action was taken as a result upon receiving an urgent letter from Thomas Kench, a member of an artillery regiment serving on Castle Island. Kench referred to the fact that there were divers of Negroes in the battalions mixed with white men, but he thought that the blacks would have a better esprit de corps should they be organized in companies by themselves. But the feeling that slaves should not fight the battles of freemen and a confusion of the question of enlistment with that of emancipation for which Massachusetts was not then prepared,[41] led to a heated debate in the Massachusetts Council and finally to blows in the coffee houses in lower Boston. In such an excited state of affairs no further action was taken. Finding recruiting difficult it is said that Connecticut undertook to raise a colored regiment[42] and in 1781 New York, offering the usual land bounty which would go to the masters to purchase the slaves, promised freedom to all slaves who would enlist for the time of three years.[43] Maryland provided in 1780 that each unit of £16,000 of property should furnish one recruit who might be either a freeman or a slave, and in 1781 resolved to raise 750 Negroes to be incorporated with the other troops.[44]

[39] Ibid., 358–360.
[40] Moore, "Historical Notes," 19.
[41] Manuscripts in the Archives of Massachusetts, CXCIX, 80.
[42] Moore, "Historical Notes," 20.
[43] Laws of the State of New York, Chapter XXXII, Fourth Session.
[44] Sparks, "Correspondence of the American Revolution," III, 331.

Farther South the enlistment of Negroes had met with obstacles. The best provision the Southern legislatures had been able to make was to provide in addition to the allotment of money and land that a person offering to fight for the country should have "one sound Negro"[45] or a "healthy sound Negro"[46] as the laws provided in Virginia and South Carolina respectively. Threatened with invasion in 1779, however, the Southern States were finally compelled to consider this matter more seriously.[47] The Continental Army

[45] Moore, "Historical Notes," 20.

[46] Ibid., 21.

[47] Taking up the Southern situation, Hamilton in 1779 wrote Jay as follows:

"*Dear Sir:* Colonel Laurens, who will have the honor of delivering you this letter, is on his way to South Carolina, on a project which I think, in the present situation of affairs there, is a very good one, and deserves every kind of support and encouragement. This is, to raise two, three, or four battalions of negroes, with the assistance of the government of that State, by contributions from the owners, in proportion to the number they possess. If you should think proper to enter upon the subject with him, he will give you a detail of his plan. He wishes to have it recommended by Congress to the State; and, as an inducement, that they would engage to take their battalions into Continental pay.

"It appears to me, that an expedient of this kind, in the present state of Southern affairs, is the most rational that can be adopted, and promises very important advantages. Indeed, I hardly see how a sufficient force can be collected in that quarter without it: and the enemy's operations there are growing infinitely serious and formidable. I have not the least doubt, that the negroes will make very excellent soldiers with proper management: and I will venture to pronounce, that they cannot be put in better hands than those of Mr. Laurens. He has all the zeal, intelligence, enterprise, and every other qualification, requisite to succeed in such an undertaking. It is a maxim with some great military judges, that, with sensible officers, soldiers can hardly be too stupid; and, on this principle, it is thought that the Russians would make the best soldiers in the world, if they were under other officers than their own. The King of Prussia is among the number who maintain this doctrine, and has a very emphatic saying on the occasion, which I do not exactly recollect. I mention this because I have frequently heard it objected to the scheme of embodying negroes, that they are too stupid to make soldiers. This is so far from appearing to me a valid objection, that I think their want of cultivation (for their natural faculties are as good as ours), joined to that habit of subordination which they acquire from a life of servitude will enable them sooner to become soldiers than our white inhabitants. Let officers be men of sense and sentiment, and the nearer the soldiers approach to machines, perhaps the better.

had been called upon to cope with the situation but had no force available for service in those parts. The three battalions of North Carolina troops, then on duty in the South,

"I foresee that this project will have to combat much opposition from prejudice and self-interest. The contempt we have been taught to entertain for the blacks, makes us fancy many things that are founded neither in reason nor experience; and an unwillingness to part with property of so valuable a kind, will furnish a thousand arguments to show the impracticability, or pernicious tendency, of a scheme which requires such sacrifices. But it should be considered, that if we do not make use of them in this way, the enemy probably will; and that the best way to counteract the temptations they will hold out, will be to offer them ourselves. An essential part of the plan is, to give them their freedom with their swords. This will secure their fidelity, animate their courage, and, I believe, will have a good influence upon those who remain, by opening a door to their emancipation.

"This circumstance, I confess, has no small weight in inducing me to wish the success of the project; for the dictates of humanity and true policy equally interest me in favor of this unfortunate class of men.

"While I am on the subject of Southern affairs, you will excuse the liberty I take in saying, that I do not think measures sufficiently vigorous are pursuing for our defence in that quarter. Except the few regular troops of South Carolina, we seem to be relying wholly on the militia of that and two neighboring States. These will soon grow impatient of service and leave our affairs in a miserable situation. No considerable force can be uniformly kept up by militia, to say nothing of the many obvious and well-known inconveniences that attend this kind of troops. I would beg leave to suggest, sir, that no time ought to be lost in making a draught of militia to serve a twelve-month, from the States of North and South Carolina and Virginia. But South Carolina, being very weak in her population of whites, may be excused from the draught, on condition of furnishing the black battalions. The two others may furnish about three thousand five hundred men, and be exempted, on that account, from sending any succor to this army. The States to the northward of Virginia, will be fully able to give competent supplies to the army here; and it will require all the force and exertions of the three States I have mentioned, to withstand the storm which has arisen, and is increasing in the South.

"The troops draughted, must be thrown into battalions, and officered in the best possible manner. The best supernumerary officers may be made use of as far as they will go. If arms are wanted for their troops, and no better way of supplying them is to be found, we should endeavor to levy a contribution of arms upon the militia at large. Extraordinary exigencies demand extraordinary means. I fear this Southern business will become a very *grave* one.

"With the truest respect and esteem,
    I am, sir, your most obedient servant,
        ALEX. HAMILTON."

consisted of drafts from the militia for nine months, which would expire before the end of the campaign. What were they to do then when this militia, which could not be uniformly kept up, should grow impatient with the service? Writing from the headquarters of the army at this time, Alexander Hamilton in discussing the advisability of this plan doubtless voiced the sentiment of the staff. He thought that Colonel Laurens's plan for raising three or four battalions of emancipated Negroes was the most rational one that could be adopted in that state of Southern affairs. Hamilton foresaw the opposition from prejudice and self-interest, but insisted that if the Americans did not make such a use of the Negroes, the British would.

The movement received further impetus when special envoys from South Carolina headed by Huger appeared before the Continental Congress on March 29, 1779, to impress upon that body the neceessity of doing something to relieve the Southern colonies. South Carolina, they reported, was suffering from an exposed condition in that the number of slaves being larger than that of the whites, she was unable to effect anything for its defense with the natives, because of the large number necessary to remain at home to prevent insurrections among the Negroes and their desertion to the enemy. These representatives, therefore, suggested that there mght be raised among the Negroes in that State a force "which would not only be formidable to the enemy from their numbers and the discipline of which they would readily admit but would also lessen the danger from revolts and desertions by detaching the most vigorous and enterprising from among the Negroes." At the same time the Committee expressed the opinion that a matter of such vital interest to the two States concerned should be referred to their legislative bodies to judge as to the expediency of taking this step, and that if these commonwealths found it satisfactory that the United States should defray the expenses.

Congress passed a resolution complying with these

recommendations.[48]   Laurens, the father of the movement, was made a lieutenant-colonel and he went immediately home to urge upon South Carolina the expediency of adopting this plan.   There Laurens met determined opposition from the majority of the aristocrats who set themselves against ''a measure of so threatening aspect and so offensive to that republican pride, which disdains to commit the defence of the country to servile bands or share with a color to which the idea of inferiority is inseparably connected, the pro-

[48] The resolutions of Congress were as follows:

''*Resolved*, That it be recommended to the States of South Carolina and Georgia, if they shall think the same expedient, to take measures immediately for raising three thousand able-bodied negroes.

''That the said negroes be formed into separate corps, as battalions, according to the arrangements adopted for the main army, to be commanded by white commissioned and non-commissioned officers.

''That the commissioned officers be appointed by the said States.

''That the non-commissioned officers may, if the said States respectively shall think proper, be taken from among the non-commissioned officers and soldiers of the continental battalions of the said States respectively.

''That the Governors of the said States, together with the commanding officer of the Southern army, be empowered to incorporate the several continental battalions of their States with each other respectively, agreeably to the arrangement of the army, as established by the resolutions of May 27, 1778; and to appoint such of the supernumerary officers to command the said negroes, as shall choose to go into that service.

''*Resolved*, That Congress will make provision for paying the proprietors of such Negroes as shall be enlisted for the service of the United States during the war, a full compensation for the property, at a rate not exceeding one thousand dollars for each active, able-bodied negro man of standard size, not exceeding thirty-five years of age, who shall be so enlisted and pass muster.

''That no pay or bounty be allowed to the said negroes; but that they be clothed and subsisted at the expense of the United States.

''That every negro, who shall well and faithfully serve as a soldier to the end of the present war, and shall return his arms, be emancipated, and receive the sum of fifty dollars.''

In connection with this Congress passed also the following resolution

''WHEREAS John Laurens, Esq., who has heretofore acted as aide-de-camp to the commander-in-chief, is desirous of repairing to South Carolina, with a design to assist in defence of the Southern States:

''*Resolved*, That a commission of lieutenant-colonel be granted to the said John Laurens, Esq.''

Journals of the Continental Congress, 1779, pp. 386, 418.

fession of arms, and that approximation of condition which must exist between the regular soldier and the militiaman.'' It was to no purpose too that Laurens renewed his efforts at a later period. He mustered all of his energy to impress upon the Legislature the need of taking this action but finally found himself outvoted, having only reason on his side and ''being opposed by a triple-headed monster that shed the baneful influence of avarice, prejudice, and pusillanimity in all our assemblies.'' ''It was some consolation to me, however,'' said he, ''to find that philosophy and truth had made some little progress since my last effort, as I obtained twice as many suffrages as before.''

Hearing of the outcome, Washington wrote him that he was not at all astonished at it, as that spirit of freedom, which at the commencement of the Revolution would have sacrificed everything to the attainment of this object, had long since subsided, and every selfish passion had taken its place. ''It is not the public but the private interest,'' said he, ''which influences the generality of mankind, nor can Americans any longer boast an exception. Under these circumstances it would have been rather surprising if you had succeeded.''[49] It is difficult, however, to determine exactly what Washington's attitude was. Two days after Hamilton wrote Jay about raising colored troops in South Carolina, the elder Laurens wrote Washington: ''Had we arms for three thousand such black men as I could select in Carolina, I should have no doubt of success in driving the British out of Georgia, and subduing East Florida before the end of July.'' To this Washington answered: ''The policy of our arming slaves is in my opinion a moot point, unless the enemy set the example. For, should we begin to form Battalions of them, I have not the smallest doubt, if the war is to be prosecuted, of their following us in it, and justifying the measure upon our own ground. The contest then must be who can arm fastest, and where are our arms? Besides I am not clear that a discrimination will not render slavery more irksome to those who remain in it. Most of the good

[49] Sparks, ''Writings of Washington,'' VIII, 322, 323.

and evil things in this life are judged by comparison; and I fear a comparison in this case will be productive of much discontent in those, who are held in servitude. But, as this is a subject that has never employed much of my thoughts, these are no more than the first crude Ideas that have struck me upon ye occasion.''[50]

What then resulted from the agitation and discussion? The reader naturally wants to know how many Negroes were actually engaged in the Continental Army. Here we find ourselves at sea. We have any amount of evidence that the number of Negroes engaged became considerable, but exact figures are for several reasons lacking. In the first place, free Negroes rarely served in separate battalions. They marched side by side with the white soldier, and in most cases, according to the War Department, even after making an extended research as to the names, organizations, and numbers, the results would be that little can be obtained from the records to show exactly what soldiers were white and what were colored.[51] Moreover the first official efforts to keep the Negroes out of the army must not be regarded as having stopped such enlistments. As there was not any formal system of recruiting, black men continued to enlist ''under various laws and sometimes under no law, and in defiance of law.'' The records of every one of the original thirteen States show that each had colored troops. A Hessian officer observed in 1777 that ''the Negro can take the field instead of his master; and, therefore, no regiment is to be seen in which there are not negroes in abundance, and among them there are able-bodied, strong and brave fellows.''[52] ''Here too,'' said he, ''there are many families of free negroes who live in good homes, have property and live just like the rest of the inhabitants.'' In 1777 Alexander Scammell, Adjutant-General, made the following report as to the number and placement of the Negroes in the Continental Army:

50 Ford, ''Washington's Writings,'' VII, 371.

51 Letter from the Adjutant General of the U. S. War Department.

52 Schloezer's ''Briefwechsel,'' IV, 365.

RETURN OF NEGROES IN THE ARMY, 24TH AUGUST, 1778

Brigades	Present	Sick, Absent	On Command	Total
North Carolina	42	10	6	58
Woodford	36	3	1	40
Muhlenburg	64	26	8	98
Smallwood	20	3	1	24
2d Maryland	43	15	2	60
Wayne	2	...	...	2
2d Pennsylvania	33	1	1	35
Clinton	33	2	4	62
Parsons	117	12	19	148
Huntington	56	2	4	62
Nixon	26	...	1	27
Paterson	64	13	12	89
Late Learned	34	4	8	46
Poor	16	7	4	27
Total	586	98	71	755

ALEX. SCAMMELL,
Adj.-Gen.[52a]

But this report neither included the Negro soldiers enlisted in several other States nor those that joined the army later. Other records show that Negroes served in as many as 18 brigades.

Some idea of the number of Negroes engaged may be obtained from the context of documents mentioning the action taken by States. Rhode Island we have observed undertook to raise a regiment of slaves. Governor Cooke said that the slaves found there were not many but that it was generally thought that 300 or more would enlist. Four companies of emancipated slaves were finally formed in that State at a cost of £10,437 7s 7d.[53] Most of the 629 slaves then found in New Hampshire availed themselves of the opportunity to gain their freedom by enlistment as did many of the 15,000 slaves in New York. Connecticut had free Negroes in its regiments and formed also a regiment of colored soldiers assigned first to Meigs' and afterward to Butler's command. Maryland resolved in 1781 to raise 750 Negroes to be incorporated with the other troops. Massachusetts thought of forming a separate battalion of Negroes and Indians but had no separate Negro regiment, the Ne-

[52a] The Washington Manuscripts in the Library of Congress.
[53] "The Spirit of '76 in Rhode Island," 186–188.

groes having been admitted into the other battalions, after
1778, to the extent that there were colored troops from 72
towns in that State. In view of these numerous facts it is
safe to conclude that there were at least 4,000 Negro soldiers
scattered throughout the Continental Army.

As to the value of the services rendered by the colored
troops we have only one witness to the contrary. This was
Sidney S. Rider. He tried to ridicule the black troops engaged in the Battle of Rhode Island and contended that only
a few of them took part in the contest.[54] On the other hand
we have two distinguished witnesses in their favor. The
Marquis de Chastellux said that "at the passage to the
ferry I met a detachment of the Rhode Island regiment, the
same corps we had with us the last summer, but they have
since been recruited and clothed. The greatest part of them
are Negroes or Mulattoes; but they are strong, robust men,
and those I have seen had a very good appearance."[55]
Speaking of the behavior of troops, among whom Negroes
under General Greene fought on this occasion, Lafayette
said the following day, that the enemy repeated the attempt
three times (tried to carry his position), and were as often repulsed with great bravery.[56] One hundred and forty-four of
the soldiers thus engaged to roll back the lines of the enemy
were, according to the Revolutionary records, Negroes.[57]
Doctor Harris, a revolutionary soldier, who took part in the
Battle of Rhode Island, said of these Negroes: "Had they
been unfaithful or even given away before the enemy all
would have been lost. Three times in succession they were
attacked with more desperate valor and fury by well disciplined and veteran troops, and three times did they successfully repel the assault and thus preserved our army from
capture."[58] A detachment of these troops sacrificed themselves to the last man in defending Colonel Greene in 1781

[54] Sidney S. Rider, "An Historical Tract in the Rhode Island Series,"
No. 10.

[55] Marquis de Chastellux, "Travels," I, 454.

[56] Moore, "Historical Notes," 19.

[57] "The Spirit of Rhode Island in '76," 186–188.

[58] Washington, "The Story of the Negro," I, 311, Note.

when he was attacked at Point Bridge, New York. A Negro slave of South Carolina rendered Governor Rutledge such valuable service that by a special act of the legislature in 1783 his wife and children were enfranchised.[59]

The valor of the Negro soldiers of the American Revolution has been highly praised by statesmen and historians. Writing to John Adams, a member of the Continental Congress, in 1775, to express his surprise at the prejudice against the colored troops in the South, General Thomas said: "We have some Negroes but I look on them in general equally serviceable with other men for fatigue, and in action many of them had proved themselves brave." Graydon in speaking of the Negro troops he saw in Glover's regiment at Marblehead, Massachusetts, said: "But even in this regiment (a fine one) there were a number of Negroes."[60] Referring to the battle of Monmouth, Bancroft said: "Nor may history omit to record that, of the 'revolutionary patriots' who on that day perilled life for their country, more than seven hundred black men fought side by side with the white."[61] According to Lecky, "the Negroes proved excellent soldiers: in a hard fought battle that secured the retreat of Sullivan they three times drove back a large body of Hessians."[62] We need no better evidence of the effective service of the Negro soldier than the manner in which the best people of Georgia honored Austin Dabney,[63] a mul-

[59] Moore, "Historical Notes," 22.

[60] Ibid., 16.

[61] Bancroft, "History of the United States," X, 133.

[62] Lecky, "American Revolution," 364.

[63] Austin Dabney, a remarkable free man of color, died at Zebulon. His remains repose, we understand, near those of his friend Harris. The following account of Dabney, as given by Governor Gilmer, may be interesting:

In the beginning of the Revolutionary conflict, a man by the name of Aycock removed to Wilkes County, having in his possession a mulatto boy, who passed for and was treated as his slave. The boy had been called Austin, to which the captain to whose company he was attached added Dabney.

Dabney proved himself a good soldier. In many a skirmish with the British and Tories, he acted a conspicuous part. He was with Colonel Elijah Clarke in the battle of Kettle Creek, and was severely wounded by a rifleball passing through his thigh, by which he was made a cripple for life. He was

atto boy who took a conspicuous part in many skirmishes with the British and Tories in Georgia. While fighting

unable to do further military duty, and was without means to procure due attention to his wound, which threatened his life. In this suffering condition he was taken into the house of a Mr. Harris, where he was kindly cared for until he recovered. He afterwards labored for Harris and his family more faithfully than any slave could have been made to do.

After the close of the war, when prosperous times came, Austin Dabney acquired property. In the year 18—, he removed to Madison County, carrying with him his benefactor and family. Here he became noted for his great fondness for horses and the turf. He attended all the races in the neighboring counties, and betted to the extent of his means. His courteous behavior and good temper always secured him gentlemen backers. His means were aided by a pension which he received from the United States.

In the distribution of the public lands by lottery among the people of Georgia, the Legislature gave to Dabney a lot of land in the county of Walton. The Hon. Mr. Upson, then a representative from Oglethorpe, was the member who moved the passage of the law, giving him the lot of land.

At the election for members of the Legislature the year after, the County of Madison was distracted by the animosity and strife of an Austin Dabney and an Anti-Austin Dabney party. Many of the people were highly incensed that a mulatto negro should receive a gift of the land which belonged to the freemen of Georgia. Dabney soon after removed to the land given him by the State, and carried with him the family of Harris, and continued to labor for them, and appropriated whatever he made for their support, except what was necessary for his coarse clothing and food. Upon his death, he left them all his property. The eldest son of his benefactor he sent to Franklin College, and afterwards supported him whilst he studied law with Mr. Upson, in Lexington. When Harris was undergoing his examination, Austin was standing outside of the bar, exhibiting great anxiety in his countenance; and when his young protégé was sworn in, he burst into a flood of tears. He understood his situation very well, and never was guilty of impertinence. He was one of the best chroniclers of the events of the Revolutionary War, in Georgia. Judge Dooly thought much of him, for he had served under his father, Colonel Dooly. It was Dabney's custom to be at the public house in Madison, where the judge stopped during court, and he took much pains in seeing his horse well attended to. He frequently came into the room where the judges and lawyers were assembled on the evening before the court, and seated himself upon a stool or some low place, where he would commence a parley with any one who chose to talk with him.

He drew his pension in Savannah where he went once a year for this purpose. On one occasion he went to Savannah in company with his neighbor, Colonel Wyley Pope. They traveled together on the most familiar terms until they arrived in the streets of the town. Then the Colonel observed to Austin that he was a man of sense, and knew that it was not suitable to be seen riding side by side with a colored man through the streets of Savannah; to which Austin replied that he understood that matter very well. Accord-

under Colonel Elijah Clarke he was severely wounded by a bullet which in passing through his thigh made him a cripple for life. He received a pension. from the United States and was by an act of the legislature of Georgia given a tract of land. He improved his opportunities, acquired other property, lived on terms of equality with some of his white neighbors, had the respect and confidence of high officials, and died mourned by all.

W. B. Hartgrove

ingly when they came to the principal street, Austin checked his horse and fell behind. They had not gone very far before Colonel Pope passed the house of General James Jackson who was then governor of the state. Upon looking back he saw the governor run out of the house, seize Austin's hand, shake it as if he had been his long absent brother, draw him from his horse, and carry him into his house, where he stayed whilst in town. Colonel Pope used to tell this anecdote with much glee, adding that he felt chagrined when he ascertained that whilst he passed his time at a tavern, unknown and uncared for, Austin was the honored guest of the governor.

White's "Historical Collections," 584.

FREEDOM AND SLAVERY IN APPALACHIAN AMERICA

To understand the problem of harmonizing freedom and slavery in Appalachian America we must keep in mind two different stocks coming in some cases from the same mother country and subject here to the same government. Why they differed so widely was due to their peculiar ideals formed prior to their emigration from Europe and to their environment in the New World. To the Tidewater came a class whose character and purposes, although not altogether alike, easily enabled them to develop into an aristocratic class. All of them were trying to lighten the burdens of life. In this section favored with fertile soil, mild climate, navigable streams and good harbors facilitating direct trade with Europe, the conservative, easy-going, wealth-seeking, exploiting adventurers finally fell back on the institution of slavery which furnished the basis for a large plantation system of seeming principalities. In the course of time too there arose in the few towns of the coast a number of prosperous business men whose bearing was equally as aristocratic as that of the masters of plantations.[1] These elements constituted the rustic nobility which lorded it over the unfortunate settlers whom the plantation system forced to go into the interior to take up land. Eliminating thus an enterprising middle class, the colonists tended to become more aristocratic near the shore.

In this congenial atmosphere the eastern people were content to dwell. The East had the West in mind and said much about its inexhaustible resources, but with the exception of obtaining there grants of land nothing definite toward the conquest of this section was done because of the handicap of slavery which precluded the possibility of a rapid expansion of the plantation group in the slave States. Separated thus by high ranges of mountains which pre-

[1] Wertenbaker, ''Patrician and Plebeian in Virginia,'' 31.

vented the unification of the interests of the sections, the West was left for conquest by a hardy race of European dissenters who were capable of a more rapid growth.[2] These were the Germans and Scotch-Irish with a sprinkling of Huguenots, Quakers and poor whites who had served their time as indentured servants in the East.[3] The unsettled condition of Europe during its devastating wars of the seventeenth and eighteenth centuries caused many of foreign stocks to seek homes in America where they hoped to realize political liberty and religious freedom. Many of these Germans first settled in the mountainous district of Pennsylvania and Maryland and then migrated later to the lower part of the Shenandoah Valley, while the Scotch-Irish took ·

[2] Exactly how many of each race settled in the Appalachian region we cannot tell, but we know that they came in large numbers, after the year 1735. A few important facts and names may give some idea as to the extent of this immigration. The Shenandoah Valley attracted many. Most prominent among those who were instrumental in settling the Valley was the Scotchman, John Lewis, the ancestor of so many families of the mountains. The Dutchmen, John and Isaac Van Meter, were among the first to buy land from Joist Hite, probably the first settler in the Valley. Among other adventurers of this frontier were Benjamin Allen, Riley Moore, and William White, of Maryland, who settled in the Shenandoah in 1734; Robert Harper and others who, in the same year, settled Richard Morgan's grant near Harper's Ferry; and Howard, Walker, and Rutledge, who took up land on what became the Fairfax Manor on the South Branch. In 1738 some Quakers came from Pennsylvania to occupy the Ross Survey of 40,000 acres near Winchester Farm in what is now Frederick County, Virginia. In the following year John and James Lindsay reached Long Marsh, and Isaac Larne of New Jersey the same district about the same time; while Joseph Carter of Bucks County, Pennsylvania, built his cabin on the Opequon near Winchester in 1743, and Joseph Hampton with his two sons came from Maryland to Buck Marsh near Berryville. But it is a more important fact that Burden, a Scotch-Irishman, obtained a large grant of land and settled it with hundreds of his race during the period from 1736 to 1743, and employed an agent to continue the work. With Burden came the McDowells, Alexanders, Campbells, McClungs, McCampbells, McCowans, and McKees, Prestons, Browns, Wallaces, Wilsons, McCues, and Caruthers. They settled the upper waters of the Shenandoah and the James, while the Germans had by this time well covered the territory between what is known as Harrisonburg and the present site of Harper's Ferry. See Maury, ''Physical Survey,'' 42; *Virginia Magazine*, IX, 337–352; Washington's Journal, 47–48; Wayland, ''German Element of the Shenandoah,'' 110.

[3] Wayland, ''German Element of the Shenandoah,'' 28–30; *Virginia Historical Register*, III, 10.

possession of the upper part of that section. Thereafter the Shenandoah Valley became a thoroughfare for a continuous movement of these immigrants toward the South into the uplands and mountains of the Carolinas, Georgia, Kentucky, and Tennessee.[4]

Among the Germans were Mennonites, Lutherans, and Moravians, all of whom believed in individual freedom, the divine right of secular power, and personal responsibility.[5] The strongest stock among these immigrants, however, were the Scotch-Irish, "a God-fearing, Sabbath-keeping, covenant-adhering, liberty-loving, and tyrant-hating race," which had formed its ideals under the influence of philosophy of John Calvin, John Knox, Andrew Melville, and George Buchanan. By these thinkers they had been taught to emphasize equality, freedom of conscience, and political liberty. These stocks differed somewhat from each other, but they were equally attached to practical religion, homely virtues, and democratic institutions.[7] Being a kind and beneficent class with a tenacity for the habits and customs of their fathers, they proved to be a valuable contribution to the American stock. As they had no riches every man was to be just what he could make himself. Equality and brotherly love became their dominant traits. Common feel-

[4] See Meade, "Old Families of Virginia," *The Transalleghany Historical Magazine*, I and II; De Hass, "The Settlement of Western Virginia," 71, 75; Kercheval, "History of the Valley," 61–71; Faust, "The German Element in the United States."

[5] Dunning, "The History of Political Theory from Luther to Montesquieu," 9, 10.

[7] Buchanan, the most literary of these reformers, insisted that society originates in the effort of men to escape from the primordial state of nature, that in a society thus formed the essential to well-being is justice, that justice is maintained by laws rather than by kings, that the maker of the laws is the people, and that the interpreter of the laws is not the king, but the body of judges chosen by the people. He reduced the power of the ruler to the minimum, the only power assigned to him being to maintain the morals of the state by making his life a model of virtuous living. The reformer claimed, too, that when the ruler exceeds his power he becomes a tyrant, and that people are justified in rejecting the doctrine of passive obedience and slaying him. See Buchanan, "De Jure Apud Scotos" (Aberdeen, 1762); Dunning, "History of Political Theories from Luther to Montesquieu"; and P. Hume Brown, "Biography of John Knox."

ing and similarity of ideals made them one people whose chief characteristic was individualism.[8]   Differing thus so widely from the easterners they were regarded by the aristocrats as "Men of new blood" and "Wild Irish," who formed a barrier over which "none ventured to leap and would venture to settle among."[9]   No aristocrat figuring conspicuously in the society of the East, where slavery made men socially unequal, could feel comfortable on the frontier, where freedom from competition with such labor prevented the development of caste.

[8] Just how much the racial characteristics had to do with making this wilderness a center of democracy, it is difficult to estimate. Some would contend that although the Western people were of races different from this aristocratic element of the East, their own history shows that this had little to do with the estrangement of the West from the East, and that the fact that many persons of these same stocks who settled in the East became identified with the interests of that section is sufficient evidence to prove what an insignificant factor racial characteristics are. But although environment proves itself here to be the important factor in the development of these people and we are compelled to concede that the frontier made the Western man an advocate of republican principles, heredity must not be ignored altogether.

Exactly how much influence the Scotch-Irish had in shaping the destiny of Appalachian America is another much mooted question with which we are concerned here because historians give almost all the credit to this race. Even an authority like Justin Winsor leaves the impression that Virginia cared little for the frontier, and that all honor is due to the Scotch-Irish. Their influence in shaping the destiny of other States has been equally emphasized. The facts collected by Hanna doubtless give much support to the claims of that people to the honor for the development of Appalachian America. His conclusions, however, are rather far-sweeping and often shade into imagination. On the other hand, a good argument may be made to prove that other people, such as the Germans and Dutch, deserve equal honor. Furthermore, few of the eulogists of the Scotch-Irish take into account the number of indentured servants and poor whites who moved westward with the frontier. Besides, it must not be thought that the East neglected the frontier intentionally simply because the Tidewater people could not early subdue the wilderness. They did much to develop it. The records of the time of the Indian troubles beginning in 1793 show that the State governments answered the call for troops and ammunition as promptly as they could, and their statute books show numerous laws which were enacted in the interest of the West during these troubles. The truth of the matter is that, whatever might have been the desire of the East to conquer the wilderness, the sectionalizing institution of slavery which the colony had accepted as the basis of its society rendered the accomplishment of such an object impossible. There was too great diversity of interest in that region.

[9] Jefferson's Works, VI, 484.

The natural endowment of the West was so different
from that of the East that the former did not attract the
people who settled in the Tidewater. The mountaineers
were in the midst of natural meadows, steep hills, narrow
valleys of hilly soil, and inexhaustible forests. In the East
tobacco and corn were the staple commodities. Cattle and
hog raising became profitable west of the mountains, while
various other employments which did not require so much
vacant land were more popular near the sea. Besides, when
the dwellers near the coast sought the cheap labor which the
slave furnished the mountaineers encouraged the influx of
freemen. It is not strange then that we have no record of an
early flourishing slave plantation beyond the mountains.
Kercheval gives an account of a settlement by slaves and
overseers on the large Carter grant situated on the west side
of the Shenandoah, but it seems that the settlement did not
prosper as such, for it soon passed into the hands of the
Burwells and the Pages.[10]

The rise of slavery in the Tidewater section, however,
established the going of those settlers in the direction of
government for the people. The East began with indentured servants but soon found the system of slavery more
profitable. It was not long before the blacks constituted
the masses of the laboring population,[11] while on the expiration of their term of service the indentured servants went
west and helped to democratize the frontier. Caste too was
secured by the peculiar land tenure of the East. The king
and the proprietors granted land for small sums on feudal
terms. The grantees in their turn settled these holdings in
fee tail on the oldest son in accordance with the law of pri-
mogeniture. This produced a class described by Jefferson
who said: "There were then aristocrats, half-breeds, pre-
tenders, a solid independent yeomanry, looking askance at
those above, yet not venturing to jostle them, and last and

---

[10] Kercheval, "History of the Valley," 47 and 48.

[11] It soon became evident that it was better to invest in slaves who had
much more difficulty than the indentured servants in escaping and passing
as freemen.

lowest, a seculum of beings called overseers, the most abject, degraded and unprincipled race, always cap in hand to the Dons who employed them for furnishing material for the exercise of their price."[12]

In the course of colonial development the people of the mountains were usually referred to as frontiersmen dwelling in the West. This "West" was for a number of years known as the region beyond the Blue Ridge Mountains and later beyond the Alleghenies. A more satisfactory dividing line, however, is the historical line of demarcation between the East and West which moved toward the mountains in the proportion that the western section became connected with the East and indoctrinated by its proslavery propagandists. In none of these parts, however, not even far south, were the eastern people able to bring the frontiersmen altogether around to their way of thinking. Their ideals and environment caused them to have differing opinions as to the extent, character, and foundations of local self-government, differing conceptions of the meaning of representative institutions, differing ideas of the magnitude of governmental power over the individual, and differing theories of the relations of church and State. The East having accepted caste as the basis of its society naturally adopted the policy of government by a favorite minority, the West inclined more and more toward democracy. The latter considered representatives only those who had been elected as such by a majority of the people of the district in which they lived; the former believed in a more restricted electorate, and the representation of districts and interests, rather than that of numbers.[13] Furthermore, almost from the founding of the colonies there was court party consisting of the rich planters and favorites composing the coterie of royal officials generally opposed by a country party of men who, either denied certain privileges or unaccustomed to participation in the affairs of privileged classes, felt that

[12] Jefferson's Works, VI, 484.
[13] This statement is based on the provisions of the first State constitutions. See Thorpe's "Charters and Constitutions."

the interests of the lowly were different. As the frontier moved westward the line of cleavage tended to become identical with that between the privileged classes and the small farmers, between the lowlanders and the uplanders, between capital and labor, and finally between the East and West.

The frontiersmen did not long delay in translating some of their political theories into action. The aristocratic East could not do things to suit the mountaineers who were struggling to get the government nearer to them. At times, therefore, their endeavors to abolish government for the people resulted in violent frontier uprisings like that of Bacon's Rebellion in Virginia and the War of Regulation in North Carolina. In all of these cases the cause was practically the same. These pioneers had observed with jealous eye the policy which bestowed all political honors on the descendants of a few wealthy families living upon the tide or along the banks of the larger streams. They were therefore, inclined to advance with quick pace toward revolution.[14] On finding such leaders as James Otis, Patrick Henry and Thomas Jefferson, the frontiersmen instituted such a movement in behalf of freedom that it resulted in the Revolutionary War.[15] These patriots' advocacy of freedom, too, was not half-hearted. When they demanded liberty for the colonists they spoke also for the slaves, so emphasizing the necessity for abolition that observers from afar thought that the institution would of itself soon pass away.[16]

In the reorganization of the governments necessitated by the overthrow of the British, however, the frontiersmen were unfortunate in that they lacked constructive leader-

[14] Grigsby, "Convention of 1788," 15, 49.

[15] The people living near the coast desired reform under British rule. The frontiersmen had to win them to the movement. A certain Scotch-Irish element in the Carolinas was an exception to this rule in that they at first supported the British.

[16] The letters and speeches of most of the revolutionary leaders show that they favored some kind of abolition. Among the most outspoken were James Otis, John Adams, Alexander Hamilton, Thomas Jefferson, and John Laurens. See also Schoepf, "Travels in the Confederation," 149; and Brissot de Warville, "New Travels," I, 220.

ship adequate to having their ideas incorporated into the new constitutions. Availing themselves of their opportunity, the aristocrats of the coast fortified themselves in their advantageous position by establishing State governments based on the representation of interests, the restriction of suffrage, and the ineligibility of the poor to office.[17] Moreover, efforts were made even to continue in a different form the Established Church against which the dissenting frontiersmen had fought for more than a century. In the other Atlantic States where such distinctions were not made in framing their constitutions, the conservatives resorted to other schemes to keep the power in the hands of the rich planters near the sea. When the Appalachian Americans awoke to the situation then they were against a stone wall. The so-called rights of man were subjected to restrictions which in our day could not exist. The right to hold office and to vote were not dependent upon manhood qualifications but on a white skin, religious opinions, the payment of taxes, and wealth. In South Carolina a person desiring to vote must believe in the existence of a God, in a future state of reward and punishment, and have a freehold of fifty acres of land. In Virginia the right of suffrage was restricted to freeholders possessing one hundred acres of land. Senators in North Carolina had to own three hundred acres of land; representatives in South Carolina were required to have a 500 acre freehold and 10 Negroes; and in Georgia 250 acres and support the Protestant religion.[18] In all of these slave States, suffering from such unpopular government, the mountaineers developed into a reform party persistently demanding that the sense of the people be taken on the question of calling together their representatives to remove certain defects from the constitutions. It was the contest between the aristocrats and the progressive westerner. The aristocrats' idea of government was developed from the "English Scion—the liberty of kings, lords, and commons,

[17] See the various State constitutions in Thorpe's "Charters and Constitutions."
[18] Ibid.

with different grades of society acting independently of all
foreign powers.'' The ideals of the westerners were principally those of the Scotch-Irish, working for ''civil liberty
in fee simple, and an open road to civil honors, secured to
the poorest and feeblest members of society.[19]

The eastern planters, of course, regarded this as an attack on their system and fearlessly denounced these rebel-
lious wild men of the hills. In taking this position, these
conservatives brought down upon their heads all of the ire
that the frontiersmen had felt for the British prior to the
American Revolution. The easterners were regarded in
the mountains as a party bent upon establishing in this
country a régime equally as oppressive as the British government. The frontiersmen saw in slavery the cause of the
whole trouble. They, therefore, hated the institution and
endeavored more than ever to keep their section open to
free labor. They hated the slave as such, not as a man. On
the early southern frontier there was more prejudice
against the slave holder than against the Negro.[20] There
was the feeling that this was not a country for a laboring
class so undeveloped as the African slaves, then being
brought to these shores to serve as a basis for a government
differing radically from that in quest of which the frontiersmen had left their homes in Europe.

This struggle reached its climax in different States at
various periods. In Maryland the contest differed somewhat from that of other Southern States because of the
contiguity of that commonwealth with Pennsylvania, which
early set such examples of abolition and democratic government that a slave State near by could not go so far in forti-
fying an aristocratic governing class. In Virginia the
situation was much more critical than elsewhere. Unlike
the other Atlantic States, which wisely provided roads and
canals to unify the diverse interests of the sections, that
commonwealth left the trans-Alleghany district to continue

[19] Foote, ''Sketches of Virginia,'' 85.
[20] Hart, ''Slavery and Abolition,'' 73; Olmsted, ''The Back Country,''
230–232. *Berea Quarterly,* IX, No. 3.

in its own way as a center of insurgency from which war was waged against the established order of things.[21]   In most States, however, the contest was decided by the invention of the cotton gin and other mechanical appliances which, in effecting an industrial revolution throughout the world, gave rise to the plantation system found profitable to supply the increasing demand for cotton.   In the course of the subsequent expansion of slavery, many of the uplanders and mountaineers were gradually won to the support of that institution.   Realizing gradually a community of interests with the eastern planters, their ill-feeling against them tended to diminish.   Abolition societies which had once flourished among the whites of the uplands tended to decline and by 1840 there were practically no abolitionists in the South living east of the Appalachian Mountains.[22]

Virginia, which showed signs of discord longer than the other Atlantic States, furnishes us a good example of how it worked out.   The reform party of the West finally forced the call of a convention in 1829, hoping in vain to crush the aristocracy.   Defeated in this first battle with the conservatives, they secured the call of the Reform Convention in 1850 only to find that two thirds of the State had become permanently attached to the cause of maintaining slavery.[23] Samuel McDowell Moore, of Rockbridge County in the Valley, said in the Convention of 1829–30 that slaves should be free to enjoy their natural rights,[24] but a generation later the people of that section would not have justified such an utterance in behalf of freedom.   The uplanders of South Carolina were early satisfied with such changes as were made in the apportionment of representation in 1808, and

[21] See the Speeches of the Western members of the Virginia Convention of 1829–30, Proceedings and Debates of the Convention of 1829–30.

[22] This is proved by the reports and records of the anti-slavery societies and especially by those of the American Convention of Abolition Societies. During the thirties and forties the southern societies ceased to make reports. See Adams, ''A Neglected Period of Anti-Slavery,'' 117.

[23] The vote on the aristocratic constitution framed in 1829–30 shows this. See Proceedings and Debates of the Convention of 1829–30, p. 903.

[24] Proceedings and Debates of the Convention of 1829–30, p. 226.

in the qualifications of voters in 1810.[25]   Thereafter Calhoun's party, proceeding on the theory of government by a concurrent majority, vanquished what few liberal-minded men remained, and then proceeded to force their policy on the whole country.

In the Appalachian Mountains, however, the settlers were loath to follow the fortunes of the ardent pro-slavery element.   Actual abolition was never popular in western Virginia, but the love of the people of that section for freedom kept them estranged from the slaveholding districts of the State, which by 1850 had completely committed themselves to the pro-slavery propaganda.   In the Convention of 1829–30 Upshur said there existed in a great portion of the West (of Virginia) a rooted antipathy to the slave.[26] John Randolph was alarmed at the fanatical spirit on the subject of slavery, which was growing up in Virginia. Some of this sentiment continued in the mountains.   The highlanders, therefore, found themselves involved in a continuous embroglio because they were not moved by reactionary influences which were unifying the South for its bold effort to make slavery a national institution.[27]

The indoctrination of the backwoodsmen of North Carolina in the tenets of slavery was effected without much difficulty because of less impediment in the natural barriers, but a small proportion of the inhabitants of the State residing in the mountainous districts continued anti-slavery. There was an unusually strong anti-slavery element in Davie, Davidson, Granville and Guilford counties.   The efforts of this liberal group, too, were not long in taking organized form.   While there were several local organizations operating in various parts, the efforts of the anti-slavery people centered around the North Carolina Manumission Society.   It had over forty branches at one time, besides several associations of women, all extending into

[25] Thorpe, "Charters and Constitutions, South Carolina."

[26] Proceedings and Debates of the Convention of 1829–30, pp. 53, 76, 442, 858.

[27] See Calhoun's Works: "A Disquisition on Government," p. 1 et seq.

seven or eight of the most populous counties of the State. This society denounced the importation and exportation of slaves, and favored providing for manumissions, legalizing slave contracts for the purchase of freedom, and enacting a law that at a certain age all persons should be born free.[28] That these reformers had considerable influence is evideuced by the fact that in 1826 a member of the manumission society was elected to the State Senate. In 1824 and 1826 two thousand slaves were freed in North Carolina.[29] Among the distinguished men who at times supported this movement in various ways were Hinton Rowan Helper, Benjamin S. Hedrick, Daniel R. Goodloe, Eli W. Caruthers, and Lunsford Lane, a colored orator and lecturer of considerable ability.[30] They constituted a hopeless minority, however, for the liberal element saw their hopes completely blasted in the triumph of the slave party in the Convention of 1835, which made everything subservient to the institution of slavery.

In the mountains of Kentucky and Tennessee conditions were a little more encouraging, especially between 1817 and 1830. The anti-slavery work in Kentucky seemed to owe its beginning to certain ''Emancipating Baptists.'' Early in the history of that State six Baptist preachers, Carter Tarrant, David Darrow, John Sutton, Donald Holmes, Jacob Gregg, and George Smith, began an anti-slavery campaign, maintaining that there should be no fellowship with slaveholders.[31] They were unable to effect much, however, because of the fact that they had no extensive organization through which to extend their efforts. Every church remained free to decide for itself and even in Northern States the Baptists later winked at slavery. More effective than these efforts of the Baptists was the work of the Scotch-Irish. Led by David Rice, a minister of the Presbyterian Church, the anti-slavery element tried to exclude slavery

[28] Adams, ''Neglected Period of Anti-Slavery,'' 138.
[29] Ibid., 34.
[30] Bassett, ''Anti-Slavery Leaders of North Carolina,'' 72.
[31] Adams, ''Anti-Slavery, etc.,'' 100–101.

from the State when framing its first constitution in the
Convention of 1792.[32]   Another effort thus to amend the
fundamental law was made at the session of the legislature
of 1797–98, and had it not been for the excitement aroused
by the Alien and Sedition Laws, the bill probably would
have passed.[33]

Many successful efforts were made through the anti-
slavery bodies. The society known as "Friends of Humanity" was organized in Kentucky in 1807. It had a constitution signed by eleven preachers and thirteen laymen.
The organization was in existence as late as 1813. The
records of the abolitionists show that there was another
such society near Frankfort between 1809 and 1823.[34] Birney then appeared in the State and gave his influence to
the cause with a view to promoting the exportation of Negroes to Liberia.[35] A number of citizens also memorialized Congress to colonize the Negroes on the public lands
in the West.[36] In the later twenties an effort was made to
unite the endeavors of many wealthy and influential persons
who were then interested in promoting abolition. Lacking
a vigorous and forceful leader, they appealed to Henry
Clay, who refused.[37] They fought on, however, for years
to come. A contributor to the *Western Luminary* said, in
1830, that the people of Kentucky were finding slavery a
burden.[38] Evidently a good many of them had come to this
conclusion, for a bill providing for emancipation introduced in the Legislature was postponed indefinitely by a
vote of 18 to 11.[39] So favorable were conditions in Kentucky at this time that it was said that Tennessee was

[32] Speech of David Rice in the Constitutional Convention of Kentucky,
1792.
[33] Birney, "James G. Birney," 96–100.
[34] Reports of the American Convention of Abolition Societies, 1809 and
1823.
[35] Birney, "James G. Birney," 70.
[36] Adams, "The Neglected Period of Anti-Slavery in America," 129–130.
Annals of Congress, 17th Congress, 1st ses., 2d ses., 18th Cong., 1st ses.
[37] Ibid., 20.
[38] "The Genius of Universal Emancipation," 11. 35.
[39] Ibid., 10. 145.

watching Kentucky with the expectation of following her lead should the latter become a free State as was then expected.

The main factor in promoting the work in Tennessee was, as in Kentucky, the Scotch-Irish Presbyterian stock. They opposed slavery in word and in deed, purchasing and setting free a number of colored men. Among these liberal westerners was organized the "Manumission Society of Tennessee," represented for years in the American Convention of Abolition Societies by Benjamin Lundy.[40] The Tennessee organization once had twenty branches and a membership of six hundred.[41] Among its promoters were Charles Osborn, Elihu Swain, John Underhill, Jesse Willis, John Cannady, John Swain, David Maulsby, John Rankin, Jesse Lockhart, and John Morgan.[42] They advocated at first immediate and unconditional emancipation, but soon seeing that the realization of this policy was impossible, they receded from this advanced position and memorialized their representatives to provide for gradual emancipation, the abolition of slavery in the District of Columbia, the prevention of the separation of families, the prohibition of the interstate slave trade, the restriction of slavery, the general improvement of colored people through church and school, and especially the establishment among them of the right of marriage.[43] To procure the abolition of slavery by argument, other persons of this section organized another body, known as the "Moral Religious Manumission Society of West Tennessee."[44] It once had a large membership and tended to increase and spread the agitation in behalf of abolition.

In view of these favorable tendencies, it was thought up to 1830 that Tennessee, following the lead of Kentucky,

[40] See Proceedings of the American Convention of Abolition Societies.
[41] Adams, "The Neglected Period of Anti-Slavery," 132.
[42] Ibid., 131.
[43] "The Genius of Universal Emancipation," 1. 142; 5. 409.
[44] "The Genius of Universal Emancipation," 4. 76, 142; Birney, "James G. Birney," 77; Minutes of the American Convention of Abolition Societies, 1826, p. 48.

would become a free State.[45]   But just as the expansion of
slavery into the interior of the Atlantic States attached
those districts to the fortunes of the slaveholding class, it
happened in some cases in the mountains which to some
extent became indoctrinated by the teaching of the defenders of slavery. Then the ardent slavery debate in Congress
and the bold agitation, like that of the immediatists led by
William Lloyd Garrison, alienated the support which some
mountaineers had willingly given the cause. Abolition in
these States, therefore, began to weaken and rapidly declined during the thirties.[46] Because of a heterogeneous
membership, these organizations tended to develop into
other societies representing differing ideas of anti-slavery
factions which had at times made it impossible for them to
coöperate effectively in carrying out any plan. The slave-
holders who had been members formed branches of the
American Colonization Society, while the radical element
fell back upon organizing branches of the Underground
Railroad to coöperate with those of their number who, seeing that it was impossible to attain their end in the Southern mountains, had moved into the Northwest Territory
to colonize the freedmen and aid the escape of slaves.[47]
Among these workers who had thus changed their
base of operation were not only such noted men as
Joshua Coffin, Benjamin Lundy, and James G. Birney, but
less distinguished workers like John Rankin, of Ripley;
James Gilliland, of Red Oak; Jesse Lockhart, of Russell-
ville; Robert Dobbins, of Sardinia; Samuel Crothers, of
Greenfield; Hugh L. Fullerton, of Chillicothe, and William
Dickey, of Ross or Fayette County, Ohio. There were other
southern abolitionists who settled and established stations
of the Underground Railroad in Bond, Putnam, and Bureau
counties, Illinois.[48] The Underground Railroad was thus
enabled to extend into the heart of the South by way of the

[45] ''The Genius of Universal Emancipation,'' 11. 65, 66.

[46] See The Minutes and Proceedings of the American Convention of
Abolition Societies, covering this period.

[47] This statement is based on the accounts of a number of abolitionists.

[48] Adams, ''A Neglected Period of Anti-Slavery,'' 60, 61.

Cumberland Mountains. Over this Ohio and Kentucky route, culminating chiefly in Cleveland, Sandusky, and Detroit, more fugitives found their way to freedom than through any other avenue.[49] The limestone caves were of much assistance to them. The operation of the system extended through Tennessee into northern Georgia and Alabama, following the Appalachian highland as it juts like a peninsula into the South. Dillingham, John Brown, and Harriet Tubman used these routes.

Let us consider, then, the attitude of these mountaineers toward slaves. All of them were not abolitionists. Some slavery existed among them. The attack on the institution, then, in these parts was not altogether opposition to an institution foreign to the mountaineers. The frontiersmen hated slavery, hated the slave as such, but, as we have observed above, hated the eastern planter worse than they hated the slave. As there was a scarcity of slaves in that country they generally dwelt at home with their masters. Slavery among these liberal people, therefore, continued patriarchal and so desirous were they that the institution should remain such that they favored the admission of the State of Missouri as a slave State,[50] not to promote slavery but to expand it that each master, having a smaller number of Negroes, might keep them in close and helpful contact. Consistently with this policy many of the frontier Baptists, Scotch-Irish and Methodists continued to emphasize the education of the blacks as the correlative of emancipation. They urged the masters to give their servants all proper advantages for acquiring knowledge of their duty both to man and to God. In large towns slaves were permitted to acquire the rudiments of education and in some of them free persons of color had well-regulated schools.[51]

Two noteworthy efforts to educate Negroes were put forth in these parts. A number of persons united in 1825 to found an institution for the education of eight or ten

[49] Siebert, ''The Underground Railroad,'' 10. 346.
[50] Ambler, ''Sectionalism in Virginia,'' 107–108.
[51] Woodson, ''The Education of the Negro,'' 120–121.

Negro slaves with their families, to be operated under the direction of the "Emancipating Labor Society of the State of Kentucky." About the same time Frances Wright was endeavoring to establish an institution on the same order to improve the free blacks and mulattoes in West Tennessee. It seems that this movement had the support of a goodly number of persons, including George Fowler, and, it was said, Lafayette, who had always been regarded as a friend of emancipation. According to a letter from a clergyman of South Carolina, the first slave for this institution went from the York district of that State. Exactly what these enterprises were, however, it is difficult to determine. They were not well supported and soon passed from public notice. Some have said that the Tennessee project was a money-making scheme for the proprietors, and that the Negroes taught there were in reality slaves. Others have defended the work as a philanthropic effort so characteristic of the friends of freedom in Appalachian America.[52]

The people of Eastern Tennessee were largely in favor of Negro education. Around Maryville and Knoxville were found a considerable number of white persons who were thus interested in the uplift of the belated race. Well might such efforts be expected in Maryville, for the school of theology at this place had gradually become so radical that according to the *Maryville Intelligencer* half of the students by 1841 declared their adherence to the cause of abolition.[53] Consequently, they hoped not only to see such doctrines triumph within the walls of that institution, but were endeavoring to enlighten the Negroes of that community to prepare them for the enjoyment of life as citizens in their own or some other country.[54]

Just as the people of Maryville had expressed themselves through *The Intelligencer,* so did those of Knoxville

[52] "The Genius of Universal Emancipation," 5. 117, 126, 164, 188, 275, 301, 324, 365; 6. 21, 140, 177.

[53] The Fourth Annual Report of the American Anti-Slavery Society, 1837, p. 48; The New England Anti-Slavery Almanac for 1841, p. 31.

[54] *Ibid.*

find a spokesman in *The Presbyterian Witness.* Excoriating those who had for centuries been finding excuses for keeping the slaves in heathenism, the editor of this publication said that there was not a solitary argument that might be urged in favor of teaching a white man that might not be as properly urged in favor of enlightening a man of color. "If one has a soul that will never die," said he, "so has the other. Has one susceptibilities of improvement, mentally, socially, and morally? So has the other. Is one bound by the laws of God to improve the talents he has received from the Creator's hands? So is the other. Is one embraced in the commands search the scriptures? So is the other."[55] He maintained that unless masters could lawfully degrade their slaves to the condition of beasts, they were just as much bound to teach them to read the Bible as to teach any other class of their population.

From a group in Kentucky came another helpful movement. Desiring to train up white men who would eventually be able to do a work which public sentiment then prevented the anti-slavery minority from carrying on, the liberal element of Kentucky, under the leadership of John G. Fee and his coworkers, established Berea College. Believing in the brotherhood of man and the fatherhood of God, this institution incorporated into its charter the bold declaration that "God hath made of one blood all nations that dwell upon the face of the earth." This profession was not really put to a test until after the Civil War, when the institution courageously met the issue by accepting as students some colored soldiers who were returning home wearing their uniforms.[56] The State has since prohibited the co-education of the races.

With so many sympathizers with the oppressed in the back country, the South had much difficulty in holding the mountaineers in line to force upon the whole nation their policies, mainly determined by their desire for the continuation of slavery. Many of the mountaineers accordingly

[55] *The African Repository,* XXXII, 16.
[56] The Catalogue of Berea College, 1897.

deserted the South in its opposition to the tariff and internal improvements, and when that section saw that it had failed in economic competition with the North, and realized that it had to leave the Union soon or never, the mountaineers who had become commercially attached to the North and West boldly adhered to these sections to maintain the Union. The highlanders of North Carolina were finally reduced to secession with great difficulty; Eastern Tennessee had to yield, but kept the State almost divided between the two causes; timely dominated by Unionists with the support of troops, Kentucky stood firm; and to continue attached to the Federal Government forty-eight western counties of Virginia severed their connection with the essentially slave-holding district and formed the loyal State of West Virginia.

In the mountainous region the public mind has been largely that of people who have developed on free soil. They have always differed from the dwellers in the district near the sea not only in their attitude toward slavery but in the policy they have followed in dealing with the blacks since the Civil War. One can observe even to-day such a difference in the atmosphere of the two sections, that in passing from the tidewater to the mountains it seems like going from one country into another. There is still in the back country, of course, much of that lawlessness which shames the South, but crime in that section is not peculiarly the persecution of the Negro. Almost any one considered undesirable is dealt with unceremoniously. In Appalachian America the races still maintain a sort of social contact. White and black men work side by side, visit each other in their homes, and often attend the same church to listen with delight to the Word spoken by either a colored or white preacher.

C. G. WOODSON

ANTAR, THE ARABIAN NEGRO WARRIOR, POET AND HERO

That men of Negro blood should rise to distinction in Arabia is not at all singular. By language and ethnological conformation the people of the Arabian Peninsula belong to the great Semitic group of the human family. But the proximity of Africa to Arabia carried the slave trade at a very early period to that soil. Naturally, as a result of intermarriage, thousands of Negroes with Arabian blood soon appeared in that part of Asia. This was especially true of the midland and southern districts of the peninsula. To-day, after several centuries of such unions, there is found in southwestern Arabia, in northern and central Africa an ever-increasing colored population of vast numbers, known as Arabised Negroes. Many of these have become celebrities whose achievements form an integral part of Arabian civilization and Mohammedan culture.[1] Emerging from this group came Antar, the most conspicuous figure in Arabia, a man noble in thought, heroic in deed, an exemplar of ideals higher than those of his age and a model for posterity.

Antarah ben Shedad el Absi (Antar the Lion, the son of the Tribe of Abs), the historic Antar, was born about the middle of the sixth century of our era, and died about the year 615. Some accounts give the year 525 as the date of his birth. By Clement Huart, a distinguished Orientalist, he is described as a mulatto.[2] "Goddess born, however," says Reynold A. Nicholson, "he could not be called by any stretch of the imagination. His mother was a black slave."[3] All authorities agree that Shedad, his father, was a man of noble blood and that his mother was an Abyssinian slave.

The manner in which they became attached to each other

1 Palgrave, "Essays on Eastern Questions," 37 et seq.
2 Huart, "A History of Arabian Literature," 13.
3 Nicholson, "Literary History of the Arabs," 114.

151

is interesting. As a result of tyrannical action upon the part of King Zoheir, chief of the Absians, several chieftains seceded to attack and rob other tribes and establish their own kingdom. Among these chieftains was one Shedad. In their wanderings they attacked and conquered a certain tribe, among the prisoners of which was a black woman of great beauty named Zebiba. Shedad fell in love with this woman and to obtain possession of her yielded all rights to the spoils. She then had two sons. Shedad lived in the fields with her for a time, during which she gave birth to a son. As a boy his strength was prodigious and courage unparalleled.

In his early life Antar was assigned to the lowly task of a keeper of camels. Here he followed the usual routine incident to such a task while the clan of his father roved from place to place, clashing with rivals in quest of the prizes of the chase or the spoils of war, or rested in some vale of Arabia and devoted itself to the simpler pastoral life. Following this sort of occupation, he so distinguished himself as to impress the woman whom he later married. This was Ibla, the beautiful daughter of Malek, another son of King Zoheir. She was, therefore, Antar's cousin. Antar's growth in courage, in bodily strength, sense of justice, and sympathy for the weak excited her admiration and high esteem. His love for Ibla found expression in deeds of valor and poems dedicated to her virtues, but the jealousy of chieftains and his lowly birth prevented their union. The magnanimity of Antar in the face of bitter opposition, however, and his undying love finally won him Ibla as his bride.

Favored by great strength and a leonine courage, Antar soon passed from the duties of a keeper of camels to those of a first-class fighting man. By these virtues, so highly prized by the warlike Arabs, he ingratiated himself both with his father and his tribe. Much of the life of Antar is lost to authentic history, but that part which remains shows that he followed the career of a great chieftain endowed with military qualities, poetic gifts, and a talent for leadership of extraordinary order. According to Huart, he took part in the terrible wars of the horses arising out of the rivalry between the stallion Dahis and the mare Ghabra.[4] Treachery alone prevented the famous courser from winning the race, and in his vengeance Qais, chief of the tribe of Abs, waged bitter war against his enemies. Antar was the rhapsodist as well as a participant in these contests. Success in war rapidly followed. His kinsmen forgot his lowly birth and former menial occupation and regarded him as the first warrior of his day. His deeds of heroism increased his prestige and after his father's death he became the protector of his tribe and the pattern of Arabic chivalry.

Meanwhile he had shown such rare poetic gifts that his fame spread beyond the circle of his clan and in due course of time he was selected as a contestant in those poetic trials that were peculiar to the Arabs in the pre-Islamic days. So successful was Antar's effort that he was acknowledged the greatest poet of his time and one of his odes was selected as one of the Mu 'Allakât, the seven suspended poems, which were judged by the assemblage of all the Arabs worthy to be written in letters of gold and hung on high in the sacred Kaabah at Mecca, as accepted models of Arabian style.[5]

[4] Huart, "A History of Arabian Literature," 14.

[5] These are two selections from Antar's Mu 'Allakât:

A FAIR LADY

'Twas then her beauties first enslaved my heart—
Those glittering pearls and ruby lips, whose kiss
Was sweeter far than honey to the taste.
As when the merchant opes a precious box
Of perfume, such an odor from her breath
Comes toward me, harbinger of her approach;
Or like an untouched meadow, where the rain
Hath fallen freshly on the fragrant herbs
That carpet all its pure untrodden soil:
A meadow where the fragrant rain-drops fall
Like coins of silver in the quiet pools,
And irrigate it with perpetual streams;
A meadow where the sportive insects hum,
Like listless topers singing o'er their cups,
And ply their forelegs, like a man who tries
With maimed hands to use the flint and steel.

The death of Antar is enshrouded in obscurity. Antar perished about the year 615 while fighting against the tribe of the Tai. According to one authority he had grown old and his youthful activity had forsaken him. He is said to have fallen from his horse and to have been unable to regain his feet in time. His death was a signal for peace and the end of the long-drawn hostility. In spite of the tribe's desire to avenge its hero and its bard, a compensation of 100 camels was accepted for the murder of one of its scions and the poets celebrated the close of the long struggle. Another author says the hero, stricken to death by a poison shaft sped by the hand of a treacherous and implacable foe, remounted his horse to insure the safe retreat of his tribe and died leaning on his lance. His enemies, smitten with terror by the memory of his prowess, dared not advance, till one cunning warrior devised a strategem which startled the horse out of its marble stillness. The creature gave a

THE BATTLE

There where the horsemen rode strongest
I rode out in front of them,
Hurled forth my battle-shout and charged them;
No man thought blame of me.
Antar! they cried; and their lances
Well-cords in slenderness, pressed to the breast
Of my war-horse still as I pressed on them.
Doggedly strove we and rode we.
Ha! the brave stallion! Now is his breast dyed
With blood drops, his star-front with fear of them!
Swerved he, as pierced by the spear points.
Then in his beautiful eyes stood the tears
Of appealing, words inarticulate.
If he had our man's language,
Then had he called to me.
If he had known our tongue's secret,
Then had he cried to me.

.   .   .   .

Deep through the sand drifts the horsemen
Charged with teeth grimly set,
Urging their war-steeds;
I urged them spurred by my eagerness forward
To deeds of daring, deeds of audacity.

bound and Antar's corpse, left unsupported, fell upon the ground.[6]

His fame as a literary character transcends that of the modern authors of black blood, such as Pushkin in Russia, and the elder Dumas in France. After his death the fame of Antar's deeds spread across the Arabian Peninsula and throughout the Mohammedan world. In time these deeds, like the Homeric legends, were recorded in a literary form and therein is found that Antar, the son of an Abyssinian slave, once a despised camel driver, has become the Achilles of the Arabian Iliad, a work known to this day after being a source of wonder and admiration for hundreds of years to millions of Mohammedans as the "Romance of Antar." The book, therefore, ranks among the great national classics like the "Shah-namch" of Persia, and the "Nibelungen-Lied" of Germany. Antar was the father of knighthood. He was the champion of the weak and oppressed, the protector of the women, the impassioned lover-poet, the irresistible and magnanimous knight. "Antar" in its present form probably preceded the romances of chivalry so common in the twelfth century in Italy and France.[7]

This national classic of the Arabian world is of great length in the original, being often found in thirty or forty manuscript volumes in quarto, in seventy or eighty in octavo. Portions of it have been translated into English, German and French. English readers can consult it best in a translation from the Arabic by Terrick Hamilton in four volumes published in London in 1820. This translation, now rare, covers only a portion of the original; a new translation, suitably abridged, is much needed. The fact that its hero is of Negro blood may have chilled the ardor of English translators to meet this need.

The original book purports to have been written more than a thousand years ago—in the golden prime of the Caliph Harún-al-Rashid (786–809)—by the famous As-Asmai

[6] Huart, "A History of Arabian Literature," 13.

[7] Holden, "Library of the World's Best Literature," 586.

(741–830). It is in fact a later compilation probably of the twelfth century. The first Arabic edition was brought to Europe by an Austro-German diplomat and scholar—Baron von Hammer Purgstall—near the end of the eighteenth century. The manuscript was engrossed in the year 1466. The verses with which the volumes abound are in many cases undoubtedly those of Antar.

One enthusiastic critic of this romance has said: ''The book in its present form has been the delight of all Arabians for many centuries. Every wild Bedouin of the desert knew much of the tale by heart and listened to its periods and to its poems with quivering interest. His more cultivated brothers of the cities possessed one or many of its volumes. Every coffee-house in Aleppo, Bagdad, or Constantinople had a narrator who, night after night, recited it to rapt audiences. The unanimous opinion of the East has always placed the romance of Antar at the summit of such literature. As one of their authors well says: ''The Thousand and One Nights'' is for the amusement of women and children; ''Antar'' is a book for men. From it they learn lessons of eloquence, of magnanimity, of generosity and of statecraft.'' Even the prophet Mohammed, well-known foe to poetry and poets, instructed his disciples to relate to their children the traditions concerning Antar, ''for these will steel their hearts harder than stone.''[9]

Another critic has said: ''The Romance of Antar is the free expression of real Arab hero-worship. And even in the cities of the Orient today, the loungers over their cups can never weary of following the exploits of this black son of the desert who in his person unites the great virtues of his people, magnanimity and bravery, with the gift of poetic speech. Its tone is elevated; it is never trivial, even in its long and wearisome descriptions, in its ever-recurring outbursts of love. Its language suits its thought: choice and educated, and not descending—as in the 'Nights'—to the common expressions or ordinary speech. It is the Arabic

[9] Edward S. Holden, ''Library of the World's Best Literature,'' I, p. 587.

romance of chivalry and may not have been without influence in the spread of the romance of mediæval Europe."[10]

An idea of this romance may be obtained from the following:

Years and years ago King Zoheir ruled Arabia. Now Shedad,
a son, nettled under the stern sway of his sire and longed for the
chase and the combat. The green plains becked, the murmuring
streams sang until the heart of Shedad grew sad. When the sun
rose one morn he gathered his camels and warriors and departed.

Far from the home of King Zoheir dwelt the tribe Djezila in
peace but Shedad fell upon them and slew them. As beautiful as
a goddess was a black woman named Zebiba who was captured.
Now it came to pass that Shedad loved Zebiba and dwelt with her
and her two sons in the fields. In time she bore him a son, as dark
as an elephant, with eyes as black as night and a head of shaggy
hair. They called him Antar.

Antar grew in strength, in courage and in mind until the chieftains disputed his possession, for his mother was a slave and Antar
must tend the herds. Zoheir summoned the chieftains and Antar
and when he was brought before him he marveled and threw him a
piece of meat. But a dog that chanced to be in the tent was quicker
than he and seized it and ran off. Rage gave Antar the fleetness of
the wind. With mighty leaps he bounded after the dog. Swifter
darted no eagle upon its prey than Antar pursued the rogue.
With a mighty spring he caught it and seizing its jaws tore them
asunder down to the beast's shoulders, and in triumph he held the
meat aloft. But the King grew afraid and let Shedad depart with
Antar. At ten years of age he slew a wolf that harassed his flock
and later killed a slave who had beaten an old woman. Thus did
the women find in him a protector and they hung upon his words
and recounted his deeds and his acts of justice.

Now Shedad's brother, Malek, had a daughter named Ibla, who
was as fair as the moon. The ladies were wont to drink camel's
milk morning and evening when Antar had cooled it in the winds.
It chanced one morning that Antar entered Ibla's tent just as her
mother was combing her hair, and the beauty of her form trans-
fixed him. A thing of loveliness fairer he had never seen, nor
ringlets of darker hue grace a human head. His heart beat wildly
at the birth of a great passion and the hot blood burned his dark

[10] Richard Gottheil, "Library of the World's Best Literature," II, 674.

cheeks. But Ibla fled and Antar left with a light heart. For days
he sang in measures sweet of Ibla's beauty and his arm burned to
do deeds. The weeds of the field became the fairest of flowers;
the limpid pools mirrored Ibla's face in images beautiful and pure
and the zephyrs whispered of love. But Antar had dared love a
princess and his father became wroth and came to the fields one
day with some chiefs to punish him.

When they arrived they found Antar in combat with a lion.
With a roar like thunder the beast lashed its tail and advanced.
But Antar knew not fear. He stepped forward to the fray. The
snarling creeping beast scratched furrows in the ground and bided
the time for the spring. Then it leaped. Like a flash Antar
hurled his lance and leaped aside. A gleam of light and iron met
flesh as the mighty body hurtled by. Quickly he seized the shaft
and held it firmly while the beast lashed furiously and growled in
its death struggles, and then it lay still. But the heart of Shedad
was softened and he invited Antar and the chieftains to sup with
him. Long into the night recounted Shedad Antar's deeds but the
dark eyes of Antar saw only Ibla and his heart yearned for the
morrow and the end of the feasting.

Not far from the land of King Zoheir dwelt the tribe of Temin
and Zoheir and his warriors departed to war against them. To
Antar was entrusted the care and protection of the women during
Zoheir's absence. Antar swore to protect them with his life and the
women were not afraid. But the days are long when lords are
away and the women burned for entertainment. Then it was that
Semiah, the lawful wife of Shedad, called the women together and
spoke of a feast on the shores of a near by lake. When the day came
Ibla and her mother attended and as Antar saw her his heart
leaped with joy. Just then shouts were heard and from afar appeared a cloud of dust which grew larger and filled the sky as it
drew near. Out from the cloud of dust sprang the tribesmen called
Cathan and with yells they seized and carried off the women.

But Antar sped up like the wind when he heard the shrieks of
his beloved Ibla and saw her anguished face and frenzied struggles.
Horse he had none but love and despair gave him the swiftness of
a steed, the courage of a lion and the strength of the elephant.
Across the plains he coursed as swiftly as the wind but the steeds
were as swift as he. Clouds of dust choked him and hid him from
view but double burdens on tired coursers could not continue the
mad pace. Antar overtook one horseman, threw him off and slew

him. Then a cry arose among the tribesmen of Cathan to kill
Antar, but Antar lusted for battle and donning the armor of the
slain man, he slew warrior after warrior until the tribesmen of
Cathan loosed the woman and fled. Then Antar comforted the
women and drove many horses home before him, among them a
black charger.

When Shedad returned with Zoheir he went to visit his flocks
and saw Antar upon a black horse guarding the herds. Shedad
inquired whence came the horse, but Antar did not wish to betray
the imprudent action of his father's wife and remained silent.
Thereupon Shedad called him a robber and struck him with such
violence that the blood ran. But Semiah saw the cruel act and her
heart went out to Antar. She clasped him in her arms and throw-
ing herself at her lord's feet, she raised her veil and told the story
of the attack and rescue and Antar's courage. Antar's silence and
magnanimity so touched Shedad that he wept. The news of Antar's feat soon reached the king, who gave him a robe of honor and
rich presents.

But jealousies among the chieftains toward Antar grew and
plots were made to kill him. Again and again he circumvented
his foes and in triumphs showed infinite pity and mercy. Deeds
of darkness but increased the mutual love between Ibla and Antar
and the name of Antar was heard far into distant lands.

Now it happened that a youth of wealth and lineage sought
Ibla's hand in marriage. But pride choked him and he basked
in the glory of his fathers' deeds. When Antar heard of the boast-
ful youth's suit he swore a great oath to kill him and he fell upon
him. But the youth escaped. Now the chieftains saw a chance to
destroy Antar's power and encompass his destruction. They appeared before Zoheir and demanded Antar's life. Then Zoheir
stripped him of his high estate and favors and sent him back to the
fields to attend the herds and Antar bowed his great head in shame
and left. But the love he bore for Ibla was as meat to his body and
refreshment to his mind and his great spirit died not.

Soon the tribe of Tex fell upon Zoheir and his warriors and
sorely pressed them. The pride of Zoheir, however, was great and
Antar stayed far from the battle, for his heart was heavy and he
was again a tender of herds. Then the day went against Zoheir
and his warriors and many fell and sadness came upon the land.
And the men of Tex pressed the men of Zoheir harder and carried
off the women and with them Ibla. Still Antar tended the herds

and came not. But the mighty chieftains of Zoheir came to him and begged him to cloak his wrath and do battle with them against the men of Tex. And Antar heard the men of Tex in silence and his heart gave a bound when they spoke of Ibla, but still he stayed in his tent and came not. Then the chieftains sought to move him by his great love for Ibla. Thereupon Antar's face beamed and he spoke and laid down the condition that Ibla must be given him as a wife. Shedad and Malek agreed and Antar girt himself and with the remnant of Zoheir's army went against the men of Tex. Now the strength of Antar was that of a hundred men and his courage that of a thousand and animated by his great burning passion and with the ardor of battle in his nostrils he fell upon the tribe of Tex. Redder sank never a sun than the plains blushed with the blood of men after that battle. Tears filled Ibla's eyes when she beheld Antar and in triumph he led her back to the land of King Zoheir. But the heart of Malek was false, and bitter plots were rife, and even Shedad viewed in despair the rise of a black slave. Malek demanded that Antar should give his bride a present of a thousand camels of a certain breed that could be found only in distant lands. Now Antar read his heart and saw his wicked artifice but he set out. Far from the land of King Zoheir wandered Antar, far from the wiles of Malek and jealous suitors, far from the tent of his beloved Ibla. But the heart of Antar was not cast down nor did hope die.

Now it happened that Antar entered the country of Persia where he was taken prisoner. His captors bound him upon a horse and departed for the village of their king. Tidings came of the ravages of a fierce lion and no warriors dared to give it battle. Fiercer had roamed no lion in the land of King Zoheir nor in Persia. Whole villages fled before it and herds were but as chaff. But Antar begged that he be loosed and they untied his bonds and gave him a lance and he departed to attack the lion.

Courage is half victory and the arm of Antar was skilled in the art of the lance and his heart was stout. But the strength of the lion was of the body whilst that of Antar was of the body and the mind. With a mighty throw Antar hurled the lance and it found its mark, but the lion bounded forward and Antar stood unarmed. Then with a mighty wrench he jerked a young tree from the ground and with powerful blows beat down the attack of the lion. He gave a mighty swing and cleft the beast's skull and it fell down and died, and Antar departed for the tent of the king. Then the men marvelled, for none dared follow to see the terrible combat nor did people believe until they saw the beast.

Then the king loaded Antar with rich gifts and honors and gave him the thousand camels which he sought, and Antar departed for the land of King Zoheir. Great was the rejoicing of Ibla when messengers brought tidings of Antar's return. Great was the surprise of Malek and the rage of the chieftains. But Shedad's heart softened and he yearned for his son and the fair Ibla gave him her hand and Antar and Ibla married and dwelt in the land of King Zoheir.

To this day the fame of Antar still persists. Rimsky-Korsakoff, a modern Russian composer, has given us in his symphony "Antar" a tone picture of this Arabian Negro's life that opens and closes with an atmospheric eastern pastorale of great beauty. It has been played during the past winter with marked success in Boston, New York, Philadelphia and Washington, at the concerts of the Boston Symphony Orchestra, that representative body of great musicians. The remarkable career of Antar and the perpetuation of his memory in history, literature and music, though removed by many centuries from the life of the American Negro of today, offers to him many thoughts for reflection.

While Arabia of the pre-Islamic days is not America of this generation nor the Semitic people of the East like the Germanic races of the West, still those human qualities that make for valor, for greatness of spirit, that reflect genius devoted to literature and social service are compelling forces in all climes and in all races. An opportunity for a free expression of them and a recognition of their potent effect in the sum total of human culture should be the mission of scholarship in all lands. Those elements of character which the Arabs of Antar's day regarded as their *beau ideal* were found not unworthy of admiration when manifested in one of Negro blood. When his poetic fancy reflected the spirit of Arab life his works were not rejected because his mother was an African slave but one of the best was placed among the immortal poems of his father's country. When his genius for warfare was shown it was given an opportunity to develop and serve the cause of all who preferred valiant deeds to arguments of race.   When his life was spent it was not looked upon as one of an unusual Negro rising above a sphere previously limited to his fellows of the same blood but as an epic of success crowning human effort and worthy to be embodied in the literature of Arabia as the exploits of a hero who exemplified the spirit of the people, acceptable for all time as their model for valor, poetic genius, hospitality, and magnanimity.

A. O. STAFFORD

DOCUMENTS

EIGHTEENTH CENTURY SLAVES AS ADVERTISED BY THEIR MASTERS

In some respects the eighteenth century slave was better off than the Negro of today. As a rule no Negro can now get his name into the leading newspapers unless he commits a heinous crime. At that time, however, masters in offering slaves for sale and advertising fugitives unconsciously spoke of their virtues as well as their shortcomings, that the public might be fully informed as to the character of the blacks. Through these advertisements, therefore, we can get at the very life of the Negro when slavery was still of the patriarchal sort and can thus contrast his then favorable condition with the wretchedness of the institution after it assumed its economic aspect in the nineteenth century. We observe that the eighteenth century slave was rapidly taking over modern civilization in the West Indies and in the thirteen colonies on the American continent. The blacks were becoming useful and skilled laborers, acquiring modern languages, learning to read and write, entering a few of the professions, exercising the rights of citizens, and climbing the social ladder to the extent of moving on a plane of equality with the poor whites.

To emphasize various facts these advertisements have been grouped under different headings, but each throws light on more than one phase of the life of the eighteenth century slave. The compiler will be criticised here for publishing in full many advertisements which contain repetitions of the same phraseology. The plan is deemed wise in this case, however, because of the additional value the complete document must have. The words to which special attention is directed appear in his own capitals.

163

LEARNING A MODERN LANGUAGE

RAN away from Austin Paris of Philadelphia, Founder, on the 22do this Instant, A Negro Boy called Bedford or Ducko, aged about Sixteen or Seventeen Years; SPEAKS VERY GOOD ENG- LISH wears a dark brown colored Coat and Jacket, a Pair of white Fustian Breeches, a grey mill'd Cap with a red Border, a Pair of new Yarn Stockings, with a Pair of brown worsted under them, or in his Pockets. Whoever brings him to his said Master, or informs him of him so that he may be secured, shall be satisfied for their Pains, by me. Austin Paris.
The American Weekly Mercury (Philadelphia), Jan. 31, 1721.

To be Sold, Three Very likely Negro Girls being about 16 years of age, and a Negro Boy about 14, SPEAKING GOOD ENGLISH, enquire of the Printer hereof.
The American Weekly Mercury (Philadelphia), June 20, 1723.

RAN away from Joseph Coleman in the Great Valley in Ches- ter County, a Negro Man, named Tom, aged about 30 Years, of a middle Stature, HE SPEAKS VERY GOOD ENGLISH, haveing on a white Shirt, Stockings and Shoes, a great riding Coat tyed round him with blew Girdles. He was seen by several Persons in New York, about the latter end of June last, who was well ac- quainted with him and suspected his being a Run away but he told them his former Master Capt. Palmer had sold him to a Person in the Great Valley, who had given him his Freedom, then he pulled out a forged pass, which to the best of his remembrance was signed by one William Hughes. Whosoever takes up the said Negro and puts him into any Gaol, and gives notice thereof to his said Master or to William Bradford in New York, or to Messrs. Steel or Bethuke Merchants in Boston, shall have Three Pounds Reward and all Reasonable Charges.
Those that take him are desired to secure the pass.
The American Weekly Mercury (Philadelphia), July 11, 1723.

RAN away from his Master, Capt. John Steel, *at the North End of* Boston, *the 17th Instant, a Young Negro Fellow, named* Pom- pey *SPEAKS PRETTY GOOD ENGLISH is about 19 or 20 Years of Age, is short in Stature and pretty long visaged, has been used to change his name; he had on a great Ratteen Coat, Waistcoat and Breeches, the coat pretty old, with white Metal Buttons, a Cotton* and linnen Shirt, and ordinary Worsted Cap, and grey Yarn Stockings, he took with him an old Hat, and a Leather Jockey Cap, a pair of old black Stockings, and a new Ozenbrigs Frock: He has made several Attempts to get off in some Vessel, therefore all Masters of Vessels are cautioned not to entertain him.

Whoever shall apprehend the said Negro and carry him to said Master shall have Five Pounds old Tenor, and necessary Charges paid by   JOHN STEEL.

The Boston Weekly News-Letter, Jan 23, 1746.

RAN away on the 19th of this Instant SEPTEMBER, from his Master JOHN JOHNSON, of Boston, Jack-maker, a Negro Man Servant, named Joe, about 23 Years of Age, a likely Fellow, who had on when he went away, a dark colored Fly Coat, with flat white Metal Buttons, a Swan Skin double breasted Jacket, Leather Deer Skin Breeches, a pair of high heel'd thick soled Shoes. He can play on the Flute, has a Scar on his upper Lip and SPEAKS GOOD ENGLISH. Whoever shall take him up and deliver him to his said Master, shall have Ten Pounds Reward, Old Tenor, and all reasonable Charges paid. All Masters of Vessels and others, are hereby cautioned against harbouring, concealing or carrying off said Negro, as they will avoid the Penalty of the Law.

The Boston Evening Post, Oct. 3, 1748.

RAN-AWAY from Luykas Joh. Wyngaard, of the City of Albany, Merchant, a certain Negro Man named SIMON, of a middle size, a slender spry Fellow, has a handsome smooth Face, and thick Legs; SPEAKS VERY GOOD ENGLISH: Had on when he went away a blue Cloth Great Coat. Whoever takes up the said Negro. and brings him to his Master, or to Mr. JOHN LIVINGSTON, at NEW YORK, shall receive Three Pounds, New York Money, Reward, and all reasonable Cost and Charges paid by

JOHN LIVINGSTON.

The New York Gazette Revived in the Weekly
Post-Boy, Nov. 28, 1748.

A Likely Negro Boy about 14 Years of Age, country born, CAN SPEAK DUTCH OR ENGLISH, to be sold: Enquire of Printer hereof.   The New York Gazette Revived in the Weekly

Post-Boy, Feb. 26, 1750.

RAN away from the Subscriber living near the Head of South River, in Anne Arundel County, on the 16th of June, a Negro Man, named *Joseph Marriott*, lately convicted from London; he is a tall slim Fellow, and TALKS VERY PLAIN *ENGLISH*. Had on a black Cloth Coat, a short white Flannel Waistcoat, a Check Shirt, a Pair of red Everlasting Breeches, a Pair of Yarn Stockings, a Pair of Old Cannell'd Pumps, a Worsted Capt, and an old Castor Hat; and took sundry other Cloaths with him.

Whoever apprehends the said Fellow, and brings him to the Subscriber shall have Two Pistoles Reward.

BENJAMIN WELSH.

The Maryland Gazette, July 4, 1754.

RAN away from his Master, James Dalton of Boston, on the first Instant, a Negro Man named Ulysses, SPEAKS GOOD ENG-LISH, about 5 feet 8 Inches high, turns his Toes a little in, somewhat bow-legged.

The Boston Evening Post, Oct. 10, 1757.

Cranstown, May 2, 1760.

RAN-away from his Master Capt Edward Arnold of Crans-town, the 20th of April, A Negro Man named Portsmouth, about 27 Years of Age, about 5 Feet 6 Inches high, strait limb'd SPEAKS PRETTY GOOD ENGLISH: * * * * * * * * * *

EDWARD ARNOLD.

The Boston Gazette and Country Journal, May 19, 1760.

RAN-away on the 28th Day of June 1761, from his Master, Ephraim Swift of Falmouth in the County of Barnstable, A Negro Man Servant named Peter, about 27 or 28 Years old, SPEAKS GOOD ENGLISH: had on when he went away a Beaveret Hat, a green worsted Capt, a close bodied Coat coloured with a green narrow Frieze Cape, a Great Coat, a black and white homespun Jacket, a flannel checked Shirt, grey yarn Stockings; also a flannel Jacket, and a Bundle of other Cloaths, and a Violin. He is very tall Fellow.

Whosoever shall apprehend the said Negro Fellow and commit him to any of his Majesty's Gaols, or secure him so as that his Master may have him again, shall have Five Dollars Reward, and all necessary Charges paid.

EPHRAIM SWIFT.

All Masters of Vessels and others are cautioned not to carry off or conceal the said Negro, as they would avoid the Penalty of the Law.

The Boston Gazette and Country Journal, July 6, 1761.

EIGHT DOLLARS REWARD

RAN away from the Subscriber, the 17th instant, a likely Negro Fellow, (named CATO) about five feet seven inches high, about twenty years old, had on when he went away, a grey bear-skin double-breasted Jacket with large white metal buttons, and striped under ditto, long striped trowsers, with leather breeches under them, a sailor's Dutch Cap; he has pimples in his face, SPEAKS GOOD ENGLISH, very nice about the hair, tells a very plausible story, upon any extraordinary occasion, and pretends to have a pass signed by John Nelson.

Whosoever may take up said servant, and return him, to his Master, shall have Eight Dollars reward, and all necessary Charges paid by

GEORGE WATSON.

Plymouth March 25, 1769.

Post Script to the Boston Weekly News-Letter, Apr. 20, 1769.

TEN DOLLARS REWARD

RUN away on the 14th instant, a Negro Woman named Lydia, aged about forty, SPEAKS GOOD ENGLISH, is remarkably tall and stout made, has a large mark on her right cheek where she has been burnt; she had on her a blue negro cloth jacket and coat, a blue shalloon gown, a red and white cotton handkerchief round her head, a blue and white ditto about her neck, and a pair of men's shoes, and a ditto men's clowded stockings. She has belonged to Mrs. Derise, sen. and to Mr. Dalziel Hunter. The Reward will be paid on delivery of the said Wench, by Mr. McDowell, No 27 Broad-street; and any person harbouring her after this notice will be prosecuted according to law.

Few. 18th, 1783.

The South-Carolina Weekly Advertiser, Feb. 19, 1783.

RAN AWAY

From the Subscribers, the 28th of June, A short old Negroe-man named Tom, marked with the small pox, SPEAKS VERY GOOD ENGLISH, late the property of Capt. Richard Estes; and having reason to believe that he is gone to the former plantation, or embarked himself for Bermuda, where he has children belonging to a Mr. Robinson; therefore all captains of vessels, or others are forbid harbouring or carrying off said Negroe, on forfeit according

to law. Whosoever will send or deliver said Negro to us or the
Warden of the Work-house, shall be generously rewarded.
Charleston, June 29.   ROCH & CUSTER.
*The South Carolina Gazette and General
Advertiser*, July 1, 1784.

TWO GUINEAS REWARD

RAN AWAY a Negro Man named Prince about twenty-three
years old, and about five feet six inches high, small featured, of a
dark complection, his Guinea country marks on his face, SPEAKS
VERY GOOD ENGLISH, has a down look; had on when he went
away a light coloured surtout coat, a pair of yellow stocking
breeches, and a round black hat; he has been seen skulking about
this city since Saturday last. Two Guineas reward will be given
and all reasonable charges paid to any one delivering the said Negro to the Warden of the Work-house, or to the Subscriber, and the
utmost rigour of the law will be inflicted on conviction of any person harbouring the said Negroe.
Charleston, July 6, 1784.   SAMUEL BOAS, No. 5 Church Street.
The South Carolina Gazette and General Advertiser, July 6, 1784.

BROUGHT TO THE WORKHOUSE

A Negro fellow named March, of the Guinea country, five feet
one inch high, SPEAKS VERY MUCH BROKEN ENGLISH,
forty or forty-five years of age, says his master's name is Mr. Gerry,
of Santee.

Also a negroe fellow named Sambo, of the Guinea country, five
feet four inches high, twenty or twenty-five years of age, pitted a
little with the small pox; has on a check shirt, a white cloth sailor
jacket, with black binding, and a pair of Osnaburg trowsers.

Also a negro fellow named Abraham, born on John's Island in
this State, thirty or thirty-five years of age, five feet three inches
high, SPEAKS PROPER ENGLISH, and says his masters name
is Thomas Cleay, and lives at Cullpepper, in Virginia.

                                        JOHN GERLEY, Warden.
July 9, 1784.
The South-Carolina Gazette and General Advertiser, July 10, 1784.

TO BE SOLD
On Tuesday Next,
By Messrs. Colcock & Gibbons.
A YOUNG NEGRO.

Between fourteen and fifteen years of age, who is an exceedingly good hair dresser, and understands very well to keep horses, CAN SPEAK FRENCH AND ENGLISH.

ROGER SMITH.

The South Carolina Gazette and General Advertiser, July 20, 1784.

RUN–AWAY

From the Subscriber
The following Negroes viz.

Moll, a tall black Wench, about 20 years old, is frequently seen in and about Charleston, and Stono, she has changed her name to Judah, and says she is free.

JAMES, a short well made fellow, with a large scar on one cheek, has also a scar on one foot, with the loss of a part of his toes, is frequently seen in Charleston and at Mr. Manigault's plantation.

JEFFERY, a middle size well made straight limb'd fellow, about 22 or 23 years old, a little pitted with the small pox, used to the coasting business.

Also JAMIE, a short well made fellow, a little bough legged, about 20 years old. THE ABOVE NEGROES ARE VERY ARTFUL, SPEAK GOOD ENGLISH, and most probably have changed their names. A Reward of THREE GUINEAS will be paid for each of the said negroes on delivery to the Warden of the Workhouse, in Charleston, or to the subscriber in Georgetown.

This is therefore to forewarn all persons from harbouring, or Masters of vessels from carrying off said Negroes, as they may depend on conviction, to be treated with the utmost rigour of the law, by

LEWIS DUTARQUE.

The State Gazette of South Carolina, Jan. 26, 1786.

BROUGHT TO THE WORKHOUSE

A Negro Girl named Hannah, this country born, 4 feet 8 inches high, 13 or 14 years of age, dark complexion, SPEAKS GOOD ENGLISH, has on a blue Negro Cloth Wrapper and petticoat, much faded, says her master's name is Mr. Rose, and lives at Asbepoo. Taken up by James Ackett in this City, February 2, 1786.

JOHN GERLEY, Warden.

State Gazette of South-Carolina, Feb. 20, 1786.

THREE GUINEAS REWARD
RUNAWAY

From the Subscriber's Plantation called Mrs. Wright's Place near Dorchester, A MULATTO FELLOW named JOE, about 20 years of age, five feet five inches high, SPEAKS EXCEEDINGLY GOOD ENGLISH, had on when he went away a brown jacket and overalls. Whoever will deliver the said fellow to the subscriber, shall have the above reward.   A. PLEYM.

The State Gazette of South Carolina, April 20, 1786.

RUN-AWAY

From the Subscriber on September last, Scipio, a likely black fellow, about 25 years old, has a few of his country marks on each side of his face, which can be perceived on examining closely, HE SPEAKS REMARKABLY GOOD ENGLISH FOR A NEGRO, AND IS EXCEEDINGLY ARTFUL, he formerly belonged to Captain Ogier, at which time was his waiting man, he is in all probability on Santee river, or Stono, as he is well acquainted there, and indeed everywhere else in the State, he generally keeps with a negro fellow belonging to the Reverend Mr. Lewis, deceased, by the name of Brutus, who is likewise runaway. Whoever will deliver said fellow or secure him, so that the subscriber can get him, either dead or alive, shall receive Ten Pounds.

Andrew a likely fellow, of a yellowish complexion, about 30 years old, his particular marks are not recollected, he formerly belonged to the estate of Thomas Sullivan, deceased, and was sold about 12 months ago to Mr. Hubert Hodson, of the Round O, he has a wife in Charleston, who belongs to a free negro carpenter, who lives now in King Street, named James Miles, and it is suspected that he is harboured there. Whoever will deliver said fellow or secure him in the Work-House of Charleston, so that the subscriber gets him shall receive Five Pounds.

Nancy, a very likely black Guinea wench, SPEAKS GOOD ENGLISH, very artful, and no doubt will change her name, and master's too; she is branded on the breast something like L blotched, about 5½ feet high, went away in 1784, at which time she belonged to John Logan Esq, deceased, she has been in Charleston the greatest part of her time since her absence, passes for a free wench, and it is said washes and irons for a livelihood. Whoever will deliver said wench, or secure her, so that the subscriber gets her safe shall receive Five Pounds.

All persons are hereby cautioned from harbouring either of these negroes, as they may depend on being prosecuted with the utmost rigour of the law. A handsome reward will be paid any person who will give information of their being harboured by any white person, so that the evidence will admit of a prosecution.

HENRY BELL.
Round O in St. Bartholomew's Parish,
Aug. 4, 1786.
The State Gazette of South Carolina, Aug. 21, 1786.

NEGRO IN CUSTODY

CHARLES THOMAS, very black, has white teeth, is about 5 feet 10 inches high, and about 26 or 27 years of age, has had his left leg broke, which bends in a little about the ancle, SPEAKS BOTH FRENCH AND ENGLISH, and is a very great rogue.

THOMAS ACKEN Gaoler.
New Castle Delaware, Aug. 28, 1793.
The Maryland Journal and Baltimore Advertiser, Sept. 20, 1793.

100 DOLLARS REWARD

Absented himself on Thursday 16th instant, from the subscriber, a Mustee Fellow named James, well known about town, being formerly the Property of Mr. Sarazin; of a Yellow Complexion, bushy hair, pitted with small pox, a remarkable scar over his right eye, SPEAKS VERY PROPER, AND CAN AT ANY TIME MAKE OUT A PLAUSIBLE TALE; had on an old green plush coat, with yellow cuffs and cape, but will no doubt change his dress, as he took a variety with him. Any person apprehending the said fellow, and deliver him to the Master of the Work-House, or to the Subscriber, shall be entitled to the above reward.

JOHN GEYER.
The City Gazette and Daily Advertiser, June 22, 1797.

20 DOLLARS REWARD

RAN-away from the Subscriber, on the evening of the 5th instant, a Negro Fellow named Lando; he is about 5 feet 7 inches high, 18 or 19 years of age, remarkably likely Fellow, rather slim made; HE SPEAKS FRENCH TOLERABLE WELL, and is too fond of the French Negroes, it is supposed he is harboured by some of them.   He had on when he went away a pair of brown trowsers, and a jacket of the same colour, with green cape and cuffs and white metal buttons, but it is very probable he may have changed his dress, as he carried other clothes with him.

A reward of Fifty Dollars will be paid to any person that will give information of his being harbored by a White and Twenty-five Dollars if by a Black Person, on conviction of the offender.

DAVID HAIG.

City Gazette and Daily Advertiser (Charleston, S. C.), June 27, 1797.

TEN DOLLARS REWARD

RAN-away from his Master on the 6th ultimo, a MULATTO FELLOW named DICK, about 20 years old, five feet nine or ten inches high; a stout well-built Fellow, SPEAKS ENGLISH VERY WELL.   It will be difficult to describe his dress, as he carried a quantity of clothing with him, when he absented himself.

The above reward will be paid to whoever shall have secured him, so that he may be returned to his Master.

Masters of vessels and all other persons are cautioned against harbouring said fellow, as they will incur the penalties of the law in that case.

JAMES MORISON.

City Gazette and Daily Advertiser (Charleston, S. C.), Nov. 12, 1798.

THIRTY DOLLARS REWARD

Absented themselves sometime since, the following slaves, viz.

Bob, a carpenter Fellow, of a yellowish complexion, mustee, has bushy hair, is about five feet six inches high, and 35 years of age; is well made, AND SPEAKS RATHER MORE PROPER THAN NEGROES IN GENERAL.

Dorcas, his Wife, also has a Yellowish complexion and bushy hair, is about 26 years of age, is a good cook, VERY SMART, AND SPEAKS VERY PROPERLY.

They have with them their two Children; one a Girl called Willoughby, about 8 or 10 years old; and another infant only a few months old.

One half the above sum will be paid for Bob, and the other half for Dorcas and the children, on their being lodged in any gaol in the State, or being delivered to Captain PAUL HAMILTON on

Salimas Island or Mr. William P. Smith at Ponpon; and One Hundred Dollars will be paid on conviction of their being harboured by a White person.

MARY EDDINGS.

City Gazette and Daily Advertiser (Charleston, S. C.), July 31, 1799.

500 DOLLARS REWARD

Absented themselves from the subscriber the following Negroes, viz.

Tom on the 23 January ult. from the City of Charleston; he is about 42 years of 'age, of a black complexion, SPEAKS GOOD ENGLISH, a little knock-kneed, had on when he went away an iron on one leg, and another on his neck.

Cyrus, from Chehaw, in the month of August last past. He is about five feet six or eight inches high, SPEAKS GOOD ENGLISH, about 38 years of age, well made, and is remarkably bow-legged.

Also Hercules from Chehaw in the month of February 1797. He is about five feet eight or nine inches high, stout and well made, SPEAKS GOOD ENGLISH, is about 36 years old, has remarkable thick lips, and has a small impediment in his speech when frightened, and of a yellowish complexion.

The above Negroes are harboured on the Ashley river, where Tom and Hercules had been for three years past, and are now between Wappoo-cut and Ashley ferry.

One Hundred dollars will be paid on conviction of a white person taking or having taken Tom's irons off, and twenty if by a Negro. Also fifty dollars will be paid on delivery of him to the master of the work house; fifty dollars will also be paid on delivery of Cyrus, and one hundred for Hercules; and a further reward of two hundred dollars will be paid on conviction of their being harboured by a white person.

February 15,   ARTHUR HUGHES.

The City Gazette and Daily Advertiser, March 5, 1800.

RAN-away from the subscribed on the 6th of July, a Negro man named PETER, formerly the property of Dr. Guion. He is very black and SPEAKS GOOD ENGLISH. He is about forty-five years of age, and has a free wife in this town, at whose house I have reason to suppose he is harboured. As he is well known in New bern I need not describe him more particularly.

I will give a reward of Ten Dollars to any person who will deliver him to Mr. Dudley, the gaoler, or to the subscriber. All person are forwarned from harbouring or employing said fellow at their peril.

August 8.   THOMAS CURTIS.

The Newbern Gazette, Aug. 15, 1800.

TWENTY DOLLARS REWARD

Absented himself from the Subscriber on Friday, his Waiting Man, named YORK, well known in Charleston, as he has been accustomed to drive a carriage and worked out the last year. He is a likely fellow, of a dark complexion, about five feet ten inches high, of a thin visage, about twenty-seven years of age, SPEAKS VERY PROPER, and may pass for a freeman. He had on when he went away, oznaburg overalls and a white shirt, with a brown negro cloth coat, and corduroy waistcoat, faced with green on the pockets, also a blue surtoutt, lined with green boise.

All masters of vessels are requested not to carry him off the State; and a reward of Twenty Dollars will be given to any person who will deliver him to the Master of the Work-house, or to

August 3.   THOMAS WARING.

City Gazette and Daily Advertiser (Charleston, S. C.), Aug. 18, 1800.

·FIVE DOLLARS REWARD

Absented himself from the Subscriber's plantation, in St. Thomas Parish, the 15th ult. BUTLER. He is a thin black fellow, about five feet seven inches high, and about 26 years of age, is remarkably civil when spoken to, AND SPEAKS VERY GOOD ENGLISH; is something of a shoemaker; he has of late threatened to go and see his mother, who belongs to the state of gen. Greene, and lives on one of his plantations in the State of Georgia, where it is probable he is gone; he also has a wife in Charleston, who works at the Distillery, (formerly Mr. Fitzsimmon's) where he may be concealed by her. The above reward will be paid to any person who will deliver him to the Master of the Work-House, or to the Subscriber in Boundary Street.

N.B. If the above Negro Fellow is taken up in the country, Ten Dollars will be paid, and all reasonable traveling expenses.

October 1.   THOMAS WIGFALL.

The City Gazette and Daily Advertiser
(Charleston, S. C.), Oct. 3, 1800.

ADVERTISEMENT

Confined in Barnwell Gaol, on the 21st day of July 1802; two NEGRO FELLOWS, Jacob and Enox. Jacob is about five feet ten inches high and very trim built, about twenty-one years of age, SPEAKS PLAIN ENGLISH, is a good deal scared on the back, has some very good clothes, such as a blue coat, new lining shirt, white ribbed stockings, several waistcoats, pair of striped overalls, two blankets, and several other things not worth mentioning; and upon examination says he was born in Virginia and was brought from thence by John Fellows, and sold by John Eaves, in the State of Georgia, on the South of Ogeehie, from whom he has absconded.

Enox is spare built and low in stature, appears to be about twenty-five years of age, SPEAKS ENGLISH, THOUGH SOME-WHAT NEGROISH had a white plain coat and home spun jacket and overalls; and upon examination says he belongs to James Hogg, about fourteen miles below Coosawhatchie Court House.

WILLIAM GOODE, Gaoler,
Barnwell District.

City Gazette and Daily Advertiser, Aug. 12, 1802.

RUN away from Sassafras River on the 9th of November, a lusty Negro Man, named Prince, about 25 Years old, full faced and pitted with the Small Pox, AND SPEAKS ENGLISH. He had on when he went away, a home spun Kersey Jacket blue Waistcoat under it, Oznabrigs shirt, new shoes, and old Yarn Stockings: He pretends to have a certificate for his Freedom, which is supposed he had from one of the Sailors on board of the Vessel he ran from.

Whoever takes up the said Negro and brings him to the Printers at Annapolis or to the Subscriber at Sassafras, shall have four Pistoles Reward and necessary charges, paid by

SAMUEL ALLYNE.

N. B.   It is probable he is in Baltimore or some other part of the Western Shore as he went away in a Canoe.

LEARNING TO READ AND WRITE

RUN away on the 4th Inst., at Night from James Leonard in Middlesex County East-New-Jersey, a Negro Man named Simon, aged 40 years, is a well-set Fellow, about 5 feet 10 inches high, has large Eyes, and a Foot 12 inches long; he was bred and born in this Country, TALKS GOOD ENGLISH, CAN READ AND

WRITE, is very slow in his speech, can bleed and draw Teeth * * *
  Whoever takes up and secures the said Negro, so that his Master
may have him again shall have Three Pounds Reward and reasonable charges, paid by

JAMES LOENARD.

The Pennsylvania Gazette, Sept. 11, 1740.

  RAN-away from Capt. Joseph Hale of Newbury, a Negro Man,
named *Cato*, the 6th Instant, about 22 Years of Age, short and
small, SPEAKS GOOD ENGLISH AND CAN READ AND
WRITE, understands farming Work carry'd with him a striped
homespun Jacket and Breeches, and Trousers, and an outer Coat
and Jacket of home-made Cloth, two Pair of Shoes, sometimes wears
a black Wigg, has a smooth Face, a sly Look, TOOK WITH A
VIOLIN, AND CAN PLAY WELL THEREON. Had with him
three Linnen Shirts, home-made pretty fine yarn Stockings. Whoever shall bring said Negro to his Master or secure him so that he
may have him again shall have *five Pounds* Reward and all necessary Charges paid by me.

JOSEPH HALE.

Newbury, July 8th, 1745.

The Boston Gazette or Weekly Journal, July 9, 1745.

  RAN-away from his Master Eleazer Tyng, Esq at Dunstable, on
the 26th May past, a Negro Man Servant call'd Robbin, almost of
the Complexion of an Indian, short thick square shoulder'd Fellow,
a very short Neck, and thick Legs, about 28 Years old, TALKS
GOOD ENGLISH, CAN READ AND WRITE, and plays on the
Fiddle; he was born at Dunstable * * * Whoever will apprehend
said Negro and secure him, so that his Master may have him again,
or bring him to the Ware-House of Messiers Alford and Tyng in
Boston, shall have a reward of Ten Pounds, old Tenor, and all reasonable Charges.
  N. B. And all Masters of Vessels or others are hereby cautioned
against harbouring, concealing or carrying off said Servant, on Penalty of the law.

The New York Gazette Revived in the Weekly
Post-Boy, July 18, 1748.

  RAN away from the Subscriber, the 20th of *November* last,
living on *Patuxent* River, near Upper Marlborough, in *Prince
George's* County, a dark Mulatto Man, named *Sam,* about 5 feet

9 or 10 Inches high, about 30 Years of Age, a Carpenter by Trade, has a down Look, and low Voice. Had on when he went away a new Cotton Jacket and Breeches, and osnabrigs Shirt; he is supposed to have taken with him, one Cotton Coat lined with blue, one red Waistcoat and Breeches, one blue Silk Coat, one light Cloth Coat, some fine Shirts, and one or two good Hats. He is supposed to be lurking in *Charles County* near *Bryan-Town*, where a Mulatto Woman lives, whom he has for some Time called his Wife; BUT AS HE IS AN ARTFUL FELLOW, AND CAN READ AND WRITE, it is probable he may endeavour to make his Escape out of the Province.

Whoever takes up the said Runaway, and secures him so as his Masters may get him again, shall have, if taken out of this Province, Three Pounds; and if within this Province, Forty Shillings, besides what the Law allows paid by

WILLIAM DIGGES, JUNIOR.
The Maryland Gazette, Feb. 27, 1755.

RAN away from Jonathan Sergeant, at Newark, in New-Jersey, A young negro man, named Esop, of middle size, with round forehead, strait nose, and a down guilty look; HE CAN WRITE, AND IT IS LIKELY HE MAY HAVE A COUNTERFEIT PASS: Had with him a beaver hat, light grey linsey-wolsey jacket, two trowsers, new pumps, and an old purple colour'd waist coat. It is supposed he went away in company with a white man, named John Smith, who is an old lean, tall man, with a long face and nose, and strait brown hair; who had on an old faded snuff-coloured coat. Whoever takes up and secures said man and Negro, so that their master may have them again, shall have Forty Shillings reward for each and all reasonable Charges, paid by

JONATHAN SERGEANT.
The Pennsylvania Gazette, Aug. 28, 1755.

FORTY DOLLARS REWARD

And all reasonable charges shall be paid to any Person that secures and brings to William Kelly, of the City of New York, merchant a Negro man named Norton Minors, who ran away from his masters Messrs. Bodkin and Ferrall of the Island of St. Croix, on the 1st day of July last; is by trade a Caulker and ship-carpenter; has lived at Newbury, in New-England; was the property of Mr. Mark Quane, who sold him to Mr. Craddock of Nevis, from whom the above gentlemen bought him about three years ago; is about 5 feet 8 inches high; age about 37 years; SPEAKS GOOD ENG-LISH, CAN READ AND WRITE; AND IS A VERY SENSIBLE FELLOW: And his masters suspect he came off in the sloop Bos-cawen, Andrew Ford, Master, who sailed from the above Island the very day this fellow eloped, bound for Louisbourg.

The New York Gazette, Nov. 10, 1760.

Ran away on the 9th Instant, October, in the Morning from the Subscriber, a Negro Man named JACK, a well set Fellow, about 5 feet 8 Inches high, full fac'd, much pitted with the Small-pox, snuffles when he speaks, READS ENGLISH, PRETENDS MUCH TO UNDERSTAND THE SCRIPTURES. Had on when he went away a Pair of Course Trowsers, stripp'd Jacket, and a Frock over it Whoever takes up said Fellow and brings him to the subscriber shall have FORTY SHILLINGS and all reasonable Charges paid.— All Matters of Vessels &c. are desired not to harbour him, or carry him off, as he or they may depend on being prosecuted as the Law directs.

MANUEL MYERS,
Linging in Stone Street.
The New York Gazette, Nov. 10, 1760.

Ran away in August last from the Subscriber, living in North-ampton County, Virginia, a Molatto Man Slave, about Five Feet Nine Inches high, and hath a large Scar on one Side of his Face. IT IS PROBABLE HE WILL ENDEAVOUR TO PASS FOR A FREE MAN, AS HE CAN WRITE. Whoever takes up, and se-cures the said slave, so that the Subscriber can have him again, shall have TWENTY DOLLARS; and if delivered to me, at Northamp-ton, FORTY DOLLARS Reward paid by

MICHAEL CHRISTIAN.
The Maryland Gazette, Oct. 27, 1769.

St. Mary's County, January 16, 1776.

TWENTY DOLLARS REWARD

RAN away from the subscriber near Chaptico, the 4th instant, a small Negro Man named *Dickison,* otherwise *Joe,* he has been frequently used to both names, he is about 5 feet 2 or 3 inches high: Had on when he went away three country cloth jackets, the under one lappelled and checked, another striped in length, the other warped with white and filled with black, his breeches the same, country shoes and stockings, felt hat half worn; he took with him a mill-bag half worn: It is likely he may have changed his name and cloths, HE IS A VERY ARTFUL FELLOW AND CAN READ, and likely may endeavour to pass for a freeman. Any person bringing him home, or securing him so as his master may get him again, shall receive if out of the Province the above reward; if sixty miles from home Five Pounds, if taken in the county or at a small distance Three Pounds and all reasonable charges, paid by   THOMAS NICHOLS.

Dunlap's Maryland Gazette or The Baltimore General Advertiser, July 23, 1776.

Perry-Hall, Baltimore County, Sept. 13, 1785.
FORTY DOLLARS REWARD, for apprehending and delivering to the suscriber, Negro Will. He left my service the 3rd inst., is short and well made, has remarkably small hands and feet, about 26 years of age, has a large beard for a Negro. HE ATTEMPTS TO READ AND WRITE, BUT HE PERFORMS VERY IMPERFECTLY. HE IS BY TRADE A BLACKSMITH; HAS DROVE A CARRIAGE, CAN SHAVE AND DRESS HAIR, AND IS A COBBLING SHOEMAKER. He is fond of strong liquor and when intoxicated is very quarrelsome. The above-described ungrateful rogue I manumitted some years past, with a number of other slaves, who were free at different periods, and I am apprehensive he has got one of their discharges. He is not free by manumission till next Christmas, and from that time he was to serve me 6 months, by agreement, for the expenses of a former elopement, about two years past, which cost me upwards of Twenty Pounds.   H. D. GOUGH.

The Maryland Journal and Baltimore Advertiser, Sept. 20, 1785.

RANAWAY on the Monday the 7th of June, a likely mulatto man named Francis, of a middle stature; he is about 25 years old, has a small scar on one of his cheeks, and some time ago received a fall from a horse, which has caused the skin about one of his eyes to be somewhat darker than the rest of his face. HE CAN WRITE A PRETTY GOOD HAND; PLAYS ON THE FIFE EXTREMELY WELL, and is an incomparable good house servant · He had when he left home, 6 good linen shirts, a fine new brown

broad cloth coat, a green shaggy jacket, breeches of several kinds, with shoe-boots and shoes. I do suppose that he intends to ship himself for Europe or elsewhere. I therefore forewarn all masters and captains of vessels as well as all other persons, from having any thing to say to the servant above described, and will give a reward of Five Guineas to any Person or Persons who will either deliver him to me in Halifax town, North Carolina, or secure him in any jail so that I get him again.   HALCOT B. PRIDE.
June 24, 1790.

The Norfolk and Portsmouth Chronicle, July 10, 1790.

100 DOLLARS REWARD

Run away from the subscriber the 9th inst., a negro man slave named WILL about 40 years of age 5 feet 8 or 10 inches high; has two remarkable scars on his breast and is much scarified about the neck and throat, caused by a disorder he was cured of some years ago; CAN READ A LITTLE, and a very dissembling fellow. He took with him sundry cloaths, among which are a blue cotton coat, with metal buttons, a striped jacket, a pair of blue cotton, and a pair of corduroy breeches. It is probable he will endeavor to pass for a freeman, and try to get on board some vessel; all masters of vessels are hereby forewarned from carrying him off. Whoever will deliver the said slave to me in Southampton county, near South Quay, or secure him in any gaol, so that I get him again, shall receive the above reward.   SAMUEL BROWNE.
Feb. 25, 1791.

The Norfolk and Portsmouth Chronicle, March 19, 1791.

TEN DOLLARS REWARD

ABSCONDED from my service on Tuesday evening, the 10th instant, a black Negro Man, named Manuel, by trade a blacksmith, about 21 Years of age, 5 feet 7 or 8 inches high, of a strong lusty make, full faced, and somewhat round shouldered; he is sober and intelligent and CAN BOTH READ AND WRITE. He had on and took with him, a grey cloth coat, an old short grey napped do., one pair nankeen breeches and vest, and one pair of corduroy breeches, and black vest. Whoever apprehends and brings home the above described Manuel, shall have the above reward.
Sept. 12, 1793.   ADAM FONERDEN.

The Maryland Journal and Baltimore Advertiser, Oct. 1, 1793.

RAN AWAY

On the 25th ultimo, from the subscriber, living near Culpepper Court-house, *A Negro Man* named *JACK*, about 30 years old, 5 feet 10 or 11 inches high, very muscular, full faced, wide nostrils, large eyes, a down look, speaks slowly and wore his hair cued; had on when he eloped, a white shirt, grey broad cloth coat, mixed cassimere waistcoat and breeches, a brown hat, faced underneath with green, and a pair of boots. He formerly belonged to Mr. *Augustin Baughan*, of Fredericksburg, now of Baltimore, and I am told was seen making for Alexandria, with the intention of taking the stage thither: HE IS ARTFUL CAN BOTH READ AND WRITE AND IS A GOOD FIDDLER; it is therefore probable that he may attempt a forgery and pass as a free man. He is most commonly known by the name of *Jack Taylor*, was originally from Essex County, has a father living there, and it is said he has a wife, the property of Mrs. Dalrymple of Dumfries. Whoever secures him in any jail so that I get him again shall have Ten Dollars Reward, and if taken above sixty and not more than one hundred miles distant, and brought home, shall receive Twelve Dollars, and for any greater distance, Fifteen Dollars, with all reasonable expenses borne. Masters of Vessels and stage drivers are forewarned carrying him out of the State, under penalty of the law.

Carter Beverley.

The Virginia Herald (Fredericksburg), Jan. 21, 1800.

TWENTY DOLLARS REWARD

Ran-away from the Subscriber's plantation at Ponpon, about the beginning of last September, a young *Mulatto Fellow* named cyrus, about five feet six or seven inches high, 25 years old, very short and strong built. The said fellow is very well known about town, as he served four years apprenticeship to Mr. Donaldson, house carpenter. IT IS PROBABLE THAT HE HAS FORGED A PASS FOR HIMSELF, AS HE WRITES; he sometimes calls himself James and says he belongs to Mr. Savage. Any person apprehending and delivering him to the Master of the Work House, or at the Subscriber's on South Bay, shall receive the above reward and all reasonable expenses paid   Thomas Osborn.

The City Gazette and Daily Advertiser
(Charleston), March 7, 1801.

EIGHT HUNDRED DOLLARS REWARD

Montgomery County, near Sugar Loaf
Mountain, Oct. 10, 1780.

Ran away, from the Subscriber, the 23rd of September last, a Negro Man named Frederick, about 26 years of age, about 6 feet high, and is a black country born likely well-set fellow. Had on, when he went away, a coarse shirt and short trousers; and carried with him, one old lightish-coloured lagathee or duroy patched coat, with a slit on the shoulders, one pair of black everlasting breeches, one pair of white cotton ditto, patched and darned before, one pair of white corded linen ditto, one striped linsey jacket, with sleeves, one linen ditto, without sleeves, one pair white yarn stockings, one pair of shoes and buckles, AND A TESTAMENT AND HYMN BOOK. HE CAN READ PRINT, IS VERY SENSIBLE AND ARTFUL, delights much in traffic, and it is probable he will change his name and cloaths, and endeavour to pass for a freeman. Whoever taks up said Negro and secures him, so that I get him again, shall receive One Hundred and Fifty Pounds Reward; if 30 miles from home, One hundred Twenty Five Pounds, and so on in proportion as far as the above Reward, paid by

JOHN WILSON.

The Maryland Journal and Baltimore Advertiser, Oct. 17, 1780.

Ran away from the subscribers living near the Queen Tree, St. Mary's County, on the fifth day of the present month, being Easter Sunday, the following three negro men, viz.

George, the property of John Edeley, aged twenty-three years, of a dark complexion, about six feet high, fleshy and well looking; had on when he went away, a blue great coat, a good ruffled shirt, a pair of country linen trousers, his other cloaths are uncertain.

David, the property of Nathaniel Ewing, aged about twenty-one years, five feet seven inches high, of a dark complexion, well made, has a burn on one of his arms near the shoulder, a sharp nose; had on when he went away a dark coloured cloth coat, whitish breeches, Irish linen shirt, old boots, a new hat with a black ribbon around the crown, other cloaths uncertain.

Charles, the property of Cornelius Wildman, aged about twenty-six years, five feet seven inches high, dark complexion, down looking fellow, thick lips; had on when he went away a cotton and woolen country coat, a striped silk jacket, a pair of white breeches and stockings, a new wool hat with a ribbon around it. IT IS

PROBABLE THAT THESE FELLOWS WILL ATTEMPT TO
GET TO PENNSYLVANIA, AS DAVID HAS ONCE BEEN
THERE WITH HIS MASTER; IT IS ALSO APPREHENDED
THAT THEY MAY HAVE SUPPLIED THEMSELVES WITH
PASSES EITHER FROM SOME ILL–DESIGNING WHITE
PERSON, OR THAT GEORGE HAS CONTRIVED TO EXE–
CUTE SOME KIND OF PASSES HIMSELF, AS HE CAN
READ WRITING, ALSO WRITE SOME LITTLE. We are like-
wise of the opinion they may endeavour to pass by the name of
BUTLER, as George had some time in his possession before he went
off a pass granted to CLEM BUTLER, who was a free negro, from
which it is likely he might take copies. Whoever takes up and
secures said Negro slaves in any gaol, so that their masters may get
them again, shall receive TWENTY FOUR DOLLARS, including
what the law allows for the three Negroes or the sum of EIGHT
DOLLARS, also including what the law allows, for either of them.
April 11, 1795.   JOHN EDELEY
                                         NATHANIEL EWING
                                         CORNELIUS WILDMAN.
                    The Maryland Gazette, May 21, 1795.

                      FORTY DOLLARS REWARD

    Ran away from the subscriber living near Stafford court-house
in the commonwealth of Virginia, about the middle of May last, a
Negro fellow named JACK, about five feet eight or nine inches
high, nineteen years old, thick made and well set, stoops in the
shoulders, and his complexion black, has a remarkable scar on the
top of one of his feet, but I forget whether right or left; he carried
with him the following cloaths, a greenish coloured great coat of
elastic cloth, with buff cuffs and cape, a white casimer vest and
breeches, a brown cloth vest, and a calico vest, but these he may
change for other cloaths; this negro lately belonged to the estate
of Mr. Thomas Stone, in Charles County, Maryland, and may pass
himself for one of the Thomas family of negroes belonging to the
said estate, who make pretention to their freedom, but the fallacy
of the attempt may be easily detected, as he is quite black, whereas
the Thomas family are all of mulatto colour; HE CAN ALSO
READ A LITTLE. I suspect he is lurking about Baltimore or
Annapolis; his mother is in the former city, who is also a run-

away, and named Rachel. I will give the above reward of fifty dollars to any person who will deliver him to me at my place of residence, or forty dollars for securing him in any gaol so that I may get him again.   TRAVERS DANIEL, JUN.
Stafford County, Virginia, Oct. 28, 1797.
The Maryland Gazette, January 4, 1798.

EIGHTY DOLLARS REWARD

Ran away from the subscriber's farm about seven miles from Annapolis, on Wednesday the 5th instant, two slaves, Will and Tom; they are brothers. Will, a straight tall well made fellow, upwards of six feet high, he is generally called black, but has rather a yellowish complexion, by trade a carpenter and cooper, and in general capable of the use of tools in almost any work; saws well at the whip saw, about thirty years of age, when he speaks quick he stammers a little in his speech. Tom a stout well made fellow, a bright mulatto, twenty-four years of age, and about five feet nine or ten inches high; he is a complete hand at plantation work, and can handle tools pretty well. Their dress at home, upper jackets lined with flannel, and overalls of a drab colour, but they have a variety of other clothing, and it is supposed they will not appear abroad in what they wear at home. WILL WRITES PRETTY WELL, AND IF HE AND HIS BROTHER ARE NOT FUR-NISHED WITH PASSES FROM OTHERS, THEY WILL NOT BE AT A LOST FOR THEM, BUT UPON PROPER EXAMI-NATION MAY BE DISCOVERED TO BE FORGED. These people it is imagined, are gone for Baltimore town as Tom has a wife living there with Mr. Thomas Edwards. For taking up and securing the two fellows in the gaol of Baltimore town, or any other gaol, so that I get them again, shall receive a reward of eighty dollars, and for either forty dollars.
Annapolis, April 10, 1797.   THOMAS HOWARD.
The Maryland Gazette, Feb. 1, 1798.

200 DOLLARS REWARD

Run away in the spring of the last year, from this place, a Young fellow belonging to me, named John, sometimes called John-son, at times calling himself John Hill, at other times John Howe. This fellow is about 5 feet 5 inches high, 23 years old, and is of a dull copper-colour, being the son of a mulatto man and negro woman; his features are generally ugly; his eyes remarkably large and prominent; he is sensible and shrewd, civil in his manners, and plausible in conversation; he served his time with a cabinet maker, and has worked as journeyman with a Windsor Chair-maker; he is very ingenious, and well acquainted with the use of the joiners tools. JOHN READS AND I BELIEVE CAN WRITE A LITTLE. He probably made some one of the Northern ports the place of his destination, or perhaps Charleston. I will pay the above reward to any person who will deliver John to me or to the Jailor in this place.   W. H. Hill.

The Charleston Courier, June 29, 1803.

EDUCATED NEGROES

RAN away on Saturday Night last, from Moorhall in Chester County, a Mulatto Man Slave, aged about 22, has a likely whitish countenance, of a middle Stature; having on a chocolate colour'd Cloth coat, Linnen Waistcoat, Leather Breeches, grey Stockings, a Pess-burnt Wig, and a good Hat; has with him several white Shirts, and some Money: HE SPEAKS SWEDE AND ENGLISH WELL. Whoever secures the said Slave, so that his Master may have him again, shall be very handsomely Rewarded, a.nd all reasonable Charges paid by   William Moore.

Wilmington, N. C., June 10, 1803.

The Pennsylvania Gazette, July 31, 1740.

RUN away the 23rd of August, from his Master Philip French of New Brunswick, in East-New-Jersey, a Negro Man *Claus,* of middle Stature yellowish complexion, about 44 Years of Age, SPEAKS DUTCH AND GOOD ENGLISH.   Philip French.

The Pennsylvania Gazette, Sept. 24, 1741.

RUN away the 15th of May from John Williams, of Trenton Ferry, a Negro Man, named James Bell, about 30 Years of Age, middle stature, SPEAKS VERY GOOD ENGLISH, AND VERY FLUENT IN HIS TALK; he formerly belonged to Slator Clay.

John Williams.

The Pennsylvania Gazette, June 21, 1744.

Philadelphia May 29, 1746.

RUN away the 2nd Instant, from John Pawling, at Perkiomen, a likely lusty, Negroe Man, named Toney, 6 Foot high, about 24 Years of Age, and SPEAKS GOOD ENGLISH AND HIGH

DUTCH. Had on when he went away, a striped Linsey Woolsey Jacket, Tow Shirt and Trowsers, an old Felt Hat. Whoever takes up and secures said Negroe, so that his Master may have him again shall have Twenty-five Shillings Reward, and reasonable Charges, paid by   JOHN PAWLING.

The Pennsylvania Gazette, June 5, 1746.

RAN AWAY about the Middle of July last from the subscriber, living in King's County, Long Island, a Negro Man named Jack, he is about 35 Years of Age, slim made, about 5 Feet 8 Inches in height, SPEAKS GOOD ENGLISH AND DUTCH, and has been used to attending a Grist-Mill.—Whoever secures him in any gaol or brings him to me shall be rewarded, and all reasonable Charges paid by
New York, August 15, 1766.   ABRAHAM SCHENK.
The New York Gazette or the Weekly Post-Boy, Aug. 21, 1766.

THREE GUINEAS REWARD

Ran-away from the subscriber on Wednesday evening last, a Mulato Fellow named Harry (sometimes calls himself Waters), speaks good English and tolerable German, he is about five feet 8 inches high, well made, and about 25 years of age, has taken away with him, a blue broadcloth coat, with a red cape, a pair of blue Negro Cloth trowsers and a short jacket, with oznaburg jacket and trowsers, much stained with tar. AS HE IS A SMART SENSIBLE FELLOW, HE MAY PROBABLY PASS FOR A FREEMAN. A Reward of Three Guineas will be given to any person who will deliver the said fellow to the Warden of the Work-house, or to the subscriber in Charleston.   GEORGE DENER.
N. B. Captains of Vessels and others are cautioned from carrying off, or concealing the said Mulatto, as they may depend upon being treated with the utmost rigour of the law.—If he returns of his own accord he will be forgiven.
Feb. 11, 1786.
The State Gazette of South Carolina, Feb. 20, 1786.

ONE HUNDRED DOLLARS REWARD

Ran away from Elk Forge Caecil County, Maryland, on the 2nd inst., Aug. 1784, Negro George about 35 or 40 years of age 5 feet 7 or 8 inches high, slender bodied, thin visage, not very black,

PLAUSIBLE, AND COMPLACENT; CAN SPEAK PRETTY
GOOD ENGLISH, A LITTLE FRENCH, AND A FEW WORDS
OF HIGH DUTCH, HAS BEEN IN THE WEST INDIES AND
IN CANADA, AND HE WAS FORMERLY A WAITING MAN
TO A GENTLEMEN, HAS THEREBY HAD AN OPPORTU-
NITY OF GETTING ACQUAINTED WITH THE DIFFERENT
PARTS OF AMERICA. His chief employ, lately, has been in the
kitchen and at cooking, at which he is very complete: is also a
barber. He has a variety of cloaths with him, and probably may
procure a pass. 'Tis thought he will endeavour to get off by water;
therefore, all concerned in that way are desired to take notice.
Whoever will secure said fellow in any gaol and give notice to the
subscriber, so that he may have him again, shall receive the above
reward, and reasonable charges if brought home.

THOMAS MAY.

The Maryland Gazetto, August 19, 1784.

TWENTY DOLLARS REWARD

Ran-away on Saturday the 23rd March, LEWIS, well known in
this city where he has been a Hair Dresser these several years, is of
a good size, a stout well-made fellow, well-featured, and between 24
and 25 years of age, SPEAKS BOTH FRENCH AND ENGLISH
FLUENTLY, IS VERY ARTFUL, AND WILL PROBABLY
ATTEMPT TO PASS AS A FREEMAN.

Whoever will apprehend him and deliver him to the Master of
the Work-house, in Charleston, or to any of the gaolers in this State,
shall be entitled to a Reward of Twenty Dollars, and all reasonable
expenses.

All Masters of Vessels and others are forbid employing, harbouring or carrying him off, as on conviction they will be prosecuted to the extent of the law.

Apply to the Printers of the City Gazette.

April 1, 1799.

The City Gazette and Daily Advertiser, April 1, 1799.

CITY SHERIFF'S SALE

*Will be sold before the Store of Messrs. Aerstein & Co., on
Thursday next the 10th inst., at twelve o'clock, a valuable negro
named WILL about 22 years of age; he is well adopted for a Waiting Man for a single gentleman who travels or as a Steward of a*

Ship of Packet. HE SPEAKS FRENCH AND SPANISH, READS AND WRITES and *never known to be guilty of any mean or bad tricks which blacks in common are addicted to, such as pilfering or drinking. His deportment is agreeable and polite. Seized by virtue of an execution for Drain Assessment and Arrearages of Taxes, and to be sold as the Property of Col.* Alexander Moultrie.

Condition, cash payable in dollars, at 4s 8d, the property not to be altered until the terms are complied with.[1]

ALSO WILL BE SOLD.—

A few articles of Household Furniture *as the property of the estate of* James Paterson, *deceased, for arrearages of State and City Taxes. Condition, cash, purchasers to pay for Sheriff's bills of sale.* City Sheriff's Office, Jan. 4.   J. H. STEVENS,
                                            City Sheriff.
City Gazette & Daily Advertiser, Jan. 5, 1799.

TWENTY DOLLARS REWARD

For Jack who has again Run-Away.

The Subscriber's Servant JACK, who calls himself John Leech, again absconded last night. He is a short well made young Mulatto, probably about five feet five inches high, about twenty-five years of age, and plausible; he has a thick bushy head of hair, like a negro's; thick lips, a film on his left eye, over which he sometimes wears a peace of green silk. He belonged when he was a child, to the late Ephraim Mitchell, esq. deceased, and afterwards to Francis Bremar, esq. from whom the subscriber bought him.

He is well acquainted all over the state, having waited upon his former masters when traveling, and also upon the subscriber when he went on the Circuits. HE CAN WRITE HIMSELF AND MAY FORGE A PASS OR CERTIFICATE OF FREEDOM. He had on, when he went off, a pair of overalls, and waistcoat of servant's cloth of a light grey mixed colour almost new, and carried several changes with him nearly of the same colour, and several coatees like them, with capes, cuffs and welts to the pockets of green cloth; but he may change his clothes; he also carried away a great coat of a drab colour spotted. He may go to Goose-creek or to the vicinity of Belville, Statesburg or Columbia, or attempt to go to the northward, but if its most suspected, that he will en-

---

[1] This advertisement appears also under another heading.

deavour to get on board of some vessel. Whoever will deliver him to the subscriber, or to the Master of the Work-house or lodge him in any gaol of the State, shall receive the above reward, and if he should be harboured by any one that the reward will be doubled upon the harbourers being prosecuted to conviction by the informer. All Masters of Vessels and others are warned against employing him or carrying him out of the city.   LEWIS TREZVANT.

The Carolina Gazette, Feb. 4, 1802.

SLAVES IN GOOD CIRCUMSTANCES

TWENTY DOLLARS REWARD

Ran away from Mr. Davis Stone in Loudoun County, Virginia, on Saturday the 19th ult., a Virginia-born NEGRO MAN, named WILL between 5½ and six feet high, stout made twenty seven years old, of a black, complexion, round shouldered and down look, when spoken to is apt to grin, is an artful sensible fellow, much accustomed to driving a wagon, is good at any kind of plantation business, tolerably ingenious, and I am informed, has a pass; had on, and took with him one white hat, one white cassimere coat, a little worn, one blue broadcloth ditto, almost new, a drab coloured coat and breeches, quite new, one red waistcoat, one cassimere ditto, one striped ditto, one pair cassimere breeches, a pair of fustian ditto, several shirts, both coarse and fine, one pair of mixed yarn stockings, blue and white, shoes with buckles, and the soles are nailed; it is probable that he may change his clothes, AS HE HAS PLENTY OF MONEY. Whoever takes up the said fellow and secures him in any gaol, so that I may get him again or deliver him to me near the Falls Church shall receive the above Reward and all reasonable charges, paid by   JOHN DULIN.
N. B. He crossed the ferry at Elk Ridge-Landing on his way to Baltimore, on Sunday the third instant.
☞All masters of vessels and others are forewarned from harbouring him, at their peril.
Nov. 5, 1793.

The Maryland Journal and Baltimore Advertiser, Nov. 5, 1793.

SIXTEEN DOLLARS REWARD

Ran away, from the subscriber, on Monday evening last, a NEGRO LAD, named TOWER, about 18 or 19 years of age, 5 feet

3 or 4 inches high, rather square or heavy in his built, somewhat bow legged, and walks with a considerable swing, has a full round face and thick lips, talks slow and not very plain. Had on and took with him, a green broadcloth coat, almost new, a new striped jacket, with sleeves in the fashion of a sailor's, a striped crossbarred printed-cotton vest of an olive colour, buckskin breeches, and striped silk and cotton hose; BUT AS HE IS KNOWN TO HAVE TAKEN A CONSIDERABLE SUM OF MONEY WITH HIM, it is probable that he may change his clothes. Whoever brings home said negro, or secures him in gaol, shall receive the above Reward and all reasonable charges.

It is supposed that he will try to go to Philadelphia; and as he speaks a little French and is known to have put a striped ribbon round his hat, it is probable that he will attempt to pass as one who lately came in the street from Cape François.

N. B. All Masters of vessels and others, are cautioned against taking him at their peril.

Baltimore, Sept. 19, 1793.   DAVID HARRIS.

The Maryland Journal and the Baltimore Advertiser, Sept. 20, 1793.

FIFTEEN DOLLARS REWARD

Ran away on the 20th instant, from the subscriber, living in Patapsco Neck, a NEGRO MAN named SALISBURY, but may assume some other name; he is about 21 years of age; 5 feet 8 or 9 inches high, stout and well made, has a smiling countenance and very thick lips; he has lately been under the doctor's hands for a sore on his right arm, which he generally carries in his bosom: Had on and took with him a blue broadcloth coat with yellow buttons, a fustian jacket, a red and white striped do., a coarse and white country cloth upper-jacket, and breeches, a pair of nankeen do., a white shirt and an oznaburg do., with a pair of good shoes. AS I EXPECT HE HAS A SUM OF MONEY WITH HIM, PROBABLY HE MAY GET SOME ONE TO FORGE A PASS FOR HIM, AND PASS AS A FREE MAN. Whoever takes up said NEGRO and secures him in any Gaol, so that I may get him again, shall have the above reward, and reasonable charges, if brought home, paid by   ROBUCK LYNCH.

N. B. All masters of vessels, and others, are forewarned at their peril not to harbour or conceal said Negro.

Baltimore County, May 25, 1793.

The Maryland Journal and Baltimore Advertiser, June 11, 1793.

Ran away from the subscriber living in Annapolis, on the 24th of May, a Negro man named Willis Bowzer, about thirty-four years of age, a full faced well looking fellow, who had the small pox in March last, and is much marked with it, he is very remarkable about the ancles and feet, his ancles look as they had been hurt,

they turn in looked swelled with knots on them, his feet are flat, or rather round instead of hollow; he is about five feet ten or eleven inches high, has a flat nose, and is a smooth spoken fellow; he appears to be religious and I suppose will endeavour to pass for a free man. As he has money and a variety of cloaths. Whoever takes up and secures the said fellow, so that I get him again, shall receive a Reward of Forty Dollars.   JOHN STUART.
N. B. All masters of vessels and others, are forbid carrying, or in any anywise harbouring, entertaining or employing the said negro at their peril.

The Maryland Gazette, June 11, 1795.

NEGROES BROUGHT FROM THE WEST INDIES

Philadelphia, June 17, 1745.
RUN away from the Sloop Sparrow, lately arrived from Barbadoes, Joseph Perry Commander, a Negro Man named John; he WAS BORN IN DOMINICA AND SPEAKS FRENCH, BUT VERY LITTLE ENGLISH, he is a very ill-featured Fellow, and has been much cut in his Back by often Whipping; his Clothing was only a Frock and Trowsers. Whoever brings him to John Yeats, Merchants in Philadelphia, shall have Twenty Shillings Reward, and reasonable Charges, paid by   JOHN YEATS.

The Pennsylvania Gazette, July 4, 1745.

RAN away, the 24th of last Month from Bennet Bard, of Burlington, a Mulatto Spanish Slave, named George, aged about 24 years, about 5 feet 10 Inches high, smooth faced, well-set, and has his Hair lately cutt off, speaks tolerable good English, BORN AT HAVANNA, SAYS HE WAS SEVERAL YEARS WITH DON BLASS, and is a good Shoemaker. Had on when he went away a corded Dimity Waistcoat, Ozenbrigs shirt and Trowsers, no Stockings, old Shoes, and a new Hat. Whoever takes up and secures said Fellow so that his Master may have him again, shall have Forty Shillings Reward and reasonable Charges paid by

BENNET BARD.

The Pennsylvania Gazette, Aug. 1, 1745.

RAN away on the Ninth of this instant September, from the subscriber, a Negroe Man, named Frank, alias Francisco, about 5 Feet 7 or 8 Inches high, well-set, about 25 Years of Age, walks remarkably upright, CAN TALK BUT LITTLE ENGLISH, HAVING LIVED AMONG THE SPANIARDS, AND TALKS IN THAT DIALECT * * * * * * * * * * * * * It is supposed he is gone off in Company with a Negroe Fellow that has been lurking about this city some Time (supposed to be a Runaway) as he was seen in Company with the Negro the Night before he went off.

THOMAS PRYOR.

The Pennsylvania Gazette, Sept. 20, 1764.

RAN away from the Subscriber living in New-York, the Beginning of June Inst. a Negro Fellow named Charles, about five Feet ten Inches, very black, Pock-pitted, and remarkable for his white Teeth; SPEAKS BOTH FRENCH AND ENGLISH, JAMAICA BORN, marked under his left Breast P. C. Count; had on when he went away, a brown Jacket, and a blue short Waistcoat under it; a Pair of Trowsers, and a Sailor's round Hat.—Whoever takes up said Negro, and secures him so that he may be had again shall have FORTY SHILLINGS Reward and all reasonable Charges paid by   ANDREW MYER in Dock-Street.

N. B. All Masters of Vessels and others are hereby warned not to carry off said Servant, at their Peril, as they will answer as the law directs.

The New York Gazette or the Weekly Post-Boy, July 31, 1766.

Ran away about a Year ago, a Negro Man, goes by the name of Antigua George, WAS BORN IN ANTIGUA, TALKS GOOD ENGLISH, is betwixt 50 and 60 Years old, about 5 Feet 5 Inches high, grey headed, and bends much in his legs when he walks. Had on a Cotton Jacket and Breeches, Country made Shoes and Stockings, and an Osnabrigs Shirt. He has since been taken up twice in TALBOT and made his Escape; and now imagine he passes for a free Negro.

Whoever takes up the said Negro, if in Talbot, shall have Twenty Shillings Reward, if brought home; if at any farther Distance, Four Dollars Reward, and reasonable Charges if brought home, paid by the subscriber living at Nye River.

MARTHA BRYAN.

The Maryland Gazette, April 9, 1767.

Ran away from the Subscriber, since the 22nd July last, a Negro fellow named Daniel. WAS BORN IN THE WEST-INDIES, SPEAKS GOOD FRENCH AND ENGLISH; is about 5 feet high, likely face and Knock Knees. Whoever will apprehend the said fellow and take him to the Warden of the Workhouse, or to the subscriber, at No. 95 Broadstreet, shall receive a handsome reward. This is to forbid all persons whatsoever from harbouring said Negro, as they may depend upon being prosecuted by law.

DE L CANTREE & SELLS.

The Gazette of the State of South Carolina, Aug. 16, 1784.

TWO GUINEAS REWARD

RAN away from the Subscriber a few days ago, a tall thin Negro-man of the name of Will about 20 years of age, remarkable by a cut or scar on the left side of his mouth; SPEAKS GOOD ENGLISH. THE FELLOW WAS BORN IN THE ISLAND OF ST. CHRISTOPHER and has served some time to cooper's trade, as well as having gone several voyages to sea. He had on when he ran off, a speckled waistcoat and breeches, and a snuff-colourd coat; but having took all his Cloaths with him, it is probable he may have changed his dress.

The above Reward will be paid to any person that delivers him to the Subscriber, or the Warden of the Sugar House.—Masters of Vessels are hereby warned at their peril not to harbour, or to take him off.

WILLIAM MARSHALL,

No. 48 Queen Street.

The South Carolina Gazette and General Advertiser, July 10, 1784.

THIRTY DOLLARS REWARD

Ran away on Saturday last a FRENCH NEGRO WOMAN, NAMED SOBETT, about 23 years old, marked on her breast thus Annette Chambis, about 4 feet 4 inches high, of a yellow complexion. She is slender made, tolerable likely, somewhat pitted with Small-pox; her hair remarkably short, and her clothing cannot be described. The above reward will be paid to any person or persons who will deliver said negro woman to the subscriber at the house of Mr. Changeur.

D. DAMCOURT.

The Baltimore Telegraph, Oct. 18, 1796.

RAN-AWAY, a MULATTO GIRL named CATHERINE about 18 years old, BY BIRTH FRENCH, but being a number of years in this country, has acquired the English pretty fluent. She is well known about town, therefore, this is to caution all persons from harbouring her, as they will be dealt with as the law orders in such case.

JACOB DE LEON.

N. B. A reward of Ten Dollars will be paid on proving where she is haboured.

The City Gazette and Daily Advertiser, March 5, 1800.

TEN DOLLARS REWARD

Run away from the subscriber, on the Euhaw, South Carolina, a Boy about sixteen years of age, SUPPOSED FORMERLY FROM ST. DOMINGO. As he was purchased from a Frenchman, HE MAY SPEAK FRENCH FOR WHAT I KNOW, BUT SPEAKING ENGLISH, HE STUTTERS AND STAMMERS; he also beats well upon the drum. I do forwarn all captains of vessels not to carry him off, or any other persons not to harbour him upon their peril.   ELIZABETH COLLETON.
September 11.

The City Gazette and Daily Advertiser, Sept. 18, 1800.

VARIOUS KINDS OF SERVANTS

A very likely Negro Woman to be sold, aged about 28 Years, fit for Country or City Business. SHE CAN CARD, SPIN, KNIT AND MILK; AND ANY OTHER COUNTRY-WORK. Whoever has a mind for the said Negro, may repair to Andrew Beadford in Philadelphia.

A Young Negro Woman to be sold by Samuel Kirk in the Second Street, Philadelphia.

The American Weekly Mercury (Philadelphia), Oct. 26, 1721.

A Likely Negro Man about Twenty two Years of Age, speaks good English, has had the Smallpox and the Measles, has been seven Years with a LIME BURNER: To be sold, Inquire of John Langdon, Baker, next Door to John Clark's at the North End, Boston.

A Likely Negro Man about Twenty-five Years of Age, has had the Small Pox, and speaks pretty good English, suitable for a Farmer, &C. To be sold, Enquire of the Printers.

The Boston Weekly News-Letter, March 21, 1734.

TO BE SOLD

A likely Young Negro Fellow, by TRADE A BRICKLAYER AND PLASTERER, has had the Small Pox. Enquire of the printer hereof.

The Pennsylvania Gazette, Jan. 29, 1739.

RAN away about two months, aged 19 Negro Woman, known by the name of Elizabeth Gregory; she was born in Long Island and has relations there and FORMERLY SERVED IN GOVERNOR MORRIS' FAMILY AT TRENTON; she was taken out of prison about 18 months ago by Thomas Lawrence, Esq. of whom the subscriber purchased her time.   JOHN KEARSLEY, JUN.

The Pennsylvania Gazette (No. 1090), 1749.

TEN POUNDS REWARD

Fairfax County, Virginia, July 5, 1784.

RAN away from the Subscriber, about six weeks ago, two slaves, viz: DICK, a stout lusty Mulatto Fellow about twenty two years of age, has large features and eyes, and a very roguish down look; he beats a drum pretty well, is artful and plausible, and well acquainted in most parts of Virginia and Maryland, HAVING FORMERLY WAITED UPON ME. CLEM, a well-set black negro lad of about nineteen years of age, has a remarkable large scar of a burn, which covers the whole of one of his knees. 'Tis impossible to describe their dress, as I am told they have stolen a variety of cloaths since their elopement. I suspect they have made towards Baltimore or Philadelphia, or may have got on board some bay or river craft. I will give the above reward to any person who will bring them to me in Fairfax County or secure them in any gaol, and give me notice so that I get them again, or Five Pounds for either of them.   GEORGE MASON, JUN.

The Maryland Gazette, Aug. 26, 1784.

TEN POUNDS REWARD, for apprehending and delivering in any gaol, so that the owner gets him, a Negro Man Slave, named George, BY TRADE A BLACKSMITH. He made his elopement last October from Port Royal Virginia. He is a black Virginia-born, speaks plain, and is very sensible, about 6 feet high, well made, has a brisk walk, large legs and arms, small over the belly, small face, somewhat hollow-eyed, about 28 years of age, is fond of smok-

13

ing the pipe; he was well cloathed when he went away, but his dress I can not describe. I expect he will change his name, pass a free-man, *AND GET EMPLOYMENT IN THE SMITH'S BUSINESS, AT WHICH HE IS A VERY GOOD HAND.* The above reward will be given, with reasonable Charges, if delivered to the subscriber, in Port Royal Virginia.

JOSEPH TIMBERLAKE, JUN.

Baltimore, Sept. 15, 1785.

The Maryland Journal and Baltimore Advertiser, Sept. 20, 1785.

TWO GUINEAS REWARD
RUNAWAY

A stout well made Negro Fellow named BOB, about 28 years of age, 5 feet 8 or 9 inches high, this country born, rather bow-legged, sensible and artful, speaks quick, and sometimes stutters a little; HE MAY POSSIBLY HAVE A TICKET THAT I GAVE HIM TWO DAYS BEFORE HE WENT AWAY, DATED THE 6TH OF APRIL, MENTIONING HE WAS IN QUEST OF A RUNAWAY, AS I DID NOT MENTION WHEN HE WAS TO RETURN, HE MAY ENDEAVOUR TO PASS BY THAT; he was seen on the road towards Goose Creek, where he has relations at Mr. John Parkers, and at Cane Acre, at Mr. John Gough's, at either or both places he may be harboured, or in Charleston at Mr. Benjamin Villepontour's, where he formerly had a wife. The above reward will be given and all reasonable charges paid on his being delivered in St. Stephens Parish to Thomas Cooper.

April 13, 1786.

The State Gazette of South Carolina, May 1, 1786.

RUN–AWAY

From the Subscriber
About ten days ago
A Negro Fellow Named
BILLY

BY TRADE A TAYLOR, of a yellowish complexion, and has a very remarkable bushy head of hair, he is well known about Santee, where he formerly lived, and had a wife, especially at Mr. Isaac Dubose's and also in Charleston, where he was worked at his trade for four or five years past. The above fellow is very artful and plausible, and may perhaps by telling a good tale, endeavour to

pass for a freeman. A guinea reward will be paid to any person who will secure him in the Work-house in Charleston, or deliver him to the subscriber at Stono.   JOSEPH BEE.
March 21, 1789.

N. B. All persons whatever are hereby cautioned against harbouring the above fellow, as they shall and may expect to be prosecuted with the utmost rigor of the law; and in case of his not returning home within a month from this date, a reward of Five Guineas will be paid to any person, either white or black, who will produce his head to his said master, whose lenity and indulgence hitherto, has been the cause of his present desertion and ingratitude.

The Columbian Herald, April 30, 1789.

FIVE DOLLARS REWARD

Absented himself from the subscriber about the 10th of April, a likely young NEGRO FELLOW, named CAROLINA; HE HAS ALWAYS BEEN ACCUSTOMED TO WAIT IN THE HOUSE; he was seen in the city about ten days ago, dressed in a sailor jacket and trowsers. CAROLINA plays remarkably well on the violin.

The above reward will be paid to any person delivering him to the Master of the Work-House or at No 11 East Bay.

All Masters of vessels and others are hereby cautioned against carrying said Negro out of the State, as they will, on conviction, be prosecuted to the utmost rigor of the law.   ROBERT SMITH.
June 13.

The City Gazette and Daily Advertiser, July 30, 1799.

SEVEN DOLLARS REWARD

Ran-away on Monday the 17th instant, A NEGRO MAN named ABERDEEN, is WELL KNOWN IN TOWN AS A SAWYER, was seen on Tuesday morning about three miles from town, had on an osnaburg coatee and trowsers, and a black hat, is about five feet four or five inches high, smooth faced, a little wide at the knees, is about forty years of age, speaks pretty good English, and can speak Creole French, is of the Cromantee Country, he is very artful and may have a forged pass to where he intends to go, or as being free.

Whoever will deliver the said Negro to the Master of the Work-House in Charleston, or to the Subscriber, shall receive the above reward and all reasonable Charges,   WILLIAM RESIDE.

City Gazette and Daily Advertiser, Oct. 5, 1798.

Ran-away about the 24th of June last, a MULATTO MAN named Will, about 5 feet 10 inches high, speaks good English, was raised by Townsend, in Christ Church parish and purchased lately from Mr. Hance Farley, *CABINET MAKER*, Queen Street.

L. CAMERON

SAMUEL SHAW.

The City Gazette and Daily Advertiser, July 31, 1799.

NEGRO PRIVATEERS AND SOLDIERS PRIOR TO THE AMERICAN REVOLUTION

Whereas Negro Jo (who formerly lived with Samuel Ogle, Esq; then Governor of Maryland, as his cook) about 13 Months ago run away from the Subscriber, who was then at Annapolis, AND HAS SINCE BEEN OUT A VOYAGE IN ONE OF THE PRIVATEERS BELONGING TO PHILADELPHIA, and is returned there: These are to desire any Person to apprehend the said Negro, so that he may be had again, for which on their acquainting me therewith, they shall be rewarded with the Sum of Five Pounds, current Money: Or if the said Negro will return to me, at my House in St. Mary's County, he shall be kindly received, and escape all Punishment for his Offence.   PHILIP KEY.

The Pennsylvania Gazette, Nov. 7, 1745.

Philadelphia, July 3, 1746.

Run away from Samuel M'Call, jun. a Negro Man, named Tom, a very likely Fellow, about 22 or 23 Years of Age, about 5 Foot 10 Inches high, speaks good English, HAS BEEN A PRIVATEERING; has several good Cloaths on, with Check Shirts, some new; formerly belonged to Dr. Shaw of Burlington. Whoever secures the said Negro in any County Gaol so that his Master may have him again, shall have a Pistole Reward and reasonable Charges paid by   SAMUEL M'CALL.

N. B. He is a sensible, active Fellow, and runs well.

The Pennsylvania Gazette, July 3, 1746.

Philadelphia, June 23, 1748.

RUN AWAY FROM JOHN POTTS OF Colebrookdale, Philadelphia county, Esq., about the 10th inst., a Spanish Negro Fellow, named John, of middle stature, about 30 years of age: Had on when he went away, only a shirt and trowsers, a cotton cap, a pair of old shoes; he is a cunning fellow and subject to make game at the cere-

monial part of all religious worship except that of the papists; he is proud, and dislikes to be called a negroe, HAS FORMERLY BEEN A PRIVATEERING, and talks much (with a seeming pleasure) of the cruelties he then committed. Whoever takes up said Negroe, and takes him to his Master at Colebrookdale aforesaid, or secures him in any gaol shall have *Thirty Shilling* reward, and reasonable charges, paid by said John Potts or Thomas York.
The Pennsylvania Gazette, June 23, 1748.

RAN away from his Master *Eleazer Tyng, Esq. at Dunstable, on the 26th May past, a Negro Man Servant Call'd Robbin, almost of the complexion of an Indian, short thick square shoulder'd Fellow, a very short neck, and thick legs, about 28 Years old, talks good English, can read and write, and plays on the Fiddle; he was born at Dunstable and IT IS THOUGHT HE HAS BEEN EN-TIC'D TO ENLIST INTO THE SERVICE, or to go to* Philadelphia: *Had on when he went away, a strip'd cotton and Linnen blue and white Jacket, red Breeches with Brass Buttons, blue Yarn Stockings, a fine Shirt, and took another of a meaner Sort, a red Cap, a Beaver Hat with a mourning Weed in it, and sometimes wears a Wig. Whoever will apprehend said Negro and secure him, so that his Master may have him again, or bring him to the Ware-House of Messiers* Alford *and* Tyng, *in* Boston, *shall have a reward of* Ten Pounds, *old Tenor, and all reasonable Charges.*

N. B. And all Masters of Vessels or others are hereby cautioned against harbouring, concealing or carrying off said Servant, on Penalty of the Law.
The New York Gazette Revived in the Weekly Post-Boy, July 18, 1748.

N. B. N. B. This Fellow was advertisel in the New York papers the 5th of June and in New Haven the 11th of June, 1759, was afterward taken up in Waterbury, and was put into Litchfield Gaol, from thence he was brought to Belford, and there made his Escape from his master again. Those who apprehend him are desired to secure him in Irons. He was taken up by Moses Foot of North Waterbury in New England. It is likely that he will change his cloaths as he did before. The Mole above mentioned is something long.

N. B. By information he was in Morris County in the Jerseys all winter AND SAID HE WOULD ENLIST IN THE PROVINCIAL SERVICE.[1]
The New York Gazette August 11, 1760.

[1] This advertisement appears in full on pages 213–214.

Ran-away from his Master Mr. James Richardson of Stonington, in the County of New London, a Molatto or Mustee Servant, of about 24 Years of Age, much Pox-broken, about 6 Feet high, brought up in North Kingston in Rhode Island Government; AND WAS A SOLDIER LAST SUMMER: He had on when he went away, a Leather Jockey Cap, a good Pair of Leather Breeches, a new large Duffil Coat, of a blue Colour, a strait-bodiced ditto, a white Broad Cloth Coat and Jacket. Whoever will take up said Fellow and secure him in any of his Majesty's Gaols in *North America,* or return him to his Master, shall have Twelve Dollars Reward and all necessary Charges paid by me,   JAMES RICHARDSON.

All Masters of Vessels are hereby cautioned not to carry off said Fellow upon the Peril of the Law.

May 7, 1763.

Supplement to the Boston Evening Post, May 23, 1763.

RELATIONS BETWEEN THE SLAVES AND THE BRITISH DURING THE REVOLUTIONARY WAR

A Negro Man, by name of JEMMY now in my possession, ONE WHO FOLLOWED THE BRITISH TROOPS, and has a wife at my house; he is about 5 feet 8 or 9 inches high, speaks well and sensible, says his master's name is Captain Kealing, from Yorktown, in Virginia. Any person claiming said Negro may have him, by applying on James Island, to   JAMES WITTER.

The South Carolina Weekly Advertiser, April 2, 1783.

Brought to the Work House

A Negro Wench named Sarah, of the Popah country 5 feet 1 inch high, speaks broken English, she has three of her country marks on her cheeks, 30 or 35 years of age, and says her master's is Timothy Ford, and lives near George-town; the said Wench SAID SHE WAS CARRIED OFF BY THE BRITISH TO CHARLESTON.   JOHN GERLEY WARDEN.

June 21, 1784.   *The South Carolina Gazette and General Advertiser,* July 27, 1784.

Brought to the Work House

A Negro Fellow named Dick of the Eoboe country, five feet five inches high, 35 years of age, speaks good English, says his master's name is *John Hill,* and lives near New Charleston in Boston; THE

SAID NEGRO FELLOW WAS CARRIED OFF BY A BRITISH
MAN OF WAR, TO SAVANNAH IN GEORGIA; he says his
master is dead, but that his old mistress is living:

JOHN GERLEY WARDEN.

June 21, 1784.

*The South Carolina Gazette and General
Advertiser, July 24, 1784.*

"The following is a List of Two Hundred and Forty-one Negroes
that were taken off AT THE EVACUATION OF CHARLESTON,
in one transportship the Scimtar. *They were put on board by
Colonel Muncreef and carried to* ST. LUCIA. Their families were
also carried off at the same time in different vessels."[1]

The Gazette of the State of South Carolina,
November 22 and December 6, 1784.

RELATIONS BETWEEN THE SLAVES AND THE FRENCH DURING THE COLONIAL WARS

Run-away the 2nd of July from Richard Colegate, of Kent
County on Delaware, a Molatto Man, named James Wenyam, of
Middle Stature, about 37 Years of Age, has a red Beard a Scar on
one Knee: Had on when he went away, a Kersey Jacket, a Pair of
Plain Breeches, a Tow Shirt, and a Felt Hat. He swore when he
went away to a Negro Man, whom he wanted to go with him, that
he had often been in the back Woods with his Master, AND THAT
HE WOULD GO TO THE FRENCH AND INDIANS AND
FIGHT FOR THEM. Whoever secures the said Molatto Man, and
gives Notice thereof to his Master, or to Abraham Gooding, Esq.; or
to the High Sheriff of New Castle County, so that his Master may
have him again, shall have Three Pounds Reward, and reasonable
Charges, paid by   RICHARD COLEGATE.

The Pennsylvania Gazette, July 31, 1746.

TEN PISTOLES REWARD

Kent County Maryland, March 19, 1755.

Whereas there were several Advertisements, (some of which were
printed, and others of the same Signification written), dispersed
through this Province, describing and offering a Reward of Two

---

[1] The list is not given here for the reason that the names are not written
in full. They are such as: "Cato," "Pompey," "Cicero," "Sam," etc.

Pistoles, &c. for taking up a Servant Man, named James Francis, and a Mulatto Man Slave call'd Tobby, both belonging to the sub-scriber; and ran away on the 11th Instant ∷ * * * * * * * * * * *

That this Slave shou'd run away and attempt getting his liberty, is very alarming, as he has always been too kindly used, if any Thing, by his Master, and one in whom his Master has put great Confidence, and depended on him to overlook the rest of the Slaves, and he had no Kind of Provocation to go off. IT SEEMS TO BE THE INTEREST AT LEAST OF EVERY GENTLEMAN THAT HAS SLAVES, TO BE ACTIVE IN THE BEGINNING OF THESE ATEMPTS, FOR WHILST WE HAVE THE FRENCH SUCH NEAR NEIGHBORS, WE SHALL NOT HAVE THE LEAST SECURITY IN THAT KIND OF PROPERTY. I shall be greatly obliged to any Gentlemen that shall hear of these Fellows, to endeavour to get certain Intelligence which Way they have taken, and to inform me of it by Express, and also to employ some active ·Person or Persons immediately, to take their Track and pursue them and secure them, and I will thankfully acknowledge the Favour and immediately answer the Expence attending it.

THOMAS RINGGOLD.
The Maryland Gazette, March 20, 1755.

COLORED METHODIST PREACHERS AMONG THE SLAVES
FORTY DOLLARS REWARD

A Young negro man slave, the property of the subscriber, named Sam, left the service of Charles Gosnell near Soldiers Delight, in Baltimore County, on Sunday last, to whom he was hired; he was · seen the same day traveling towards Baltimore, where he has sev-eral relations (manumitted blacks) who will conceal and assist him to make his escape: HE WAS RAISED IN A FAMILY OF RELIGIOUS PERSONS, COMMONLY CALLED METHODISTS, AND HAS LIVED WITH SOME OF THEM FOR YEARS PAST, ON TERMS OF PERFECT EQUALITY; the refusal to continue him on these terms, the subscriber is instructed, has given him offence, and is the sole cause of his absconding. Sam is about twenty-three years old, 5 feet 8 or 9 inches high, pretty square made, has a down look, very talkative among persons whom he can make free with, but slow of speech; HE HAS BEEN IN THE USE OF INSTRUCTING AND EXHORTING HIS FELLOW CREA-TURES OF ALL COLORS IN MATTERS OF RELIGIOUS

DUTY: Had on and took with him when he went off, the following clothes, a country-made cloth jacket, with sleeves, a red under jacket, an old striped vest, and striped Holland trousers, two pair of coarse linen trousers, one two-linen, and one other coarse linen shirt, a pair of new shoes, and an old hat; but it is supposed he will change his clothes with his relations.   Whoever will take the said slave and deliver him to the subscriber, or secure him in Baltimore County Gaol, shall receive TEN DOLLARS, if taken within ten miles, or any shorter distance from home; FIFTEEN DOLLARS. if above fifteen miles; TWENTY DOLLARS, if 30 miles; THIRTY DOLLARS. if above 40 miles; and in the State; and if out of the State, the above Reward from   THOMAS JONES.

   N. B. It is not improbable but that he will endeavor to get over to Dorset County, on the Eastern Shore.   All skippers of Vessels and others are forbid to hire or assist him in any manner. Baltimore, June 6, 1793.

The Maryland Journal and Baltimore
Advertiser, June 14, 1793.

   Went away on the 9th inst. from the subscriber living in the city of Annapolis, a negro man named JEM, a lively, brisk, active fellow when he pleases, 28 years of age, about 5 feet 8 inches high, slender made, rather thin face, has a great hesitation in his speech, and when he laughs shows his gums very much, takes snuff, one of his legs is sore; he is very artful and can turn his hand to any thing; he has been used to waiting, to taking care of horses and driving a carriage, is something of a gardener, carpenter and bricklayer; IS OR PRETENDS TO BE OF THE SOCIETY OF METHODISTS, HE CONSTANTLY ATTENDED THE MEETINGS, AND AT TIMES EXHORTED HIMSELF; he took with him a watch of his own, a fine hat, a new drab coloured surtout coat, lined about the body with green, light cloth waistcoat, buckskin breeches; a black coat lapelled is missing from the house; it is probable he may change his dress; he had some time in the summer from me a pass for a limited time (three or four days) to go to Baltimore, it is not improbable but he may get the date altered and make use of it. Whoever takes him up and delivers him to me, or secures him in any gaol so that I get him again, shall receive TWENTY DOLLARS. December 16, 1797.   JAMES BRICE.

The Maryland Gazette, January 4, 1798.

Ran-away from the subscriber on the 19th of October last, Negro
Jacob, 35 years of age, about 6 feet high, smooth face, high forehead, his wool growing in a peak leaves his temples bare, speaks low
and rather hoarse, had on and took with him when he went away,
a brownish cotton coat, a blue coarse short coat with metal buttons,
old breeches, osnabrig shirt, and a match coat blanket; his Sunday
apparel, a purple cloth coat with rimmed buttons, nankeen breeches,
mixed worsted stockings, and half boots; HE PROFESSES TO BE
A METHODIST, AND HAS BEEN IN THE PRACTICE OF
PREACHING OF NIGHTS; it is expected he is harbouring about
the city of Annapolis, West river, South river, South river Neck,
or Queen Anne, as he has a wife at Miss Murdoch's. Whoever
takes up and secures said fellow in any gaol so that I get him again,
shall receive the above reward paid by

THOMAS GIBBS, living near
Queene Anne.

N. B. All masters of vessels and others are forewarned harbouring
employing or carrying off said fellow at their peril.
March 7, 1800.   T. G.

The Maryland Gazette, September 4, 1800.

Ran away from the subscriber, living in Anne Arundel county,
on the 21st of February, a negro man named Dick, about forty
years of age, five feet six inches high, round full face, large eyes,
very bow legged, slow of speech, and fond of smoking a pipe, HE
IS A METHODIST PREACHER, took along with him a country
cloth coat, and one gray coloured, and breeches, two osnabrig shirts,
short kersey coat and trousers, shoes nailed. Whoever takes up the
said negro, and secures him in any gaol shall receive the above reward, and if brought home all reasonable charges paid by me
Feb. 24, 1800.   HUGH DRUMMOND.

The Maryland Gazette, Sept. 4, 1800.

Philadelphia, Sept. 4, 1746.

Run away on the 16th of July from Thomas Rutter, of this
city, a Negro Man, named Dick, commonly CALLED PREACH-
ING DICK,[2] aged about 27 Years. * * *

THOMAS RUTTER.

The Pennsylvania Gazette, Sept. 4, 1746.

---

[2] It is not known whether Dick was a Methodist or Baptist Preacher.

FORTY DOLLARS REWARD

Ran-Away from the subscriber on the 8th of November last, a negro fellow named Simbo. He was formerly the property of Francis Burns dec. of Onslow County, HE IS A METHODIST PREACHER, AND CAN READ AND WRITE.—He is about 6 feet high, very black and smooth skin, and speaks very distinct.

He is supposed to be lurking some times down Neuse river, and at others up the same, and so he ranges through Craven, Jones, and Onslow Counties.

Any person apprehending the said negro, and delivering him to the subscriber, within five miles of Swansborough, shall be entitled to the above reward.—Or any person who will so secure him that I get him again, shall receive Twenty Dollars.

The most probable method to catch him, will be at Methodist meetings.—All masters of vessels and others are forewarned from harbouring employing or carrying him away, at their peril.

June 27.   HENRY LOCKEY.

The Newbern Gazette, August 15, 1800.

SLAVES IN OTHER PROFESSIONS

RUN AWAY ON THE 4TH INST., AT NIGHT FROM *James Leonard* in Middlesex County, *East-New-Jersey*, a Negro Man named *Simon*, aged 40 Years, is well-set Fellow, about 5 feet 10 Inches high, has large Eyes, and a Foot 12 inches long; he was bred and born in this Country, talks good English, can read and write, is very slow in his speech, CAN BLEED AND DRAW TEETH PRETENDING TO BE A GREAT DOCTOR AND VERY RELIGIOUS, AND SAYS HE IS A CHURCHMAN. Had on a dark grey Broadcloth Coat, with other good Apparel, and peeked toe'd Shoes. He took with him a black Horse, about 13 Hands and a Half high, a Star in his Forehead, branded with 2 on the near Thigh or Shoulder, and trots; also a black hunting Saddle about half worn.

Whoever takes up and secures the said Negro, so that his Master may have him again shall have *Three Pounds Reward* and reasonable Charges, paid by

JAMES LEONARD.

The Pennsylvania Gazette, Sept. 11, 1740.

Whereas Cambridge, *a Negro Man belonging to* James Oliver *of* Boston *doth absent himself sometimes from his Master: SAID NEGRO PLAYS WELL UPON A FLUTE, AND NOT SO WELL*

ON A VIOLIN. This is to desire all Masters and Heads of Families not to suffer said Negro to come into their Houses to teach their Prentices or Servants to play, nor on any other Accounts. All Masters of Vessels are also forbid to have anything to do with him on any Account, as they may answer it in the Law.
N. B. Said Negro is to be sold: Enquire of said Oliver.
                              The Boston Evening Post, Oct. 24, 1743.

SIX DOLLARS REWARD

Absconded on or about the 1st instant, a Negro Fellow, named Pero. He is remarkably tall being nearly 6½ feet in height, his hands have been frost bitten, in consequence of which he has lost several of his finger nails. He speaks the French and English languages; PASSES FOR A DOCTOR AMONG PEOPLE OF HIS COLOR, AND IT IS SUPPOSED PRACTICES IN THAT CAPACITY ABOUT TOWN. The above reward will be paid on his delivery at the Work-House, or the Subscriber

                                        JAMES GEORGE.

N. B. All masters of vessels are forewarned from carrying him off the State as they will be prosecuted to the utmost rigor of the law.
        The City Gazette and Daily Advertiser, June 22, 1797.

CLOSE RELATIONS OF THE SLAVES AND INDENTURED SERVANTS

Run away in April last from RICHARD TILGHMAN of QUEEN ANNE County in MARYLAND a Mulatto slave, Named RICHARD MOLSON, of Middle stature, about forty years old, and has had the Small Pox, HE IS IN COMPANY WITH A WHITE WOMAN NAMED MARY, WHO IS SUPPOSED NOW GOES FOR HIS WIFE; AND A WHITE MAN NAMED *GARRETT CHOISE,* AND *JANE* HIS WIFE, which said White People are servants to some Neighbors of the said RICHARD TILGHMAN. The said fugatives are Supposed to be gone to CAROLINAS or some other of his Majestys Plantations in AMERICA. Whoever shall apprehend the said Fugatives and cause them to be committed into safe custody, and give Notice thereof to their Owners shall be well rewarded. The White man has one of his fore fingers disabled.

Whoever shall carry them to the Sheriff of PHILADELPHIA shall have Twenty Pounds current money paid him or them or shall convey the Molatta to the said sheriff shall have Ten Pounds, or whoever shall convey the Molatta to the said Richard Tilghman shall have Fifteen Pounds reward.—

The American Weekly Mercury (Philadelphia), Aug. 11, Aug. 25 and Sept. 1, 1720.

Ran away from the Subscribers in *Baltimore County* in *Maryland*, a Negro Man named Charles, of middle stature, aged about 28 or 30 Years, talks tolerable English: Had on when he went away, an Ozenbrigs Frock with brass Buttons on it, dark colour'd Kersey Jacket, a Cotton Jacket, old Leather Breeches, Ozenbrig Trowsers, Felt Hat, and old Shoes. HE IS SUPPOSED TO BE IN COMPANY WITH TWO SERVANT MEN belonging to *John Fuller,* sen., the one of them is a Scotch Man, named *James M'Cornet*, of middle stature, age about 26 Years, long black Hair if not cut off, and a black Beard; has with him a dark Kersey Jacket and a Cotton Jacket, old Leather Breeches, a pair of Ozenbrigs Trowsers and a pair of Crocus Trowsers, Ozenbrigs Shirt and a Dowlass Shirt, Country made Shoes and Stockings and an old Felt Hat bound round with the same. The other named *Charles King* of middle Stature, aged about 23 Years; has with him a Drugget Coat much worn, of a Cinnamon Colour, Cotton Jacket, Leather Breeches with Pewter Buttons on one Knee covered with Leather and none on the other, two ozenbrigs Shirts, a pair of Trowsers, Country made Shoes and Stockings of a bluish grey Colour, topt with black and white Yarn.

NOTE James M'Connet speaks broad Scotch very thick, and snuffles a little.

Whoever takes up the said Negro together with his Companions, shall have Twenty Shillings Reward for each besides what the Law directs paid by us   Darby Hernly

The Philadelphia Gazette, June 26, 1740.   John Fuller.

Run away 21st of August, from the Subscribers, of Kingsess, Philadelphia County, A WHITE MAN AND A NEGRO, IT IS SUPPOSED THEY ARE GONE TOGETHER, the White Man's Name is Abraham Josep, a Yorkshire Man, a Shoemaker by Trade aged about 24 Years * * *

The Negroe's Name is Tom, of a yellowish colour, pretty much pitted with Small Pox, thick set * * *

Two nights before there were several things stolen, and it is supposed they have them   James Hunt

Peter Elliot.

The Pennsylvania Gazette, Sept. 10, 1741.

RUN AWAY FROM TALBOT COUNTY School, Maryland, on Monday, the 5th of this instant August, George Ewings, MASTER OF SAID SCHOOL, WHO TOOK WITH HIM A NEGROE MAN, named Nero and two Geldings, the one of a grey, the other of a black Colour, the Property of the Visitors of said School. The said Ewings is an Irishman, of a middling Stature, and thin Visage, is pitted with Small-pox, and has the Brogue upon his Tongue, and had on when he went away a light blue new coat.

Whoever apprehends and secures said Ewings, Negro and Geldings, so that they may be had again, shall receive a Reward of Five Pounds, Maryland Currency, paid by the Visitors of said School

Signed by order,

WILLIAM GOLDSBOROUGH, Register of Said School.

The Pennsylvania Gazette, Aug. 15, 1745.

RUN away on Saturday the 26th of October, from Cadwalder, of Trenton, a Negro Man, named Sam, a likely Fellow, about 26 Years of Age, speaks very good English: Had on when he went away, a good Duroy Coat, a fine Hat, almost new, a Pair of good Leather Breeches with Trowsers over them; but as he has other Clothes with him, he may have changed them since. HE WAS ENTICED AWAY BY ONE ISAAC RANDALL, AN APPREN-TICE OF THOMAS MERRIOT, jun. They took with them a likely bay Gelding, six Years old, thirteen Hands and a Half high, paces well, and is shod before: And they are supposed to have gone with a Design to enter on board a Privateer, either at New York or Philadelphia. Whoever takes them up, and secures the Negro and Gelding shall be rewarded, by

THOMAS CADWALDER.

The Pennsylvania Gazette, Oct. 31, 1745.

RUN away, the 2nd of last month from the subscriber, living at the old town Potomack, Frederick county, Maryland, a mulattoe servant man named Isaac Cromwell, about 40 years of age, a tall slim fellow, very smooth tongued, by which some people may perhaps be imposed upon: Had on when he went away, a blanket coat, leather breeches, worsted Stockings, new shoes, with brass buckles on them.

RUN AWAY AT THE SAME TIME, AN ENGLISH SERV-ANT WOMAN, named Anne Greene, about 45 years of age, short and well set, one of her legs much shorter than the other, much pock-marked: Had on when she went away, a white jacket, striped linsey coat. They took with them the following goods, viz. blankets, a striped cotton gown, and petticoat, several shirts and skirts, with other clothing, too tedious here to mention, also a small bay horse not branded, a large bay pacing horse, his hind feet both white, about 7 years old, branded on the near buttock with a heart and a T through it; and a small old black horse, his brand not known, with some white spots on his back. Whoever takes up the said servants, and secures them, so that their master may have them again, shall have Five Pounds, if taken in Maryland, and if in Pennsylvania, or the Jerseys, Seven Pounds and reasonable Charges, paid by Thomas Cresap or James Whitehead, Work-house-keeper in Philadelphia.

Pennsylvania Gazette, June 1, 1749.

RUN AWAY FROM FRANCIS MINES, APPOQUINIMY, New Castle county, a servant woman, named Ann Wainrite: She is short, well-set, fresh colour'd, of a brown complexion, round visage, was brought up in Virginia, speaks good English and bold. Had on when she went away, a blue linsey-wolsey gown, a dark brown petticoat, and a Bath bonnet. She hath taken with her a striped cotton shirt, and some white ones, a drab coloured great coat, a silver hilted sword, with a broad belt, and a cane; with a considerable parcel of other goods: Also a large bay pacing horse, roughly trimmed, shod before, and branded on the near buttock S.R. THERE WENT AWAY WITH HER, A NEGRO WOMAN belonging to Jannet Balvaird, named Beck; she is lusty strong and pretty much pock-broken; had on when she went away, a brown linnen gown, a striped red and white linsey-wolsey petticoat, the red very dull, a coarse two petti-coat, and calico one, with a great piece tore at the bottom, and stole a black crape gown: Also a bay horse with three white feet, a blaze down his face, and a new russet hunting saddle. Whoever takes up the above mentioned women and horses, and secures them, so as they may be had again, shall have Four Pounds reward and reason-able Charges, paid by

FRANCIS MINES
JANNET BALVAIRD.

The Pennsylvania Gazette, Oct. 8, 1747.

RUN away from the subscriber, on Elkridge, in Anne Arundel county, Maryland, TWO WHITE SERVANTS, AND A NEGRO;

one of the servants named John Wright, a shoemaker by trade, has a red nose, and a crooked finger; Had on, an ozenbrigs shirt, and breeches of the same, and a dark colour'd coat, with a large cape. The other a Yorkshire-man, named William Cherryhome, a stout fellow, with yellowish har: Had on ozenbrigs shirts and trowsers, a white fustian coat: they both have hats and shirts. The Negro named Sam, is a lusty young fellow, with large scars on his breast and back. Whoever takes up and secures the said servants and Negro, so that they may be had again, shall have NINE POUNDS, besides what the law allows, paid by

JOHN HAMMOND.

N.B. They were seen coming from Lancaster to Philadelphia.

The Pennsylvania Gazette, Aug. 2, 1750.

RUN away from James West, the first of April last a servant man, named Willis M'Coy, a small short fellow, his right eye looks red; he had on when he went away, a blue jacket and a striped flannel jacket under it, a pair of trowsers, and under them a pair of cloth breeches, too long for him, and were ripped at the knee; he had two shirts on, one ozenbrigs, the other check linnen, he is supposed to have run away with a Negro man, named Toby, WHO LEFT HIS MASTER THE SAME DAY THE OTHER DID; the Negro has on a dark coloured duffil great coat much torn, he is a lusty well-set fellow, betwixt 40 and 50 years old, has sundry jackets, and coarse and fine shirts; they have no doubt changed their apparel; the Negro speaks good English, born in Philadelphia. Whoever takes up the white servant, shall have Three Pounds reward, and reasonable charges, paid by James West; and whoever takes up the Negroe above, shall have Forty Shillings paid by James Mockey, and Charges.

The Pennsylvania Gazette, Aug. 2, 1750.

RUN away from the Subscriber, living at *Cambridge* in Dorchester County, on the 15th of this Instant July, a dark Mulatto Man Slave, named Prince: HE WENT OFF IN COMPANY WITH A WHITE SERVANT MAN whose name is John, but his surname forgot, belonging to Mr. William Horner, Merchant of the same Town. The said slave is of middle Stature, well made, well featured, and is a pert lively Fellow and plays well on the Banjer. He had on a country Linnen Shirt, short Linnen Breeches, and an old Felt Hat.

Whoever takes up the said slave and brings him to the Subscriber, shall have Four Pounds Reward, besides what the Law allows paid by

JOHN WOOLLFORD.

If the White Man is secured, so that he may be had again, I doubt not but they who secure him will have a handsome Reward paid by *William Horner.*

The Maryand Gazette, July 25, 1754.

RAN away from Jonathan Sergeant, at Newark, in New-Jersey, A young Negro man, named Esop, of middle size, with round forehead, strait nose, and a down guilty look; he can write, and it is likely he may have a counterfeit pass: Had with him a beaver hat, light grey linsey-wolsey jacket, tow trowsers, new pumps, and an old purple colour'd waistcoat. IT IS SUPPOSED HE WENT AWAY IN COMPANY WITH A WHITE MAN, named John Smith, who is an old lean, tall man, with a long face and nose, and strait brown hair; who had on an old faded snuff-coloured coat. Whoever takes up and secures said man and Negro, so that their master may have them again, shall have Forty Shillings reward for each and all reasonable Charges, paid by

JONATHAN SERGEANT.

The Pennsylvania Gazette, Aug. 28, 1755.

FORTY SHILLINGS REWARD

RUN away from the manor of Eaton in Suffolk County on the 18th of November, a negro named Caesar, about 40 Years of age, near 5 feet 8 inches high; has thick lips, bandy legs, walks lame, and speaks very bad English; had on when he went away, a blue jacket, check flannel shirt, tow Cloth trowsers, black and white yarn stockings, half worn shoes, and an old felt hat; has formerly lived in some part of West Jersey, where 'tis suspected he is gone; HE WENT OFF IN COMPANY WITH ONE THOMAS CORN-WELL, WHO CALLS HIMSELF A BRISTOL MAN, and who 'tis feared has forged a pass for the Negro. Whoever secures the Negro so that the subscriber may have him again, shall have the above reward and all reasonable Charges, paid by

JOHN SLOSS HOBART.

All masters of vessels, and others are forbid to conceal or transport said Negro at their peril.

The New York Gazette or Weekly Post-Boy, Dec. 5, 1765.

14

RAN away on the 25th of April last, from a Mine Bank, belonging to *Alexander Lawson* and Company, in *Anne Arundel* County, near *Elk Ridge,* Landing, a Convict Servant Fellow, who came in the County last Year in Captain *James Dobbins*: He is an Englishman about 6 Feet high, and of a black complexion. Had on two Cotton Jackets, the under one without Sleeves, a Pair of Cotton Breeches, an Osnabrigs Shirt, a Felt Hat, a white Linnen Cap, a Silk Handkerchief, white Yarn Stockings, and Country made Shoes.

A NEGRO FELLOW BELONGING TO THE SAID COMPANY WENT AWAY WITH HIM, who is acquainted with the back Roads, and is supposed to be conducting him that Way. He is about 5 Feet 6 Inches high, pretty aged, and speaks good English. Had on a Cotton Jacket and Breeches, and Osnabrigs Shirt, an old Felt Hat, a white Linnen Cap, white Yarn Stockings, and Country made Shoes. They took with them a Drugget Coat of a light Colour, lined with Shalloon, and trimmed with Metal Buttons.

Whoever apprehends the said two Fellows, and secures them in any Gaol, so that the Subscriber may have them again, shall have, if taken within the Province, Four Pistoles Reward, for each, and reasonable Charges, if brought to   *Alexander Lawson.*

The Maryland Gazette, May 9, 1754.

FIFTY PISTOLES REWARD

Annapolis, in Maryland, March 25, 1754.

RAN away on the 18th Instant with the Sloop Hopewell, belonging to the Subscriber, William Curtis, Master, the TWO FOLLOWING CONVICT SERVANTS, AND NEGRO MAN, viz:

John Wright, a White Man, of a swarthy Complexion, very lusty, talks hoarse, and is much pitted with the Small Pox.

John Smith, also a lusty White Man, with short black Hair.

Toney, a yellowish Negro, and not quite so lusty, pretends to be a Portugese, speaks good English and pertly, is a good Hand by Water, also can do Cooper's Work, Butchering, &c. Had on or with him, a Dove colour'd Surtoot Coat.

They may have sundry Cloaths, Wigs, Linnen, Cash &c. belonging to the Captain, as it is believed they have murdered him; and the above Wright was seen with the Captain's Cloaths on, which were red; though he had Cloaths of sundry Colours with him: He also had a neat Silver hilted Sword, and Pistols mounted with Silver.

The Captain had the Register of the Sloop with him, but he was not endorsed thereon, as he was to return here to make up his Load, and clear at the proper Office.

They were seen off Patuxent on the 22nd Instant, at which time the said Wright assumed Master, and took two Men with them, belonging to Schooner of Mr. James Dick's and Company one a White Man belonging to Capt. William Strachan, of London Town, who went on board with some Bread for them, at which Time they hoisted Sail, and cut their Boat adrift, and carried them off.

They had some Lumber on board, such as Staves, Heading, and Plank; also Rum, Molasses, Sugar, Linnen &C. &C.

The Sloop is about 45 Tons, Square sterned, with a Round House, with a Partition under dividing the Cabin and Steerage, the Waste black, yellow Gunwales and Drift Rails, and the Drift and Stern blue.

Whoever secures the said sloop and Goods so that the Owner may have her again, and the three White Servants and two Slaves, so that they may be brought to Justice, shall have FIFTY PIS— TOLES Reward, paid by

Patrick Creagh.

Maryland Gazette, April 11, 1754.

New-York, July 10, 1760.

RUN away from Dennis Hicks, of Philipsburgh in Westchester County, and Province of New York, a mulatto man Slave named Bill, aged about 20 Years has a long sharp Nose, with a black Mole on the Right side of his Face, near his Nose, has very large Ears, speaks good English, and pretends to be free, and can read and write well: SAYS HE HAS A WHITE MOTHER AND WAS Born in NEW—ENGLAND. He is of a middle size, and has a thin Visage, with his Hair cut off. All person are forbid to harbour him, and all Masters of Vessels are forbid to carry him off, as they will answer it at their Peril. TWENTY—FIVE POUNDS Reward for securing him in any Gaol, or bringing him to me so that I may have him again, and reasonable Charges paid by

Dennis Hicks.

N.B. This Fellow was advertised in the New York Papers the 5th of June and in Newhaven the 11th of June 1759, was afterward taken up in Waterbury, and was put into Litchfield Gaol, from thence he was brought to Belford, and there made his escape from his master again. Those who apprehend him are desired to secure him in Irons. He was taken up by Moses Fort, of North Waterbury in New England. It is likely he will change his Cloaths as he did before. The Mole above mentioned is something long.

N.B. By information he was in Morris County in the Jerseys all the Winter; and said he would enlist in the provincial service.[3]

The New York Gazette, Aug. 11, 1760.

TEN PISTOLES REWARD

Kent County Maryland, March 19, 1755.

WHEREAS THERE WERE SEVERAL Advertisements, (some of which were printed, and others of the same Signification written), dispers'd through this Province, describing and offering a Reward of Two Pistoles, &c. for taking up a SERVANT MAN, NAMED JAMES FRANCIS, AND A MULATTO MAN SLAVE call'd Toby, both belonging to the subscriber, and ran away on the 11th Instant: And whereas it has been discovered since the Publishing of the said Advertisements, that they carried with them many more Things than is therein described, I do hereby again and farther give Notice that the White Man James Francis, is aged about 21 years, his Stature near five Feet and and half, slender bodied, with a smooth Face, almost beardless, born in England and bred a Farmer. The Mulatto is a lusty, well-set Country born Slave with a great Nose, wide Nostrils, full mouth'd, many Pimples in his Face; very slow in Speech, he is a tolerable Cooper and House Carpeter, and no doubt will endeavour to pass for a Free-Man; Each hath a Felt Hat, Country Cloth Vest and Breeches, and Yarn Stockings: one of them has a light coloured loose Coat of Whitney or Duffel: The White Man a dark close bodied Coat, a striped short Vest of Everlasting, another of blue Fearnothing, with other Cloaths. The Slave has also many other valuable Garments; they took with them likewise a Gun, Powder and Shot, and are suppos'd either to cross, or go down Bay in a Pettiauger.

Whoever brings the said Servant and Slave to the Subscriber on the Mouth of Chester River or to Thomas Ringgold at Chester-Town, shall have for a Reward Ten Pistoles and all reasonable Charges in taking and securing the said Servant and Slave, paid by[4]

JAMES RINGGOLD.

THOMAS RINGGOLD.

The Maryland Gazette, March 20, 1755.

[3] This advertisement appears under another heading on page 199.

[4] This advertisement occurs also under the heading of ''The Relations of the French and Negroes.''

ONE HUNDRED DOLLARS REWARD

RAN away from Hagerstown, Washington County, Maryland in September last, a Negro wench named PEGGY, but sometimes calls herself NANCY, about 26 years of age, talks on the Welsh accent, her complexion of a yellowish cast, the wool on her head is longer than negroes commonly have: Had on a blue petticoat of Duffil cloth, old shoes and stockings, her other clothes uncertain. IT IS SUPPOSED SHE WENT OFF WITH A PORTUGESE FELLOW WHO SERVED HIS TIME WITH MR. JACOB FUNK: they probably may be in the neighborhood of Georgetown or Alexandria or gone towards camp, and that she will attempt to pass for a free woman, and wife to the Portugese fellow. Whoever takes her up and secures her in any gaol, so that the subscriber get her again, or delivers her to Daniel Hughes, Esq., in Hagerstown, shall have the above reward, and reasonable charges,

JOHN SWAN.

The Maryland Journal and Baltimore
Advertiser, Oct. 19, 1779.

SIX DOLLARS REWARD

On Monday night, the 18th instant, ran away, from the subscriber, living in Montgomery County, near Georgetown, a likely, bright MULATTO MAN named GEORGE PINTER, about 21 years of age, 5 feet 9 or 10 inches high, spare made, with long bushy hair; he is remarkably talkative, and generally smiles when spoken to; he had on, and took with him, a drab-coloured country-cloth surtout, one white broad-cloth coat with plated buttons, one striped nankeen ditto, two striped silk and cotton waistcoats with gilt buttons, one pair of blue yarn stockings, all of them about half worn, and a pretty good felt hat, with a very wide but shallow crown; his other clothes unknown. It is highly probable he is furnished with a pass and will assume the character of a free man; he went off, IT IS SUSPECTED IN COMPANY WITH A COUPLE OF IRISH SERVANTS WHO LEFT THE LITTLE FALLS ON THE SAME DAY, where they had been at work together for some time past. Whoever apprehends and secures the said Runaway, in any gaol, so that his master may get him again, shall receive the above reward, with reasonable charges, if brought home.

March 25, 1793.   WILLIAM WALLACE.

The Maryland Journal and Baltimore
Advertiser, March 29, 1793.

Westmoreland County, Virginia, Aug. 17, 1749.

RUN away from subscriber on Monday last, a Convict Servant named Thomas Winey; he professes farming, was imported lately from Maidstone gaol in the County of Kent, Great Britain—* * *

THE ABOVE MENTIONED SERVANT TOOK WITH HIM A MOLATTOE SLAVE named James, a well set fellow, 23 years old * * * * * * * * * * * * I have been informed by their confederates since they went off, that they intend to go to Pennsylvania and from thence to New England, unless they can on their way get passage in some vessel to Great Britain where the Molattoe slave pretends to have an UNCLE WHO ESCAPED FROM HIS MASTER IN THIS COLONY NEAR 23 YEARS AGO, AND IS SAID TO KEEP A COFFEE HOUSE IN LONDON.

The Pennsylvania Gazette, Sept. 14, 1749.

REVIEWS OF BOOKS

The Negro. By W. E. B. DuBois. New York: Henry Holt and Co. 1915. Pp. 254. 50 cents.

In this small volume Dr. DuBois presents facts to show that, contrary to general belief, the Negro has developed and contributed to civilization the same as all other groups of the human race. The usual arguments that the backward state of Negro culture is due to the biological inferiority of the race he shows to be without foundation, since these arguments have been largely abandoned by creditable scholars. Much of the material in the book has been known for several years to readers of works of scholars on race questions. As is commonly the case, truths which tend to destroy deep-rooted prejudices reach general readers with considerable slowness. While it is not possible to treat but briefly a large subject in such small compass, the facts set forth by the author will put many persons on their guard against individuals who continue to spread misinformation about the Negro race.

The book is divided into twelve chapters, contains a helpful index, has a topically arranged list of books suggested for further reading, and an index. All of the chapters make interesting reading; but those treating of the achievements in state building and general culture of the ancient African Negro are especially stimulating. The author points out that in Egypt, both as mixed Semitic-Negroids and pure blacks from Ethiopia, Negro blood shared in producing the civilization of Egypt. Another center of Negro civilization was the Soudan. There strong Negro empires like Songhay and Melle developed under Mohammedan influence and existed for many centuries. In West Africa there was a flourishing group of Negro city states, the most famous of these being the Yoruban group. Recent discoveries of Frobenius in these parts of the continent show that the people reached a high stage of development in the terra cotta, bronze, glass, weaving, and iron industry. In the regions about the Great Lakes, inhabited largely by the Bantu, are found many worked over gold and silver mines, old irrigation systems, remains of hundreds of groups of stone buildings and fortifications. The author explains that the decline of this ancient culture was due to internal wars, Mohammedan conquest, and especially the ravages of the slave trade. The fact of the existence of such culture in the past stands as evidence of the capacity of the race to achieve.

It is worth noting what the author thinks about "the future relation of the Negro race to the rest of the world." He states that the "clear modern philosophy . . . assigns to the white race alone the hegemony of the world and assumes that other races, and particularly the Negro race, will either be content to serve the interests of the whites or die out before their all-conquering march." Of the several plans of solutions of the Negro problems since the emancipation from chattel slavery he tells us that practically all have been directed by the motive of economic exploitation for the benefit of white Europe. Because all dark races, and the white workmen too, are included in this capitalistic program of economic exploitation, he believes there is coming "a unity of the working classes everywhere," which will apparently know no race line. But the colored peoples are more largely the victims of this economic exploitation. In answer to it the author concludes: "There is slowly arising not only a strong brotherhood of Negro blood throughout the world, but the common cause of the darker races against the intolerable assumptions and insults of Europeans has already found expression." He expresses the hope that "this colored world may come into its heritage, . . . the earth," may not "again be drenched in the blood of fighting, snarling human beasts," but that "Reason and Good will prevail."

J. A. BIGHAM.

The American Civilization and the Negro. By C. V. ROMAN, A.M., M.D. F. A. Davis Company, Philadelphia, 1916. 434 pages.

This volume is a controversial treatise supported here and there by facts of Negro life and history. The purpose of the work is to increase racial self respect and to diminish racial antagonism. The author has endeavored to combine argument and evidence to refute the assertions of such writers as Schufeldt and agitators like Tillman and Vardaman. But although on the controversial order the author has tried to write "without bitterness and bias." The effort here is directed toward showing that humanity is one in vices and virtues as well as in blood; that the laws of evolution and progress apply equally to all; that there are no diseases peculiar to the American Negro nor any debasing vices peculiar to the

African; that there are no cardial virtues peculiar to the European; and that all races having numerous failings, one should not give snap judgment of the other, especially when that judgment involves the welfare of a people.

The work contains an extensive zoological examination of man as an inhabitant of the world, the differences in the separate individuals composing races, the forces with which they must contend, the morals of mankind, and the general principles of human development. The question of Negro slavery in America is discussed as a preliminary in coming to the crucial point of the study, the presence of the colored man in the South. The author frankly states what the colored man is struggling for. Making a review of the history of the Negroes in the United States, he justifies their claim to political rights on the ground that they are reacting successfully to their environment.

The book abounds with illustrations of prominent colored Americans, successful Negroes, individual types, typical family groups, arts and crafts among the Africans, public schools and colleges.

J. O. BURKE.

The Police Control of the Slave in South Carolina. By H. M. HENRY, M.A., Professor of History and Economics, Emory and Henry College, Emory, Virginia, 1914. 216 pages.

This work is a doctoral dissertation of Vanderbilt University. The author entered upon this study to show to what extent the southern people "sought to perpetuate, not slavery, but the same method of controlling the emancipated Negro which was in force under the slavery regime, the difficulties which were met with from without and the measure of success attained." He was not long in discovering that the laws on the statute books did not adequately answer the question. It was necessary, therefore, to determine to what extent these laws were in force and what extralegal method may have been resorted to in a system so flexible as slavery.

One of the first influences discovered was the Barbadian slave code and then the evolution of slave control from that of the white indentured servant. Soon then the status of the slave as interpreted by the court was that of no legal standing in these tribunals. The overseer is then presented as a Negro driver, referred to in contemporary sources. The author devotes much space to the patrol system, the various kinds of punishment, the court for the trial of slaves, the relations between the Negroes and the whites, the question of trading with slaves, slaves hiring their time, the slave trade, the stealing, harboring and kidnapping of free Negroes, the runaway slaves, the Seamen Acts, the gatherings of Negroes, slave insurrections, the abolition of incendiary literature, the prohibition of the education of the blacks, manumission, and the legal status of the free Negro.

The author shows by his researches that although amended somewhat, the slave code agreed upon in 1740 continued as a part of the organic law. At times some effort was made to ameliorate the condition of the blacks. The kidnapping of free Negroes, at first permitted, was later declared a crime, the murder of a Negro by a white man, which until 1821, was punishable only by a fine, was then made a capital offence, the court for the trial of Negroes became more inclined to be just, the privileges of trading and hiring their time, although prohibited by law, became common, and some efforts were made to give the blacks religious instruction. At the same time the Negro suffered from reactionary measures restricting their emancipation, prohibiting free Negroes from entering the State, and proscribing their education. The author can see why the rich planters for financial reasons supported this system, but wonders why non-slaveholders who formed the majority of the white population, "should have assisted in upholding and maintaining the slavery status of the Negro with its attendant inconveniences, such a patrol service, when they must have been aware in some measure, at least, that as an economic regime it was a hindrance to their progress."

In this study the author found nothing "to indicate that there was any movement or any serious discussion of the advisability of abolishing slavery or devising any plan that would eventually lead to it." In that State there never were many anti-slavery inhabitants. The Quakers who came into the State soon left and the Germans who at first abstained from slavery, finally yielded. There probably was an academic deprecation of the evils of the institution but hardly any tendency toward agitation; and if there had been such, the promoters would not have secured support among the leading people. A few men like Judge O'Neall favored the emancipation of worthy slaves, but the agitation from without gave this sentiment no chance to grow. Yet the author is anxious not to leave the impression that, had it not been for outside interference, slavery in South Carolina would have been modified. This would not have happened, he contended, because unlike the States of North Carolina and Virginia, South Carolina did not find slaves less valuable. The condition of the slave in the upper country was better than that in the low-lands, but no section of the State showed signs of abolition.

This work is a well-documented dissertation. It has an appendix containing valuable documents, and a critical bibliography of the works consulted. It could have been improved by digesting documents which appear almost in full throughout the work. Another defect is that it has no index.

C. B. WALTER.

Gouldtown. By WILLIAM STEWARD, A.M., and REV. THEOPHILUS G. STEWARD, D.D.   J. B. Lippincott Co., Philadelphia, 1913. 237 pages. $2.50.

There are hundreds of thousands of mulattoes in the United States Anyone interested in this group of the American people will find many illuminating and suggestive facts in Gouldtown. It is the history of the descendants of Lord Fenwick, who was a major in Oliver Cromwell's army, and of Gould a Negro man. Fenwick's will of 1683 contains the following: ''I do except against Elizabeth Adams of having any ye leaste part of my estate, unless the Lord open her eyes to see her abdominable transgression against him, me and her good father, by giving her true repentance, and forsaking yt *Black* yt hath been ye ruin of her, and becoming penitent for her sins; upon yt condition only I do will and require my executors to settle five hundred acres of land upon her.'' Elizabeth did not forsake this Negro by the name of Gould and the remarkable mulatto group of Gouldtown is the result of this marriage. Gouldtown is a small settlement in southwest New Jersey.

In 1910 there were 225 living descendants from this union scattered throughout the United States from the Atlantic to the Pacific; many in Canada, others in London, Liverpool, Paris, Berlin and Antwerp. For over 200 years these descendants have married and inter-married with Indian, Negro and White with no serious detriment except the introduction of tuberculosis into one branch of the family by an infusion of white blood. It is interesting to note that crime, drunkenness, pauperism or sterility has not resulted from these two hundred years of miscegenation. Thrift and intelligence, longevity and fertility have been evident. In every war except the Mexican, the community has been represented; one member of the group became a bishop in the A. M. E. Church; one, chaplain in the United States army, and many, now white, are prominent in other walks of life. Several golden weddings have been celebrated. Several have reached the aged of a hundred years while many seem not to have begun to grow old until three score years have been reached.

If one enters into the spirit of Gouldtown, and reads hastily the dry, Isaac-begat-Jacob passages, the study moves like the story of a river that loses itself in the sands. ''Samuel 3rd. when a young man went to Pittsburgh then counted to be in the far west and all trace of him was lost.'' ''Daniel Gould . . . in early manhood went to Massachusetts, losing his identity as colored.'' Such expressions are typical of the whole study. A constant fading away, a losing identity occurs. The book is clearly the story of the mulatto in the United States.

Aside from an occasional lapse in diction, it is a careful study with 35 illustrations and many documents such as copies of deeds, wills, family-bible and death records.

WALTER DYSON.

NOTES

"*The Creed of the Old South*," by Basil Gildersleeve, has come from the Johns Hopkins Press. This is a presentation of the Lost Cause to enlarge the general appreciation of southern ideals.

From the same press comes also "*The Constitutional Doctrines of Justice Harlan*," by Floyd B. Clark. The author gives an interesting survey of the decisions of the Supreme Court of the United States, tracing the constitutional doctrine of the distinguished jurist.

The Neale Publishing Company has brought out "*The Aftermath of the Civil War in Arkansas*," by Powell Clayton. The author was governor of the State from 1868 to 1871. Not desiring to take radical ground, he endeavors to be moderate in sketching the work of different factions.

From the press of Funk Wagnalls we have "*Samuel Coleridge-Taylor; Musician, His Life and Letters*," by W. C. Berwick Sayres.

Dean B. G. Brawley, of Morehouse College, contributed to the January number of "*The South Atlantic Quarterly*," an article entitled, "*Pre-Raphaelitism and Its Literary Relations.*"

C. F. Heartman, New York, has published the poems of Jupiter Hammon, a slave born in Long Island, New York, about 1720. Nothing is known of Hammon's early life. It is probable that he was a preacher. His first poem was published December 25, 1760. They do not show any striking literary merit but give evidence of the mental development of the slave of the eighteenth century.

Dr. B. F. Riley, the noted Birmingham preacher and social worker, is planning to bring out a biography of Booker T. Washington. Dr. Riley is a white man and is the author of "*The White Man's Burden*," an historical and sociological work written in behalf of the rights of all humanity irrespective of class or condition.

Dr. C. G. Woodson has been asked to write for the revised edition of the "*Encyclopaedia Americana*" the article on "*Negro Education.*"

The Cambridge University Press has published "*The Northern Bantu*," by J. Roscoe. This is a short history of some central African tribes of the Uganda Protectorate.

J. A. Winter contributed to the July number of "*The South African Journal of Science*" a paper entitled "*The Mental and Moral Capabilities of the Natives, Especially of Sekukuniland.*"

In "*Folk Lore,*" September 30, 1915, appeared "*Some Algerian Superstitions noted among the Shawai Berbers of the Aurès Mountains and their Nomad Neighbors.*"

Murray has published in London "*A History of the Gold Coast and Ashanti*" in two volumes, by W. W. Claridge. The introduction is written by the Governor of the Gold Coast, Sir Hugh Clifford. It covers the period from the earliest times to the commencement of the present century. The volume commences with an account of the Akan tribes and their existence in two main branches —Fanti and Ashanti. Beginning with the early voyages, the author gives an extensive sketch of European discovery and settlement.

"*A History of South Africa from the Earliest Days to the Union,*" by W. C. Scully, has appeared under the imprint of Longmans, Green and Company.

Fisher Unwin has published "*South West Africa,*" by W. Eveleigh. The volume gives a brief account of the history, resources and possibilities of that country.

HOW THE PUBLIC RECEIVED THE JOURNAL OF NEGRO HISTORY

My dear Dr. Woodson:

I thank you cordially for sending me a copy of the first issue of THE JOURNAL OF NEGRO HISTORY. It is a real pleasure to see a journal of this kind, dignified in form and content, and conforming in every way to the highest standards of modern historical research. You and your colleagues are to be congratulated on beginning your enterprise with such promise, and you certainly have my very best wishes for the future success of an undertaking so significant for the history of Negro culture in America and the world.

I feel it a duty to assist concretely in work of this kind, and accordingly I enclose my check for sixteen dollars, of which fifteen dollars are in payment of a life membership fee in the Association for the Study of Negro Life and History, and one dollar for a year's subscription to the JOURNAL.

Very sincerely yours,

J. E. SPINGARN

Dear Dr. Woodson:

Thank you for sending me the first number of your QUARTERLY JOURNAL. Mr. Bowen had already loaned me his copy and I had been meaning to write to you, stating how much I liked the looks of the magazine, the page, the print, and how good the matter of this first number seemed to me to be. I am going to ask the library here to subscribe to it and I shall look over each number as it comes out. Enclosed is my cheque for five dollars which you can add to your research fund.

Very truly yours,

EDWARD CHANNING,
Mclean Professor of Ancient
and Modern History,
Harvard University

My dear Dr. Woodson:

No words of mine can express the delight with which I am reading the first copy of your JOURNAL, nor the supreme satisfaction I feel that such an organization as the Association for the Study of Negro Life and History is in actual and active existence.

Inclosed find check for sixteen dollars for one year's subscription to the JOURNAL and a life membership in the Association.

Very truly yours,

LEILA AMOS PENDLETON

Washington, D. C.

Dear Sir:

I have read with considerable interest Number I of THE JOURNAL OF NEGRO HISTORY. The enterprise seems to me to be an excellent one and deserving of enthusiastic support.

Yours sincerely,

A. A. GOLDENWEISER,

Department of Anthropology,

Columbia University

Dear Sir:

Last week I chanced to see a copy of THE JOURNAL OF NEGRO HISTORY, January number, and while I didn't have opportunity to read it fully, I was very favorably impressed with it; so much so that I am sending my check for one year's subscription, including the January number. Allow me to hope much success may attend this undertaking and that subsequent numbers be as elegant and attractive as this one. Yours very truly,

T. SPOTUAS BURWELL

Dear Sir:

I want to congratulate you on the appearance and contents of this first number. It has received most favorable comment from every one to whom I have shown it. I certainly wish it every success. Yours truly,

CAROLINE B. CHAPIN

Englewood, N. J.

Dear Mr. Woodson:

I have examined with more than usual interest the copy of THE JOURNAL OF NEGRO HISTORY which has just reached me through your courtesy. It certainly looks hopeful and I trust that the venture may prove its usefulness very quickly. I am sending you my check for a subscription as I shall be glad to receive subsequent issues.

Wishing you great success in your editorial position and hoping that the idea of the organization may be attained, I remain,

Yours very truly,

F. W. SHEPARDSON,

Professor of American History,

The University of Chicago

My dear Dr. Woodson:

I looked over the first number of THE JOURNAL OF NEGRO HISTORY with much interest. It bears every evidence of a scientific disposition on the part of the editor and his board.

Yours sincerely,

FERDINAND SCHEVILL,

Professor of European History,

The University of Chicago

My dear Dr. Woodson:

Your magazine is excellent. I am noting it in the current *Crisis.*

Very sincerely Yours,

W. E. B. DuBois,

Editor of the Crisis

My dear Dr. Woodson:

Enclosed find my check for $1 for one year's subscription to THE JOURNAL OF NEGRO HISTORY. I am enjoying the reading of the first issue and shall look forward with interest to the coming of each successive one.

With best wishes for the work, I am,

Very truly yours,

T. C. WILLIAMS,

Manassas, Va.

My dear Dr. Woodson:

I have read THE JOURNAL OF NEGRO HISTORY with pleasure, interest, profit and withal, amazement. The typographical appearance, the size and the strong scholastic historical articles reveal research capacity of the writers, breadth of learning and fine literary taste. Having been the editor of the *Voice of the Negro* and knowing somewhat of the literary capacity of the best writers of the race, I cannot but express satisfaction and amazement with this new venture under your leadership. I sincerely hope and even devoutly pray that this latest born from the brain of the Negro race may grow in influence and power, as it deserves, to vindicate for the thinkers of the race their claim to citizenship in the republic of thought and letters. Count upon me as a fellow worker.

Yours sincerely,

J. W. E. BOWEN

Vice-President of Gammon Theological Seminary

My dear Dr. Woodson:

I have examined with interest the first number of THE JOURNAL OF NEGRO HISTORY, which you so kindly sent me. It is a credit to

15

its editors and contributors and I hope it may continue to preserve high standards and to prosper.

Sincerely yours,
FREDERICK J. TURNER,
Professor of American History in Harvard University

My dear Dr. Woodson:

I am obliged to you for your copy of THE JOURNAL OF NEGRO HISTORY and am interested in knowing that you have undertaken this interesting work. I shall endeavor to see that it is ordered for our library. I should suppose that if you could manage to float it and keep it going for a few years, at least, that it would have considerable historical value.

Very sincerely yours,
A. C. McLAUGHLIN,
Head of the Department of American History, The University of Chicago

My dear Dr. Woodson:

Thank you for sending me the JOURNAL OF NEGRO HISTORY, which I have examined with interest and which I am calling to the attention of the Harvard Library. You have struck a good field of work, and I am sure you can achieve genuine results in it.

Sincerely yours,
CHARLES H. HASKINS,
Dean of the Harvard Graduate School

My dear Dr. Woodson:

Please accept my thanks for an initial copy of THE JOURNAL OF NEGRO HISTORY which you were kind enough to send me. I am delighted with it. Its mechanical makeup leaves nothing to be desired and its contents possess a permanent value. It should challenge the support of all forward-looking men of the race and command the respect of the thinking men of the entire country regardless of creed or color. I wish you the fullest measure of success in this unique undertaking.

Your friend,
J. W. SCOTT,
Principal of the Douglass High School, Huntington, W. Va.

My dear Mr. Woodson:

I wish to acknowledge the receipt of the first number of THE JOURNAL OF NEGRO HISTORY. I have read it with much interest and congratulate you, as the editor, upon your achievement. The more I think of the matter, the more do I believe there is a place for such a publication. The history of the Negro in Africa, in the West Indies, in Spanish America, and in the United States offers a large field in which little appears to have been done.

Very truly yours,
A. H. BUFFINTON,
Instructor in History, Williams College

My dear Sir:

A copy of THE JOURNAL OF NEGRO HISTORY was received yesterday and I wish to thank you and the gentlemen associated with you for this magnificent effort. There is ''class'' to this magazine, more ''class'' than I have seen in any of our race journals. May I say, notwithstanding the fact that I edited a race magazine once myself, the whole magazine is clean and high and deserves a place in our homes and college libraries alongside with the great periodicals of the land.

Yours very truly,
J. MAX BARBER

Dear Sirs:

Please find enclosed my subscription of one dollar in cash to THE JOURNAL OF NEGRO HISTORY, and permit me to congratulate you on your first publication.

Very truly yours,
OSWALD GARRISON VILLARD

Dear Sir:

The first number of your magazine reached me a few days ago. It is a fine publication, doing credit to its editor and to the association. I think it has a fine field.

Sincerely yours,
T. G. STEWARD,
Captain, U. S. Army, Retired

Dear Dr. Woodson:

I have the first number of THE JOURNAL OF NEGRO HISTORY. Permit me to congratulte you and to earnestly hope that it may live long and prosper. It is excellent in purpose, matter and method. If the present high standard is maintained, you and your friends will not only make a most valuable contribution to a dire need of the Negro, but you will add in a substantial measure to current historical data.   Truly yours,

D. S. S. GOODLOE,
Principal, Maryland Normal and Industrial School

"Why then, should the new year be signalized by the appearance of a magazine bearing the title THE JOURNAL OF NEGRO HISTORY? How can there be such a thing as history for a race which is just beginning to live? For the JOURNAL does not juggle with words; by 'history' it means history and not current events. The answer is to be found within its pages. . . ."

"But the outstanding feature of the new magazine is just the fact of its appearance. Launched at Chicago by a new organization, the Association for the Study of Negro Life and History, it does not intend 'to drift into the discussion of the Negro Problem,' but rather to 'popularize the movement of unearthing the Negro and his contributions to civilization . . . believing that facts properly set forth will speak for themselves.' "

"This is a new and stirring note in the advance of the black man. Comparatively few of any race have a broad or accurate knowledge of its part. It would be absurd to expect that the Negro will carry about in his head many details of a history from which he is separated by a tremendous break. It is not absurd to expect that he will gradually learn that he, too, has a heritage of something beside shame and wrong. By that knowledge he may be uplifted as he goes about his task of building from the bottom."

The New York Evening Post.

When men of any race begin to show pride in their own antecedents we have one of the surest signs of prosperity and rising civilization. That is one reason why the new JOURNAL OF NEGRO HISTORY ought to attract more than passing attention. Hitherto the history of the Negro race has been written chiefly by white men; now the educated Negroes of this country have decided to search out and tell the historic achievements of their race in their own way and from their own point of view. And, judging from the first issue of their new publication, they are going to do it in a way that will measure up to the standards set by the best historical publications of the day.

The opinions which the American Negro has hitherto held concerning his own race have been largely moulded for him by others. Himself he has given us little inkling of what his race has felt, and thought and done. Any such situation, if long enough continued, would make him a negligible factor in the intellectual life of mankind. But the educated leaders of the race, of whom our colleges and universities have been turning out hundreds in recent years, do not propose that this shall come to pass. They are going to show the Negro that his race is more ancient than the Golden Fleece or Roman Eagle; that Ethiopia had a history quite as illustrious as that of Nineveh or Tyre, and that the Negro may well take pride in the rock from which he was hewn. The few decades of slavery form but a small dark spot in the annals of long and great achievements. That embodies a fine attitude and one which should be thoroughly encouraged. It aims to teach the Negro that he can do his own race the best service by cultivating those hereditary racial traits which are worth preserving, and not by a fatuous imitation of his white neighbors.

At any rate, here is a historical journal of excellent scientific quality, planned and managed by Negro scholars for readers of their own race, and preaching the doctrine of racial self-consciousness. That in itself is a significant step forward.

The Boston Herald.

A new periodical, to be published quarterly, is the journal of "The Association for the Study of Negro Life and History," a society organized in Chicago in September, 1915. The commendable aim of the Association is to collect and publish historical and sociological material bearing on the Negro race. Its purpose, it is claimed, is not to drift into discussion of the Negro problem, but to publish facts which will show to posterity what the Negro has so far thought, felt, and done.

The president of the association, George C. Hall, of Chicago; its secretary-treasurer, Jesse E. Moorland, of Washington, D. C.; the editor of the JOURNAL, Carter G. Woodson, also of Washington; and the other names associated with them on the executive council and on the board of associate editors, guarantee an earnestness of purpose and a literary ability which will doubtless be able to maintain the high standard set in the first issue of the JOURNAL. The table of contents of the January number includes several historical articles of value, some sociological studies, and other contributions, all presented in dignified style and in a setting of excellent paper and type. The general style of the JOURNAL is the same as that of the *American Historical Review.*

The Southern Workman.

An undertaking which deserves a cordial welcome began in the publication, in January, of the first number of the *Journal of Negro History*, edited by Mr. Carter G. Woodson, and published at 2223 Twelfth Street, N. W., Washington, by the Association for the Study of Negro Life and History, formed at Chicago in September, 1915. The price is but $1 per annum. The objects of the Association and of the journal are admirable—not the discussion of the "negro problem," which is sure, through other means, of discussion ample in quantity at least, but to exhibit the facts of negro history, to save and publish the records of the black race, to make known by competent articles and by documents what the negro has thought and felt and done. The first number makes an excellent beginning, with an article by the editor on the Negroes of Cincinnati prior to the Civil War; one by W. B. Hartgrove on the career of Maria Louise Moore and Fannie M. Richards, mother and daughter, pioneers in negro education in Virginia and Detroit; one by Monroe N. Work, on ancient African civilization; and one by A. O. Stafford, on negro proverbs. The reprinting of a group of articles on slavery in the *American Museum* of 1788 by "Othello," a negro, and of selections from the *Baptist Annual Register*, 1790–1802, respecting negro Baptist churches, gives useful aid toward better knowledge of the American negro at the end of the eighteenth century.—*The American Historical Review.*

THE JOURNAL

OF

NEGRO HISTORY

VOL. I—JULY, 1916—No. 3

COLORED FREEMEN AS SLAVE OWNERS IN VIRGINIA[1]

Among the quaint old seventeenth century statutes of
Virginia may be found the following significant enactment:

No negro or Indian though baptized and enjoyned their own
ffreedome shall be capable of any purchase of Christians *but yet
not debarred from buying any of their owne nation.*[2]

"Christians" in this act means persons of the white race.
Indented servitude was the condition and status of no small
part of the white population of Virginia when this law was
enacted. While it is not a part of our purpose in this article
to show that white servants were ever bound in servitude to
colored masters, the inference from this prohibition upon
the property rights of the free Negroes is that colored freemen had at least attempted to acquire white or "Christian"
servants. In a revision of the law seventy-eight years later
it was deemed necessary to retain the prohibition and to
annex the provision that if any free Negro or mulatto "shall
nevertheless presume to purchase a Christian white servant,
such servant shall immediately become free."[3]

[1] Acknowledgments are due to the Johns Hopkins Press for permitting
the use in this article of data included in the author's monograph entitled
"The Free Negro in Virginia, 1619–1865."

[2] Hening's Statutes at Large of Virginia, Vol. II, p. 280 (1670). Italics
my own.

[3] Hening, Vol. V, p. 550.

If we see in these laws nothing more than precautionary measures against a possible reversal of the usual order of white master and black servant to that of black master and white servant, they are nevertheless significant as commentaries on the extent of the remaining unimpaired property rights of black freemen. Only in the light of these prohibitions do we see the full significance of the last clause of the act which reads: "but yet not debarred from buying any of their owne nation."

With no evidence beyond this explicit admission in the written law of the right of free Negroes to own servants and slaves of their own race it could scarcely be doubted that there were in the colony colored men known to the framers of this law who held to service persons of their own race and color. But when the court records are opened and the strange story of the free Negro Anthony Johnson and his slave John Casor is read and understood we are forced to a realization of the impartial attitude of the law toward black masters not only in its outward expression but also in its actual application. The story of the relation of these two black settlers in the young colony is worth relating in the quaint language of the times word for word as it appears in the manuscript records.

The deposition of Capt. Samll. Goldsmyth taken in open court 8th of March [16]54 sayeth that being att ye house of Anth. Johnson Negro about ye beginning of November last to receive a Hogsd of tobac, a negro called Jno. Casor came to this depo [nen]t & told him yt hee came into Virginia for seaven or eight years of Indenture; yt hee had demanded his freedome of Antho. Johnson his mayster & further sd yt hee had kept him his serv[ant] seaven years longer than hee should or ought; and desired that this Depont would see yt hee might have noe wronge; whereupon your depont demanded of Anth. Johnson his Indenture. the sd Johnson answered hee never saw any. The negro Jno. Casor replyed when hee came in he had an Indenture. Anth. Johnson sd hee had ye Negro for his life, but Mr. Robert & George Parker sd they knewe that ye sd Negro had an Indenture in one Mr. S[andys?] hand on ye other side of ye Baye. Further sd Mr. Robert Parker & his

Brother George sd (if the sd. Anth. Johnson did not let ye negro go free) the said negro Jno Casor would recover most of his Cows from him ye sd Johnson.   Then Anth. Johnson (as this dep't. did suppose) was in a great feare. . . . Anth. Johnsons sonne in Law, his wife & his own two sonnes persuaded the old negro Anth. Johnson to sett the sd. Jno. Casor free . . . more sth not.

SAMLL GOLDSMYTH.

Eight March Anno 1654.[4]

John Casor was not, however, permitted to enjoy long his freedom.   Johnson decided to petition the county court to determine whether John Casor was a slave for life or a servant "for seven years of indenture."   The court-record of the suit is as follows:

Whereas complaint was this daye made to ye court by ye humble peticion of Anth. Johnson Negro ag[ains]t Mr. Robert Parker that hee detayneth one John Casor a Negro the plaintiffs Serv[an]t under pretense yt the sd Jno. Casor is a freeman the court seriously considering & maturely weighing ye premises doe fynd that ye sd Mr. Robert Parker most unrightly keepeth ye sd Negro John Casor from his r[igh]t mayster Anth. Johnson as it appeareth by ye Deposition of Capt. Samll Gold smith & many probable circumstances.   be it therefore ye Judgement of ye court & ordered that ye sd Jno. Casor negro, shall forthwith bee turned into ye service of his sd master Anthony Johnson and that the sd Mr. Robert Parker make payment of all charges in the suite and execution.[5]

In thus sustaining the claim of Anth. Johnson to the perpetual service of John Casor the court gave judicial sanction to the right of Negroes to own slaves of their own race. Indeed no earlier record, to our knowledge, has been found of judicial support given to slavery in Virginia except as a punishment for crime.   Additional gleanings from the records show that this black slavemaster was a respected citizen of wealth and one of the very earliest Negro arrivals upon this continent, if, indeed, he was not one of the first

[4] Original MS. Records of the County Court of Northampton.   Orders, Deeds and Wills, 1651–1654, p. 20.

[5] Original MS. Records of the County Court of Northampton.   Orders, Deeds and Wills, 1651–1654, p. 10.

twenty brought in on the Dutch man-of-war in 1619. Every doubt of the correctness of this assertion should be banished by a perusal of the somewhat detailed evidence upon which the conclusion is based.

The discovery of the fact that Anthony Johnson was a slaveowner led to a further examination of court records and land patents for additional information concerning him. In the court records of Northampton County in 1653 it was found recorded that "Anth. Johnson negro hath this daye made his compl[ain]t to ye court that John Johnson, Senr. most unrightly detayneth a pattent of his for 450 acres of land (which pattent sd. Jno. Johnson negro claymeth & boldly affirmeth to bee his land."[6]

A search in the early land patents of the State revealed a grant by the authorities of the State of two hundred and fifty acres of land in Northampton County to Anthony Johnson a Negro. The grant was made as "head rights" upon the importation by the Negro of five persons into the colony.[7] Still pursuing the record of this black freeman, who was able to maintain a slave, the following was discovered in the records of the county court of Northampton:

Upon ye humble pet[ition] of Anth. Johnson negro & Mary his wife & their Information to ye Court that they have been Inhabitants in Virginia above thirty years, consideration being taken of their hard labor and honored service performed by the petitioners in this Country for ye obtayneing of their Livelyhood and ye great Llosse they have sustained by an unfortunate fire with their present charge to provide for. Be it therefore fitt and ordered that from the day of the debate hearof during their natural lives the sd Mary Johnson & two daughters of Anthony Johnson Negro be disingaged and freed from payment of Taxes and leavyes in Northampton County for public use.[8]

Subtracting thirty years from 1652, the date of this order of the court, it appeared that this Negro and his wife were in Virginia in 1622. Examination of a census taken in Vir-

6 Original MS. Records of Northampton Co., 1651-1654, p. 200.
7 MS. Land Patents of Virginia, 1643-1651, 326.
8 MS. Court Records of Northampton Co., 1651-1654, p. 161.

ginia after the Indian massacre of 1622 and called ''The
Lists of Living and Dead in Virginia'' revealed the fact that
there were only four Negroes in the colony beside the sur-
viving nineteen out of the twenty that came in in 1619. The
name of one of these four was Mary and the name of one of
the first twenty was Anthony.[9] It may with good reason be
surmised, if it cannot be proved, that Mary became the wife
of Anthony and that in the course of the next thirty years
they acquired the surname Johnson as well as a large tract
of land and a slave by the name of John Casor.

The Existence of Black Masters after Colonial Times

Some readers may be inclined to regard the case of the
slave John Casor as altogether exceptional and peculiar to
an early period in the growth of slavery before custom had
fully crystallized into law. It is true that similar examples
are hard to find in the seventeenth century when the free
Negroes were few in number. But if from the paucity of
examples it is argued that such a case was a freak of the
seventeenth century and that nothing similar could have
occurred after slavery became a settled and much regulated
institution, the answer is that slave-owning by free Negroes
was so common in the period of the Commonwealth as to
pass unnoticed and without criticism by those who con-
sciously recorded events of the times. For abundant proof
of the relation of black master and black slave we must refer
again to court records and legislative petitions from which
events and incidents were not omitted because of their common occurrence. Deeds of sale and transfer of slaves to
free Negroes, wills of free Negroes providing for a future
disposition of slaves, and records of suits for freedom
against free Negroes, all relate too well the story of how
black masters owned slaves of their own race, to require
additional proof.

The following record of the court of Henrico County
under date of 1795 is an example of what is to be found in
the records of any of the older counties of Virginia:

[9] J. C. Hotten, ''Lists of Emigrants to America,'' pp. 218–258.

Know all men by these presents that I, James Radford of the County of Henrico for and in consideration of the sum of thirty-three pounds current money of Virginia to me in hand paid by George Radford a black freeman of the city of Richmond hath bargained and sold unto George Radford one negro woman aggy, to have and to hold the said negro slave aggy unto the said George Radford his heirs and assigns forever.

JAMES RADFORD (seal)[10]

Judith Angus, a well-to-do free woman of color of Petersburg, was the owner of two household slaves. Before her death in 1832 she made a will which provided that the two slave girls should continue in the service of the family until they earned money enough to enable them to leave the State and thus secure their freedom according to law.[11]

From the records of the Hustings Court of Richmond may be gotten the account of a suit for freedom begun by Sarah, a slave, against Mary Quickly, a free black woman of the city. It is worthy of note that no claim was made by the plaintiff that Mary Quickly, being a black woman, had no right to own a slave. The grounds for the suit had no relation whatever to the race or color of the defendant, Mary Quickly.[12]

The only evidence at hand of the kind of relations that existed between black masters and their chattel slaves is supplied by the word of old men who remember events of the last two decades before the war. All that have been heard to speak of the matter are unanimously of the opinion that black masters had difficulty is subordinating and controlling their slaves. William Mundin, a mulatto barber of Richmond, seventy-five years of age, when interviewed, but still of trustworthy memory and character, is authority for the statement that Reuben West, a comparatively wealthy free colored barber of Richmond went into the slave market and purchased a slave cook, but because of the spirit of insub-

[10] MS. Deeds of Henrico County, No. 5, p. 585.
[11] MS. Legislative Petitions, Dinwiddie County, 1833, A 5123, Virginia State Library.
[12] Orders of the Hustings Court of Richmond, Vol. 5, p. 41.

ordination manifested by the slave woman toward him and his family he disposed of her by sale. James H. Hill, another free colored man to whose statements a good degree of credence is due, corroborates in many points this story about Reuben West as a slaveowner. His statement is that Reuben West was a free colored barber of some wealth and the owner at one time of two slaves, one of whom was a barber working in his master's shop on Main Street. So much of these statements has been confirmed by reference to tax books and court records that the entire story may be accepted as true.

A Truly Benevolent Slavery

The type of black master represented by Reuben West or Anthony Johnson must be distinguished from the colored slaveowner who kept his slaves in bondage, not for their service, but wholly in consideration of the slaves. A very considerable majority of black masters, unlike the examples above cited, were easily the most benevolent known to history. It was owing to a drastic state policy toward freedmen that this unusually benevolent type of slavery arose.

During the last quarter of the eighteenth century slaveowners in Virginia possessed unrestricted powers to bestow freedom upon their slaves. Under such circumstances free blacks became instrumental in procuring freedom for many of their less fortunate kinsmen. They frequently advanced for a slave friend the price at which his white master held him for sale and, having liberated him, trusted him to refund the price of his freedom. A free member of a colored family would purchase whenever able his slave relatives. The following deed of sale is a striking example of such a purchase:

Know all men of these presents that I David A. Jones of Amelia County of the one part have for and in consideration of the sum of five hundred dollars granted unto Frank Gromes a black man of the other part a negro woman named Patience and two children by name Phil and Betsy to have and to hold the above named negroes to the only proper use, behalf and benefit of him and his heirs forever.

DAVID JONES (seal)[13]

Phil Cooper, of Gloucester County, in 1828 was the chattel slave of his free wife. Janette Wood of Richmond was manumitted in 1795 by her mother, "natural love" being the only consideration named in the legal instrument. John Sabb, of Richmond, purchased in 1801 his aged father-in-law Julius and for the nominal consideration of five shillings executed a deed of manumission.[14]

Purchases of this kind before 1806 were usually followed immediately by manumission of the slave. Scattered through the deeds and wills of Virginia County records in the quarter century ending with 1806 are to be found numerous documents of which the following is an example:

> To all whom these presents may come know ye, that I Peter Hawkins a free black man of the city of Richmond having purchased my wife Rose, a slave about twenty-two years of age and by her have had a child called Mary now about 18 mo. old, for the love I bear toward my wife and child have thought proper to emancipate them and for the further consideration of five shillings to me in hand paid . . . I emancipate and set free the said Rose and Mary and relinquish all my right . . . as slaves to the said Rose and Mary.

PETER HAWKINS (seal)[15]

Indeed the kindness of free Negroes toward their friends and relatives seeking freedom afforded such an accessible avenue to liberty that those vigilant white citizens who desired to preserve the institution of slavery deemed it necessary to put obstructions in the way. A law which required any slave manumitted after May 1, 1806 to leave the State within the space of twelve months was passed in 1806 and remained in force until the war rendered it obsolete. Forfeiture of freedom was the penalty for refusal to accept

[13] MS. Deeds of Henrico County, No. 4, p. 692.
[14] MS. Deeds of Henrico County, No. 6, p. 274.
[15] MS. Deeds of Henrico County, No. 6, p. 78.

banishment. From this act dates the beginning of this benevolent type of slavery. Free Negroes continued to purchase their relatives but held them as slaves, refusing to decree their banishment by executing a deed or will of manumission.

A pathetic example of this kind was the case of Negro Daniel Webster of Prince William County. At the age of sixty when an illness forced him to the conclusion that life was short, he sent a petition to the legislature saying that he had thus far avoided the evil consequences of the law of 1806 by retaining his family in nominal slavery but that then he face the alternative of manumitting his family to see it disrupted and banished or of holding his slave family together till his death, when its members like other property belonging to his estate would be sold as slaves to masters of a different type. He begged that exception be made to the law of 1806 in the case of his wife and children so that he might feel at liberty to manumit them.[16]

A similar petition to the Legislature in 1839 by Ermana, a slave woman, stated that her husband and owner had been a free man of color, that he had died intestate and that she, her children and her property had escheated to the literary fund. Scores of similar petitions to the Legislature for special acts of relief tell the story of how black men and women who owned members of their families neglected too long to remove from them the status of property.

A case more amusing than pathetic was that of Betsy Fuller, a free Negro huckstress of Norfolk and her slave husband. The colored man's legal status was that of property belonging to his wife. Upon the approach of the Civil War he was blatant in his advocacy of Southern views, thus evincing his indifference to emancipation.[17]

Feeble efforts were made by the legislature for a score of years before the war to limit the power of free Negroes to acquire slaves for profit. By an act of 1832 free Negroes

[16] MS. Legislative Petitions, Prince William Co., 1812, Virginia State Library.
[17] *Lower Norfolk County Antiquary*, Vol. IV, p. 177.

were declared incapable of purchasing or otherwise acquiring permanent ownership, except by descent, of any slaves other than husband, wife, and children. Contracts for the sale of a slave to a black man were to be regarded as void.[18] But even this attempt at limitation was passed by a bare majority of one.[19] Within three years of the beginning of the War the law was revised to read: "No free negro shall be capable of acquiring, except by descent, any slave."[20] In the opinion of a judge who passed upon this law, its object was "to keep slaves as far as possible under the control of white men only, and to prevent free negroes from holding persons of their own race in personal subjection to themselves. Perhaps also it is intended to evince the distinctive superiority of the white race."[21]

Whatever may have been their object these acts are of more significance because of the story they tell than they ever were in accomplishing the emancipation of slaves from masters of the black race. The period of the existence of the black master was conterminous with the period of the existence of slavery. By the same immortal proclamation which broke the shackles of slaves serving white masters were rent asunder, also, the bonds which held slaves to masters of their own race and color.

JOHN H. RUSSELL, PH.D.,

(Professor of Political Science, Whitman College, Walla Walla, Washington.)

[18] Acts of Assembly, 1831–1832, p. 20.
[19] Senate Journal, 1832, p. 176.
[20] Acts of Assembly, 1857–1858.
[21] Grattan's Reports, Vol. 14, p. 260.

THE FUGITIVES OF THE PEARL

The traditional history of the Negro in America, during nearly three hundred years, is one in which the elements of pathos, humor and tragedy are thoroughly mixed and in which the experiences encountered are of a kind to grip the hearts and consciences of men of every race and every creed. Just as colonial Americans resented their enforced enlistment for maritime service under the flag of King George, so it may be assumed that with equal vigor did the little band of Africans object to a forced expatriation from their native wilds, even though, as it happened, they were destined to be, in part, the builders of a great and prosperous nation and the progenitors of a strong and forward-looking race.

There are few incidents that distinguish the bondage of the descendants of that first boat load of involuntary African explorers, that evince, in so large a degree the elements alluded to, as do those which cluster about the story of the "Edmondson Children." There were altogether fourteen sons and daughters of Paul and Amelia who passed as devoutly pious and respectable old folks. Paul was a freeman who hired his time in the city. Amelia was a slave. Their little cabin, a few miles out of the city of Washington proper, was so neat and orderly that it was regarded as a model for masters and slaves alike for many miles around. They were thus permitted to live together by the owners of Amelia, who realized how much more valuable the children would be as a marketable group after some years of such care and attention as the mother would be sure to bestow. Milly, as she was familiarly called, reared the children, tilled the garden, and, being especially handy with the needle, turned off many a job of sewing for the family of her mistress. She was entirely ignorant so far as books go, but Paul read the Bible to her when visiting his loved ones

243

on Sunday and what he explained she remembered and treasured up for comfort in her moments of despair.

The older boys and girls were hired out in prominent families in the city and by their intelligence, orderly conduct and other evidences of good breeding came to be known far and wide as "The Edmondson Children," the phrase being taken as descriptive of all that was excellent and desirable in a slave. The one incurable grief of these humble parents was that in bringing children into the world they were helping to perpetuate the institution of slavery. The fear that any day might bring to them the cruel pangs of separation and the terrible knowledge that their loved ones had been condemned to the horrors of the auction block was with them always a constant shadow, darkening each waking moment. More and ever more, they were torn with anxiety for the future of the children and so they threw themselves with increasing faith and dependence upon the Master of all, and no visit of the children was so hurried or full of other matters but that a few moments were reserved for prayer. At their departure, one after another was clasped to the mother's breast and always this earnest admonition followed them, "Be good children and the blessed Lord will take care of you." Louisa and Joseph, the two youngest, were still at home when there occurred events in which several of their older brothers and sisters took so prominent a part and which are here to be related.

The incidents of this narrative which are reflected in its title are contemporary with and in a measure resultant from the revolution out of which came the establishment of the first French Republic and the expulsion of Louis-Philippe in 1848. The citizens of the United States were felicitating their brothers across the water upon the achievement of so desirable a result. In Washington especially, the event was joyously acclaimed. Public meetings were held at which representatives of the people in both houses of Congress spoke encouragingly of the recent advance toward universal liberty. The city was regally adorned with flags and bunting and illumination and music everywhere. The

White House was elaborately decorated in honor of the event and its general observance, scheduled for April 13. A procession of national dignitaries, local organizations and the civic authorities, accompanied by several bands of music and throngs of citizens, made its way to the open square (now Lafayette Park) opposite the White House. Speeches were in order. Among the addresses which aroused the large crowd to enthusiasm were those of Senator Patterson of Tennessee and Senator Foote of Mississippi.[1] The former likened the Tree of Liberty to the great cotton-wood tree of his section, whose seed is blown far and wide, while the latter spoke eloquently of the universal emancipation of man and the approaching recognition in all countries of the great principles of equality and brotherhood.

Here and there huddled unobtrusively in groups on the fringe of the crowd were numbers of slaves. The enthusiasm of the throng, frequently manifested in shouts of approval, was discreetly reflected in the suppressed excitement of the slaves, who whispered among themselves concerning the curious and incredible expressions they had heard. Could it possibly be that these splendid truths, this forecast of universal liberty, might include them too? A few of the more intelligent, among whom was Samuel Edmondson, drew together to discuss the event and were not long concluding that the authority they had listened to could not be questioned and that they should at once contribute their share towards so desirable a consummation.

Coincident with this celebration there had arrived at Washington the schooner *Pearl* with Daniel Drayton[2] as

[1] *The Washington Union*, April 14, 1848.

[2] Daniel Drayton was a native of New Jersey who had spent several years following the water. He had risen from cook to captain in the wood-carrying business from the Maurice River to Philadelphia. Eventually he engaged in coast traffic from Philadelphia southward. He seemed to have drifted quite naturally from strong humane impulses, intensified by an old-time spiritual conversion, into a settled conviction that the fatherhood of God and the brotherhood of man was a reality and that it was his duty to do what he could to assist those in bondage.

Latterly his voyages had carried him into the Chesapeake Bay and thence up the Potomac. His first successful effort to assist the slaves was made on an

super-cargo, Captain Sayres, owner, and a young man, Chester English, as sailor and cook. Drayton witnessed the great demonstration near the White House and, as might have been expected, the sentiment that seemed to have won all Washington found a natural and active response, for when the news of the purpose of his visit was communicated by the woman for whose deliverance he had agreed to make the trip, he was appealed to on behalf of others and consented to take all who should be aboard by ten o'clock that night.

The Edmondson boys actively promoted the scheme and, rightly in so just a cause, abused the privileges which their integrity and unusual intelligence had won for them. The news was passed to an aggregate of 77 persons, all of whom faithfully appeared and were safely stowed away between decks before midnight. Samuel sought his sisters Emily and Mary at their places of employment and acquainted them with his purpose. They at first hesitated on account of the necessity of leaving without seeing their mother, but were soon persuaded that it was an opportunity they should not be willing to neglect.

The *Pearl* cast free from her moorings shortly after midnight Saturday and silently, with no sign of life aboard, save running lights fore and aft, crept out to mid-stream and made a course towards the lower Potomac. The condition that obtained on Sunday morning after the discovery of the absence of so many slaves from their usual duties may be accurately described as approaching a panic. Had the evidences of a dreadful plague become as suddenly manifest, the community could not have experienced a greater sense of horror or for the moment been more thoroughly paralyzed. A hundred or more families were affected

earlier trip when he agreed to take away a woman and five children. The husband was already a free man. The woman had under an agreement with her master more than paid for her liberty, but when she had asked for a settlement, he had only answered by threatening to sell her. The mother and five children were taken aboard at night and after ten days were safely delivered at Frenchtown, where the husband was in waiting for them. Memoir of Daniel Drayton, Congressional Library.

through the action of these seventy and seven slaves and the stern proofs of their flight were many times multiplied.

The action of the masters in this emergency is eloquent testimony that the fine orations of two days before concerning the spread of liberty and universal brotherhood had been nothing more than so many meaningless conversations. When confronted on Sunday morning with the fact that theirs and their neighbors' slaves, in so great numbers, had disappeared during the night, the realization of the difference between popular enthusiasm for a sentiment and a real sacrifice for a principle, was borne in upon them and they found that while they enjoyed the former they were not at all ready to espouse the latter.

As a result the day was but little advanced when an excited cavalcade of the masters, after scouring every portion of the city, broke for the open country to the North, designing to cover each of the roads leading from the city. They had not reached the District limits, however, when they whirled about and galloped furiously in the opposite direction and never checked rein, until panting and foaming, their horses were brought up at the wharves. A vessel was chartered and steamed away almost immediately on its mission to capture the party of runaway slaves.

Fate, which occasionally plays such strange and cruel tricks in the lives of men, presented in this instance a Machiavellian combination of opposing forces, that was disastrous to the enterprise of the fugitives. Judson Diggs,[3] one of their own people, a man who in all reason might have been expected to sympathize with their effort, took upon himself the rôle of Judas. Judson was a drayman and had hauled

[3] The only punishment meted out to Judson Diggs for his act of betrayal, so far as is known, was that by a party of young men who, shortly after the occurrence, took him from his cart and after considerable rough handling, threw him into the little stream that in those days and indeed for many years thereafter, took its way along the north side of the old John Wesley Church, then located at a spot directly opposite the north corner of the Convent of the Sacred Heart on Connecticut Avenue, between L and M Streets.

A number of old citizens now living distinctly remember Judson Diggs, who lived, despised and avoided, until late in the sixties. One of these is Mr. Jerome A. Johnson of the Treasury Department.

some packages to the wharf for one of the slaves, who was without funds to pay the charge, and although he was solemnly promised that the money should be sent him, he proceeded at once to wreak vengeance through a betrayal of the entire party.

Even so, it would seem they might have had an excellent chance to escape, but for the adverse winds and tides which set against them towards the close of Sunday. They were approaching the open waters of the Bay and the little vessel was already pitching and tossing as from the lashing of a gale. The captain decided that it was the part of prudence to remain within the more quiet waters of the Potomac for the night and make the open sea by light of day. Under these circumstances they put into Cornfield Harbor and here in the quiet hours before midnight the pursuing masters found them.

It is difficult to realize the consternation felt by the fugitives when the noise of tramping feet and the voices of angry men broke upon their ears. They seemed to realize at once that they were lost and many gave themselves up to shrieks and tears until wise council prevailed. Captain Drayton and his mate were immediately the storm center of the infuriated masters, many of whom were loud in the demand that summary vengeance be wreaked upon them and that these two at least should be hung from the yard arm. It was easily possible that this demand might have been acceded to, had not a diversion been caused by some of the others who were anxious to locate the slaves.

To satisfy themselves as to their safety they proceeded to break open the hatchways when, so suddenly as to create something of a panic, Richard Edmondson bounded on deck and in a voice of suppressed excitement exclaimed, ''Do yourselves no harm, gentlemen, for we are all here!'' Richard was young, muscular and of splendid proportions and seeing him thus by the poor light of smoky lanterns, with flashing eyes and swinging arms, leaping into their midst with an unknown number of others following, some of the masters experienced a feeling of terror, and dropping their guns, scurried away to safety among the dark shadows of the vessel.

By the time the others reached the deck, the shock of Richard's strange appearance had somewhat died away and when Samuel, who was one of the last, appeared, a sharp blow which, but for a sudden lurch of the vessel, would have laid him low fell on one side of his head. Drayton and Sayres,[4] who were witnesses of this incident, were horrified to think that, having not so much as a penknife with which to defend themselves, these poor creatures might be brutally murdered, and, notwithstanding the serious aspect of their own fortunes,[5] protested vigorously against such violence. But for this timely interference, there is but little doubt that some of these poor people would have been cruelly if not fatally injured.

The true condition of affairs, however, was speedily recognized and seeing there was nothing to fear in the way of resistance, order was soon evolved out of the general chaos and then came the decision to make an early start on the return trip. Among the slaves, the reaction from a feeling of hope and joyous anticipation of the delights of freedom was terrible indeed. The bitter gall and wormwood of failure was the sad and gloomy portion of these seventy and seven souls. Among them then there were but few who were not completely crushed, their minds a seething torrent, in which regret, misery and despair made battle for the mastery. Children weeping and wailing clung to the skirts of their elders. The women with shrieks, groans and tearful lamen-

[4] Memoir of Daniel Drayton, Congressional Library.

[5] The case against Drayton and Sayres was prosecuted by Philip Barton Key, the District Attorney, before Judge Crawford, and on appeal the prisoners were sentenced to pay a fine of $10,000 and to remain in jail until the same should be paid.

English was absolved from all criminal responsibility and given his liberty.

After an imprisonment of more than four years they were pardoned by President Filmore, to whom such application had been presented by Charles Sumner.—Memoir of Daniel Drayton.

The fare at the jail was insufficient and of poor quality and a more wholesome and generous diet was frequently surreptitiously furnished by Susannah Ford, a colored woman, who sold lunches in the lobby of the Court House.

tations deplored their sad fate, while the men, securely chained wrist and wrist together, stood with heads dropped forward, too dazed and wretched for aught but to turn their stony gaze within upon the wild anguish of their aching hearts.

Their arrival at Washington was signalized by a demonstration vastly different but little short of that which had taken place a few days before. The wharves were alive with an eager and excited throng all intent upon a view of the miserable folks who had been guilty of so ungrateful an effort. So disorderly was the mob that the debarkation was for some time delayed. This was finally accomplished through the strenuous efforts of the entire constabulary of the city.

The utmost watchfulness and care was, however, unavailing to prevent assaults. The most serious instance of this kind was the act of an Irish ruffian, who so far forgot the traditions and sufferings of his own people as to cast himself upon Drayton with a huge dirk and cut off a piece of his ear.[6] For a few moments all the horrors incident to riot and bloodshed were in evidence. The air was filled with the screams of terrorized women and children and the curses and threats of vengeful men. The whole was a struggling, swaying mass, which for a season had been swept beyond itself by brutish passion.

Numerous arrests were made and in due course the march to the jail was begun with the accompanying crowd hurling taunts and jeers at every step. While they were proceeding thus, an onlooker said to Emily, "Aren't you ashamed to run away and make all this trouble for everybody?" To this she replied, "No sir, we are not and if we had to go through it again, we'd do the same thing."

The controversy that was precipitated through the attempted escape, between the advance guard of abolition and the defenders of slavery, was most bitter and violent. The storm broke furiously about the offices of *The National Era*. In Congress, Mr. Giddings of Ohio moved an "inquiry into

6 Stowe, "Key to Uncle Tom's Cabin."

the cause of the detention at the District jail of persons merely for attempting to vindicate their inalienable rights.'' Senator Hale of New Hampshire moved a resolution of ''inquiry into the necessity for additional laws for the protection of property in the District.'''[7] A committee consisting of such notable characters as the Channings, Samuel May, Samuel Howe, Richard Hildreth, Samuel Sewell and Robert Morris Jr., was formed at Boston to furnish aid and defense for Drayton. These men were empowered to employ counsel and collect money. Horace Mann, Wm. H. Seward, Salmon P. Chase and Fessenden of Maine volunteered to serve gratuitously.[8]

Other philanthropists directed their attention to the liberation of these slaves. The Edmondsons were owned by an estate. The administrator, who was approached by John Brent,[9] the husband of the oldest sister of the children, agreed to give their friends an opportunity to effect their purchase, as he was unwilling to run any further risk by keeping them. He failed to keep this promise and when Mr. Brent went to see them the next day he was informed that they had been sold to Bruin and Hill, the slave-dealers of Alexandria and Baltimore and had been sent to the former city. A cash sum of $4,500 had been accepted for the six children and when taxed with the failure to keep his promise, he simply said he was unwilling to take any further risk with them. Bruin also refused to listen to any proposals, saying he had long had his eyes on the family and could get twice what he paid for them in the New Orleans market.

[7] *The National Era*, April 16, 1848.
[8] Memoir of Daniel Drayton.
[9] John Brent, the husband of Elizabeth, the oldest of the Edmondson girls, had first bought himself, earning the money chiefly by sawing wood; had then bought the freedom of his father, Elton Brent, for whom he paid $800, and finally bought Elizabeth's freedom, after which they were married. He purchased the ground at the southwest corner of 18th and L streets, now owned by his heirs, and erected a small frame dwelling. This was later enlarged and there the John Wesley A. M. E. Zion Church was established. He was a laborer in the War Department during forty years and died in 1885.—From interviews with Mr. Brent and other members of the family.

They were first taken to the slave pens at Alexandria, where they remained nearly a month. Here the girls were required to do the washing for a dozen or more men with the assistance of their brothers and were at length put aboard a steamboat and taken to Baltimore where they remained three weeks. Through the exertions of friends at Washington, $900 was given towards their freedom by a grandson of John Jacob Astor, and this was appropriated towards the ransom of Richard, as his wife and children were said to be ill and suffering at Washington. The money arrived on the morning they were to sail for New Orleans but they had all been put aboard the brig *Union,* which was ready to sail, and the trader refused to allow Richard to be taken off. The voyage to New Orleans covered a period of seven days, during which much discomfort and suffering were experienced. There were eleven women in the party, all of whom were forced to live in one small apartment and the men numbering thirty-five or forty, in another not much larger. Most of them being unaccustomed to travel by water were afflicted with all the horrors of sea-sickness. Emily's suffering from this cause was most pitiable and so serious was her condition at one time that the boys feared she would die. The brothers, however, as in all circumstances, were very kind and would tenderly carry her out on deck whenever the heat in their close quarters became too oppressive and would buy little comforts that were in their reach and minister in all possible ways to her relief.

In due course they arrived at New Orleans and were immediately initiated into the horrors of a Georgia pen. The girls were required to spend much time in the show room, where purchasers came to examine them carefully with a view to buying them. On one occasion a youthful dandy had applied for a young person whom he wished to install as housekeeper and the trader decided that Emily would just about meet the requirements, but when he called her she was found to be indulging in a fit of weeping. The youth, therefore, refused to consider her, saying that he had no room for the snuffles in his house. The loss of this transaction so incensed the trader, who said he had been offered $1,500 for the proper person, that he slapped Emily's face and threatened to send her to the calaboose, if he found her crying again.

Here also the boys had their hair closely cropped and their clothes, which were of good material, exchanged for suits of blue-jeans. Appearing thus, they were daily exhibited on the porch for sale. Richard, who was in reality free, as his purchase money was on deposit in Baltimore, was allowed to come and go at will and early bent his energies toward the discovery of their elder brother Hamilton,[10] who was living somewhere in the city. His quest was soon rewarded with success and one day to the delight of his sisters and brothers he brought him to see them. Hamilton had never seen Emily, as he had been sold away from his parents before her birth, but his joy, though mingled with sorrow, could not be suppressed. He was soon busy with plans for the increase of their meager comforts. Finding upon inquiry that Hamilton was thoroughly responsible, the trader consented to the girls' spending their nights at their brother's home. He was also at pains to secure good homes for the unfortunate group and was successful in inducing a wealthy Englishman to purchase his brother Samuel.

In consequence of an epidemic of yellow fever, which increased in virulence from day to day, the traders decided to bring the slaves North without further delay and so a few days later they were reembarked on the brig *Union* with Baltimore as their destination. Samuel was the only one of the brothers and sisters left behind. As he was pleasently situated with humane and kindly owners, the parting from him was not so sad as otherwise it might have been. Sixteen days were required for the trip and upon their arrival they were again placed in the same old prison. Richard was almost immediately freed and, in company with

10 Hamilton Edmondson was sold in the New Orleans slave market about the year 1840 and took the name of his purchaser and was thereafter known as Hamilton Taylor. He learned the trade of cooper and was allowed a percentage of his earnings, but was unfortunate in having his first savings stolen. He eventually acquired his freedom through the payment of $1,000.

a Mr. Bigelow, of Washington, was enabled to rejoin his wife and children.

Paul Edmondson visited his children at the Baltimore jail in company with their sister.[11] He had been encouraged to hope that in some way a fund might be raised for their ransom, but it was not until some weeks later, after they had been returned through Washington and again placed in their old slave quarters at Alexandria, that an understanding as to terms could be had with Bruin and Hill. They finally agreed to accept $2,250 if the amount was raised within a certain time and gave Paul a signed statement of the terms, which might be used as his credentials in the matter of soliciting assistance. Armed with this document, he arrived at New York and found his way to the Anti-Slavery office, where the price demanded was considered so exorbitant that but little encouragement was given him. From here he went to the home of Rev. Henry Ward Beecher, where he arrived foot-sore and weary. After ringing the bell, he sat upon the doorstep weeping. Here Mr. Beecher found him and, taking him into his library, inquired his story.

As a result there followed a public meeting in Mr. Beecher's Brooklyn church, at which he pleaded passionately as if for his own children, while other clergymen spoke with equal interest and feeling. The money was raised, an agent appointed to consummate the ransom of the children, and Paul, with a sense of happiness and relief to which he had long been a stranger, started with the good news on his way homeward.

Meanwhile the girls were torn with doubt and anxiety as to the success of their father's mission. Several weeks had elapsed and the traders were again getting together a coffle of slaves for shipment to the slave market, this time to

[11] He continued in the cooperage business, was highly respected and became comparatively wealthy, having a place of business on Girard near Camp street. John S. Brent, who is his nephew and the son of the John Brent heretofore mentioned in this narrative, spent a week with his uncle, Hamilton Taylor, in 1865, on his return from Texas, when, as a member of the Fifth Massachusetts Cavalry, he was mustered out of the service.—Interview with John S. Brent.

that in South Carolina. The girls too, had been ordered to be in readiness and the evening before had broken down in tears when Bruin's young daughter, who was a favorite with the girls, sought them out and pleaded with them not to go. Emily told her to persuade her father not to send them and so she did, while clinging around his neck until he had not the heart to refuse.

A day or two later, while looking from their window, they caught sight of their father and ran into his arms shouting and crying. So great was their joy that they did not notice their father's companion, a Mr. Chaplin, the agent appointed at the New York meeting to take charge of the details of their ransom. These were soon completed, their free papers signed and the money paid over. Bruin, too, it is said, was pleased with the joy and happiness in evidence on every hand and upon bidding the girls good-bye gave each a five dollar gold piece.

Upon their arrival at Washington they were taken in a carriage to their sister's home, whence the news of their deliverance seemed to have penetrated to every corner of the neighborhood with the result that it was far into the night before the last greetings and congratulations had been received and they were permitted, in the seclusion of the family circle, to kneel with their parents in prayer and thanksgiving.[12]

[12] The fame of the Edmondson children through the incident of the *Pearl* was now wide indeed, and after the Brooklyn meeting there had been made many suggestions looking to their education and further benefit. The movement for the education of Emily and Mary was crystallized into a definite proposition and they were both placed in a private school a short distance out of New York. Miss Myrtilla Miner had already established her school for girls at Washington and had moved to a new location at about what is now the square bounded by 19th, 20th, N and O streets. Here, after returning from New York, Emily assisted Miss Miner in the school and it was in one of the little cabins on this place that the Edmondson family established their home after moving in from the country. Miss Miner, speaking of the establishment of her school at its new location, says: "Emily and I lived here alone, unprotected except by God, the rowdies occasionally stoning the house at evening and we nightly retired in the expectation that the house would be fired before morning. Emily and I have been seen practicing shooting with a pistol."— Myrtilla Miner, "A Memoir," Congressional Library; "Key to Uncle Tom's Cabin."

In the meantime what had become of Samuel? When Hamilton Edmondson was seeking to locate his sisters and brothers in desirable homes in New Orleans, he first saw Mr. Horace Cammack, a prosperous cotton merchant, whose friendship and respect he had long since won and who, upon the further representation of Samuel's proficiency as a butler, agreed to purchase him. In this wise, it came to pass that Samuel was duly installed as upper houseman in the Cammack home. Although situated more happily than most slaves he was fully determined, as ever, that the world should one day know and respect him as a free man, and patiently waited and watched for the opportunity to accomplish his purpose.

Meanwhile another element had thrust itself into the equation and must be reckoned with in the solution of the problem of his after life. It happened that Mrs. Cammack, a lady of much beauty and refinement of manner, had in her employ as maid, a young girl of not more than eighteen years named Delia Taylor. She was tall, graceful and winsome, of the clear mulatto type, and through long service in close contact with her mistress, had acquired that refinement and culture, which elicit the admiration and delight of those in like station and inspire a feeling much akin to reverence in those more lowly placed. With some difficulty Samuel approached her with a proposal and, although at first refused, finally won her as his bride.

Matters now moved along on pleasant lines for Samuel

The parents of the children, however, were not yet entirely relieved of the fears that had so long haunted them, for there were still the two youngest children, Louisa and Joseph, whom the good mother frequently alluded to as "the last two drops of blood in her heart," and although she had scarcely ever seen a railroad train, she determined to go to New York herself to see what could be done and to thank the good people who had already brought so much of happiness to herself and family. While the mother was in that city the girls were brought to see her and in later years she often delighted to tell of their happy meeting and of the good white folks who were brought together to hear her story. She returned to Washington at the end of a week, carrying the assurance that the money would be provided for the redemption of the last two of her children.

Mrs. Louisa Joy, the last of the "Edmondson Children," died only a short while ago.

and Delia during several months, but with the advent of Master Tom, Cammack's son who had been away to college, there was encountered an element of discord, which was for a while to destroy their happiness. This young gentleman took a violent dislike to Samuel from the very first meal the latter served him. They finally clashed and Samuel had to run away. His master, however, sent his would-be-oppressor with the rest of the family to the country and ordered Samuel to return home. This he did and immediately entered upon his duties.

The year following, Mr. Cammack went to Europe on cotton business and not long after his arrival was killed in a violent storm while yachting with friends off the coast of Norway. After this event, affairs in the life of Samuel gradually approached a crisis, while in the meantime an additional responsibility had been added to himself and Delia in the person of a little boy, whom they named David.

Master Tom, being now the head of the house, left little room for doubt as to the authority he had inherited and proceeded to evince the same in no uncertain way, especially towards those against whom he held a grievance. To get rid of Samuel was first in order. This was the easiest possible matter, for there was not a wealthy family on the visiting list of the Cammacks who would not, even at some sacrifice, make a place for him in their service. Through the close intimacy of Mrs. Cammack and Mrs. Slidell, the latter was given the refusal and Samuel told to go around and see his future Mistress. To her he expressed a desire to serve in her employ but he was now determined more than ever that his next master should be himself. Accordingly he proceeded directly to a friend from whom he purchased a set of free-papers, which had been made out and sold him by a white man. These required that he should start immediately up the river but upon a full consideration of the matter he decided that the risks were too great in that direction. The problem was a serious one. An error of judgment, a step in the wrong direction, would not only be a serious, if not fatal blow to his hopes, but might lead to untold hardships to others most dear to him.

Somewhat irresolutely he turned his steps towards the river front, gazing with longing eyes at the stretch of water, the many ships in harbor, some entering, others steaming away or being towed out to open water. The thought that in this direction, beyond the wide seas, lay his refuge and ultimate hope came to him with so much force as to cause him to reel like one on whom a severe blow had been dealt. He stood for some time, seemingly bewildered, in the din and noise of the wharf, noting abstractedly the many bales of cotton, as truck after truck-load was rushed aboard an outward bound steamer. The bales seemed to fascinate him completely. A stevedore yelled at him to move out of the way and aroused him into action, but in that interval an idea which seemed to offer a possible means of escape had been evolved. He would impersonate a merchant from the West Indies in search of a missing bale of goods and endeavor to get passage to the Islands, where he well knew the flag of free England was abundant guarantee for his protection. The main thought seemed a happy one, for he soon found a merchantman that was to clear that night for Jamaica. It was not a passenger vessel, but the captain, a good-natured Briton, said that he had an extra bunk in the cabin and if the gentleman did not mind roughing it, he would be glad to have his company. The first step towards his freedom was successfully taken, the money paid down for the passage and with the injunction from the captain to be aboard by nine o'clock he returned ashore.

Only a few hours now remained to him, before a long, perhaps a lasting separation from his dear wife and baby, and thinking to pass these with them he hurried thence by the most unfrequented route, but had hardly crossed the threshold when Delia, weeping bitterly, implored him to make good his escape, as Master Tom had already sent the officers to look for him. With a last, fond embrace and a tear, which, falling upon that cradled babe, meant present sorrow, but no less future hope, the husband and father made his way under the friendly shadows of the night, back to the waiting ship.

When the officer from the custom house came aboard to inspect the ship's papers Samuel was resting, apparently without concern, in the upper bunk of the little cabin.

The captain seated himself at the center table, opposite the officer, and spread the papers before him. "Heigho, I see you have a passenger this trip," and then read from the sheet: "Samuel Edmondson, Jamaica, W. I., thirty years old. General Merchant."

"Yes," said the captain as he concluded. "Mr. Edmondson asked for passage at the last moment and as he was alone and we had a bunk not in service, I thought I'd take him along. He has a valuable bale of goods astray, probably at Jamaica, and is anxious to return and look it up."

"Well I hope he may find it. Where is he? let's have a look at him."

"Mr. Edmondson, will you come this way a moment?" called the captain.

As may be imagined the subject of this conversation had been listening intently and now when it was demanded that he present himself, he murmured a fervent "God help me" and jumped nimbly to the deck.

"This is my passenger," said the Captain, and to Samuel he said: "The customs officer simply wished to see you, Mr. Edmondson."

Samuel bowed and stood at ease, resting one hand upon the table and in this attitude without the quiver of an eyelash or the flinching of a muscle, bore the searching look of the officer, which rested first upon his face and then upon his hand. The flush of excitement still mounting his cheek and brow, gave a bronzed swarthiness and decidedly un-American cast to his rich brown color, while his features, clean-cut and but slightly of the Negro type, with hands well shaped and nails quite clean, were a combination of conditions rarely met in the average slave. The first glance of suspicion was almost immediately lost to view in the smile of friendly greeting with which the officer's hand was extended. "I hope you may recover your goods," were the words he said and, rising, ad'ded: "I must be off." The captain had meanwhile placed his liquor chest on the table and, in a glass of good old Jamaica rum, a hearty *"Bon voyage"* and responsive *"Good wishes"* were exchanged.

The subsequent story of Samuel, interesting and adventurous as it is, scarcely comes within the scope of the purpose of this article. After a brief stay at Jamaica, Samuel sailed before the mast on an English schooner carrying a cargo of dye-wood to Liverpool. Two years were passed here in the service of a wealthy merchant, whom he had served while a guest of his former master in New Orleans. During the third year he was joined by his wife and boy who had been liberated by their mistress. Subsequently the family took passage for Australia under the protection of a relative of his Liverpool employer, who was returning to extensive mining and sheep-raising interests near the rapidly growing city of Melbourne.[13]

JOHN H. PAYNTER, A.M.

13 *Note.*—This personal narrative of Samuel Edmondson was related by himself at his home in Anacostia where he died several years ago.

Children	Grandchildren	Great Grandchildren	G. G. Grandchildren	G. G. G. Grandchildren
1. Hamilton Edmondson 2. Elizabeth Edmondson m. John Brent	1. Catharine Brent m. James H. Paynter '60 d. 64	1. John H. Paynter m. Minnie H. Pillow 2. Minerva Paynter	1. Verden T. Paynter 2. Brent Paynter 3. Cary Paynter	

	2. Martha Brent m. Wm. H. Bell	1. Claude DeWitt Bell
		2. Adelbert Bell m.
		  1.
		  2.
			1. Marie ———
			2. Albertine Bell	

	3. Amelia Brent m. Garrett Smith Wormley	1. James Wormley m.
		  1. Lena Champ, 2. Emma Davis
		2. Garrett Wormley m.
		  1. Rebecca Webster,
		  2. Cora Nickens, 3. Emily
		3. C. Sumner Wormley m.
		4. Edith Wormley m. Harry S. Minton
		5. Smith Wormley m. ——— Cheatham
		6. Clem Wormley m.
		7. Roscoe Wormley m.
		8. Leon Wormley m. ——— Anderson
			1. Amelia Wormley
			2. Julian Wormley
			
			1. Lowell Wormley
			2. Edith Wormley
			1. Swan Leon Wormley
			1. Clementine Wormley
			1. Sumner Wormley
			2. Roscoe Wormley
			1. Elizabeth Wormley	

	4. Emily Brent m. Wm. L. Freeman	1. Corinne Freeman 2. Olive Freeman 3. Fred. Dent Freeman m. Lucy Stannard	1. Reginald Freeman m. ———	1. ——— Freeman

THE EDMONDSONS (continued)

Descendants of Paul and Amelia Edmondson

Children	Grandchildren	Great Grandchildren	G. G. Grandchildren	G. G. G. Grandchildren
	5. John S. Brent m. 1. Margaret, 2. Rebecca	1. Ellsworth Brent m. Jennie Howard 2. Mon 3. Julia 4. Edna		
	6. Rebecca Brent m. John Wright	1. Ella Wright m. James H. Payne 2. Ira Wright m. Ruth Taylor 3. Afie Wright m. Robt. E. Syphax	1. Francis Ennis Syphax 2. Robt E. Syphax	
	7. Calvin Brent m. Albertine Jones 2. ——	1. Marguerite Brent 2. Ethel Brent 3. Ralph Brent 4. Alfred Brent m. 5. Clarence Brent m. 6. Ernestine Brent 7. John Brent m. —— Cook	1. Janice Brent 1. ——	
3. Ephraim Edmondson m. ——	8. Wm. Brent 1. Narcissa Edmondson m. George Tossett, 2. Massey 2. Oliver Edmondson m. ——	1. —— Edmondson		
4. Richard Edmondson m. ——	1. Sophoenia Edmondson m. —— Fairfax 2. Sallie Edmondson m. Benj. Freeman	1. Wm. Freeman m. 2. George Freeman		

THE EDMONDSONS (continued)

Descendants of Paul and Amelia Edmondson

Children	Grandchildren	Great Grandchildren	G. G. Grandchildren	G. G. G. Grandchildren
5. Martha Edmondson m. 1. Edward Young, 2. Levi Pennington	1. Edward Young m. Josephine Johnson	1. Walter Young m. Belle Steves	1. Dorothy Maxwell Young 2. Alex. Helene Young 3. Elizabeth Martha Young 4. Edward Owen Young 5. Isabel Young	
6. Eveline Edmondson m. Wm. B. Ingram	1. Julia Ingram m. Joseph Becket	2. Mollie Young m. —— Thomas		
	2. Martha Ingram m. Mason Coxton	1.		
		1. William Coxton 2. Fred Coxton 3. Mason Coxton 4. Joseph Coxton 5. Mary Corton 6. Julia Coxton 7. Eva Coxton m. Carl Seward		
	3. Eveline Ingram m. Wm. Johnson	1. Mie Johnson m. —— Mosely		
	4. William Ingram m.			
	5. Joseph Ingram			
7. Saml. Edmondson	1. David Edmondson			
	2. Amelia Edmondson			
	3. Robt. Wellington Edmondson m. Evie Bastien	1. Albion Edmondson 2. Delia Edmondson 3. Hugh Edmondson		

THE EDMONDSONS (*concluded*)

Descendants of Paul and Amelia Edmondson

Children	Grandchildren	Great Grandchildren	G. G. G. Grandchildren	G. G. G. G. Grandchildren
8. Emily Edmondson m. Larkin Johnson	1. Ida Johnson m. Jas. Berry	1. Irene Berry 2. Annita Berry 3. Ilce Berry		
	2. Fannie Johnson m. Rezin H. Shipley	1. _____		
	3. Emma Johnson m. Wallace Chapman	1. Bernard Chapman 2. Garrett Chapman		
	4. Robt. Johnson m. _____	1. _____ Johnson 2. _____ Johnson		
9. Henrietta Edmondson 10. John Edmondson 11. Eliza Edmondson 12. Mary Edmondson 13. Joseph Edmondson m. Alice				
14. Louisa Rebecca Edmondson m. Gilbert L. Joy	1. Annita L. Joy m. Wm. A. Clark 2. Lula Joy m. Arthur Brooks 3. Gilbert L. Joy, Jr., m. Margaret Jones	1. Corelli Dancy Joy		

LORENZO DOW[1]

This is the record of a remarkable and eccentric white man who devoted himself to a life of singular labor and self-denial. In any consideration of the South one could not avoid giving at least passing notice to Lorenzo Dow as the foremost itinerant preacher of his time, as the first Protestant who expounded the gospel in Alabama and Mississippi, and as a reformer who at the very moment when cotton was beginning to be supreme, presumed to tell the South that slavery was wrong.

He arrests attention—this gaunt, restless preacher. With his long hair, his flowing beard, his harsh voice, and his wild gesticulation, he was so rude and unkempt as to startle all conservative hearers. Said one of his opponents: "His manners (are) clownish in the extreme; his habit and appearance more filthy than a savage Indian, his public discourses a mere rhapsody, the substance often an insult upon the gospel." Said another as to his preaching in Richmond: "Mr. Dow's clownish manners, his heterodox and schismatic proceedings, and his reflections against the Methodist Episcopal Church, in a late production of his on church government, are impositions on common sense, and furnish the principal reasons why he will be discountenanced by the Methodists."

But he was made in the mould of heroes. In his lifetime

---

[1] Very little has been written about Lorenzo Dow. There is an article by Emily S. Gilman in the *New England Magazine,* Vol. 20, p. 411 (June, 1899), and also one by J. H. Kennedy in the *Magazine of Western History,* Vol. 7, p. 162. The present paper is based mainly upon the following works: (1) "Biography and Miscellany," published by Lorenzo Dow, Norwich, Conn., 1834; (2) "History of Cosmopolite;" or "The Four Volumes of Lorenzo Dow's Journal concentrated in one, containing his Experience and Travels," Wheeling, 1848; (3) "The Dealings of God, Man, and the Devil; as exemplified in the Life, Experience, and Travels of Lorenzo Dow," 2 Vols. in one. With an Introductory Essay by the Rev. John Dowling, D.D., of New York. Cincinnati, 1858.

he traveled not less than two hundred thousand miles, preaching to more people than any other man of his time. He went from New England to the extremities of the Union in the West again and again. Several times he went to Canada, once to the West Indies, and three times to England, everywhere drawing great crowds about him. Friend of the oppressed, he knew no path but that of duty. Evangel to the pioneer, he again and again left the haunts of men to seek the western wilderness. Conversant with the Scriptures, intolerant of wrong, witty and brilliant, he assembled his hearers by the thousands. What can account for so unusual a character? What were the motives that prompted this man to so extraordinary and laborious a life?

Lorenzo Dow was born October 16, 1777, in Coventry, Tolland County, Connecticut. When not yet four years old, he tells us, one day while at play he "suddenly fell into a muse about God and those places called heaven and hell." Once he killed a bird and was horrified for days at the act. Later he won a lottery prize of nine shillings and experienced untold remorse. An illness at the age of twelve gave him the shortness of breath from which he suffered more and more throughout his life. About this time he dreamed that the Prophet Nathan came to him and told him that he would live only until he was two-and-twenty. When thirteen he had another dream, this time of an old man, John Wesley, who showed to him the beauties of heaven and held out the promise that he would win if he was faithful to the end. A few years afterwards came to the town Hope Hull, preaching "This is a faithful saying, and worthy of all acceptation, that Christ Jesus came into the world to save sinners"; and Lorenzo said: "I thought he told me all that ever I did." The next day the future evangelist was converted.

But he was to be no ordinary Christian, this Lorenzo. Not satisfied with his early baptism, he had the ceremony repeated, and with twelve others formed a society for mutual watch and helpfulness. At the age of eighteen he had still another dream, this time seeing a brittle thread in the air suspended by a voice saying, "Woe unto you if you

preach not the gospel.'' Then Wesley himself appeared
again to him in a dream and warned him to set out at once
upon his mission.

The young candidate applied to the Connecticut Conference of the Methodist Church. He met with a reception
that would have daunted any man less courageous. He best
tells the story himself: ''My brethren sent me home. Warren and Greenwich circuits, in Rhode Island, were the first
of my career. I obeyed, but with a sorrowful heart. Went
out a second time to New Hampshire, but sent home again;
I obeyed. Afterwards went to Conference by direction—
who rejected me, and sent me home again; and again I
obeyed. Was taken out by P. W. on to Orange circuit, but
in 1797 was sent home again: so in obedience to man I went
home a fourth time.''

As a matter of fact there was much in the argument of
the church against Lorenzo Dow at this time. The young
preacher was not only ungraceful and ungracious in manner, but he had severe limitations in education and frequently assumed toward his elders an air needlessly arro-
gant and contemptuous. On the other hand he must reasonably have been offended by the advice so frequently given
him in gratuitous and patronizing fashion. Soon after the
last rebuff just recorded, however, he says, on going out on
the Granville circuit, ''The Lord gave me souls for my
hire.'' Again making application to the Conference, he was
admitted on trial for the first time in 1798 and sent to
Canada to break fresh ground. He was not satisfied with
the unpromising field and wrote, ''My mind was drawn to
the water, and Ireland was on my mind.'' His great desire
was to preach the gospel to the Roman Catholics beyond the
sea. Accordingly, on his twenty-second birthday, acting
solely on his own resources, the venturesome evangelist
embarked at Montreal for Dublin. Here he had printed
three thousand handbills to warn the people of the wrath to
come. He attracted some attention, but soon caught the
smallpox and was forced to return home. Back in America,
he communicated to the Conference his desire to ''travel

the country at large." The church, not all impressed in his favor by his going to Ireland on his own accord, would do nothing more than admit him to his old status of being on trial, with appointment to the Dutchess, Columbia, and Litchfield circuits. Depressed, Dow gave up the work, and, desiring a warmer climate, he turned his face toward the South. From this time forth, while he constantly exhibited a willingness to meet the church half way, he consistently acted with all possible independence, and the church as resolutely set its face against him.

Dow landed in Savannah in January, 1802. This was his first visit to the region that was to mean so much to him and in whose history he himself was to play so interesting a rôle. He walked on foot for hundreds of miles in Georgia and South Carolina, everywhere preaching the gospel to all classes alike. Returning to the North, he found that once more he could not come to terms with his conference. He went back to the South, going now by land for the first time. He went as far as Mississippi, then the wild southwestern frontier, and penetrated far into the country of Indians and wolves. Returning in 1804, he became one of the first evangelists to cultivate the camp-meeting as an institution in central Virginia. Then he threw down the gauntlet to established Methodism, daring to speak in Baltimore while the General Conference of the church was in session there. The church replied at once, the New York Conference passing a law definitely commanding its churches to shut their doors against him.

Notwithstanding this opposition Dow continued to work with his usual zeal. About 1804 he was very busy, speaking at from five hundred to eight hundred meetings a year. In the year 1805, in spite of the inconveniences of those days, he traveled ten thousand miles. Then he made ready to go again to Europe. Everything possible was done by the regular church to embarrass him on this second visit, and when he arrived in England he found the air far from cordial. He did succeed in introducing his camp-meetings into the country, however; and although the Methodist

Conference registered the opinion that such meetings were "highly improper in England," Dow prolonged his stay and planted seed which, as we shall see, was later to bear abundant fruit. Returning to America, the evangelist set out upon one of the most memorable periods of his life, journeying from New England to Florida in 1807, from Mississippi to New England and through the West in 1808, through Louisiana in 1809, through Georgia and North Carolina and back to New England in 1810, spending 1811 for the most part in New England, working southward to Virginia in 1812, and spending 1813 and 1814 in the Middle and Northern states, where the public mind was "darkened more and more against him." More than once he was forced to engage in controversy. Typical was the judgment of the Baltimore Conference in 1809, when, in a matter of difference between Dow and one Mr. S., without Dow's having been seen, opinion was given to the effect that Mr. S. "had given satisfaction" to the conference. Some remarks of Dow's on "Church Government" were seized upon as the excuse for the treatment generally accorded him by the church. In spite of much hostile opinion, however, Dow seems always to have found firm friends in the State of North Carolina. In 1818 a paper in Raleigh spoke of him as follows: "However his independent way of thinking, and his unsparing candor of language may have offended others, he has always been treated here with the respect due to his disinterested exertions, and the strong powers of mind which his sermons constantly exhibit."[2]

His hold upon the masses was remarkable. No preacher so well as he understood the heart of the pioneer. In a day when the "jerks," and falling and rolling on the ground, and dancing still accompanied religious emotion, he still knew how to give to his hearers, whether bond or free, the wholesome bread of life. Frequently he inspired an awe that was almost superstitious and made numerous converts. Sometimes he would make appointments a year beforehand and suddenly appear before a waiting congregation like an

[2] "Dealings," II, 169.

apparition. At Montville, Connecticut, a thief had stolen an axe. In the course of a sermon Dow said that the guilty man was in the congregation and had a feather on his nose. At once the right man was detected by his trying to brush away the feather. On another occasion Dow denounced a rich man who had recently died. He was tried for slander and imprisoned in the county jail. As soon as he was released he announced that he would preach about "another rich man." Going into the pulpit at the appointed time, he began to read: "And there was another rich man who died and—." Here he stopped and after a breathless pause he said, "Brethren, I shall not mention the place this rich man went to, for fear he has some relatives in this congregation who will sue me." The effect was irresistible; but Dow heightened it by taking another text, preaching a most dignified sermon, and not again referring to the text on which he had started.

Dow went again to England in 1818. He was not well received by the Calvinists or the Methodists, and, of course, not by the Episcopalians; but he found that his camp-meeting idea had begun twelve years before a new religious sect, that of the Primitive Methodists, commonly known as "ranters." The society in 1818 was several thousand strong, and Dow visited between thirty and forty of its chapels. Returning home, he resumed his itineraries, going in 1827 as far west as Missouri. In thinking of this man's work in the West we must keep constantly in mind, of course, the great difference made by a hundred years. In Charleston in 1821 he was arrested for "an alleged libel against the peace and dignity of the State of South Carolina." His wife went north, as it was not known but that he might be detained a long time; but he was released on payment of a fine of one dollar. In Troy also he was once arrested on a false pretense. At length, however, he rejoiced to see his enemies defeated. In 1827 he wrote: "Those who instigated the trouble for me at Charleston, South Carolina, or contributed thereto, were all cut off within the space of three years, except Robert Y. Hayne, who was then the Attorney- General for the state, and is now the Governor for the *nullifiers.*"[3]

The year 1833 Dow spent in visiting many places in New York, and in this year he made the following entry in his Journal: "I am now in my fifty-sixth year in the journey of life; and enjoy better health than when but 30 or 35 years old, with the exception of the callous in my breast, which at times gives me great pain. . . . The dealings of God to me-ward, have been good. I have seen his delivering hand, and felt the inward support of his grace, by faith and hope, which kept my head from sinking when the billows of affliction seemed to encompass me around. . . . And should those hints exemplified in the experience of Cosmopolite be beneficial to any one, give God the glory. Amen and Amen! Farewell!" He died the following year in Georgetown, District of Columbia, and rests under a simple slab in Oak Hill Cemetery in Washington.

There is only one word to describe the writings of Lorenzo Dow—Miscellanies. Anything whatsoever that came to the evangelist's mind was set down, not always with good form, though frequently with witty and forceful expression. . Here are "Hints to the Public, or Thoughts on the Fulfilment of Prophecy in 1811"; "A Journey from Babylon to Jerusalem," with a good deal of sophomoric discussion of natural and moral philosophy; "A Dialogue between the Curious and the Singular," with some discussion of religious societies and theological principles; "The Chain of Lorenzo," an argument on the eternal sonship of Christ; "Omnifarious Law Exemplified: How to Curse and Swear, Lie, Cheat and Kill according to Law," "Reflections on the Important Subject of Matrimony," and much more of the same sort. "Strictures on Church Government" has already been referred to as bringing upon Dow the wrath of the Methodist Church. The general thesis of this publication, regarded at the time as so sensational, is that the Methodist mode of church government is the most arbitrary

[3] "Dealings," I, 178.

and despotic of any in America, with the possible exception
of that of the Shakers.

"A Cry from the Wilderness—intended as a Timely
and Solemn Warning to the People of the United States"
is in every way one of Dow's most characteristic works. At
this distance, when slavery and the Civil War are viewed in
the perspective, the mystic words of the oracle impress us
as almost uncanny: "In the rest of the southern states, the
influence of these Foreigners will be known and felt in its
time, and the seeds from the HORY ALLIANCE and the DE-
CAPIGANDI, who have a hand in those grades of GENERALS,
from the INQUISITOR to the Vicar General and down. . . .
☞The STRUGGLE will be DREADFUL! the CUP will
be BITTER! and when the agony is over, those who survive
may see better days! FAREWELL!"[4]

A radical preacher of the Gospel, he could not but be
moved with compassion on observing the condition of the
Negroes in the South during these years. When denied
admission to white churches because of his apparent fanat-
icism he often found it pleasant to move among the blacks.
Arriving in Savannah, one day, he was accosted by a Negro,
who, seeing that he had no place to stop, inquired as to
whether he would accept the hospitality of a black home.
He embraced this opportunity and found the people by
whom he was entertained "as decent as two thirds of the
citizens of Savannah."[5]   When on another occasion in
Savannah he learned that Andrew Bryan, the Negro minister of the city, had, because of his preaching, been whipped
unmercifully and imprisoned, Dow preached to the congregation himself.[6] He moved among Negroes, lived with them
socially, distributed tracts among them, preached to them
the Word, counted them with pride among his converts and
treasured in his memory his experiences among them.[7]

[4] "Dealings," II, 148.
[5] "Perambulations of Cosmopolite, or Travels and Labors in Europe and
America," 95.
[6] Ibid., 93.
[7] Ibid., passim.

As a result this liberal-minded man was naturally opposed to slavery. He was as outspoken a champion of freedom as lived in America in his day. "Slavery in the South," said he, "is an evil that calls for national reform and repentance." He thought that this "national scourge in this world," might "be antidoted before the storm" gathered and burst.[8] "As all men are created equal and independent by God of Nature," contended he, "Slavery must have Moral Evil for its foundation, seeing it violates the Law of Nature, as established by its author." "Ambition and avarice on the one hand," thought he, "and social dependence upon the other, affords the former an opportunity of being served at the expense of the latter and this unnatural state of things hath been exemplified in all countries, and all ages of the world from time immemorial." He further said, "Pride and vain glory on the one side, and degradation and oppression on the other creates on the one hand a spirit of contempt, and on the other a spirit of hatred and revenge, preparing them to be dissolute: and qualifying them for every base and malicious work!" He believed that "the mind of man is ever aspiring for a more exalted station; the consequence is the better slaves used the more saucy and impertinent they become: of course the practice must be wholly abolished or the slaves must be governed with absolute sway." He had discovered that "the exercise of an absolute sway over others begets an unnatural hardness which as it becomes imperious contaminates the mind of the governor; while the governed becomes factious and stupefied like brute beasts, which are kept under by a continual dread and hence whenever the subject is investigated, the evils of despotism presents to view in all their odious forms."[9]

His attack on slavery, however, was neither so general nor universal as would be expected of such a radical. He saw that "there is a distinction admissible in some cases, be-

[8] Biography and Miscellany, 30.
[9] "A Journey from Babylon to Jerusalem or the Road to Peace and True Happiness," 71.

tween Slavery itself and the spirit of slavery.'' ''A man may possess slaves by inheritance or some other way; and may not have it in his power either to liberate them or to make better their circumstances, being trammelled by the Laws and circumstances of the country,—yet whilst he feels a sincere wish to do them all the justice he can.'' He remarked too that ''we have no account of Jesus Christ saying one word about emancipation. Onesimus ran away from Philemon to Rome; whence finding Paul, whom he had seen at his master's, he experienced religion, and was sent back by the apostle with a letter—but not a word about setting him free.''[10]

Contrasting then the unhappy state with that of the past, he said, ''The first and primitive Christians had all things common, not from commandment but from spirit by which they were influenced day by day; so when the time of restitution takes place, which will be long before the consummation of all things, then the Law of Nature, from Moral principles will be practiced and the world will be as one concentrated Family.'' ''The openings to Providence preparatory to that day should be attended to, from principles of duty—lest judgments should perform what offered mercy if not rejected may be ready to accomplish. To feed and clothe another is both the interest and duty of all Masters—and the sixth chapter of Ephesians is an excellent tract on the subject to all who wish for advice, both as masters and servants.''[11]

It was likewise in keeping with Dow's fearlessness to denounce the efforts to discriminate against Negroes in the early Churches. He questioned the far-reaching authority of Bishop Coke, Asbury, and McKendree, and accused Asbury of being jealous of the rising power of Richard Allen, founder of the African Methodist Church.[12] He refers at considerable length to the incident in a Philadelphia church which ultimately made Absalom Jones a rector and Richard

[10] ''A Journey from Babylon and Jerusalem,'' 71.
[11] *Ibid.*, 72.
[12] ''History of Cosmopolite,'' 544–546.

Allen a bishop: "The colored people were considered by some persons as being in the way. They were resolved to have them removed, and placed around the walls, corners, etc.; which to execute, the above expelled and restored man, at prayer time, did attempt to pull Absolom Jones from his knees, which procedure, with its concomitants, gave rise to the building of an African meeting house, the first ever built in these middle or northern states."

Here at least was a man with a mission—that mission to carry the gospel of Christ to the uttermost parts of the earth. He knew no standard but that of duty; he heeded no command but that of his own soul. Rude, and sharp of speech he was, and only half-educated; but he was made of the stuff of heroes; and neither hunger, nor cold, nor powers, nor principalities, nor things present, nor things to come, could daunt him in his task. After the lapse of a hundred years he looms larger, not smaller, in the history of our Southland; and as of old we seem to hear again "the voice of one crying in the wilderness, Prepare ye the way of the Lord."

BENJAMIN BRAWLEY

THE ATTITUDE OF THE FREE NEGRO TOWARD
AFRICAN COLONIZATION

In the midst of the perplexities arising from various plans for the solution of the race problem one hundred years ago, the colonization movement became all things to all men. Some contended that it was a philanthropic enterprise; others considered it a scheme for getting rid of the free people of color because of the seeming menace they were to slavery. It was doubtless a combination of several ideas.[1] Furthermore, the meaning of colonization varied on the one hand according to the use the slave-holding class hoped to make of it, and on the other hand according to the intensity of the attacks directed against it by the Abolitionists and the free colored people because of the acquiescent attitude of colonizationists toward the persecution of the free blacks both in the North and South.[2]

Almost as soon as the Negroes had a chance to express themselves they offered urgent protest against the policy of removing them to a foreign land. Before the American Colonization Society had scarcely organized, the free people of Richmond, Virginia, thought it advisable to assemble under the sanction of authority in 1817, to make public expression of their sentiments respecting this movement. William Bowler and Lenty Craw were the leading spirits of the meeting. They agreed with the Society that it was not only proper, but would ultimately tend to benefit and aid a great portion of their suffering fellow creatures to be colonized; but they preferred being settled "in the remotest corner of the land of their nativity." As the presi-

[1] *The African Repository*, XXVI, 246, and XXIX, 14.
[2] Jay, "An Inquiry into the Character and Tendencies of the American Colonization and American Anti-Slavery Societies," p. 26 *et passim;* Stebbins, "Facts and Opinions Touching the Real Origin, Character, and Influence of the American Colonization Society," p. 63 *et seq.; The African Repository,* and Colonization Society Letters in the Library of Congress.

dent and board of managers of the Society had been pleased to leave it to the entire discretion of Congress to provide a suitable place for carrying out this plan, they passed a resolution to submit to the wisdom of that body whether it would not be an act of charity to grant them a small portion of their territory, either on the Missouri River or any place that might seem to them most conducive to the public good and their future welfare, subject, however, to such rules and regulations as the government of the United States might think proper.[3] Many Negroes, however, emigrated from this State during later years. Subsequent accounts indicate, too, that this increasing interest in colonization among the colored people of that Commonwealth extended even into North Carolina.[4]

Farther north we observe more frequent and frank expressions of the attitude of the colored people toward this enterprise. When the people of Richmond, Virginia, registered their mild protest against it, about 3,000 free blacks of Philadelphia took higher ground.[5] Because their ancestors not of their own accord were the first successful cultivators of the wilds of America, they felt themselves entitled to participate in the blessings of its "luxuriant soil," which their blood and sweat had moistened. They viewed with deep abhorrence the unmerited stigma attempted to be cast upon the reputation of the free people of color, "that they are a dangerous and useless part of the community," when in the state of disfranchisement in which they lived, in the hour of danger, they "ceased to remember their wrongs and rallied around the standard of their country." They were determined never to separate themselves from the slave population of this country as they

[3] Garrison, "Thoughts on Colonization," 8.

[4] Colonization Society Letters, 1826, Letter of J. Gales, of Raleigh, North Carolina. Niles Register, XXXV, 386; XLI, 103.

[5] The leaders of this meeting were: James Forten, chairman, Russell Parrott, secretary, Rev. Absalom Jones, Rev. Richard Allen, Robert Douglass, Francis Perkins, Rev. John Gloucester, Robert Gordon, James Johnson, Quamony Clarkson, John Sommerset, and Randall Shepherd. See Garrison's "Thoughts on African Colonization." Niles Register, XVII, 30.

were brethren by the "ties of consanguinity, of suffering, and of wrong."[6] They, therefore, appointed a committee of eleven persons to open correspondence with Joseph Hopkinson, member of Congress from that city, to inform him of the sentiments of the meeting, and issued an address to the "Humane and Benevolent Inhabitants of Philadelphia,"[7]

[6] Stebbins, "Origin, Character and Influence of the American Colonization Society," 194.

[7] The address was as follows:

"Relieved from the miseries of slavery, many of us by your aid, possessing benefits which industry and integrity in this prosperous country assures to all its inhabitants, enjoying the rich blessings of religion, by opportunities of worshipping the only true God, under the light of Christianity, each of us according to his understanding; and having afforded us and our children the means of education and improvement; we have no wish to separate from our present homes, for any purpose whatever. Contented with our present situation and condition, we are desirous of increasing the prosperity, by honest efforts, and by the use of the opportunities, for their improvement, which the constitution and laws allow.

"We, therefore, a portion of those who are the objects of this plan, and among those whose benefits, with them of others of color, it is intended to promote; with humble and grateful acknowledgments to those who have devised it, renounce and disclaim every connection with it; and respectfully and firmly declare our determination not to participate in any part of it.

"Nor do we view the colonization of those who may become emancipated by its operation among our southern brethren, as capable to produce their happiness. Unprepared by education and a knowledge of the principles of our blessed religion, for their new situation, those who will thus become colonized will thus be surrounded by every suffering which can affect the members of the human family.

"Without arts, without habits of industry, and unaccustomed to provide by their own exertions and foresight for their wants, the colony will soon become the abode of every vice, and the home of every misery. Soon will the light of Christianity, which now dawns among that portion of our species, be cut out by the clouds of ignorance, and their day of life be closed, without the illumination of the gospel.

"To those of our brethren who shall be left behind, there will be assured perpetual slavery and augmented sufferings. Diminished in numbers, the slave population of the southern states, which by their magnitude alarms its proprietors, will be easily secured. Those who among their bondsmen, who feel that they should be free, by right which all mankind have from God and from nature, will be sent to the colony; and the timid and submissive will be retained, and subjected to increasing rigor. Year after year will witness those means to assure safety and submission among their slaves, and the southern masters will colonize only those who it may be dangerous to keep among them. The bondage of a large portion of our members will thus be rendered perpetual.

disclaiming all connection with the society, questioning the professed philanthropy of its promoters, and pointing out how disastrous it would be to the free colored people, should it be carried out.[8]

Although a few persecuted Negroes of Maryland from the very beginning believed it advisable to emigrate, the first action of importance observed among the colored people of Baltimore, favoring colonization in Africa, was that of a series of meetings held there in 1826. The sentiment of these delegates as expressed by their resolutions was that the time had come for the colored people to express their interest in the efforts which the wise and philanthropic were making in their behalf. Differing from the people of Richmond they felt that, although residing in this country, they were strangers, not citizens, and that because of the difference of color and servitude of most of their race, they could not hope to enjoy the immunities of freemen. Believing that there would be left a channel through which might pass such as thereafter received their freedom, they urged emigration to Africa as the scheme which they believed would offer the quickest and best relief.[9]

We have not been able to find many records which give proof that in the States far South there was much opposition of the Negroes to the plan of removing the free people

"Disclaiming, as we emphatically do, a wish or desire to interpose our opinions and feelings between the plan of colonization and the judgment of those whose wisdom as far as exceeds ours as their situations are exalted above ours, we humbly, respectfully, and fervently intreat and beseech your disapprobation of the plan of colonization now offered by the American Society for colonizing the free people of color of the United States. Here in the city of Philadelphia, where the voice of the suffering sons of Africa was first heard; where was first commenced the work of abolition, on which heaven has smiled, for it could have had success only from the Great Maker; will not a purpose be assisted which will state the cause of the entire abolition of slavery in the United States, and which may defeat it altogether; which proffers to those who do not ask for them what it calls benefits, but which they consider injurious and which must insure to the multitudes whose prayers can only reach you through us, misery, sufferings, and perpetual slavery.

"JAMES FORTEN, *Chairman,*
"RUSSELL PARROTT, *Secretary.*"

[8] Garrison, "Thoughts on Colonization," p. 10.
[9] *The African Repository,* II, 295 *et seq.*

of color from the United States. We must not conclude,
however, that this absence of protest from the free colored
people in that section of the country was due to the fact that
they almost unanimously approved the plan of African
Colonization.[10]   Consideration must be given to the fact
that the free colored people in the Southern States did not
exercise the privilege of free speech. Consequently, if
there were even a large minority who opposed the plan, they
were afraid to make their views known, especially when this
movement was being promoted by some of the leading white
people of that section.

Occasionally there arose among the colored people of the
South advocates of colonization, setting forth the advantages of emigration in all but convincing style.[11] Such was
a free man of color of Savannah in the year 1832. He had
always viewed the principles on which the American Colonization Society was grounded as one of large policy, though
he saw it was "aided by a great deal of benevolence." And
when viewing his situation with those of his colored brethren
of the United States he had often wondered what prevented
them from rising with one accord to accept the offer made
them, although they might sacrifice the comforts of their
present situation. He had often almost come to the conclusion that he would make the sacrifice, and had only been prevented by unfavorable accounts of the climate. Hearing
that Liberia needed help, he desired to go. He and the
Negroes for whom he spoke seemed to be of an enterprising
kind. He understood the branches of "wheel-wright, blacksmith, and carpentry," and had made some progress in
machinery. He did not expect to go at the expense of the
Society and therefore hoped to take with him something
more than those who had emigrated on those terms.[12]

Another such freeman spoke from Charleston the same
year. He had observed with much regret that Northern

---

[10] It must be borne in mind, too, that *The African Repository*, in which
appeared most of the letters of Negroes favoring emigration to Africa, was the
organ of the American Colonization Society.

[11] *The African Repository*, VII, 216.

[12] *Ibid.*, XII, 149–150.

States were passing laws to get rid of the free people of color driven from the South on account of hostile legislation.[13] He was also fearful as to the prospects of the free blacks even in favorable Southern cities like Charleston, where they were given a decided preference in most of the higher pursuits of labor. He believed, therefore, that emigration to Africa was the solution of their problem. He urged this for the reason that the country offered them and their posterity forever protection in life, liberty, "and property by honor of office with the gift of the people, privileges of sharing in the government, and finally the opportunity to become a perfectly free and independent people, and a distinguished nation."[14] The letters of Thomas S. Grimké written to the Colonization Society during these years show that other freedmen of Charleston driven to the same conclusions were planning to emigrate.[15]

Conditions in that State, however, forced some free Negroes to emigrate to foreign soil. A number of free colored people left Charleston, and settled in certain free States. After residing two or three years in the North they found out that their condition instead of improving had grown worse, as they were more despised, crowded out of every respectable employment, and even very much less respected. They, therefore, returned to their former home. On reaching Charleston, however, they were still dissatisfied with their condition. Changes, which had taken place during their absence from the State, made it evident that in this country they could never possess those rights and privileges which all men desire. Some of them resolved, therefore, to try their fortunes in Liberia.[16]

The Negroes in Alabama had also become interested in the movement during these years.[17] In writing to Mr. McLain, of Washington, S. Wesley Jones, a colored man of

[13] During these years conditions were becoming intolerable for the free blacks in the South.
[14] The African Repository, VII, 239.
[15] Colonization Society Letters, 1832.
[16] The African Repository, XXIII, 190.
[17] Colonization Society Letters, 1848–1851.

Tuscaloosa, said that save the Christian religion there was no subject of so much importance and that lay so near his heart as that of African Colonization. All that was necessary to change the attitude on the part of the colored people was a "move by some one in whom the people have confidence to put the whole column in motion," and just "when there is a start made in Alabama the whole body of the free people of color will join in a solid phalanx." As for himself he had fully made up his mind to go to Liberia, but could not leave the United States until he had closed up a ten years' business, and if successful in collecting "tolerably well" what was due him he would be able to go without expense to the Society.[18]

In July, 1848, this same writer addressed to Mr. McLain another letter in which he gave details of a trip he had made in an adjoining county in the interest of emigration to Liberia. During this trip he said he had found a few free colored people who, after he had talked with them on the subject, were of one accord that the best thing they could do for themselves was to emigrate to Liberia.[19] In another letter addressed to McLain by the same writer December 29, 1851, it was stated that the colonization movement was still growing in the State. He also said that "those of us who want to go to Liberia are men who have been striving to do something" for themselves and consequently have "more or less business to close up." Mention was also made of the fact that there were at Huntsville, in the northern part of the State, several who had in part "made up their minds to go and only wanted a little encouragement to set them fully in favor of Liberia."[20]

Although thus favorably received in the South, however, the Colonization Society met opposition in other parts. The spreading of the immediate abolition doctrine by men like Garrison and Jay had a direct bearing on the enterprise. The two movements became militantly arrayed against each

18 *The African Repository*, XXVI, 276.
19 Ibid., XXVI, 194.
20 *Ibid.*, XXVIII (July 12, 1848).

other and tended to inflame the minds of the colored people throughout the country. The consensus of opinion among them was that the Colonization Society was their worst enemy and its efforts would tend only to exterminate the free people of color and perpetuate the institution of slavery.[21] So general was this feeling that T. H. Gallaudet, a promoter of the colonization movement, writing to one of its officers in 1831, said that something must be done to calm the feelings of the colored people in the large cities of the North.[22] Their resentment seemed to be due not so much to the fact that they were urged to emigrate, but that a large number of the promoters of the enterprise seemed to feel that the free Negroes should be forced to leave.[23] Considering themselves as much entitled to the protection of the laws of this country as any other element of its population, they took the position that any free man of color who would accept the offers of the colonization movement should be branded as an enemy of his race. They not only demonstrated their unalterable opposition but expressed a firm resolve to resist the colonizationists even down to death.

The proceedings of these meetings will throw much light on the excitement then prevailing among the free people of color in the border and Northern States. In 1831 a Baltimore meeting led by William Douglass and William Watkins, expressed the belief that the American Colonization Society was founded "more upon selfish policy than in the true principles of benevolence; and, therefore, as far as it regards the life-giving spring of its operations," that it was not entitled to their confidence, and should be viewed by them with that caution and distrust which their happiness demanded. They considered the land in which they had been born and bred their only "true and appropriate home," and declared that when they desired to remove they would apprise the public of the same, in due season.[24] That same

[21] Colonization Society Letters, 1831, *passim.*

[22] Letter of T. H. Gallaudet in the Colonization Society Letters, 1831.

[23] Jay, "An Inquiry into the Character and Tendencies of the American Colonization Society," 28 *et passim.*

[24] Garrison, "Thoughts on African Colonization," 22.

year a large meeting of colored people of Washington, in
the District of Columbia, convened for the purpose of expressing their opinion on this important question. Although they knew that among the advocates of the colonizing system, they had many true and sincere friends, they
declared that the efforts of these philanthropists, though
prompted no doubt by the purest motives, should be viewed
with distress. They further asserted that, as the soil which
gave them birth, was their only true and veritable home,
it would be impolitic, if they should leave their home without the benefit of education.[25] A meeting of the very same
order of the free people of color of Wilmington, Delaware,
that year, led by Peter Spencer and Thomas Dorsey,
took the position that the colonization movement was inimical to the best interests of the colored people, and at
variance with the principles of civil and religious liberty,
and wholly incompatible with the spirit of the Constitution
and the Declaration of Independence of the United States.[26]

A meeting of free colored people held in Boston, Massachusetts, in 1831, was of the opinion that none should leave
the United States, but if there were or should be any ex-
patriated in consequence of abuses from their white countrymen, it was advisable to recommend them to Haiti or Upper
Canada where they would find equal laws. In regard to
their being sent to Africa, because they were natives of that
land, they asked: "How can a man be born in two countries at the same time?" In refutation of the argument
made by the Colonization Society, that the establishment of
the colony in Liberia would prevent the further operation
of the slave trade, they said: "We might as well argue that
a watchman in the city of Boston would prevent thievery
in New York; or that the custom house officers there would
prevent goods being smuggled into any other port of the
United States."[27] Because there were in the United States
much better lands on which a colony might be established,

[25] Garrison, ''Thoughts on Colonization,'' 22.
[26] Ibid., 23.
[27] Ibid., 11.

and at a much cheaper expense to those who promoted it, than could possibly be had by sending them into "a howling wilderness across the seas," they questioned the philanthropy of the promoters of African colonization and adopted resolutions in opposition to the movement.[28]

A public meeting of colored citizens of New York, with Samuel Ennals and Philip Bell as promoters, referred to the Colonizationists as men of "mistaken views" with respect to the welfare and wishes of the colored people. The meeting solemnly protested against the bold effort to colonize the oppressed free people of color on the ground that it was "unjust, illiberal and unfounded; tending to excite prejudice of the community."[29] At a meeting of the free colored people of Brooklyn, promoted by Henry C. Thompson and George Hogarth, it was resolved that they knew of no other country in which they could justly claim or demand their rights as citizens, whether civil or political, but in the United States

[28] The resolutions were as follows

"*Resolved*, That this meeting contemplate, with lively interest, the reported progress of the sentiments of liberty among our degraded brethren, and that we legally oppose every operation that may have a tendency to perpetuate our present political condition.

"*Resolved*, That this meeting look upon the American Colonization Society as a clamorous, abusive and peace-disturbing combination.

"*Resolved*, That this meeting look upon those clergymen, who have filled the ears of their respective congregations with the absurd idea of the necessity of removing the free colored people from the United States, as highly deserving the just reprehension directed to the false prophets and priests, by Jeremiah, the true prophet, as recorded in the twenty-third chapter of his prophesy.

"*Resolved*, That this meeting appeal to the generous and enlightened public for an impartial hearing relative to the subject of our present political condition.

"*Resolved*, That the gratitude of this meeting, which is so sensibly felt, be fully expressed to those whose independence of mind and correct views of the rights of man have led them so fearlessly to speak in favor of our cause; that we rejoice to behold in them such a strong desire to extend towards us the inestimable blessings in the gift of a wise Providence which is deemed by all nature, and for which their valiant fathers struggled in the Revolution.

"ROBERT ROBERTS, *Chairman,*
"JAMES G. BARBARDOES, *Secretary.*"
—Garrison, "Thoughts on African Colonization," 20.

[29] *Ibid.*, 13.

of America, their native soil; and that they would be active
in their endeavors to convince the members of the Colonization Society, and the public generally, that being men,
brethren, and fellow citizens, they were like other citizens
entitled to an equal share of protection from the Federal
Government.[30]

The sentiment of a meeting at Hartford, Connecticut, in
1831, was that the American Colonization Society was actuated by the same motives which influenced the mind of
Pharaoh, when he ordered the male children of the Isra-
elites to be destroyed. They believed that the Society was
the greatest of all foes to the free colored people and slave
population; and that the man of color who would emigrate
to Liberia was an enemy to the cause and a traitor to his
brethren. As they had committed no crime worthy of
banishment, they would resist all attempts of the Colonization Society to banish them from their native land.[31] A
New Haven meeting of the Peace and Benevolent Society of
Afric-Americans, led by Henry Berrian and Henry N. Mer-
riman, expressed interest in seeing Africa become civilized
and religiously instructed, but not by the absurd and in-
vidious plan of the colonization society to send a "nation
of ignorant men to teach a nation of ignorant men." They
would, therefore, resist all attempts for their removal to the
torrid shores of Africa, and would sooner suffer every drop
of their blood to be taken from their veins than submit to
such unrighteous treatment. From the colored people of
Lyme, Connecticut, came the sincere opinion that the Colonization Society was one of the wildest projects ever patronized by enlightened men. The colored citizens of Middle-
town, chief among whom were Joseph Gilbert and Amos G.
Beman, inquired "Why should we leave this land, so dearly
bought by the blood, groans and tears of our fathers?
Truly this is our home," said they, "here let us live and
here let us die."[32]

[30] Garrison, "Thoughts on Colonization," 23–24.
[31] Ibid., 28–29.
[32] Ibid., 30–31.

The meeting in Columbia, Pennsylvania, the leaders of which were Stephen Smith and James Richard, expressed the opinion that African colonization was a scheme of the Southern planters and wicked device of slaveholders who were desirous of riveting more firmly, and perpetuating more certainly, the fetters of slavery by ridding themselves of a population whose presence, influence and example had a tendency (as they supposed) to produce discontent among the slaves, and to furnish them with inducements to rebellion.[33] A few weeks later a meeting was held at Pittsburgh under the leadership of J. B. Vashon and R. Bryan. The colored people of this city styled themselves as brethren and countrymen as much entitled to the free exercise of the elective franchise as any other inhabitants and demanded an equal share of protection from the Federal Government. They informed the Colonization Society that should their reason forsake them, then might they desire to remove. They would apprise them of that change in due season. As citizens of the United States, they mutually pledged to each other their lives, their fortunes, and their sacred honor, not to support a colony in Africa nor Upper Canada, nor yet emigrate to Haiti. Here they were born—here they would live by the help of the Almighty God—and here they would die.[34] Early in 1832, the colored people of Lewiston, Pennsylvania, in a meeting called by Samuel and Martin Johnston, expressed practically the same sentiments.[35] Through

[33] Garrison, ''Thoughts on African Colonization,'' 31–32.

[34] Ibid., 34–35.

[35] Ibid., 49. Among the resolutions passed were:

''Resolved, That we hold these truths to be self-evident (and it is the boasted declaration of our independence), that all men (black and white, poor and rich) are born free and equal; that they are endowed by their Creator with certain inalienable rights, that among these are life, liberty and the pursuit of happiness.

''Resolved, That we feel it to be our duty to be true to the constitution of our country, and are satisfied with the form of government under which we now live; and, moreover, that we are bound in duty and reason to protect it against foreign invasion; that we always have done so and will do so still.

''Resolved, That we view the efforts of the Colonization Society as officious and uncalled for. We have never done anything worthy of banishment from our friends and home.''—Garrison, ''Thoughts on African Colonization,'' 41.

the influence of Jacob D. Richardson and Jacob G. Williams, an indignation meeting of the same kind was held at Harrisburg.[36]

The free people of color, assembled at Nantucket, Rhode Island, in 1831, under the leadership of Arthur Cooper and Edward J. Pompey, saw no philanthropy in the colonization movement, but discovered in it a scheme gotten up to delude them from their native land into a country of sickness and death.[37] A Trenton meeting promoted by Lewis Cork and Abner H. Francis, viewed the American Colonization Society as the most inveterate foe both to the free and slave man of color. These memorialists disclaimed all union with the Society and, once for all, declared that they would never remove under its patronage either to Africa or elsewhere.[38]

In New York there had been various expressions pro and con as to emigration to Liberia, but it does not seem that a large number of colored people of that city ever favored it. They believed rather in emigration to Canada. The attitude of the people of that State was shown in 1834 by the troubles of Reverend Peter Williams, Rector of St. Phillip's Church in the city of New York. Working through the Phoenix Society and the Anti-Slavery Society he had endeavored to convince the free colored people that the idea held out to men of color that no matter how they might strive to become intelligent, virtuous and useful, they could never enjoy the privilege of citizens in the United States, was erroneous. On the contrary, he believed that the Declaration of Independence, which his father had helped to maintain, and the Gospel of Jesus Christ had sufficient power to raise the people of color at some time to the rank of citizenship. Although his opposition never extended further than the expression of his views, there arose so much antagonism to him that he was asked by his bishop to resign from the Anti-Slavery Society, because of a disturbance in

[36] Garrison, "Thoughts on African Colonization," 40–41.
[37] Ibid., 33–34.
[38] Ibid., 45–47.

his church.[39] There remained others, however, to continue
the attack. At a meeting in 1839 the free people of color of
New York entered a unanimous protest against the efforts
of this body, reiterating the sentiment that the American
Colonization Society was the source from which came the
various proscriptions and oppressions under which they
groaned.[40]

The attitude of the free blacks of New York was probably better demonstrated on the occasion of the appearance
of W. S. Ball, who had been sent to Liberia by the free
colored people of Illinois to secure definite information concerning the advisability of emigrating to Africa. On his
return to New York, he made a speech to a large assembly
of colored people, some of whom desiring to see Liberia for
themselves, had made preparations for a company to sail
September, 1848. Ball expressed himself as well pleased
with the country and after interesting the colored people of
Illinois[40a] he hoped to return to Liberia with a large emigration. The colored people of New York received him in good
faith. While the Liberian Commissioners were in session,
President Roberts and his comrades were invited to come
to the Anthony Street Church to inform them of the country.
After several speeches had been made, opportunity was
given to the colored people to ask questions that had not
been touched upon. This continued for some time and
seemed to elicit information highly favorable to the cause,
until a Mr. Morrill made his way up the aisle toward the
platform. After having gained the attention of the audience
with an air of superiority which showed he was accustomed
to control audiences of colored people, he said that he had
just come into town and was surprised to find his friends

[39] Believing it his duty to aid any free person or persons of color who
thought it best and wished to emigrate, instead of opposing them he had given
his personal support in their efforts to leave the country. Records would show
that he had helped the most prominent men of the Colony to get there, among
them being John B. Russwurm and James M. Thompson, two excellent men and
good scholars.—*African Repository*, X, 187.

[40] Cornish and Wright, ''The Colonization Scheme Considered,'' 7.

[40a] *African Repository*, XXIV, 158.

engaged in holding a colonization meeting. "That question," said he, "has been settled long ago! and the Liberia humbug—" At this point the hisses were so loud he could not be heard. Finally after much yelling and shouting of "hear him," the meeting became a bedlam and the presiding officer attempted to leave the chair. Finding order impossible the meeting was adjourned in an uproar. Amid cries of "a fight, a fight," women leaped over the pews and made their way to the doors. After some time had elapsed order was restored by clearing the house, but Morrill, who seemingly had come with the expressed purpose of breaking up the meeting, was not found in the chaos that ensued.[41]

Doubtless the best expression of antagonism to the American Colonization Society came from the Annual Convention of the Free Colored People held first in 1830 and almost annually thereafter in Philadelphia and other Northern cities almost until the Civil War. The Second Annual Convention showed an attitude of militant opposition by emphatically protesting against any appropriation by Congress in behalf of the movement. The Third Annual Convention, which met in Philadelphia in 1833, probably represented the high water mark of their antagonism to this enterprise. There were 59 representatives of the free people of color from eight different States, namely, Pennsylvania, Maryland, New Jersey, Delaware, Rhode Island, New York, Connecticut, and Massachusetts. The leaders of the movement were James Forten, Robert Douglas, Joseph Cassey, Robert Purvis, and James McCrummell. At an early stage in the proceedings of this Convention there prevailed a motion that "a committee consisting of one delegate from each of the States represented in the Convention, be appointed to draft resolutions expressive of the sentiments of the people of color in regard to the subject of colonization." Although these men were opposed to emigration to Africa, they favored a sort of colonization in some part of America, for the relief of such persons as might leave the United

[41] The African Repository, XXIV, 261.

States on account of oppressive laws like those of Ohio.[42] The colored people would in this case give such refugees all aid in their power.

After having divested themselves of "all unreasonable prejudice," and reviewed the whole ground of their opposition to the American Colonization Society, with all the candor of which they were capable, they still declared to the world that they were unable to arrive at any other conclusion than that the life-giving principles of the Society were totally repugnant to the spirit of true benevolence; that the doctrines which the Society inculcated were hostile to those of their holy religion and in direct violation of the golden rule, and that "the inevitable tendency of this doctrine was to strengthen the cruel prejudice of their opponents, to still the heart of sympathy to the appeals of suffering Negroes, and retard their advancement in morals, literature and science, in short, to extinguish the last glimmer of hope, and throw an impenetrable gloom over their fears and most reasonable prospects." All plans for actual colonization, therefore, were rejected.[43]

The movement thereafter continued to receive the attention of the people in the various parts of the country, being generally denounced. The Negroes of Ohio were prominent among those who opposed it.[44] Invited to hear a lecture by Mr. Pinney, a former governor of Liberia, then on a tour in the United States raising funds to purchase land there, the free blacks of Cincinnati held a meeting to protest. Arrogating to themselves the privilege of expressing the opinion of all the colored people of the United States, they respectfully declined the invitation for the reasons that the scheme was iniquitous in that it implied the assumption of the inequality of the free people of color.[45] They ac-

[42] Reference is here made to the "Black Laws" of Ohio, passed to prevent the immigration of persecuted blacks from the South into that commonwealth.

[43] Proceedings of the Third Annual Convention of the Free People of Color.

[44] At this time the free blacks throughout the country were being urged by Abolitionists to redouble their attacks on the American Colonization Society. The Negroes merely needed to follow their lead.

[45] The African Repository, XX, 316, 317.

cordingly urged that such sums as their so-called friends might give for the purchase of land in Africa might be used for establishing schools and asylums for colored children in this country.[46]   At a series of meetings of free colored people, held in the city of Cleveland, Ohio, during the winter of 1845–46, the Colonization Society was denounced as an organization whose proceedings tended to aggravate the injustice with which the free colored people were treated in this country. It was called the greatest antagonist which colored people had to meet and put down, before they could "stand erect in this country." During the meeting a very bitter spirit was shown toward the white race. They passed resolutions declaring that the colored people were entitled to all the privileges and immunities enjoyed by the whites and pledged themselves never to rest until they had redressed their wrongs and gained their rights.[47]

Another important instance of the opposition of the colored people of the North and West may be observed in the proceedings of a meeting held in Cincinnati. Mr. Vashon, a free man of color of Pittsburgh, had a motion passed in one of their anti-slavery meetings in that city, "declaring the Colonization Society inimical to the best interests of the free colored population of the country, and unworthy of the support of the churches." After speeches had been made by Vashon and Henry Gloster, a free man of color from Michigan, the original motion was passed with but one or two dissenting voices in spite of the efforts to amend it. It is probable that the amendments proposed were to soften the tone of the original motion, but no mention was made of them other than to state that they were offered by the opposition.[48]

Numerous other meetings were held to continue the expression of the same sentiments. At a meeting in Boston in 1847 the Colonization Society was referred to as the expa-

[46] Having the idea that the colonization scheme meant the expatriation of the free Negroes, several of their eminent leaders and anti-slavery friends advocated the colonization of the colored people on the western public lands.

[47] *The African Repository*, XXII, 265.

[48] *Ibid.*, XXVI, 221.

triating institution which would never be able to expel
"Americans by birth" pledged never to leave their native
land.[49]   A State convention of colored people of New York
held during three days in the capital at Albany, 1851, unanimously expressed their pleasure at the failure of the Colonization Society of that State to obtain an appropriation from
the Legislature.[50]   At another meeting at Albany in 1852,
Reverend J. W. C. Pennington, and Dr. J. McCune Smith
were instrumental in inducing the meeting to adopt an able
refutation of Governor Hunt's views in favor of a similar
appropriation.[51]   Another State Convention of Colored
People of Ohio convened in Cincinnati, unconditionally condemned the Society because its policy of expatriating the
free colored people was merely to render slave property
more secure and valuable.[52]   John M. Langston was the
chairman of this meeting.   Other such meetings held in
Rochester, New York, and New Bedford, Massachusetts,
about the same time, expressed similar sentiments.[53]   On
the occasion of the formation of a County Colonization
Society as a result of a visit of J. B. Pinney to Syracuse,
resolutions expressing deep regret that the influence of the
Society had extended to that section[54] were unanimously
passed.   At another meeting of Providence, the same year,
the Colonization Society was denounced because of the plea
that its motive in promoting emigration to Africa was to
Christianize the heathen.[55]

A series of meetings were held in Ohio to oppose the
efforts of colonization agents.[56]   A Columbus meeting of
1849 considered such workers inveterate enemies.   Another
meeting in the same place in 1851 referred to one of their

[49] Stebbins, "Facts and Opinions Touching the Real Origin and Influence
of the American Colonization Society," 196.

[50] Ibid., 197.

[51] Ibid., 202.

[52] Ibid., 199.

[53] Ibid., 200.

[54] Ibid., 201.

[55] Ibid., 206.

[56] Ibid., 206.

memorials as containing the false statement that the colored people of Ohio were prepared to go to Liberia. They considered N. L. Rice and David Christy, promoters of the colonization scheme in that State, avowed friends of slavery and slaveholders.[57] In a subsequent State Convention in 1853, they urged every free black to use his influence against any bill offered in any State, or national legislature to appropriate money for this enterprise.[58] When "Cushing's Bill" to facilitate colonization was offered, the free people of Cincinnati, Ohio, held an indignation meeting in 1853 to organize their friends to prevent its passage.[59]

The most distinguished Negroes of the country, too, were using the rostrum and the press to impede the progress of the American Colonization Society. Prominent among these protagonists were Samuel E. Cornish, and Theodore S. Wright, who without doubt voiced the sentiments of the majority of the free colored people in the North. These leaders took occasion in 1840 to attack Theodore Frelinghuysen and Benjamin Butler who had been reported as saying that the colonization project had been received with delight by the colored people.[60] Answering this assertion, they maintained that "if it was said of Southern slaves— if it had been asserted that they yearned for Africa or indeed, any part of the world, even more unhospitable and unhappy, where they might be free from their masters, there probably would have been no one to dissent from that opinion." But to prove that this was not the situation among the free people of color these spokesmen related numerous facts, showing that in various conventions from year to year the free blacks had protested against emigration to Africa.[61]

[57] Stebbins, "Facts and Opinions Touching the Real Origin, Character and Influence of the American Colonization Society," 207.

[58] Ibid., 208.

[59] Ibid., 208.

[60] Cornish and Wright, "The Colonization Scheme Considered," 7.

[61] "Having now done what we could," said they, "we ask you in view of the whole case whether you ought longer to take advantage of our weakness and press on us an enterprise that we have rejected from the first? Whether you ought to persist in a scheme which nourishes an unreasonable and un-

The greatest enemy of the Colonization Society among the freedmen, however, was yet to appear. This was Frederick Douglass. At the National Convention of Free People of Color, held at Rochester, New York, in 1853, he was called upon to write the address to the colored people of the United States. A significant expression in this address was: "We ask that no appropriation whatever, State or national, be granted to the colonization scheme. We would have our right to leave or remain in the United States placed above legislative interference."[62] He had already gone on record in writing to Mrs. Harriet Beecher Stowe in reply to her inquiry as to the best thing to be done for the elevation of the colored people. "Evidently the Society," said he, "looks upon our extremity as their opportunity and whenever the elements are started against us they are stimulated to immeasurable activity. They do not deplore our misfortunes but rather rejoice in them."[63] He referred to the Society as the twin sister of slavery, still at her post fostering prejudice against the colored man and scattering abroad her hateful unphilosophical dogmas as to the inferiority of the Negro and the necessity of his expatriation for his elevation and that of his white country men. "The truth is," said he, "we are here and here we are likely to remain. Individuals emigrate, nations never. We have grown up with this republic and I see nothing in her character or find in the character of the American people as yet, which compels the belief that we must leave the United States."[64]

All the free persons of color, however, did not continue to think on this wise. After the ebullitions of sentiment

christian prejudice—which persuades legislatures to continue their unjust enactments against us in all their rigor—which exposes us to the persecution of the proud and profligate—which cuts us off from employment, and straitens our means of subsistence—which afflicts us with the feeling that our condition is unstable—and prevents us from making efforts for our improvement, or for the advancement of our own usefullness and benefits and with our families.''— Cornish and Wright, "The Colonization Scheme Considered," 8.

[62] Stebbins, "Facts and Opinions Touching the Real Origin, Character and Influence of the American Colonization Society," 208.

[63] *The African Repository*, XXVI, 294.

[64] Douglass, "Life and Times of Frederick Douglass," 260.

had ceased, a few Negroes began to think that emigration was not an unmixed evil. They were driven to this position in various ways. Some desired to flee from increasing persecution then afflicting free Negroes both in the North and in the South; others were won over by such inducements for commercial advancement as a pacification of Yoruba seemed to offer in opening up the Soudan; and not a few like Alexander Crummell[65] and Daniel A. Payne, who, although opposed to the expatriation of their race, favored colonization so far as it would redeem Africa. Even Frederick Douglass, in answering the charge that the free people of color had been prejudiced against efforts to redeem Africa, stated that they were very much in favor of such a work, but objected to the efforts of the Colonization Society because of its "defect of good motives."[66] A number of Negroes yielded also to the logic of the Colonizationists, who in trying to disabuse their minds of the thought that it would be a disgrace to leave this country as exiles, held up to them the example of the Pilgrim Fathers who left their native land to obtain political and religious liberty. Furthermore, some Negroes like Martin R. Delaney, who had at first fearlessly opposed the colonization of the blacks in Africa, began during the fifties to promote the emigration of the free people of color to other parts. Many of this persuasion went to Canada West and some few to Trinidad.[67]

Although antagonism to African Colonization was pronounced in the Northern free States, there were several intelligent colored men who were strongly in favor of it. It was said, however, that such Negroes had usually been educated or aided in some way by the American Colonization Society. One of this class of spokesmen was George Baltimore, of Whitehall. In reading in the *National Watchman* a notice for a call for a national convention of colored people to be held in Troy, in 1847, he availed himself of the

[65] Crummell thought so well of it that he went to Africa for this purpose. See *The African Repository*, XXX, 125.

[66] *Ibid.*, LXIII, 273.

[67] Niles' Register, LVI, 165 and 180.

opportunity to speak for the Colonization Society. Referring to the suggestions set forth in the call, the writer said
that he could adopt all of them excepting the one to recommend emigration and colonization not of Africa, Asia, or
Europe. He considered this a fling at the American Colonization Society, and those people of color who were desirous
of going to their fatherland.[68] Another spokesman of this
order was Alphonso M. Sumner, of Philadelphia. Personally he was in favor of emigrating from the United States
and was of the opinion that, at that time at least, colonization in Liberia offered the only tangible means of attaining
their wishes. He believed that the abolition of the slave
trade could be attained in no other way, but like most
colored men in the free States, favoring colonization, he was
desirous of knowing something about the land before emigrating thereto.[69]

Writing from Hartford in 1851, Augustus Washington
stated that he was well aware that there could be nothing
more startling than that a Northern colored man, considered
intelligent and sound in faith, should declare his opinion
and use his influence in favor of African colonization. He
maintained, however, that the novelty of the thing did not
prove it false any more than it would be to say that because
one breaks away from a long-established custom he may not
have the least reason for doing so. He urged the free
colored people to emigrate from the crowded cities to less
populous parts of the United States, to the Great West or
to Africa, or to any place where they might secure an equality of rights and liberties with a mind unfettered and space
in which to rise. Moreover, from the time he was a lad of
fifteen years of age, and especially since the Mexican War,
he had advocated the plan of a separate State for the colored
people.[70] In a letter addressed to the editor of the *African*

[68] *The African Repository*, XXIII, 374.

[69] *Ibid.*, XXIV, 243.

[70] Mr. Washington had been active in securing the assistance of a few men
of superior ability and high ideals and finally entered into negotiations with
the authorities for a tract of land in Mexico on which he proposed to colonize

Repository, in 1853, Nathaniel Bowen undertook to express similar views. Although they possessed only partial freedom in this country, the free colored people of his city, Rome, New York, were generally against colonization. Moreover, he found many colored people who talked of and favored going to Canada, but he believed if those persons would take their interests into consideration, they would not hesitate to go to Africa.[71]

The efforts toward emigration too took organized form during the forties and fifties. In 1848 the free colored people of Dayton, Ohio, held a meeting to express their sentiments in favor of emigration to Africa, and to ask the white citizens to aid them in going there.[72] The movement also reached the colored people of Cincinnati, Ohio.[73] At a meeting held in that city on the 14th of July, 1850, they adopted a preamble and resolutions expressing similar sentiments. Going a step further, in 1850 a number of free Negroes of New York formed an organization called the New York and Liberian Agricultural and Emigration Society to coöperate with the Colonization Society. Considerable money was collected by the organization to aid emigrants whom they sent to Liberia.[74]

In July, 1852, there was held in Baltimore, a meeting of delegates from the city and different sections of the State of Maryland. After heated discussion and much excitement they passed resolutions to examine the different foreign localities for emigration, giving preference to Liberia. It seemed that although a majority of the delegates present

the free Negroes of the United States, but the war in that country prevented the execution of the plan. He was compelled finally to abandon the plan of a separate state in America, but gave all his time, voice and pen and means to the cause of emigration to Liberia. See *New York Tribune*, ——, and *The African Repository*, XXVII, 259.

[71] Anthony Bowen, who was at that time a messenger in the Patent Office at Washington, D. C., was the uncle of Nathaniel Bowen. See *The African Repository*, XXVIII, 164.

[72] *The African Repository*, XXI, 285.

[73] *The Cincinnati Gazette*, July 14, 1841.

[74] Stebbins, "Facts and Opinions Touching the Real Origin, Character and Influence of the American Colonization Society," 200–201.

desired to coöperate with the American Colonization Society, they were afraid to do so because of the opposition of the Baltimore people, who in a state of excitement almost developed into a mob intent upon breaking up the meeting.[75] As this meeting of delegates from the whole State seemed to be favorable to the colonization enterprise, the people of Baltimore felt it incumbent upon them to hold another meeting a few days thereafter, maintaining that they did not know that a previous meeting was called for the consideration of the questions brought before it, and denounced it as being unrepresentative. They said that they were not opposed to voluntary emigration but did not at any time elect delegates to the so-called Colored Colonization Convention.[76]

To carry out more effectively the work of ameliorating the condition of the colored people, a National Council composed of two members chosen by election at a poll in each State, was organized in 1853. As many as twenty State conventions were to be represented. Before these plans could be well matured, however, those who believed that emigration was the only solution of the race problem called another convention to consider merely that question. Only those who would not introduce the question of African emigration but favored colonization in some other parts were invited. Among the persons thus interested were Reverend William Webb and Martin R. Delaney of Pittsburgh, Doctor J. Gould Bias and Franklin Turner of Philadelphia, Reverend Augustus R. Greene of Allegheny, Pennsylvania, James M. Whitfield of New York, William Lambert of Michigan, Henry Bibb, James Theodore Holly of Canada, and Henry M. Collins of California.[77] Frederick Douglass criticised this step as uncalled for, unwise, unfortunate, and premature. "A convention to consider the subject of emigration," said he, "when every delegate must declare himself in favor of it before hand, as a condition of taking

[75] The Baltimore Sun, July 27, 28 and 29, 1852.
[76] Stebbins, "Facts and Opinions, etc.," 200–201.
[77] Cromwell, "The Negro in American History," 42.

his seat, is like the handle of the jug, all on one side.''[78] James M. Whitfield, the Negro poet of America, came to the defense of his co-workers, he and Douglass continuing the literary duel for a number of weeks. The convention was accordingly held. In it there appeared three parties, one led by Doctor Delaney who desired to go to the Niger Valley in Africa, another by Whitfield, whose interests seemed to be in Central America, and a third by Holly who showed a preference for Haiti. The leaders of these respective parties were commissioned to go to these various countries to do what they could in carrying out their schemes.[79] Holly went to Haiti and took up with the Minister of the Interior the question of admitting Negro emigrants from the United States.[80]

Among the colored people of the Northwest there appeared evidence of considerable interest in emigration. This was especially true of Illinois and Indiana, from which commissioners had been sent out to spy the land.[81] This is evidenced too by the sentiment expressed by delegates attending the Cleveland Convention in 1854. The next emigration convention was held at Chatham, Canada West, in 1856. One of the important features of this meeting was the hearing the report of Holly who went to Haiti the previous year. From this same meeting Martin R. Delaney proceeded on his mission to the Niger Valley in Africa. There he concluded a treaty with eight African kings, offering inducements to Negroes to emigrate. In the meantime James Redpath had gone to Haiti and accomplished some things that Holly failed to achieve. He was appointed Haitian Commissioner of Emigration in the United States, with Holly as his co-worker. They succeeded in sending to Haiti as many as two thousand emigrants, the first sailing

[78] *The North Star,* 1853.

[79] Letter of Bishop Holly in Cromwell's ''Negro in American History,'' 43–44.

[80] *Ibid.,* 44.

[81] *The African Repository,* XXIV, 261.

in 1861. Owing to their unpreparedness and the unfavorable climate, not more than one third of them remained.[82]

Considering the facts herein set forth we are compelled to say that the colonization movement was a failure. Although it did finally interest a number of free Negroes their concern in it did not materialize on account of the outbreak of the Civil War occurring soon thereafter. On the whole, the movement never appealed to a large number of intelligent free people of color. With the exception of those who hoped to be especially benefited thereby, few leading Negroes dared to support the enterprise. The most weighty evidence we can offer is statistics themselves. The report of the Colonization Society shows that from 1820 to 1833[83] only 2,885 colored persons had been sent out by the Society. More than 2,700 of this number were taken from the slave States, and about two thirds of these were slaves manumitted on the condition of their emigrating. Of the 7,836[84] sent out of the United States up to 1852, 2,720 were born free, 204 purchased their freedom, 3,868 were emancipated in view of removing them to Liberia, and 1,044 were liberated Africans sent out by the United States Government. When we consider the fact that there were 434,495[85] free persons of color in the United States in 1850 and 488,070 in 1860, this element of the population had not been materially decreased by the efforts of the American Colonization Society.

LOUIS R. MEHLINGER

[82] Letter of Bishop Holly in Cromwell's ''The Negro in American History,'' 44.

[83] *The Liberator*, 1833.

[84] *The African Repository*, XXIII, 117.

[85] United States Census, 1850 and 1860.

DOCUMENTS

TRANSPLANTING FREE NEGROES TO OHIO FROM 1815 TO 1858[1]

Brown county was one of the first parts of Ohio to be invaded by free Negroes. In the "Historical Collections of Ohio" Howe says:

"In the county (Brown) there are two large settlements of colored persons, numbering about 500 each. One of these is 3 miles north of Georgetown; the other is in the NE. part of the county, about 16 miles distant. They emigrated from Virginia, in the year 1818, and were originally the slaves of Samuel Gist, who manumitted and settled them here, upon two large surveys of land. Their situation, unfortunately, is not prosperous."—Howe, Historical Collections of Ohio, 71.

Referring to these settlements some years later another historian said:

"The colored settlement in Eagle Township was made in 1818, by a number of the former slaves of Samuel Gist, a wealthy banker, resident of London, England, and an extensive land-owner and slaveholder in the United States.

"It is not known that Gist ever visited his plantation here, or that he ever saw a single slave that cultivated his lands, but all was left to the management of resident agents appointed by him. These lands lay in the counties of Hanover, Amherst, Goslin, and Henrico, Va., and included some of the first plantations in the 'Old Dominion.'

"In 1808 desiring to make ample provision for the future of those who had so abundantly filled his coffers by their servitude, Gist made a will, the intent of which was certainly benevolent, but which has been most wretchedly executed. This document of fifty-eight closely written pages is a study within itself. It begins thus:

[1] For a more detailed account of these settlements see Woodson's "The Education of the Negro, Prior to 1861," 243–244; and Hickok, "The Negro in Ohio," 85–88.

This is the last will and testament of me Samuel Gist, of Gower street, in the Parish of St. Giles, in the city of London, of the county of Middlesex, England.

"After bequeathing various valuable estates, large sums of money to his only daughter, he designated what property and sums of money shall fall to the numerous persons who have been in his employ, and most explicitly does he provide for his slaves in Virginia, who numbered nearly one thousand souls!

"Relative to them the will provides that at his death his 'slaves in Virginia shall be free.' That his lands shall be sold and comfortable homes in a free State be purchased for them with the proceeds. That the revenue from his plantations the last year of his life be applied in building school houses and churches for their accommodation. That all money coming to him in Virginia be set aside for the employment of ministers and teachers to instruct them. That 'care be taken to make them as comfortable and happy as possible.'

"In 1815 Samuel Gist died, and Wickham of Richmond, Va. (in conjunction with his father-in-law, Page), who had been appointed Gist's agent, proceeded to execute his will. Accordingly through parties in Hillsboro, Ohio, 1,112 acres of land near Georgetown, and 1,200 acres west of Fincastle, in Eagle Township, were purchased for homes for these slaves. These lands were covered with thickets of undergrowth and sloughs of stagnant water and were almost valueless at that time for any purpose other than pasturage. Here in June, 1818, came nearly 900 persons, a part of whom located on the Georgetown lands, the remainder on the Fincastle purchase. Their 'comfortable homes' lay in the wild region about them; the education they received was in the stern school of adversity. As a matter of course, they did not prosper. Some who were able returned to Virginia. Others built rude huts and began clearing away the forest. What little money they had was soon spent. Scheming white men planned to get their personal property. They became involved in numerous law suits among themselves, and so from various causes they were reduced almost to pauperism. In later years their lands have been sold, so that at present but few families remain as relics of this once large settlement. Among the first families that settled in this township were the following, most of whom had families:

"Jacob Cumberland, George Cumberland, Samuel Hudson, Gabriel York, James Gist, Gabriel Johnson, Joseph Locust, James

Cluff, —— Davis, Sol Garrison, —— Pearsons, —— Williams, Glascow Ellis, and Tom Fox. 'Old Sam Hudson,' as he was familiarly known, was an odd character, and many anecdotes are yet related of him. At one time he was sent to the State Prison at Columbus for making unlawful use of another man's horse, and so it happened that a white man named Demitt accompanied him for a like offense. Upon being interrogated as to his occupation, Sam answered, 'Preacher ob de Gospel!' Turning to Demitt, the officer asked, 'What's your occupation?' 'I clerk for Sam,' was the shrewd reply.

"Richmond Cumberland ('Blind Dick'), Meredith Cumberland, Taylor Davis, Moses Cumberland, Ephraim Johnson, and Winston Cumberland were also born in Virginia."—History of Brown County, Ohio (edition 1883), p. 592.

"During these years according to the letter below another group of Negroes found their way into Jefferson County, Ohio."

Dear Sir:

Every body with whom I have talked about this colony of Negroes, referred me to Judge Mansfield as one knowing more about it than anybody else. He, therefore, is my chief informer. In 1825 a colony of slaves was sent up from Charles City County, Virginia, to Smithfield, in Jefferson County, Ohio, about twenty miles southwest of Steubenville. They were the slaves of Thomas Beaufort of the Virginia County above named. So far as I could learn not all of Beaufort's slaves were sent to Smithfield. Another colony I was told was located at Stillwater in Harrison County, Ohio, but I have not yet been in that community. How the slaves traveled from Virginia to Smithfield could not be told. The number sent up is not known—about thirty or forty families, they said. They were a tribe, as it were, Nattie Beaufort being the patriarch. They were sent in charge of a man named McIntyre, an overseer, who supposedly had been sent to see to the locating of the slaves on a tract of land which the master had bought for them through Benjamin Ladd, a Quaker of the Smithfield community. McIntyre returned to Virginia after a few days stay. He was never in the community again, nor was any other representative of the Beaufort's so far as anybody knows. The land was bought in Wayne Township—about 200 acres, about five miles out from Smithfield. It is quite rolling, of stiff clay character. There are fine farms all about it and coal fields not far away. It was bought of Thomas Mansfield whose son, a prominent lawyer in Steubenville, still owns land contiguous to the Beaufort tract, and owns now a part of what his father sold the slaves.

According to Judge Mansfield the tract of land was laid out in five-acre plots. A cabin was built on each and a family placed in each cabin. The families were the married sons and daughters of Nathaniel Beaufort who had been his master's "nigger driver," was the way one of his granddaughters put it. The whole colony was under Nathaniel Beaufort's control as long as he lived, during which time it prospered. Two of the original colony, both women, are still living and own their little tracts, one residing on her property and the other in the infirmary. The descendants of the first settlers owned most of the land but some of it has been lost. Whether they had any teams and money to start with it is not known to Judge Mansfield, but he thought that they did not. Both men and women had to "work out" much of the time for means to go upon, the girls toiling as servants in the community for twenty-five to fifty cents per week and their keep, the men receiving forty to fifty cents per day often paid in such provisions as meal and meat.

Judged by the management of their own plots they are not a success as farmers, most of their soil being now practically worthless. "The land which was bought for the slaves was never recorded in their names," says Judge Mansfield. It was deeded to Benjamin Ladd as trustee and so stands in the record now. Judge Mansfield's last words were: "There has been no clash over that land because of its run down condition, but if coal or oil should be found about there, I cannot tell what will happen." The financial condition of the colony is no better than it was seventy-five years ago, the physical condition is far from being as good. Two or three of these Negroes, however, showing evidence of thrift are very good farmers. They have increased their holdings and built new cabins, although most of the old dwellings are still there and are occupied by the descendants of the original settlers. They have rapidly increased in numbers and have extensively intermarried. From the first the people were religious, regular church goers. They have two churches among them, one Methodist and the other Baptist. Their morals have been good, having seldom committed crime. Officers of the law have found very little to do in this community. During the life of the colony there have been

only two arrests for serious crimes, one of which was for stealing
a horse and the other for stealing wool. Both of the accused were
sent to the penitentiary. No other serious charge has ever been
brought against any member of the community so far as Judge
Mansfield knew. The original set were fine physical specimens,
"as fine," says Judge Mansfield, "as the community ever saw."

Separate schools for white and blacks have been maintained
from the start. Nearly all the teachers have been white. The
preachers have been members of the colony. None of them, however, have gained any particular prominence in any line. Not
even any of the children, so far as could be learned, had ever been
sent off to school. The best known of them now are two brothers,
William and Wilson Toney, both preachers. Just what acreage
they now own I could not learn. How much is owned by the best
of them also could not be determined.

The community is called by some "McIntyre" after the man
who carried the slaves up into Ohio, and by others it is called
"Haiti." The latter term is almost wholly used by white people
throughout the county and has always been offensive to the Negroes.
Although I went to "Haiti" and talked with one of the men,
Judge Mansfield gave me practically all the information. I will
send you more in a few days gathered at other points. I have
tried to cover your questions and to include other vital ones.
Please call my attention to anything that I might mention to add
to the interest or thoroughness of the story. I have reported here
almost word for word as the facts were given me by the Judge and
hope the story will have some interest for you. I expect to find
out a great deal more about that community.[1]

Very truly yours,

C. A. POWELL.

Under a protest from afar a goodly number of slaves
were settled in Lawrence county in 1827.

COMMUNICATED

"BLACKS AND MULATTOES

"On the 14th April, seventy of this description of persons, in
one company emigrated into and settled within Lawrence county.
They were a part of a stock of slaves emancipated by the last will

---

[1] Mr. Powell, a teacher of Tuskegee, wrote this letter a few years ago
while making a study of the Negroes in Ohio.

of a Mr. Ward, late of Pittsylvania county, Virginia, deceased. Those unfortunate creatures have little or no property of value— many of them ragged and dirty. It was expected that such a number together, in such condition would hardly, in Ohio, find a place where to lay their heads; yet so far from meeting with ob- stacles, facilities to settlement were extended to them. All of them have found places, and many of them have already obtained security as the law requires; and probably the balance will within twenty days. The writer of this note would censure none for acts of kindness to this unfortunate class of persons—yet as he regards the moral character and welfare of society, he cannot view these rapid accessions without some degree of alarm.''—*The Ohio State Journal and Columbus Gazette*, May 3, 1827.

Some years later there was established in Mercer county another colony, which because of its connection with friends in Cincinnati, then promoting the settlement of Negroes on public land, became the most promising of the colored com- munities in Ohio. Sketching the history of that county, Howe says:

"In the southern part of this county is a colony of colored people, amounting to several hundred persons. They live prin- cipally by agriculture, and own extensive tracts of land in the townships of Granville, Franklin, and Mercer. They bear a good reputation for morality, and manifest a laudable desire for mental improvement. This settlement was founded by the exertions of Mr. Augustus Wattles, a native of Connecticut, who, instead of merely theorizing upon the evils which prevent the moral and mental advancement of the colored race, has acted in their behalf with a philanthropic, Christian-like zeal, that evinces he has their real good at heart. The history of this settlement is given in the annexed extract of a letter from him.

" 'My early education, as you well know, would naturally lead me to look upon learning and good morals as of infinite importance in a land of liberty. In the winter of 1833–4, I providentially became acquainted with the colored population of Cincinnati, and found about 4,000 totally ignorant of every thing calculated to make good citizens. Most of them had been slaves, shut out from every avenue of moral and mental improvement. I started a school for them, and kept it up with 200 pupils for two years. I then proposed to the colored people to move into the country and purchase land, and remove from those contaminating influences which had so long crushed them in our cities and villages. They promised to do so, provided I would accompany them and teach school. I travelled through Canada, Michigan and Indiana, looking for a suitable location, and finally settled here, thinking this place contained more natural advantages than any other unoccupied country within my knowledge. In 1835, I made the first purchase for colored people in this county. In about three years, they owned not far from 30,000 acres. I had travelled into almost every neighborhood of colored people in the State, and laid before them the benefits of a permanent home for themselves and of education for their children. In my first journey through the state, I established, by the assistance and cooperation of abolitionists, 25 schools for colored children. I collected of the colored people such money as they had to spare, and entered land for them. Many, who had no money, afterwards succeeded in raising some, and brought it to me. With this I bought land for them.

" ' I purchased for myself 190 acres of land, to establish a manual labor school for colored boys. I had sustained a school on it, at my own expense, till the 11th of November, 1842. Being in Philadelphia the winter before, I became acquainted with the trustees of the late Samuel Emlen, of New Jersey, a Friend. He left by his will $20,000, for the "support and education in school learning and the mechanics arts and agriculture, such colored boys, of African and Indian descent, whose parents would give them up to the institute." We united our means and they purchased my farm, and appointed me the superintendent of the establishment, which they call the Emlen Institute.'

"In 1846, Judge Leigh, of Virginia, purchased 3,200 acres of land in this settlement, for the freed slaves of John Randolph, of Roanoke. These arrived in the summer of 1846, to the number of about 400, but were forcibly prevented from making a settlement by a portion of the inhabitants of the county. Since then, acts of hostility have been commenced against the people of this settlement, and threats of greater held out, if they do not abandon their lands and homes."—Howe's "Historical Collections of Ohio," pp. 355–356.

Coming to Shelby county the same historian did not fail to mention a settlement of prosperous Negroes who were keeping pace with their white neighbors.

"In Van Buren township is a settlement of COLORED people, numbering about 400. They constitute half the population of the township, and are as prosperous as their white neighbors. Neither are they behind them in religion, morals and intelligence, having churches and schools of their own. Their location, however, is not a good one, the land being too flat and wet. An attempt was made in July, 1846, to colonize with them 385 of the emancipated slaves of the celebrated John Randolph, of Va., after they were driven from

Mercer county; but a considerable party of whites would not willingly permit it, and they were scattered by families among the people of Shelby and Miami who were willing to take them.''—Howe's ''Historical Collections of Ohio,'' pp. 465–466.

This effort at colonizing so many Negroes in the State of Ohio led to much discussion. There arose an anti-free Negro party which sounded the alarm against such philanthropy and undertook to frighten all blacks away. The sentiment of such alarmists may be obtained from the following:

"By the following letter from a gentleman on a tour through Virginia to the editor, it will appear that we are to have a colony of free negroes (no less than five hundred) planted in our adjoining county. Much as we commiserate the situation of those who, when emancipated, are obliged to leave their country or again be enslaved, we trust our constitution and laws are not so defective as to suffer us to be overrun by such a wretched population:

" 'RICHMOND, VA., May 10, 1819.

" 'Dear Sir:—Since my arrival in this county I have understood that a large family of negroes, consisting of about five hundred, have lately been liberated and are to be marched to Ohio, and there settled on land provided for them agreeably to the will of a Mr. Gess, who formerly owned them. There are persons now engaged in collecting the poor miserable beings from different quarters and driving them like cattle to Goochland county, from whence they will take up their line of march to Ohio. I am told that they are perhaps as depraved and ignorant a set of people as any of their kind and that their departure is hailed with joy by all those who have lived in their neighborhood. Ohio will suffer seriously from the iniquitous policy pursued by the States of Virginia and Kent. in driving all their free negroes upon us. The people of Ohio are bound in justice to themselves to adopt some counteracting measure. Many people here are of the opinion that we may be compelled to introduce slavery in Ohio in self-defense, and they appear to be gratified that we are suffering many of the evils attending it, without (as they call it) any of the benefits. I have been gratified to tell them what I believe to be true—that nineteen twentieths of the people of Ohio are so opposed to slavery that they would not consent to its introduction under any circumstances; and, although they commiserate the situation of those who have been liberated and compelled to abandon their country or again be made slaves, yet in justice to themselves and their posterity they will refuse admittance to such a population.

" 'Your most ob't.,

" 'A. T.'

"(Editor) We understand from a respectable authority that 270 of said negroes have landed at Ripley and are to settle near the center of Brown county on White Oak, the residue of 500 to follow soon after.''—Quillin's ''The Color Line in Ohio,'' pp. 28–29 and *The Supporter, Chillicothe,* June 16, 1819.

In view of this alarm aroused by the so-called Negro invasion the Ohio colonizationists availed themselves of the opportunity to set forth their plan as the only solution of the problem. The following articles are interesting.

"NEW STYLE COLONIZATION

"It seems that our old friend Gerrit Smith is anxious to form a colony of colored people in the State of New York. It is not known that he pays the expenses of any to get to that happy spot, but he certainly offers them a share in the property of earth, when they arrive. Some have thought his effort in his respect, another proof of his great liberality. Perhaps it is—but of the character of those lands we know nothing. The *Journal of Commerce* seems to understand the subject from the following, which we cut from a late number:

''*Bounty of Gerrit Smith.*—Some of the newspapers are eulogizing this once sensible man, because he is giving away deeds in any number to colored men, of forty acre lots of his vast tract in Hamilton county. The considerations in the deeds are as follows:

''''For and in consideration of the sum of one dollar to me, in hand paid, and being desirious to have all share in the subsistence and happiness, which a bountiful God has provided for all, has granted, sold, etc.''

'' 'If the negroes do not run away from the bears and wolves and climate and sterility of Hamilton county, with more anxiety than they ever did from Southern slavery, then we do not understand their character. We do not blame the negroes for getting their liberty if they can, but to make them take farms in Hamilton county, is too bad. The wild beasts up there will rejoice in a negro settlement among them, especially at the beginning of winter.'

"Had Judge Leigh taken the Randolph negroes there, they might have fared as well as they have done in Ohio, and certainly he could have gotten the land much cheaper!

"After all, 'there is no place like home!' And there is no 'home, sweet home,' for the colored man, but in Liberia!''

The African Repository, XXII, 320–321.

FREEDOM IN A FREE STATE

"Facts are almost daily transpiring which show the immense importance of colonization. Among them, none are more conspicuous than those which come to us from the free States. If the colored people cannot enjoy freedom in a free State, what can they do? Where shall they go? Here is a fact:

"*Randolph's 'John.'*—We are told by the *Lynchburg Virginian*, that John, the well-known and faithful servant of the late John Randolph, who, with the emancipated slaves of his master, went to Ohio, and were there treated by the citizens in a manner of which our readers have been apprized, has returned to Charlotte with the intention of petitioning the legislature to allow him to remain in the commonwealth. He says, they have no feeling for colored people in Ohio, and, if the legislature refuse to grant his petition, he will submit to the penalty of remaining and be sold as a slave—preferring this to enjoying freedom in a free state.

"We have been repeatedly asked, why do you not send those slaves to Liberia? To this question we reply, we have had nothing to do with them, and have reason to believe that they have been prejudiced against going to Liberia. And in addition to this, it is now very doubtful whether they have money enough left to take them to Liberia; and it would be impossible for us, in the present state of our finance, to give them a free passage and support them six months after their arrival.

"We have been informed that many of the rest of them would come back to Virginia, and be slaves, rather than remain in Ohio, *if they could get back.* And yet they are now free and in a free state! But what does it all amount to?

"Suppose western Virginia and northern Kentucky, were tomorrow to emancipate their slaves, what would become of them? They could not remain in those states. They must remove. Where shall they go? To Ohio, most easily, and as there are more Abolitionists in that state than any other, more hopefully! But would they be admitted there? Where then shall they go? Let those who can, answer these questions. In view of them, and such like, the scheme of colonization rises in magnificence and grandeur beyond conception.

"This then is the time to aid this scheme, that when these thickening events shall turn the tide into Liberia, there may be strength and intelligence enough there to receive it!"

The African Repository, XXII, 321–322.

(From the Colonizationist)

THE RANDOLPH SLAVES

"PLATTSVILLE, WIS.,
"August 22, 1846.

"*Bro. Gurley:*—I have observed from time to time, with the deepest interest, the course pursued by the citizens of Ohio toward the emancipated slaves of the late John Randolph of Virginia.

"I had repeatedly remarked in my lectures, as stated in the 'Eleventh Annual Report of the Indiana Colonization Society,' that when slaves were emancipated in the south, and by the laws of those States (as is the case with most of them), they are forced to leave and not permitted to remain in any State south, to go into the north; those northern States would reject them, and leave the slave the alternative, to choose between returning into bondage or emigrating to Liberia. In other words, Liberia offers the only retreat for the slave from bondage, where he is required to leave the south. The free States, may, for a short time, tolerate the migration of a few colored people among them from the south. Especially among the Abolitionists, where they are allowed to have the satisfaction of abducting them from their masters. But if the master comes and offers them, and especially in large numbers, they will be refused.

"On my way to this place, I met with a citizen of Indiana, formerly of Virginia, who gave me some singular facts on this subject. There is living in Ohio, said he, a worthy citizen, a Mr. G., a native of Virginia, who, after a residence there of some eight or ten years, returned to Virginia, on a visit to see a brother who still remained in the 'Old Dominion.' Mr. G. gave his brother an interesting account of the prospects and policy of Ohio, with which he was much pleased. The Virginia brother remarked to Mr. G. that he found his slaves a great burden to him and requested him to take them all to Ohio and set them free! 'I cannot do it,' said Mr. G. 'Why?' asked his brother. 'The citizens of Ohio will not allow me to bring 100 negroes among them to settle,' said Mr. G. 'But,' said he, 'I can put you upon a plan by which you can get rid of them and get them into Ohio very easy. Do you take them to Wheeling and there place them on a steamboat for Cincinnati, and speak of taking them to New Orleans; and while you are looking out for another boat, give the chance, and the Abolitionists will steal the whole of them and run them off, and then celebrate a perfect triumph over them. But if you take them to the same men and ask them to receive and take care of them, they will tell you to take care of them yourself.'

"The case of the Randolph slaves proves that Mr. G. was right, and that the view presented in our annual report is a just one. Mr. Randolph emancipated his slaves, and as they could not remain in Virginia, they were to be sent to Ohio—there they are not allowed to settle, and must now return to bondage, or go to Liberia.

"As yet the burden of embarrassment of a mixed population of blacks is scarcely felt in the north, as it must be soon; for just as emancipation goes on in the south, they must increase in the north, unless our plan and policy prevails. I cannot say that I regret to see a test of these practical truths. For facts speak out loudly to prove the correctness of the best system of policy on these subjects. Had Mr. Randolph's slaves been allowed to remain in Ohio, they would have been a downtrodden and oppressed people for all time to come. If they go to Liberia they will be FREE in every sense of the term.

"B. T. KAVANAUGH."
The African Repository, XXII, 322–323.

THE REPUBLIC OF LIBERIA

"The undersigned, having been appointed agent of the American Colonization Society, for the State of Ohio, to solicit funds to aid its operations, begs leave to call attention to the statistical facts, in reference to the position which this State occupies, in relation to the free colored population of the United States, and the interest which she has in sustaining the Republic of Liberia.

"From 1790 to 1810, the increase of the free colored population of the United States, was at the average rate of near 6 per cent. per annum. The average increase of the slaves has been a little over $2\frac{1}{2}$ per cent. per annum, or exactly two and sixty-hundredths. The census tables for the whole period up to 1840, indicates that the natural increase of the free colored population is somewhat less than that of the slave. I shall suppose it to be $2\frac{1}{4}$ per cent. per annum. The excess of increase over $2\frac{1}{2}$ will, therefore, represent the emancipations. In applying this rule, it appears that the work of emancipation must have been actively prosecuted from 1790 to 1810.

"From 1810 to 1820 the rate of increase was *reduced* to a

little less than 2½, or exactly two and forty-seven hundredths per cent. per annum. This indicates that emancipation had ceased to swell, in any appreciable degree, the number of free colored persons, unless we are forced to admit that there is *greater mortality amongst freedmen than slaves.* This cessation of emancipation was *before the organization of the Colonization Society.* It is supposed to have been caused by the conviction that emancipation upon the soil had wrought but little change in the colored man's condition. The sympathies of good men were therefore awakened in behalf of the colored man, and colonization proposed and adopted, as the best means of securing to him the social and political privileges of which he was deprived. The establishment of an independent republic, including a population of 80,000 souls, with foreign exports to the value of $100,000 a year, and the introduction of civilization and Christianity in Africa, with all their attendant blessings, furnishes an answer to the question of the success of the scheme.

"The period of the greatest popularity of the Colonization Society, was from 1820 to 1830. During this time, the increase of the free colored population reached to nearly 3 per cent. or a half per cent. per annum over the natural increase. But from 1830 to 1840, the period when the Society had the least popularity, the increase was but a very small fraction over *two* per cent. per annum, being two and eight hundredths, indicating that fewer bondmen had been liberated than during any other period. Indeed, the *decrease* was so great as to reduce the rate of increase *more than a half per cent. per annum below the natural increase of the slaves,* and furnished an argument in favor of the idea, that freedom in this country is unfavorable to the longevity of the colored man. From all these facts, we may infer that colonization, while its object has been to benefit the free colored man, has not been unfavorable to emancipation.

"But colonization has not removed the 450,000 free persons of color from our country. They remain as *a floating body* in our midst, drifting, as the census tables show, hither and thither, as the effects of *climate* at the north, or *foreign emigration* at the east, or *prejudice* at the south, repel it from those points. It is an interesting subject of investigation to watch the movements of the colored population, and ascertain where they are tending and whither they will find a resting place.

"In 1810, in the eastern States, they commenced a movement

from north towards the south; and in 1820, began to diverge westward, through the most southern of the free States, and penetrated into Ohio, Indiana, and Illinois. From 1830 to 1840, Pennsylvania alone retained her natural increase, while the other eastern
and northeastern free States, and also the eastern and south-
eastern slave States, all lost, or repelled, the greater part of their
natural increase, and some of them a considerable portion, besides,
of the original stock. But where have these people gone? That
is the question which deeply interests Ohio. The census tables furnish the solution.

"From 1810 to 1840, the colored population of Ohio has been
increasing at the average rate of 20 per cent. per annum. The
increase for the ten years from 1830 to 1840, was 91¼ per cent.
Supposing the emigration into Ohio since 1840 to have been no
greater than before that period, her present colored population
will be 30,000. If to this we add that of Indiana and Illinois,
allowing their increase to have been at the same rate, these three
States will have a population of near 50,000 colored persons, or
*one ninth of the present free colored population of the United
States.*

"Ohio, therefore, cannot remain inactive. *She must do something.* These men should have all the stimulants to mental and
moral action which we ourselves possess. But I shall leave to wiser
men than myself the task of devising *new* means to secure this
object, while I go forward in my labors for the *only one* which has
yet been successful in securing to any portion of the colored people
their just rights.

"The Colonization Society has in its offer, generally, more
slaves than its means will enable it to send to Liberia. Without
a large increase of means, therefore, the Society cannot send out
many *free persons of color.* Three fourths of the emigrants heretofore have been liberated by their masters, with a view of being
sent to Liberia.

"Perhaps it is well that events should have been thus ordered.
If slaves, when emancipated and instructed, and made to taste of
the sweets of liberty, and to feel the responsibilities of nationality,
can establish a prosperous and happy republic, and exert such an
extended moral influence as to accomplish infinitely more in removing the greatest curse of Africa, the slave-trade, from a large
extent of her coast, than has been done at an expense of more than
a hundred millions of dollars, by the fleets of England and France,

it reflects the greater honor upon the African race, and may serve to stimulate the free people of color of this country, to make the effort to join their brethren in a land of freedom.

"In addition to sending emigrants to Liberia, it is of the utmost importance that the Society *should purchase the greatest possible amount of territory, at the present moment,* and thus enlarge the sphere of influence which the republic exerts over the natives, and put it beyond the power of the nations, adverse to her interests, to circumscribe her in the noble efforts she is making for the redemption of Africa.

"In this connection, it may be proper to say, that the gift of *one dime* from each one of the 100,000 inhabitants of Cincinnati, or $10,000 would probably purchase *fifty-six miles square of territory* or more than *two millions of acres of land as good as that of Ohio.* Now, suppose a gift of such value were offered to the colored people of the city, or of the State, on condition that they would take possession of it, and organize *a State Government for themselves,* and be admitted as one of the members of the new republic, who will say that they should or would reject the offer? Who will say that it would not be more safe and wise to emigrate to Africa than to Canada, Oregon, California or Mexico? But the decision of this question of right belongs to the colored people themselves. If the *foreign emigration* continues to roll in upon us, the subordinate stations in society, in the west also, as is the case already in the east, will ere long be chiefly occupied by foreigners, and the colored man left, it is to be feared, without profitable employment. Dear as is the land of one's birth, if men's interests can be better promoted by a removal, the ties of country and kindred are bonds easily broken. The spirit of enterprise which characterizes the present age, if we do our duty, will in due time animate the intelligent colored man, as it is now stimulating the white race, and if he cannot secure equality of condition here, will prompt him to go where he can obtain it.

"Total number of emigrants up to January, 1848... 5,961
Number of communicants in churches in 1843,
        were, of
        Americans 1,015
        Captured Africans 116
        Converted heathen .... 353 in all.... 1,484
Present population estimated by President Roberts.80,000

Of these, are emigrants, captured Africans, etc.,
about 5,000

"The slave trade is suppressed on 400 miles of coast, excepting at one point.

"Shipping owned in the colony, 14 vessels, of from 20 to 80 tons.

"The exports annually, from the colony, are about $100,000.

"David Christy,

"*Agent Am. Col. Society.*"

The African Repository, XXIV, 179–180.

Oxford, O., April, 1848.

A TYPICAL COLONIZATION CONVENTION

CONVENTION OF FREE COLORED PEOPLE

In another column we present a Circular Address to the free colored people of Maryland, calling a Convention to assemble in Baltimore the 25th of July, to take into consideration their present condition and future prosperity, and compare them with the inducements held out to them to emigrate to Liberia. This movement may be considered indicative of the change that is going on in the minds of the colored people respecting emigration. It is well known that heretofore they have been almost entirely insensible to the advantages which they must necessarily enjoy in a land peculiarly their own. They have not been entirely free from the control of bad counsellors.—Now they seem resolved to take the matter into their own hands, and to look at their present condition and future prospects in this country as a matter in which they are personally interested. When they do this in earnest, the result can be easily foreseen. They will desire to escape from their present anomalous condition, will yearn to be free and disenthralled, to have a land of their own, to have rights unquestioned by any superiors, where character, enterprise, education, and all that is lovely and noble in life shall combine to elevate and improve them and their children after them to the latest generation.

—*African Repository,* XXVIII, 195–196.

EMIGRATION OF THE COLORED RACE

In presenting the circular, which will be found in another column, of which a committee of colored persons have undertaken the distribution, (and which was written by one of themselves,) it gives us pleasure to commend it as the evidence of a new and generally unexpected change of sentiment on the part of the colored population, or, at least, some portion of it. It is well known that for twenty-five years the Colonization Societies in this country have labored to present before that portion of our population, the advantages which must accrue to them, from emigration to a land where they might enjoy, undisturbed, those social and material privileges which it was impossible ever to expect they could obtain by a residence of centuries in this country, and that these appeals have met with comparatively little attention, and, in deed have been received with very bad grace by the great mass of those whom it was intended to benefit. The cause of this opposition was to be found in the steady and violent animosity of those white fanatics, who, setting themselves up as the peculiar friends of the blacks, represented that the prejudice against their color was merely an arbitrary sentiment, which time would weaken or entirely dissipate; and that they might still look forward to enjoying, in this country, an equality in social and political rights with the whites.

This assumption of peculiar friendliness on the part of the Abolitionists, and the plausible reasonings with which they approached their "colored friends," have acquired the confidence of the latter, who are now, however, beginning to awake to a just idea of their condition and future prespects in this country. They have discovered that the loud-mouthed protestations of the Abolitionists, are the mere effervescence of an intermeddling and dangerous faction, against whose principles the whole Union—whose destruction they have mediated—has pronounced in tones of thunder; a faction whose baleful alliance is shunned most religiously, by both of the great parties of the country. They have discovered that underground railroads are a device to inveigle the slaves from a condition of comparative comfort, into the *freedom of starvation*, with a poor display of political privileges, which are mockery in view of their exercise by an ignorant and despised minority; that the expectations fostered in behalf of the free blacks are proved to be entirely futile by the continued attitude of opposition held towards them, when there is a question of lessening the social and political gulf which divides the races. They discover that the rapid immigration of whites from every quarter, is encroaching upon their employments, and lessening their chance of gaining a thrifty livelihood, even in those menial pursuits to which they are chiefly limited.

With the spread of education, and the expansion of republican ideas, they become more sensible of their own anomalous and degraded condition, and the result is a yearning to be free like those around them, to have a land all their own, to have rights unquestioned by any superior color, to go wherever such privileges may be obtained. They see in the growing republics on the West coast of Africa, a living refutation of the calumnies of the Abolitionists against the colonizationists, a land where, from simple citizenship up to the highest post in the government, all is free and open to them, and where character, enterprise, education and honorable ambition, have all their appropriate rewards in the order of the State. What is better, no white man can hope to cast his lot there with the prospect of permanent settlement, or transmitting a healthy posterity. They see there such men as the late Gov. Russwurm or the present Gov. Roberts, sustaining their rule surrounded by their own race, with a distinction and dignity which would do honor to any white man. They see there pioneers of their own color, who in the arts of peace or of war, are striking examples of what the emancipation of the MIND can effect.

This is a crisis full of important results to the race in this country, and it behooves them now to cast aside all false issues, to take into serious consideration (in the words of the circular) their present condition and future prospects in this country, and contrast them with the inducements and prospects opened to them in Liberia, or any other country.

We have little doubt as to the quarter to which their preferences will be given, although that is as yet left an open question. Trinidad is a failure, Jamaica is a half-ruined British dependency, and in both the white man the sole source of authority. Liberia excepted, Haiti is the only point left, and here reigns a perpetual jealousy between the black and mulatto. Moreover, the imperial rule set up there is repugnant to their feelings and inclinations, for strange to say, in the midst of depression, this race in America has become imbued with a sentiment of republicanism and a love for its system, which will make them in Africa the sedulous imitators of ourselves, in all but in the misfortune of introducing another race to be perpetually subservient to themselves. In this career we are happy to believe they will run rejoicing, long after the privations of their forefathers in this country shall have been forgotten.

—*African Repository*, XXVIII, 196–197.

CIRCULAR

Pursuant to an invitation given through the columns of the Baltimore daily papers to the Free Colored Population of Baltimore, friendly to calling a State Convention, to be held in this city some time during the ensuing summer to take into consideration their present position and future prospects in this country, and to compare the same with the inducements and prospects held out to them to emigrate to Liberia or elsewhere; a respectable number assembled in the school room of St. James (colored) Church, corner of Saratoga and North streets.

The meeting being duly organized, it was resolved that a Convention of Delegates of the Free Colored Population from each county of the State of Maryland and of the City of Baltimore, be held in this city on the 25th of July next, for the purpose above stated.

Resolved, That a committee of three be appointed to issue a circular addressed to the Free Colored People of the State, setting forth the object of the Convention, the time of its commencement and the conditions upon which Delegates will be entitled to a seat in the same.

At an adjourned meeting of persons friendly to the call of the said Convention, held on the 4th of June 1852, in the room before referred to, the Committee on the Circular Address, made the following report, which was unanimously approved and adopted:

ADDRESS TO THE FREE COLORED PEOPLE OF THE STATE OF MARYLAND

Brethren:—Whereas the present age is one distinguished for inquiry, investigation and enterprise, in physical, moral and political sciences above all past ages of the world, one in which the nations of the earth seem to have arisen from the slumber of ages, and are putting forth their utmost energies to obtain all those blessings, which nature and nature's God seem to have intended that man should enjoy, and the principles set forth by the American Sages, in the Declaration of Independence of these United States, "that all men are created equal, and are endowed by their Creator with certain inalienable rights, among which are life, liberty and the pursuit of happiness," with each revolving year have extended wider and wider throughout the habitable globe, and sunk deeper and deeper into the hearts of millions of men, and as we humbly hope, are destined to revolutionize the civil and political conditions of all the nations of the earth, it would indeed be passing strange if the Free Colored man in this country, which gave birth to those elevated and sublime sentiments, should feel nothing of the force of their mighty import, and with anxious eye and panting heart, endeavor in this, or some other country, to realize the blessings so freely enjoyed by the white citizens of this land. Actuated by these feelings we have presumed to address our brethren of our native State, and we do hereby respectfully solicit them to assemble with us in this city, on the 25th of next month (July), to take into serious consideration our present condition and future prospects in this country, and contrast them with the inducements and prospects opened to us in Liberia, or any other country. In conformity with a resolution passed at the meeting held on the 24th ultimo, the Committee do hereby respectfully propose, that each county in the State shall have the privilege of sending any number of Delegates not exceeding six, as they may deem proper, and our brethren throughout the State are requested to hold meetings (by legal permission) in their several counties, for the purpose of selecting their Delegates, and to collect money to defray the expenses they may incur by attending the said Convention.

As the object for which this Convention is called, is one of vital importance to the Free Colored People of Maryland, it is greatly to be desired, and confidently expected that a full attendance of Delegates will be present on the occasion, who will calmly, deliberately and intelligently consider the object for which they have been called together, and that each Delegate will come prepared to contribute his portion of information, and fully and freely to express his views on the great subject of our future destiny.

Delegates are requested to bring credentials of their appointment from the chairman and secretary of the meeting at which they were appointed, but in counties where no formal meeting is held, Delegates are requested to procure a certificate from some respectable person, either white or colored, a well known resident of the county from whence he or they may come. All Delegates complying with the above requisitions, shall be duly admitted to the Convention.

All communications in relation to the Convention must be directed to the care of H. H. Webb, St. James' School Room, corner of Saratoga and North streets.

JAMES A. HANDY, *Chairman.*

JOHN H. WALKER, *Secretary.*

—*The African Repository,* XXXIII, pp. 197–199.

BALTIMORE, June 4, 1852.

PROCEEDINGS OF THE CONVENTION OF FREE COLORED PEOPLE OF THE
STATE OF MARYLAND

Held in Baltimore, July 26, 27, and 28, 1852

In pursuance of public notice, a meeting of delegates to the Convention of Free Colored People of the State was held in the lower room of Washington Hall. The Convention was temporarily organized at 3 o'clock, by calling James A. Handy, of Fell's Point, to the chair, John H. Walker being appointed secretary. Mr. Handy returned his thanks for the honor conferred upon him.

On motion of Charles O. Fisher, of Fell's Point, a committee of one from each delegation present was appointeed to nominate permanent officers of the Convention.

On motion of James F. Jackson, the credentials of the delegates were handed in, and the following sections of the State were found to be represented:

East Baltimore—James A. Handy, James T. Jackson, Chas. O. Fisher, Stephen W. Hill, Daniel Koburn, David G. Bailey.

Kent county—Jas. A. Jones, Isaac Anderson, Levi Rogers, Wm. Perkins.

Dorchester county—B. Jenifer, C. Sinclair, S. Green, Thomas Fuller, S. Camper, J. Hughes.

Caroline County—Jacob Lewis, Philip Canada, John Webb.

Northwest Baltimore—Samuel B. Hutchings, David P. Jones, Wm. H. White, Francis Johns, John H. Walker, Cornelius Thompson.

Frederick County—Rev. William Tasker, Perry E. Walker, Joseph Lisles, Robert Troby, Ephraim Lawson, Nicholas Penn.

Northeast Baltimore—Chas. Williamson, Rev. Darius Stokes, H. H. Webb, J. Forty, C. Perry, Fred. Harris.

Hartford County—Daniel Ross, Henry Hopkins.

Talbot County—Garrison Gibson, Charles Dobson, Joseph Bantem.

There was considerable excitement among a number of 'outsiders,' opposed to the meeting and its objects, who frequently assailed the delegates coming to the Convention and a large number of whom, having come into the room, were ripe for any further opposition they could exhibit.

The Dorchester county delegation having seen this state of things, several of them arose and remarked that they did not think that their presence here could be of any benefit, and they there proposed to withdraw and go home. This announcement was received with applause, and cries of "good" from the opponents of colonization.

A member from Kent county begged the delegates to stand firm in their position, and the result of their labors would be of much benefit. [Applause and hisses.]

John H. Walker of Baltimore, arose and read the circular calling the Convention, which was to take into consideration the present condition and future prospects of the colored race. He said they lived in the same State that their fathers had lived in, but not under the same Constitution—the new instrument not recognizing the colored people at all. They were men, but not recognized as men. He alluded to the legislation of the members of the Assembly, all of which resulted in oppression to the colored race, each consecutive session. He desired that the condition of the colored people should be considered by this convention; that they should decide on what course to take. The circular alluded to emigration to Liberia, or elsewhere, which he explained to mean that they should examine all the places and see if emigration would be beneficial. It was necessary for them to know the geographical position and resources of the different countries—of their rivers, mountains, harbors, climate, &c; and if the convention should determine on any particular place for emigration, it was necessary to ascertain all that would be wanted in such country. For one he intended now to remain where he was, but if a better place could be found why he was gone for it. The speaker was opposed at first, but finally gained the attention of the audience, and was frequently applauded.

Wm. Perkins, of Kent county, said he believed that much of the opposition and excitement which had sprung up about this convention within a few days, was caused by a report, falsely circulated, that the Colonization Society had given $700 for carrying out certain objects through its medium. He hoped that after the explanation that had been given, the Dorchester county delegation would consent to remain.

A member from Dorchester county said that if they were assured that the colored people of Baltimore desired them to remain, they would do so. Their object was to consult for the good of the colored race.

Perry E. Walker, of Frederick, said, they had come here supposing that the majority of the colored people of Baltimore were in favor of the call of the convention. (Cries of "no, they are not.") He and his associates had come to consider into the condition of their race—had no other object in view.

Rev. Darius Stokes addressed the convention, the object of which, he said, was to consult only in reference to the condition of the colored people. They had been told for thirty years past of countries which were better for them, but they had only to depend upon the representation of others as to the truths of these statements. They were a people—the colored people of the State of Maryland—who should consult about their present condition and future prospects. He said their white friends were getting tired of helping them, because they did not seem disposed, it was alleged, to help themselves. He asked where were their schools, orphan asylums? &c. As to going to Africa he was in favor of any man going where he thought he could do better. (Cries of "good," "right," "that's it.")

P. Gilman (not a delegate), asked to be heard, and after a great deal of confusion, got the attention of the audience, and spoke in opposition to what Mr. Stokes had said. He remarked that he could not talk as well as Stokes, but he could think as well. (laughter.) As for him, he came here to put down and oppose this convention. [Cries of "good," and cheers from the audience.]

Henry Zeddicks, of Frederick, said that they were here from pure motives, to consult for their good, and was received with much favor by the whole assemblage.

James A. Jones, of Kent, said he was decidedly in favor of emigration—and emigration to Africa. They expected to be honored in coming into the presence of Baltimore friends, but in this, the largest city of the State, they found a great amount of confusion. In his opinion, he believed that the colored man could never rise to eminence except in Africa—in the land of their forefathers. [A voice—"Show it in Africa."] He pointed to Liberia. He believed that Africa was the only place where the colored man could expect to be a freeman. On taking his seat he was hissed by the opponents of emigration.

The committee on nominating permanent officers, recommended the following, who were accepted:

President—Rev. William Tasker, of Frederick; *Vice Presidents* —C. Sinclair of Dorchester, Levi Rogers of Kent, E. Lawson of Frederick, S. W. Hill of East Baltimore, Charles Dobson of Talbot,

Francis Johns of West Baltimore, and John Webb of Caroline; *Secretaries*, John H. Walker of Baltimore, and Josiah Hughes of Dorchester.

Rev. Darius Stokes addressed the convention in an eloquent and fervent style in reference to its objects.

James A. Jones, of Kent, said that since he had addressed the convention, he had been informed that his head, if not his life, was in danger if he left the room. He would therefore leave under the protection of the police, and send in the morning his resignation.

Rev. Darius Stokes begged Mr. Jones to remain—that the young colored gentlemen of Baltimore were not disposed to harm him. People had said that they had met here to sell their rights and liberties, but they would show them to-morrow that they only looked to their welfare and interests. This was the first time a colored convention of the whole State and ever assembled in the State—a remarkable era in their history.

On motion of Mr. Stokes a committee of ten were appointed to prepare a "platform" for the convention. The following was the Committee:—H. H. Webb, of Baltimore; James A. Jones, of Kent; Charles O. Fisher, of Baltimore; B. Jenifer and Thomas Fuller, of Dorchester; Jacob Lewis, of Caroline; Joseph Bantem of Talbot; Perry E. Walker, of Frederick; William Williams, of Baltimore; and Henry Hopkins, of Harford.

The convention then adjourned till Tuesday morning.

SECOND DAY'S PROCEEDINGS

The Convention re-assembled at 10 o'clock on Tuesday the 27th, at Washington Hall, the Rev. William Tasker of Frederick, President, in the chair. The convention was opened with prayer by the president.

A note was received from H. H. Webb, of Baltimore, declining to serve as a delegate to the convention, stating that he was not able to attend, and did not approve of the manner in which he was elected.

In the absence of Josiah Hughes, of Dorchester, one of the Secretaries, Cornelius Campbell, was appointed to fill the vacancy.

The proceedings of Monday not being ready, on motion, the report in the "*Sun*" was read in lieu thereof.

William Williams, of Baltimore, arose and stated that his name appeared in the committee on the platform through a mistake—he was not a delegate to the convention.

On motion, James A. Handy, of Baltimore, and William Perkins, of Kent, were appointed on the platform committee, to fill the vacancies occasioned by the withdrawal of Webb and Williams.

Charles Wyman and Allen Lockerman, delegates from Caroline Co., appeared and took their seats.

Several of the delegates from Dorchester county and other places were not present, having gone home in consequence of the disturbances on Monday afternoon.

B. Jenifer, chairman of the committee on the platform, made the following report, which was read by Charles O. Fisher:

WHEREAS, The present age is one distinguished for enquiry, investigation, enterprise and improvement in physical, political, intellectual and moral sciences, we hold the truths to be self-evident that we are, as well as all mankind, created equal, and are endowed by our Creator with the right to enquire into our present condition and future prospects; and as a crisis has arisen in our history presenting a bright and glorious future, may we not hope that ere long the energies of our people may be aroused from their lethargy, and seek to obtain for themselves and posterity the rights and privileges of freemen—therefore,

Resolved, That while we appreciate and acknowledge the sincerity of the motives and the activity of the zeal of those who, during an agitation of twenty years have honestly struggled to place us on a footing of social and political equality with the white population of this country, yet we cannot conceal from ourselves the fact that no advance has been made towards a result to us so desirable; but that on the contrary, our condition as a class is less desirable than it was twenty years ago.

Resolved, That in the face of an emigration from Europe, which is greater each year than it was the year before, and during the prevalence of a feeling in regard to us, which the very agitation intended for good, has only served apparently to embitter we cannot promise ourselves that the future will do that which the past has failed to accomplish.

Resolved, That recognising in ourselves the capacity to conduct honorably, and creditably, in public affairs; to acquire knowledge, and to enjoy the refinements of social intercourse; and having a praiseworthy ambition that this capacity should be developed to its full extent, we are naturally led to enquire where this can best be done, satisfied as we are that in this country, at all events from present appearances, it is out of the question.

Resolved, That in comparing the relative advantages of Canada, the West Indies and Liberia—these being the places beyond the limits of the United States to which circumstances have directed our attention—we are led to examine the claims of Liberia particularly, where alone, we have been told that we can exercise all the functions of a free republican government, and hold an honorable position among the nations of the earth.

Resolved, That in thus expressing our opinions it is not our purpose to counsel emigration as either necessary or proper in every case. The transfer of an entire people from one country to another, must necessarily be the work of generations—each individual now and hereafter must be governed by the circumstances of his own condition, of which he alone can be the judge, as well in regard to the time of removal, as to the place to which he shall remove; but deeply impressed ourselves with the conviction that sooner or later removal must take place, we would counsel our people to accustom themselves to the idea of it, and in suggesting Liberia to them, we do so in the belief that it is there alone they can reasonably anticipate an independent national existence.

Resolved, That as this subject is one of greatest importance to us, and the consideration of which, whatever may be the result, can not be put aside, we recommend to our people in this State to establish and maintain an organization in regard to it, the great object of which shall be enquiry and discussion, which, without committing any one, shall lead to accurate information, and that a convention like the present, composed of delegates from the counties and Baltimore city, be annually held at such time and place as said convention, in their judgment, may designate.

A motion was made to accept the report, which led to debate, John H. Walker speaking at length in opposition to the resolutions, and hoped that they would be referred back to the committee, contending that there should have been a recommendation to raise a fund to fee a lawyer, or some influential citizen of this State, to go to Annapolis next winter to endeavor to obtain a change of legislation in reference to the colored race.

B. Jenifer, of Dorchester, replied to Walker, urging that his views were in opposition to the spirit of the circular which called them together, and a majority of the delegates present.

At one o'clock the convention took a recess.

Afternoon Session.—The convention re-assembled at 4 o'clock, the resolutions being again debated by various delegates—John H. Walker, B. Jenifer, C. Perry, and others.

Rev. Darius Stokes moved to lay the motion to adopt the platform on the table, which was determined in the affirmative.

On motion of Mr. Stokes the convention went into the committee of the whole, Charles Williamson in the chair, and took up the report of the committee in sections.

The two first resolutions were adopted, the third referred back to the committee, and pending the further action on the remainder of the resolutions, the convention adjourned till Wednesday morning.

THIRD DAY'S PROCEEDINGS

The convention re-assembled at 10 o'clock on Wednesday the 28th at Plowman street Hall, Ephraim Lawson, Vice President, in the chair, who opened the proceedings with Prayer.

A note was received from the President, Rev. Wm. Tasker, stating that indisposition would prevent him from presiding over the deliberations of the body the remainder of its sessions.

The attendance of the delegatees was small in the morning, and very few lookers on were present.

The platform being again taken up, F. Harris, of Baltimore, presented a protest against the adoption of the fourth resolution, which pointed out Liberia as the place of emigration for the colored people, because it recommends emigration to that place contrary to the wishes of his constituents, and a majority of the free colored people of the city and State. He contended that if they were for Liberia, they should say so at once, and tell the mob out doors that they were endeavoring to send them all there—not say one thing in the convention and another outside.

James A. Jones, of Kent, said that Harris was endeavoring to shape his course the way the wind blowed. For himself, he hoped the entire platform would be adopted, and without further debate he moved that the fourth resolution be passed.

Stephen W. Hill, of Baltimore, contended that the resolutions did not look to an immediate emigration to Africa—that they only recommended Liberia as a place where they could enjoy the blessings of liberty, and as the most suitable country for the colored man whenever they should be disposed to seek another home.

William Perkins, of Kent, in answer to the protest of Harris, said the only platform they recommended for adoption, left it to every man to go where he pleased, or to remain here if it suited him better. Let Mr. Harris go to his constituents and tell them that the convention only recommended what it thought best; its action was binding on no man.

F. Harris, in reply, asked if the convention had examined Liberia. They recommended that place for them to emigrate to, and yet they had not made any examination of Liberia to know whether it would suit. Did they know anything of the climate or agriculture of Liberia to lay before the people. Let them examine Canada, Jamaica, and other places, and then if they found Liberia the best place, why say so to the people.

Chas. Williamson said he had had it in his power to examine most countries. He had been in Canada twice; in the West Indies three times, and, under the British government in Trinidad five years. During that time he had examined the countries with a view to see which was the best for the colored people. He was sixty-seven years of age and could expect little for himself. In the West Indies capital ruled the people—the government recognized you, but the planters, who had been accustomed to drive on slaves, knew you not. If they went to Canada they would not better their condition—he had lived there seventeen months at one time. It would cost money to get to Canada—money to get to the West Indies. The Canadas are peopled with many persons from this country. The leading men were principally Yankees. In the West Indies he had to take his hat around to get the dead out of the way of the turkey-buzzards—that showed their sympathy. In Canada you cannot be recognized in office—in the West Indies it is better, and some colored persons get into office. In the Canadas he never heard of but one colored man being in office. The Canadas are a fine country, but he asserted here that he felt there could no permanent home for them except in Africa, where their children could enjoy all the blessings of liberty. That was the best country for them. In the United States they did not want the colored people any more, they had got the use of them, and now in this State the new constitution did not recognize them at all. (A voice—"Yes, as chattels.") The minister of Hayti to this country was not recognized by the President, and had to go home again. Liberia, on the west coast of Africa, had as fine, or better, climate, as regards atmosphere, than the West Indies. He wished to go where they would be free, for their moral culture here he considered out of the question.

James A. Handy, of Baltimore, remarked that they lived in an interesting age of the world—that it was the glory of our day that assistance is offered to the immortal principles of man, and it struggles to free itself from the trammels and superstitions of the past, and of the oppressions and burthens of the present. We live in an age of physical, moral and intellectual wonders; and that man is truly fortunate who lives at the present, and has the privilege of aiding in carrying forward the great enterprise of redeeming, disenthralling and restoring back in all their primitive glory three millions of down trodden people to the land of their forefathers. On the western shore of Africa there was the infant republic of Liberia attracting the attention of all the enlightened nations of the earth. For four years she had maintained her position as an independent State, and today she was prosperous, happy and free, acknowledged by England, France, Russia and Prussia—four of the greatest powers of the earth; and before this year is out the United States will be willing, ready and anxious to cultivate friendly relations with that garden spot—that heritage which a kind and overruling Providence has prepared for us, and not only for us, but for all the sable sons and daughters of Ham.

One word in relation to the inducements held out by Liberia— Asia could not exceed the variety of the productions of Africa— Europe with her numerous manufactories and internal resources, could not cope with her in physical greatness—America with her noble institutions, elements of power, facilities of improvement, promises of greatness and high hopes of immortality, was this day far, very far behind her in natural resources. Nothing can excel the value of her productions—sugar-cane grows rapidly, cotton is a native plant, corn and hemp flourish in great perfection; oranges, coffee, wild honey, lemons, limes, mahogany, cam-wood, satin-wood, rose-wood, &c., abound there; mules, oxen, horses, sheep, hogs, fowls of all kinds, are in the greatest abundance. She holds out a rich temptation to commerce and a strong inducement to emigration. To the latter the United States owed what she was, making her one of the most effective nations of the world. For years the glorious galaxy of stars which arose in the western hemisphere have been casting their generous, grateful light over the social, moral and political darkness of the East, but to-day the commanding tide of commerce is changing. From the Pacific shores the genius of

American enterprise and industry has opened a nearer highway to the Celestial Empire, and is now, by a closer interchange of fraternal relations, unbolting the massive doors, and securing the commerce of China and Japan.

On the lap of American civilization, and around the altars of this christian land, have been born the moral elements of civil and Christian power, ordained by heaven for the redemption of Africa. For the last 2,000 years, that wretched land of mystery and crime has been abandoned to the cupidity of most cruel barbarism, surpassing in degradation, guilt and woe, all other nations of the earth. Pre-eminently high on the page of prophetic scripture is chronicled in most unequivocal language the name and future redemption of Africa. For twelve centuries the problem "how shall Africa be redeemed?" has been unsolved, although earnestly sought for by the civil and religious powers of Europe; but in every instance it has been in vain, and the cloud of her wretchedness blackened on each failure. Mysterious and inscrutable are the ways of Providence to accomplish her restoration, lift her from the jaws of death, bind her as a jewel to the throne of righteousness, and give her a place among the civilized nations of mankind. God in his pity, wisdom and goodness, has opened the way for a part of her crushed children, predoomed by bloody superstitions to altars of death, to be delivered from immolation and find an asylum under a form of ameliorated service in the bosom of this country; and here their children have been born, elevated and blessed under redeeming auspices. In the lapse of time, by the same benevolent providence, many of this people have become free, and to such the voice of heaven emphatically speaks, thundering forth in invigorating terms, "Arise and depart for this is not your rest."

This makes us bold in saying that emigration is the only medium by which the long closed doors of that continent are to be opened; by her own children's returning, bearing social and moral elements of civil and religious power, by which that continent is to be resuscitated, renovated and redeemed.

Thirty-one years ago the first emigrant ship that ever sailed eastward from these shores to Africa, conveying to that dark land a missionary family of some two hundred souls—her own returning children, enriched with the more enduring treasures of the western world; there by them on the borders of that continent, overshadowed with the deepest gloom, were raised the first rude temples of civilization—the first halls of enlightened legislation—

the first christian altars to the worship of Almighty God that have ever proved successful, or of any permanent, practical utility. Then and there arose the long promised light, the star of hope to the benighted millions of Africa. Since that day the star has risen higher and higher, the light extended along the coast and reaching far back towards the mountains of the Moon, radiating, elevating and purifying; and to-day we behold a nation born on the western coast of Africa, respected, prosperous and happy. Here then is practically and beautifully solved, on the true utilitarian principles of this wonder-working age, the mysterious problem: By whom is Africa to be redeemed? The answer comes rumbling back to us, over the towering billows of the Atlantic, from the Republic of Liberia, with a voice that starts our inmost souls, falling with ponderous weight upon the ears of the free colored people of this Union—"thou art the man, thou art the woman."

James A. Jackson, of Baltimore, eulogized Hayti as standing as high above the other West India islands as the United States does above the republic of Mexico, in the point of commercial importance. This island had tried the experiment of republicanism and had changed it. It was now a question with the colored people, in their present condition, whether they were more suited to a republican than monarchical government. The productions of the soil of Hayti and of her forests were referred to, and the fact alleged that she would produce more than all the other West India islands put together. The exports and imports of the United States to and from the island were cited as an illustration of her prosperity. A comparison was made of the commerce of Liberia and that of Hayti, the latter country being held up in a very favorable light.

Nicholas Penn, of Frederick, spoke in favor of emigration to Liberia. They did not want an island. The colored population increased so fast that they needed no island but a continent for them. His constituents wished him to examine Africa, and he hoped it would be done. Liberia was the only place for them. The white man fought for and claimed this country, and he was now going to give it up to them. In the language of Patrick Henry, will we be ready tomorrow or next day to act more than now? No! Now was the time; and he hoped this enterprise would spread far and wide until the whole people should understand it and all unite in the glorious movement. Let us appoint men to go and examine Liberia, and report to us just what it is. We want a home, and we were sent here to examine and determine on what would be best to recommend.

B. Jenifer, of Dorchester, said, all these statements about Africa were theoretical—gained through geography, and went on to state that he had spent nearly eleven months in Africa, had traveled it over and examined its productions and resources. He had been sent for that purpose by a colored colonization society of his county; but did not wish to discuss Liberia at this time. Mr. Handy had so ably discussed the subject, and in all of which he fully coincided with him. The true question for this convention to decide was whether they should remain, here, or to seek a home in Liberia or elsewhere.

John H. Walker, after some difficulty, got the floor and offered a substitute for the report of the committee on the platform, which was unanimously adopted. The following is the substitute:

WHEREAS, The present age is one eminently distinguished for inquiry, investigation, enterprise and improvement in physical, political, intellectual and moral sciences; and, whereas, among our white neighbors every exertion is continually being made to improve their social and moral condition, and develop their intellectual faculties; and, whereas, it is a duty which mankind, (colored as well as white,) owe to themselves and their Creator to embrace every opportunity for the accomplishment of this mental culture and intellectual development, and general social improvement; and, whereas, we, the free colored people of the State of Maryland, are conscious that we have made little or no progress in improvement during the past twenty years, but are now sunken into a condition of social degradation which is truly deplorable, and the continuing to live in which we cannot but view as a crime and transgression against our God, ourselves and our posterity; and, whereas, we believe that a crisis in our history has arrived when we may choose for ourselves degradation, misery and wretchedness, on the one hand, or happiness, honor and enlightenment, on the other, by pursuing one of two paths which are now laid before us for our consideration and choice; may we not, therefore, hope that our people will awaken from their lethargic slumbers, and seek for themselves that future course of conduct which will elevate them from their present position and place them on an equality with the other more advanced races of mankind—may we not hope that they will consider seriously the self-evident proposition that all men are created equal, and endowed by the Creator with the same privileges of exerting themselves for their own and each other's benefit; and, whereas, in view of these considerations, and in order to commence the great and glorious work of our moral elevation, and our social and intellectual improvement, we are of the opinion that an organization of the friends of this just and holy cause is absolutely necessary for effecting the object so much to be desired, and we are therefore—

Resolved, That we will each and every one, here pledge ourselves to each other and to our God, to use on every and all occasions, our utmost efforts to accomplish the objects set forth in the foregoing preamble; and that we will, now, and forever hereafter, engraft this truth in our prayers, our hopes, our instructions to our brethren and our children—namely, that degradation is a sin and a source of misery, and it is a high, and honorable and a blessed privilege we enjoy, the right to improve ourselves and transmit to posterity happiness instead of our misery—knowledge instead of our ignorance.

Resolved, That while we appreciate and acknowledge the sincerity of the motives and the activity of the zeal of those who, during an agitation of twenty years, have honestly struggled to place us on a footing of social and political equality with the white population of the country, yet we cannot conceal from ourselves the fact that no advancement has been made towards a result to us so desirable; but that on the contrary, our condition as a class is less desirable now than it was twenty years ago.

Resolved, That in the face of an emigration from Europe, which is greater each year than it was the year preceding, and during the prevalence of a feeling in regard to us, which the very agitation intended for good has only served apparently to embitter, we cannot promise ourselves that the future will do that which the past has failed to accomplish.

Resolved, That we recognize in ourselves the capacity of conducting our own public affairs in a manner at once creditable and well calculated to further among us the cause of religion, virtue, morality, truth and enlightenment—and to acquire for ourselves the possession and enjoyment of that elevated refinement which so much adorns and beautifies social intercourse among mankind, and leads them to a proper appreciation of the relations existing between man and Deity—man and his fellow men, and man and that companion whom God has bestowed upon him, to console him in the hours of trouble and darkness, or enjoy with him the blessings that heaven vouchsafed occasionally to shower upon our pathway through life.

Resolved, That in a retrospective survey of the past, we see between the white and colored races a disparity of thought, feeling and intellectual advancement, which convinces us that it cannot be that the two races will ever overcome their natural prejudices towards each other sufficiently to dwell together in harmony and in the enjoyment of like social and political privileges, and we therefore hold that a separation of ourselves from our white neighbors, many of whom we cannot but love and admire for the generosity they have displayed towards us from time to time, is an object devoutly to be desired and the consummation of which would tend to the natural advantage of both races.

Resolved, That comparing the relative advantages afforded us in Canada, the West Indies and Liberia—these being the places beyond the limits of the United States which circumstances have directed our attention—we are led to examine the claims of Liberia particularly, for there alone, we have been told, that we can exercise all the functions of a free republican government, and hold an honorable position among the nations of the earth.

Resolved, That this Convention recommend to the colored people of Maryland, the formation of societies in the counties of the State and the city of Baltimore, who shall meet monthly, for the purpose of raising means to establish and support free schools for the education of our poor and destitute children, and for the appointment each month of a person whose duty it shall be to collect such information in relation to the condition of the colored emigrants in Canada, West Indies, Guiana and Liberia, as can be obtained by him from all available sources, which information shall be brought to these monthly meetings above alluded to, and read before them for the instruction of all, in order that when they are resolved, if they should so resolve, to remove from this country to any other, they may know what will be their wants, opportunities, prospects, &c., in order to provide beforehand for any emergencies that may meet them on their arrival in their new homes.

Resolved, That as this subject is one of the greatest importance to us, and the consideration of which whatever may be the result, cannot be put aside, we recommend to our people in this State to establish and maintain an organization in regard to it, the great object of which shall be enquiry and discussion, which, without committing any, may lead to accurate information; and that a convention like the present, composed of delegates from the respective counties of the State and from Baltimore city, be held annually at such times and places as may be hereafter designated. '

Resolved, That in thus expressing our opinions, it is not our purpose to counsel emigration as either necessary or proper in every case. The transfer of an entire people from one country to another, must necessarily be the work of generations. Each individual now and hereafter must be governed by the circumstances of his own condition, of which he alone can be the judge, as well in regard to the time of removal as to the place to which he shall remove; but deeply impressed ourselves with the conviction that sooner or later removal must take place, we would counsel our people to accustom themselves to that idea.

Resolved, That this Convention recommend to the ministers of the gospel among the free colored population of Maryland to endeavor, by contributions from their congregations and by other means, to raise funds for the purpose of forwarding the benevolent object of educating the children of the destitute colored persons in this State; and that they also impress upon the minds of their hearers the benefits which would necessarily result from development of their intellects, and the bringing into fullest use those mental powers and reasoning faculties which distinguish mankind from the brute creation; and that this be requested of them as a part of their duty as ministers of the religion of our Lord and Saviour Jesus Christ.

E. Harris entered his protest against the adoption of the fourth resolution.

A motion made to adjourn sine die at 2 o'clock P.M., was lost; and a resolution restricting each speaker to five minute speeches was adopted.

Wm. Perkins spoke of the law enforced in Kent, by which the children of free colored persons, whom the officers decided the parents were unable to support, were bound out; and also of the law which prohibited a colored person returning to the State if he should happen to leave it. They were oppressed and borne down.

James A. Jones, of Kent, thought his native county equal to any other in the State, and that colored persons were not more oppressed there than elsewhere in the State.

Charles O. Fisher moved that a committee of five be appointed to draw up a memorial to the Legislature of Maryland, praying more indulgence to the colored people of the State, in order that they may have time to prepare themselves for a change in their condition, and for removal to some other land.

Daniel Koburn, of Baltimore, in referring to the oppressive laws of the State, said the hog law of Baltimore was better moderated than that in reference to the colored people. The hog law said at certain seasons they should run about and at certain seasons be taken up; but the law referring to colored people allowed them to be taken up at any time.

Chas. Dobson, of Talbot, said that the time had come when free colored men in this country had been taken up and sold for one year, and when that year was out, taken up and sold for another year. Who knew what the next Legislature would do; and if any arrangements could be made to better their condition, he was in favor of them. He was for the appointing the committee on the memorial.

B. Jenifer, of Dorchester, opposed the resolution; he was not in favor of memorializing the Legislature—it had determined to carry out certain things, and it was a progressive work.

Chas. Wyman, of Caroline; Jos. Bantem, of Talbot; John H. Walker, Chas. O. Fisher and others discussed the resolution which was finally adopted.

The following is the committee appointed: Jno. H. Walker and Jas. A. Handy, of Baltimore; William Perkins, of Kent; Thomas Fuller, of Dorchester; and Daniel J. Ross, of Hartford county.

A resolution of thanks to the officers of the Convention, the reporters of the morning papers, and authorities for their protection, was adopted. The proceedings were also ordered to be printed in pamphlet form.

The Convention, at 3 o'clock adjourned to meet on the second Monday in November, 1853, at Frederick, Md.

—From the *Baltimore Sun*, July 27, 28, and 29, 1852.

REVIEWS OF BOOKS

The Slaveholding Indians. Volume I: As Slaveholder and Secessionist. By ANNIE HELOISE ABEL, Ph.D. The Arthur H. Clark Company, Cleveland, 1915. Pp. 394.

This is the first of three volumes on the slaveholding Indians planned by the author. Volume II is to treat of the Indians as participants in the Civil War and Volume III on the Indian under Reconstruction.

The present volume deals with a phase, as the author says, "of American Civil War history, which has heretofore been almost neglected, or where dealt with, either misunderstood or misinterpreted." It comes as a surprise to most of us that the Indian played a part of sufficient importance within the Union to have the right to have something to say about secession. Yet inconsistently enough he was considered so much a foreigner that both the South and the North, particularly the former, found it expedient to employ diplomacy in approaching him.

The South, we are assured, found the attitude of the Indians toward secession of the greatest importance. Yet it was not the Indian owner so much as the Indian country that the Confederacy wanted to be sure of possessing, for Indian Territory occupied a position of strategic importance from both the economic and the military point of view. "The possession of it was absolutely necessary for the political and institutional consolidation of the South. Texas might well think of going her own way and of forming an independent republic once again, when between her and Arkansas lay the immense reservations of the great tribes. They were slaveholding tribes, too; yet were supposed by the United States government to have no interest whatsoever in a sectional conflict that involved the very existence of the 'peculiar institution.'"

The above quotation is practically the intent of the book and the author has succeeded in carrying this out in four divisions entitled: I, "The General Situation in the Indian Country, 1830–1860." II, "Indian Territory in Its Relations with Texas and Arkansas." III, "The Confederacy in Negotiation with the Indian Tribes.'' IV, ''The Indian Nations in Alliance with the Confederacy.''

The book is essentially a work by a scholar for scholars. It is certainly not for the laity. The facts are striking but well substantiated. There can be no doubt but that much time has been spent in its compilation. The style, however, is unusually dry. It has appendices, an invaluable bibliography, a carefully tabulated index, four maps, and three portraits of Indian leaders.

It is interesting to note that the author is of British birth and ancestry and so presumably is free from sectional prejudice. Her book marks a distinct step forward, for those who are interested in Indian affairs.

JESSIE FAUSET.

The Political History of Slavery in the United States. By JAMES
    Z. GEORGE, formerly Chief Justice of the Supreme Court of
    Mississippi and later United States Senator from that State.
    The Neale Publishing Company, New York, 1915. Pp. xix, 342.

This is a discussion as well as the history of slavery and Reconstruction from the time of the introduction of the slaves in 1619 to the break-up of the carpet-bagger governments. ''Considering the jealousies and even animosities that are becoming more and more intensified between the North and South, as well as the disposition that is ever increasing in the stronger section to dominate the weaker,'' the author believes that ''it is becoming necessary to think over calmly and seriously the causes that have produced these evils, and to ascertain, if we can, the remedy, if remedy there be.''

The work begins with a sketch of ancient slavery, showing that the introduction of the institution into the Southern States was not exceptional. He then gives an account of slavery in the colonies, and the efforts to suppress the slave trade. The connection of slavery with the War of 1812 and with the Hartford Convention is noted. He then takes up the Missouri Compromise with some detail, giving almost verbatim the proceedings of Congress relative thereto. In the same way he treats the ''Repudiation of the Missouri Compromise,'' the Annexation of Texas, the Wilmot Proviso, the Kansas-Nebraska Affair, the Lincoln and Douglas Debates, John Brown's Invasion, Secession, the Civil War, and Reconstruction.

Throughout this treatise, he carefully notes the ''jealousy of sectional interest and power and the determination to maintain this power even at a cost of a dissolution of the Union.'' In other words, the whole sectional struggle grew out of what he calls the effort to maintain the balance of power between two sections of the Union, with the slavery question contributing thereto. Facts set forth bring out very clearly that the South is not to be censured as being especially hostile to the Negro when on the statute books of the North there are found numerous laws to show that persons of color were not considered desirables in those States.

He raises the question as to whether the South violated the Missouri Compromise and considers it a revolution that public functionaries disregarded the rights of the owners of slave property when the highest tribunal, the Supreme Court, had sanctioned these rights. The act of secession is palliated too on the ground that the South had developed under the influence of that peculiar political philosophy which produced there a race that could never sanction passive obedience. In seceding the South was not attempting to overturn the government of the United States. It was not contemplated to interfere with the States adhering to the Union. They sought merely to ''withdraw themselves from subjection to a government which they were convinced intended to overthrow their institutions.''

The Civil War came in spite of the fact that the Convention that framed the Constitution negatived the proposition to confer on the Federal Government the authority to exert the force of the Union against a delinquent State. It was, therefore, a mere act of coercing a section preparing for self-defense. Reconstruction is treated very much in the same way. The laws under which it was effected were unjust, the men who executed them were harsh, and the weaker section had to pay the price.

The book cannot be classed as scientific work. The topics discussed are not proportionately treated, the style is rendered dull by the incorporation of undigested material, and the emphasis is placed on the political and legal phases of history at the expense of the social and economic. In it we find very little that is new. It merely presents the well-known political theory of the Old South. The chief value of the work consists in its being an expression of the opinion of a distinguished man who participated in many of the events narrated.

J. O. Burke.

The Constitutional Doctrines of Justice Harlan. By FLOYD BAR-
ZILIA CLARK, Ph.D., Assistant Professor of Political Science in
Pennsylvania State College. Series XXXIII, No. 4, Johns
Hopkins University Studies in Historical and Political Science
under the direction of the Department of History, Political
Economy, and Political Science. The Johns Hopkins Press,
Baltimore, 1915.

This work is a legal treatise consisting of a scholarly discussion
of the doctrines advanced by Justice Harlan during his service as
a member of the Supreme Court of the United States. The book
opens with a brief biography of the jurist, emphasizing the important events of his career to furnish a basis for the study of his
theories. The author then takes up such topics as the "Suability
of States," the "Impairment of the Obligation Contracts," "Due
Process of Law," "Interstate and Foreign Commerce," "Equal
Protection of the Laws," the "Jurisdiction of Courts," "Miscellaneous Topics," and "Judicial Legislation."

The author finds that in the treatment of these important legal
questions Harlan measures up to the standard of an able jurist.
Replying to those who have charged him with emphasizing too
greatly the letter of the law, the writer says that such a contention
is based on ignorance or prejudice. "No one who so interpreted the
Eleventh Amendment," says the author, "as to maintain that a
suit against the officer of a State in his official capacity was not a
suit against a State could have held to the strict letter of the law."
The author further contends that this criticism of the jurist arises
from the fact that he did not believe in equivocation.

The interpretation of the laws relating to the Negro, the point
on which he dissented from the majority of the members of the
court, should have been given more prominence in this discussion.
The discriminations against the Negroes are treated in connection
with the chapters on "Interstate and Foreign Commerce" and
"Equal Protection of the Laws." The Fourteenth Amendment is
treated along with such miscellaneous topics as "Direct Taxation,"
"Copyrights," "Insular Cases," "Interstate Comity," and "Labor
Legislation." Stating Justice Harlan's theory as to the position
the Negro should occupy in this country, however, the author writes
very frankly. Harlan, he thought, believed that they should
occupy the position that historically they were intended to occupy
by the Thirteenth and Fourteenth Amendments. He believed that
the law should be interpreted as it was meant and not as the court

thought expedient and wise. "Though it may be true that his relation to the negro in political matters may have made him more violent in his dissents, any one who will look fairly at the question must conclude that his doctrine was legally correct. And as time passes, and as both classes become better educated and broader in their views, it may be said that the tendency of the court is likely to be to interpret the laws largely as he thought they should have been interpreted, that is, as historically they were meant."

C. B. Walter.

Reconstruction in Georgia, Economic, Social, Political, 1865–1872. By C. Mildred Thompson, Ph.D. Longmans, Green, and Company, New York, 1915. Pp. 418.

The appearance of C. M. Thompson's Reconstruction in Georgia arouses further interest in the study of that period which has been attracting the attention of various investigators in the leading universities of the United States. These writers fall into different groups. Coming to the defense of a section shamed with crime, some have endeavored to justify the deeds of those who resorted to all sorts of schemes to rid the country of the "extravagant and corrupt Reconstruction governments." Lately, however, the tendency has been to get away from this position. Yet among these writers we still find varying types, many of whom have for several reasons failed to write real history. Some have not forsaken the controversial group, not a few have tried to explain away the truth, and others going to the past with their minds preoccupied have selected only those facts which support their contentions.

What has this author in question done? In this readable and interesting work the writer has shown considerable improvement upon historical writing in this field. She has endeavored to deal not only with the political but also with the economic and social phases of the history of this period. One gets a glance at the State before the war, the transition from slavery to freedom, the problems of labor and tenancy, the commercial revival, the social readjustment, political reorganization, military rule, State economy, reorganized Reconstruction, agriculture, education, the administration of justice, the Ku Klux disorder, and the restoration of home rule.

This research leads the author to conclude that the seven years of the history of the State from 1865 to 1872 marked only the beginning of the social and economic transformation that has taken place since the war. This upheaval broke up the large plantation system, removed from power the "slave oligarchy," and exalted the yeomanry of moderate means, the uplanders now in control in the South. When the Democratic rule replaced Republicanism "one set of abnormal influences were put at rest," economic and social problems becoming the all-engrossing topics, and politics a diversion rather than a matter of self-preservation. The race problem then aroused began in another age, and not being settled, has been bequeathed to a later generation. Emancipation itself would have aroused racial antagonism but Republican Reconstruction increased it a hundred fold. This was the most enduring contribution of Congressional interference.

Politically Reconstruction in Georgia was a failure. The greatest political achievement of the period was the enfranchisement of the Negro, but this was soon undone, the Southern white man having no freedom of choice—"he had to be a democrat,—whether or no." Although establishing the Negro in freedom the government failed to establish him in political and social equality with the whites. "But still," says the author, "the race problem and the cry of Negro! Negro!—the slogan of political demagogues who magnify and distort a very real difficulty in playing upon the passions of the less educated whites—rise to curtail freedom of thought and act."

Out of this mass of material examined one would expect a more unbiased treatment. The work suffers from some of the defects of most Reconstruction writers, although the author has endeavored to write with restraint and care. One man is made almost a hero while another is found wanting. The white Southerner could not but be a Democrat but no excuse is made for the Negro who had no alternative but to ally himself with those who claimed to represent his emancipator. The State was at one time bordering on economic ruin because the Negroes became migratory and would not comply with their labor contracts. Little is said, however, about the evils arising from the attitude of Southern white men who have never liked to work and that of those who during this period, according to the author, formed roving bands for plundering and stealing. But we are too close to the history of Reconstruction to expect better treatment. We are just now reaching the period when we can tell the truth about the American Revolution. We must yet wait a century before we shall find ourselves far enough removed from the misfortunes and crimes of Reconstruction to set forth in an unbiased way the actual deeds of those who figured conspicuously in that awful drama.

NOTES

"That the idea of a "Secretary of Peace" for the United States is no new thing was brought out in the course of a paper by P. Lee Phillips, read by President Allen C. Clark before the Columbia Historical Society, which met at the Shoreham Hotel last night.

"In the course of the paper, entitled "The Negro, Benjamin Banneker, Astronomer and Mathematician," it was brought out that Banneker, who was a free Negro, friend of Washington and Jefferson, published a series of almanacs, unique in that they were his own work throughout. In the almanac for 1793 one of the articles from Banneker's pen was "A Plan of Peace Office for the United States," for promoting and preserving perpetual peace. This article was concise and well written, and contains most of the ideas set forth today by advocates of peace. Banneker took a "crack" at European military ideas, and advocated the abolishment in the United States of military dress and titles and all militia laws. He laid down laws for the construction of a great temple of peace in which hymns were to be sung each day.

"Mr. Phillips's paper brought out that Banneker helped in one of the early surveys of the District of Columbia."—*Washington Star.*

This dissertation will be brought out in the Annual Publication of the Columbia Historical Society.

Professor Alain Leroy Locke, of Howard University, has published an interesting prospectus of his lectures on the race problem.

Professor A. E. Jenks, of the University of Minnesota, has contributed to the *American Journal of Sociology* an elaborate paper on the legal status of the miscegenation of the white and black races in the various commonwealths.

Miss L. E. Wilkes, of the Washington Public Schools, has been lecturing on *"Missing Pages of American History."* This is a summary of her work treating the Negro soldier from the Colonial Period through the War of 1812. The treatise will be published in the near future.

In the Church Missionary Review has appeared "*A Survey of Islam in Africa*," by G. T. Manley.

An article entitled "*The Bantu Coast Tribes of East Africa Protectorate*," by A. Werner, has been published in the *Journal* of the Royal Anthropological Institute. In the same *Journal* has appeared also "*The Organization and Laws of Some Bantu Tribes in East Africa*."

Ashanti Proverbs, translated by R. Sutherland Rattray, with a preface by Sir Hugh Clifford, has been published by Milford in London.

A. Werner has published in London "*The Language Families of Africa*," a concise and valuable textbook of the classification, philology, and grammar of the languages.

The German African Empire, by A. F. Calvert, has appeared over the imprint of Werner Laurie.

The History of South Africa from 1795 to 1872, by G. McCall Theal, has been published in London by Allen and Unwin. This is a fourth and revised edition of a work to be completed in five volumes.

"*The Tropics*," by C. R. Enock, has been brought out by Grant Richards. This is a description of all tropical countries. It contains some valuable information but is chiefly concerned with advancing the theory that it is essential to study the capabilities of a country so as to develop all of its industries. The contention of the author is that the economic independence of each country is its safeguard from war and that commercialism is ruin.

The Methodist Book Concern has announced "*Pioneering on the Congo*," by John Springer.

Hodder and Stoughton have published "*Mary Slessor of Calabar: Pioneer Missionary*." This is an account of a factory girl who distinguished herself as a missionary and was later appointed head of a native court.

French Memories of Eighteenth Century America, by Charles H. Sherrill, has been published by Scribners. He failed to take into account the many references of French travelers to the Negroes and slavery.

In the second number of *Smith College Studies in History* appears Laura J. Webster's *Operations of the Freedmen's Bureau in South Carolina.*

About the middle of July the Neale Publishing Company will bring out *The New Negro, His Political, Civil and Mental Status,* by Dean William Pickens, of Morgan College.

Professor Sherwood, of La Crosse, Wisconsin, has for some time been making researches into *Paul Cuffee.*

AN INTERESTING COMMENT

Dear Sir:

It was very good of you to mail me a copy of the Journal of Negro History. I had seen a copy of this publication, I believe, at the library of the Institute of Jamaica. The second number is certainly an impressive issue indicative of the changed point of view. The so-called literature on slavery and the negro is, in the main, rather a hindrance than a help. The expression of mere personal opinion is of exceedingly slight value in the furtherance of any good cause. What the world needs is not mere knowledge but a better understanding of the facts and experience already available. When a race has reached a point where it realizes its own place in history, and the value of a critical analysis of its historical experience, a measurable advance has been made towards the attainment of a genuine progress. All values are relative. True history concerns itself with any and all achievements and not merely with political changes or military events. Most of the so-called historical disquisitions delivered annually before the American Historical Association fall seriously short in this respect. Ever since Green wrote his first real history of the English people the old-time historian has lost caste among men who are seriously concerned with the urgent solution of present-day problems. Unquestionably, a true political history is of real value, but the social history of mankind is infinitely more important.

The Journal of Negro History seems to meet the foregoing requirements for a social history of the negro race rather than a mere increase in the already voluminous so-called history of the political aspects of slavery reconstruction or reorganization during recent times. The article on the negro soldier in the American revolution is excellent. The prerequisite for a genuine race progress is race pride. For this reason the past achievements of the negro in this or any other country, individually or collectively, are of the utmost teaching value. It is a far cry, apparently, from the very recent high and well deserved promotion of a negro to a commanding position in the army, back to the days of the service rendered by negro soldiers in the Revolution, but in its final analysis it is all a chain of connected events. Where so much has been done and is being achieved the outlook for the future must needs be encouraging. Progress is only made by struggling, and the best results are those achieved against apparently insuperable difficulties. Race progress and race pride are practically equivalent terms. Individuals and races fail in proportion as they permit discouraging circumstances or conditions to control their destinies. A true philosophy of history never fails to bring home the conviction that lasting success is attained only through the ages by persistent effort in the right direction. The negro race has reason to be proud of its achievements, but I am sure that the future progress will rest largely upon a better understanding of the negro's place in history. Just as in the case of individuals, so in the case of races, it is, first and last, a question of finding our place in the world. Variation in type is absolutely essential to the highest development of the human species. It is not, therefore, the duty of any one race to follow blindly in the footsteps of another. It is for each race to seek for the best traits peculiarly its own, and to leave absolutely nothing undone, in season and out, to develop those particular traits to the highest possible degree. In other words, it is not for the negro to try to be as near as he can to a white man, even in his innermost thoughts and aspirations, but to interpret the lessons of his own life through the philosophy of negro history and to be true to the moral and spiritual ideals of his race and his ancestors, be they what they may.

Very truly yours,

F. L. HOFFMAN,

Statistician.

THE JOURNAL

OF

NEGRO HISTORY

VOL. I—OCTOBER, 1916—No. 4

THE WORK OF THE SOCIETY FOR THE PROPAGATION OF THE GOSPEL IN FOREIGN PARTS AMONG THE NEGROES IN THE COLONIES

The Society for the Propagation of the Gospel in Foreign Parts was organized in London in the year 1701. During the eighteenth century the British Colonies of the New World constituted the principal field of missionary endeavor for this organization. There were then in North America 250,000 settlers, whole colonies of whom were living in heathenism while others were adhering to almost every variety of strange faiths. The work of proselyting these people was too important to be intrusted to individual enterprise and too extensive to be successfully prosecuted by the heads of the Church only. The ministrations of the Established Church were then limited to a few places in Virginia, New York, Maryland and the cities of Boston and Philadelphia. To supply this deficiency the Society endeavored to use missionaries as a direct means to convert the heathen of all races, whether Europeans, Indians or Negroes. There were cruel masters who objected to the conversion of their slaves,[1] but that any race should be denied the message of salvation because of its color was ever repudiated by the Society. From the very beginning of this work the conversion of the Negroes was as important to the

[1] "An Account of the Endeavor Used by the S. P. G.," pp. 6–12; Meade, "Sermons of Rev. Thomas Bacon," pp. 31 et seq.

Society as that of bringing the whites or the Indians into the church. Such dignitaries of the church, as Rev. Thomas Bacon and Bishops Fleetwood, Lowth, Sanderson and Wilson, ever urged this duty upon their brethren at home and abroad.[2]

The first really effective work of the Society was done in South Carolina. Reverend Mr. Thomas of Goose Creek Parish in that State early instructed the Indian and Negro slaves of his vicinity. He directed his attention to the Negroes in 1695 and ten years later counted among his communicants twenty blacks, who with several others "well understanding the English tongue," could read and write. He further said, in 1705: "I have here presumed to give an account of one thousand slaves so far as they know of it and are desirous of Christian knowledge and seem willing to prepare themselves for it, in learning to read, for which they redeem the time from their labor. Many of them can read the Bible distinctly and great numbers of them were learning when I left the province."[3]

This work, however, had not proceeded without much opposition. The sentiment as to the enlightenment of the blacks was largely that of the youth who resolved never to go to the holy table while slaves were received there. Others felt like the lady who inquired: "Is it possible that any of my slaves should go to heaven, and must I see them there?"[4] The earnest workers sent out by the Society, however, did not cease to labor in behalf of the Negroes and the number of masters willing to have their slaves instructed gradually increased. Among these liberal owners were John Morris, of St. Bartholomew's, Lady Moore, Captain David Davis, Mrs. Sarah Baker at Goose Creek, Landgrave Joseph Morton and his wife of St. Paul's, the Governor and a member of the Assembly, Mr. and Mrs. Skeen,[5] Mrs. Haigue and Mrs.

---

[2] Special Report of U. S. Commission of Ed., 1871, pp. 300 *et seq.*

[3] *Journal*, Vol. I, May 30, July 18, and Aug. 15, 1707; Special Report of the U. S. Com. of Ed., 1871, p. 363.

[4] Pascoe, "Classified Digest of the Records of the Society for the Propagation of the Gospel in Foreign Parts," p. 15.

[5] *Ibid.*, 15.

Edwards. So successful were the efforts of Mrs. Haigue and Mrs. Edwards that they were formally thanked by the Society for their care and good example in instructing the Negroes of whom no less than twenty-seven prepared by them, including those of another planter, were baptized by the Reverend E. Taylor of St. Andrew's within two years.[6]

Other less liberal masters refused to allow their slaves to attend Mr. Taylor for instruction, but some of them were induced to teach the blacks the Lord's Prayer. The result even from this was so successful that there came to the church more Negroes than could be accommodated. So great was their desire for instruction that had it not been for the opposition of their owners, almost all of them would

[6] In 1713 this churchman wrote his supporters:

"As I am a minister of Christ and of the Church of England, and a Missionary of the most Christian Society in the whole world, I think it my indispensable and special duty to do all that in me lies to promote the conversion and salvation of the poor heathens here, and more especially of the Negro and Indian slaves in my own parish, which I hope I can truly say I have been sincerely and earnestly endeavoring ever since I was a minister here where there are many Negro and Indian slaves in a most pitifull deplorable and perishing condition tho' little pitied by many of their masters and their conversion and salvation little desired and endeavored by them. If the masters were but good Christians themselves and would but concurre with the ministers, we should then have good hopes of the conversion and salvation at least of some of their Negro and Indian slaves. But too many of them rather oppose than concurr with us and are angry with us, I am sure I may say with me for endeavouring as much as I doe the conversion of their slaves. . . . I cannot but honour Madame Haigue. . . . In my parish a very considerable number of Negroes . . . were very loose and wicked and little inclined to Christianity before her coming among them I can't but honor her so much . . . as to acquaint the Society with the extraordinary pains this gentle woman and one Madm. Edwards, that came with her, have taken to instruct those negroes in the principles of the Christian Religion and to instruct and reform them: And the wonderful successe they have met with, in about a half a year's time in this great and good work. Upon these gentle women's desiring me to come and examine these negroes . . . I went and among other things I asked them, Who Christ was. They readily answered. He is the Son of God and Saviour of the world and told me that they embraced Him with all their hearts as such, and I desired them to rehearse the Apostles' Creed, and the Ten Commandments and the Lord's Prayer, which they did very distinctly and perfectly. 14 of them gave me so great satisfaction, and were so very desirous to be baptized, that I thought it my duty to baptize them and therefore I baptized these 14 last Lord's Day. And I doubt not but these gentlewomen will prepare the rest of them for Baptism in a short Time." *Journal*, Vol. II, Oct. 6, 1713; A. Mss., Vol. VIII, pp. 356-7; Pascoe, "Digest of Records of S. P. G.," p. 15.

have been converted. "So far as the missionaries were permitted," says one, "they did all that was possible for their evangelization, and while so many professed Christians among the planters were lukewarm, it pleased God to raise to himself devout servants among the heathen, whose faithfulness was commended by the masters themselves. In some of the congregations the Negroes or blacks constituted one half of the communicants."[7]

This interest of the clergy in the Negroes of South Carolina continued in spite of opposition. Rev. Mr. Guy, of St. Andrew's Parish, said that he baptized "a Negro man and a Negro woman" in 1723, and Rev. Mr. Hunt, minister of St. John's Parish, reported in that same year that "a slave, a sensible Negro, who can read and write and comes to church, is a Catechumen under probation for Baptism which he desires."[8] A new impetus too was given the movement about 1740. Influenced by such urgent addresses as those of Dr. Brearcroft, and Bishops Gibson, Wilson and Secker, the workers of the Society were aroused to proselyting more extensively among the Negroes. In 1741 the Bishop of Canterbury expressed his gratification at the large number of Negroes who were then being brought into the church.[9]

A decided step forward was noted in 1743. That year a school for Negroes was opened by Commissary Garden and placed in charge of Harry and Andrew, two colored youths, who had been trained as teachers at the cost of the Society. This establishment was a sort of training school for bright young blacks who felt called to instruct their fellow countrymen. For adults who labored during the day it was an evening school. It was successfully conducted for more than twenty years. In 1763 the institution was for some unknown reason closed after being conducted in the face of many difficulties and obstructions, although this was the only educational institution in that colony for its 50,000 blacks.[10]

[7] *Journal*, II, 328; XIV, 48; XX, 132–133; XVI, 165–166.

[8] *Proceedings of the S. P. G.*, 1723, p. 46.

[9] Pascoe, "Digest of the Records of the S. P. G.," 16.

[10] Meriwether, "Education in South Carolina," p. 123; McCrady, "South Carolina," etc., p. 246; Dalcho, "An Historical Account of the Protestant Episcopal Church in South Carolina," pp. 156, 157, 164.

Some good results were obtained by the missionaries of the Society of North Carolina, but difficulties were also encountered there. The chief trouble seems to have been that missionaries of that colony were "frustrated by the slave owners who would by no means permit" their Negroes to be baptized, "having a false notion that a christened slave is by law free."[11] "By much importunity," says an investigator, Mr. Ransford of Chowan (in 1712) prevailed on Mr. Martin to let him baptize three of his Negroes, two women and a boy. "All the arguments I could make use of," said he, "would scarce effect it till Bishop Fleetwood's sermon (in 1711) . . . turned ye scale."[12] Mr. Rumford succeeded, however, in baptizing upwards of forty Negroes in one year. In the course of time, when the workers overcame the prejudice of the masters, a missionary would sometimes baptize fifteen to twenty-four in a month, forty to fifty in six months, and sixty to seventy in a year.[13] Reverend Mr. Newman, a minister in North Carolina, reported in 1723 that he had baptized two Negroes who could say the Creed, the Lord's Prayer, the Ten Commandments, and gave good sureties for their further information.[14] According to the report of Rev. C. Hall, the number of conversions there among Negroes for eight years was 355, including 112 adults, and "at Edenton the blacks generally were induced to attend service at all these stations, where they behaved with great decorum."[15]

In the Middle and Southern Colonies these missionaries had the cooperation of Dr. Thomas Bray. In 1696 he was sent to Maryland by the Bishop of London to do what he could toward the conversion of adult Negroes and the education of their children.[16] Bray's most influential supporter was M. D'Alone, the private secretary of King William. D'Alone gave for the maintenance of the cause a fund, the

11 Pascoe, "Digest of the Records of the S. P. G.," p. 22.
12 Ibid., 22.
13 Ibid., 23.
14 Proceedings of the S. P. G., 1723, p. 47.
15 Pascoe, "Digest of the Records of the S. P. G.," p. 22.
16 Smyth, "Works of Franklin," V, 431.

proceeds of which were first used to employ catechists, and later to support the Thomas Bray Mission after the cate- chists had failed to give satisfaction. At the death of this missionary the task was taken up by certain of his followers known as the "Associates of Dr. Bray."[17] They extended their work beyond the bounds of Maryland. These bene- factors maintained two schools for the benefit of Negroes in Philadelphia. About the close of the French and Indian War, Rev. Mr. Stewart, a missionary in North Carolina, found there a school for the education of Indians and Ne- groes conducted by "Dr. Bray's Associates."[18]

Georgia too was not neglected. The extension of the work of Dr. Bray's associates into the colony made an open- ing there for taking up the instruction of Negroes. The Society joined with these workers for supporting a school- master for Negroes in 1751 and an improvement in the slaves was soon admitted by their owners.[19] In 1766 Rev. S. Frink, a missionary toiling in Augusta, found that he could neither convert the Indians nor the whites, who seemed to be as destitute of religion as the former, but succeeded in converting some Negroes.[20]

In Pennsylvania the missionary movement found less obstacles to the conversion of Negroes than to that of the Indians. In fact, the proselyting of Negroes in the colony was less difficult than in some other parts of America. The reports of the missionaries show that slaves were being bap- tized there as early as 1712.[21] About this time a Mr. Yeates, of Chester, was commended by the Rev. G. Ross "for his endeavors to train up the Negroes in the knowledge of re- ligion."[22] Moved by the appeal of the Bishop of London, other masters permitted the indoctrination of their slaves in the principles of Christianity. At Philadelphia the Rev. G. Ross baptized on one occasion 12 adult Negroes, "who

[17] Wickersham, "History of Education in Pennsylvania," p. 249.
[18] Bassett, "Slavery and Servitude in North Carolina," p. 226.
[19] Journal, Vol. XI, pp. 305 and 311.
[20] Pascoe, "Digest of the Records of the S. P. G.," p. 28.
[21] Journal, Vol. XVII, p. 97.
[22] Ibid., II, 251.

were examined before the congregation and answered to the admiration of all who heard them. . . . The like sight had never been seen before in that church."[23]   Rev. Mr. Beckett, minister in Sussex County, Pennsylvania, said in 1723 that he had admitted two Negro slaves and that many Negroes constantly attended his services.[24]   The same year Rev. Mr. Bartow baptized a Negro at West Chester.[25]   Rev. Mr. Pugh, a missionary at Appoquinimmick, Pennsylvania, said, in a letter written to the Society in 1737, that he had received a few blacks and that the masters of the Negroes were prejudiced against their being Christians.[26]   Rev. Richard Locke christened eight Negroes in one family at Lancaster in 1747 and another Negro there the following year.[26a]   In 1774 the Rev. Mr. Jenney reported that there was "a great and daily increase of Negroes in this city who would with joy attend upon a catechist for instruction"; that he had baptized several, but was unable to add to his other duties; and the Society, ever ready to lend a helping hand to such pious undertakings, appointed the Rev. W. Sturgeon as catechist for the Negroes at Philadelphia.[27]   The next to show diligence in the branch of the work of the Society was Mr. Neill of Dover. He baptized as many as 162 within 18 months.[28]

The operations of the Society did not seem to cover a large part of New Jersey. The Rev. Mr. Lindsay wrote of the baptizing of a Negro at Allerton in 1736.[29]   The reports from the missions of New Brunswick show that a large number of Negroes had attached themselves to the church. This condition, however, did not obtain in all parts of that colony. Yet subsequent reports show that the missionary spirit was not wanting in that section. The baptism of black

23 *Journal*, IX, 87.
24 *Proceedings of the S. P. G.*, 1723, p. 47.
25 *Ibid.*, 1737, 50.
26 *Ibid.*, 1737, p. 41.
26a Pennsylvania Magazine of History, XXIV, 467, 469.
27 Pascoe, "Digest of the Records of the S. P. G.," p. 38.
28 *Ibid.*, 39.
29 *Proceedings of the S. P. G.*, 1736.

children and the accession of Negro adults to the church were from time to time reported from that field.[30]

The most effective work of the Society among Negroes of the Northern colonies was accomplished in New York. In that colony, the instruction of the Negro and Indian slaves to prepare them for conversion, baptism, and communion was a primary charge oft repeated to every missionary and schoolmaster of the Society. In addition to the general efforts put forth in the colonies, there was in New York a special provision for the employment of sixteen clergymen and thirteen lay teachers mainly for the evangelization of the slaves and the free Indians. For the Negro slaves a catechizing school was opened in New York City in 1704 under the charge of Elias Neau. This benevolent man, after several years' imprisonment because of his Protestant faith, had come to New York to try his fortunes as a trader. As early as 1703 he called the attention of the Society to the great number of slaves in New York "who were without God in the world, and of whose souls there was no manner of care taken"[31] and proposed the appointment of a catechist to undertake their instruction. He himself finally being prevailed upon to accept this position, obtained a license from the Governor, resigned his position as elder in the French church and conformed to the Established Church of England, "not upon any worldly account but through a principle of conscience and hearty approbation of the English liturgy."[32] He was later licensed by the Bishop of London.

Neau's task was not an easy one. At first he went from house to house, but afterwards arranged for some of the slaves to attend him. He succeeded, however, in obtaining gratifying results. He was commended to the Society by Rev. Mr. Vesey in 1706 as a "constant communicant of our church, and a most zealous and prudent servant of Christ, in

[30] Pascoe, "Digest of the Records of the S. P. G.," 55.

[31] *Ibid.*, 56.

[32] *Ibid.*, 57, and "Special Report of U. S. Com. of Ed.," 1871, 362; and "An Account of the Endeavors Used by the S. P. G.," pp. 6–12.

proselyting the miserable Negroes and Indians among them to the Christian Religion, whereby he does great service to God and his church.''[33] Further confidence in him was attested by an act of the Society in preparing at his request "a Bill to be offered to Parliament for the more effectual Conversion of the Negro and other Servants in the Plantations, to compell Owners of Slaves to cause children to be baptized within 3 months after their birth and to permit them when come to years of discretion to be instructed in the Christian Religion on our Lord's day by the Missionaries under whose ministry they live.''[34]

Neau's school suffered greatly in 1712 because of the prejudice engendered by the declaration that instruction was the main cause of the Negro riot in that city. For some days Neau dared not show himself, so bitter was the feeling of the masters. Upon being assured, however, that only one Negro connected with the school had participated in the affair and that the most criminal belonged to the masters who were openly opposed to educating them, the institution was permitted to continue its endeavors, and the Governor extended to it his protection and recommended that masters have their slaves instructed.[35] Yet Neau had still to complain thereafter of the struggle and opposition of the generality of the inhabitants, who were strongly prejudiced with a horrid motive thinking that Christian knowledge "would be a means to make the slave more cunning and apter to wickedness.''[36] Not so long thereafter, however, the support of the best people and officials of the community made his task easier. Neau could say in 1714 that "if the slaves and domestics in New York were not instructed it was not his fault.''[37] The Governor, the Council, Mayor, the Recorder and the Chief Justice informed the Society that Neau had performed his work "to the great advancement of religion in general and the particular bene-

[33] Pascoe, "Digest of the Records of the S. P. G.," p. 58.
[34] Ibid., Journal, I, Oct. 20, 1710.
[35] "Special Report of U. S. Com. of Ed.," 1871, p. 362.
[36] Pascoe, "Digest, etc.," p. 59.
[37] Journal, III, Oct. 15, 1714.

fit of the free Indians, Negro slaves, and other Heathens in those parts, with indefatigable zeal and application."[38]

Neau died in 1722. His work was carried on by Mr. Huddlestone, Rev. Mr. Whitmore, Rev. Mr. Colgan, Rev. R. Charlton, and Rev. S. Auchmutty. From 1732 to 1740 Mr. Charlton baptized 219 slaves and frequently thereafter the number admitted yearly was from 40 to 60.[39] The great care exercised in preparing slaves for the church was rewarded by the spiritual knowledge which in some cases was such as might have put to shame many persons who had had greater advantages. Rev. Mr. Auchmutty, who served from 1747 to 1764, reported that there was among the Negroes an ever-increasing desire for instruction and "not one single Black" that had been "admitted by him to the Holy Communion" had "turned out bad or been in any shape a disgrace to our holy Profession."[40]

The interest in the enlightenment of Negroes too extended also to other parts of the colony. In 1737 Rev. Mr. Stoupe wrote of baptizing four black children at New Rochelle.[41] Mr. Charlton had taken upon himself at New Windsor the task of instructing these unfortunates before he entered upon the work in New York City. At Staten Island too he found it both practical and convenient "to throw into one the classes of his white and black catechumens."[42] Rev. Charles Taylor, a schoolmaster at that place, kept a night school "for the instruction of Negroes, and of such as" could not "be spared from their work in the day time."[43] Rev. J. Sayre, of Newburgh, followed the same plan of coeducation of the races in each of the four churches under his charge.[44] Rev. T. Barclay, an earnest worker among the slaves in Albany, reported in 1714 "a great forwardness" among them to embrace Christianity

[38] Humphreys, "Historical Account of the S. P. G.," 243.

[39] Pascoe, "Digest, etc.," p. 65.

[40] Ibid., 66.

[41] Proceedings of the S. P. G., 1737.

[42] Pascoe, "Digest, etc.," p. 68.

[43] Proceedings of the S. P. G., 1723, p. 50.

[44] Journal, XIX, 452–453.

"and a readiness to receive instruction."[45]   He found much opposition among certain masters, chief among whom were Major M. Schuyler and his brother-in-law Petrus Vandroffen.   Sixty years later came the report from Schenectady that there were still to be found several Negro slaves of whom 11 were sober, serious communicants.[46]

These missionaries met with more opposition than encouragement in New England.   The Puritan had no serious objection to seeing the Negroes saved, but when the conversion meant the incorporation of the undesirable class into the state, then so closely connected with the church, many New Englanders became silent.   This opposition, however, was not effective everywhere.   From Bristol, Rev. J. Usher wrote in 1730 that several Negroes desired baptism and were able "to render a very good account of the hope that was in them," but he was forbidden by their masters to comply with the request.   Yet he reported the same year that among others he had in his congregation "about 30 Negroes and Indians," most of whom joined "in the public service very decently."[47]   At Newtown, where greater opposition was encountered, Rev. J. Beach seemed to have baptized by 1733 many Indians and a few Negroes.[48]   The Rev. Dr. Cutler, a missionary at Boston, wrote to the Society in 1737 that among those he had admitted to his church were four Negro slaves.[49]   Endeavoring to do more than to effect nominal conversions, Doctor Johnson, while at Stratford, had catechetical lectures during the summer months of 1751, attended by many Negroes and some Indians, as well as whites, "about 70 or 80 in all."   And said he: "As far as I can find, where the Dissenters have baptized 2, if not 3 or 4 Negroes or Indians, I have four or five communicants."[50]   Dr. Macsparran conducted at Narragansett a class of 70 Indians and Negroes whom he frequently catechized and in-

[45] Ibid., January 21, 1715.
[46] Pascoe, "Digest of the Records of the S. P. G.," p. 67.
[47] Ibid., 46.
[48] Ibid., 47.
[49] Proceedings of the S. P. G., 1737 and 1738, p. 39.
[50] Ibid., p. 40.

structed before the regular service.[51]   Rev. J. Honyman, of
Newport, had in his congregation more than 100 Negroes
who ''constantly attended the Publick Worship.''[52]

It appears then that the Negroes were instructed by the
missionaries in all of the colonies except some remote parts
of New England, Virginia and Maryland. The Established
Church had workers among the white persons in those colonies but they did not always direct their attention to the
slaves. This does not mean, however, that the slaves in
those parts were entirely neglected. There were at work
other agencies to bring them to the light. And so on it continued until the outbreak of the Revolution, when the work
of these missionaries was impeded and in most cases brought
to a close.

C. E. PIERRE

[51] *Proceedings of the S. P. G.*, 1723, 51.
[52] Ibid., 1723, p. 52.

PEOPLE OF COLOR IN LOUISIANA

PART I

The title of a possible discussion of the Negro in Louisiana presents difficulties, for there is no such word as Negro permissible in speaking of this State. The history of the State is filled with attempts to define, sometimes at the point of the sword, oftenest in civil or criminal courts, the meaning of the word Negro. By common consent, it came to mean in Louisiana, prior to 1865, slave, and after the war, those whose complexions were noticeably dark. As Grace King so delightfully puts it, "The pure-blooded African was never called colored, but always Negro." The *gens de couleur*, colored people, were always a class apart, separated from and superior to the Negroes, ennobled were it only by one drop of white blood in their veins. The caste seems to have existed from the first introduction of slaves. To the whites, all Africans who were not of pure blood were *gens de couleur*. Among themselves, however, there were jealous and fiercely-guarded distinctions: "griffes, briqués, mulattoes, quadroons, octoroons, each term meaning one degree's further transfiguration toward the Caucasian standard of physical perfection."[1]

Negro slavery in Louisiana seems to have been early influenced by the policy of the Spanish colonies. De las Casas, an apostle to the Indians, exclaimed against the slavery of the Indians and finding his efforts of no avail proposed to Charles V in 1517 the slavery of the Africans as a substitute.[2] The Spaniards refused at first to import slaves from Africa, but later agreed to the proposition and employed other nations to traffic in them.[3] Louisiana learned

[1] King, "New Orleans, the Place and the People during the Ancien Regime," 333.

[2] De las Casas, "Historia, General," IV, 380.

[3] Herrera, "Historia General," dec. IV, libro II; dec. V, libro II; dec. VII, libro IV.

361

from the Spanish colonies her lessons of this traffic, took over certain parts of the slave regulations and imported bondmen from the Spanish West Indies. Others brought thither were Congo, Banbara, Yaloff, and Mandingo slaves.[4]

People of color were introduced into Louisiana early in the eighteenth century. In 1708, according to the historian, Gayarré, the little colony of Louisiana, at the point on the Gulf of Mexico now known as Biloxi, in the present State of Mississippi, had been in existence nine years. In 1708, the population of the colony did not exceed 279 persons. The land about this region is particularly sterile, and the colonists were little disposed to undertake the laborious task of tilling the soil. Indian slavery was attempted but found unprofitable and exceedingly precarious. So Bienville, lacking the sympathy of De las Casas for the Indians, wrote his government to obtain the authorization of exchanging Negroes for Indians with the French West Indian islands. ''We shall give,'' he said, ''three Indians for two Negroes. The Indians, when in the islands, will not be able to run away, the country being unknown to them, and the Negroes will not dare to become fugitives in Louisiana, because the Indians would kill them.''[5]

Bienville's suggestion seems not to have met with a very favorable reception. Yet, in 1712, the King of France granted to Anthony Crozat the exclusive privilege for fifteen years of trading in all that immense territory which, with its undefined limits, France claimed as Louisiana. Among other privileges granted Crozat were those of sending, once a year, a ship to Africa for Negroes.[6] When the first came, is not known, but in 1713 twenty of these Negro slaves from Africa are recorded in the census of the little colony on the Mississippi.[7]

In 1717 John Law flashed meteor-wise across the world with his huge scheme to finance France out of difficulty with

[4] French, ''Historical Collections of Louisiana,'' Part V, 119 et seq.
[5] Gayarré, ''History of Louisiana,'' 4th Edition, I, 242, 254.
[6] French ''Historical Collections of Louisiana,'' Part III, p. 42.
[7] Gayarré, ''History of Louisiana,'' I, 102.

his Mississippi Bubble. Among other considerations mentioned in the charter for twenty-five years, which he obtained from the gullible French government, was the stipulation that before the expiration of the charter, he must transport to Louisiana six thousand white persons, and three thousand Negroes, not to be brought from another French colony. These slaves, so said the charter, were to be sold to those inhabitants who had been two years in the colony for one half cash and the balance on one year's credit. The new inhabitants had one or two years' credit granted them.[8] In the first year, the Law Company transported from Africa one thousand slaves, in 1720 five hundred, the same number the next March, and by 1721 the pages of legal enactments in the West Indies were being ransacked for precedents in dealing with this strange population. But of all these slaves who came to the colony by June, 1721, but six hundred remained. Many had died, some had been exported. In 1722, therefore, the Mississippi Company was under constraint to pass an edict prohibiting the inhabitants of Louisiana from selling their slaves for transportation out of the colony, to the Spaniards, or to any other foreign nation under the penalty of the fine of a thousand livres and the confiscation of the Negroes.[9]

But already the curse of slavery had begun to show its effects. The new colony was not immoral; it may best be described as unmoral. Indolence on the part of the masters was physical, mental and moral. The slave population began to lighten in color, and increase out of all proportion to the importation and natural breeding among themselves. La Harpe comments in 1724 upon the astonishing diminution of the white population and the astounding increase of the colored population.[10] Something was undoubtedly wrong, according to the Caucasian standard, and it has remained wrong to our own day.[11] The person of color was now, in

[8] Gayarré, "History of Louisiana," I, 242, 454.

[9] Ibid., I, 366.

[10] Ibid., I, 365–366.

[11] In 1900 a writer in Pearson's Magazine in discussing race mixture in early Louisiana made some startling statements as to the results of the miscegenation of these stocks during the colonial period.

Louisiana, a part of its social system, a creature to be legislated for and against, a person lending his dark shade to temper the inartistic complexion of his white master. Now he began to make history, and just as the trail of his color persisted in the complexion of Louisiana, so the trail of his personal influence continued in the history of the colony, the territory and the State.

Bienville, the man of far-reaching vision, saw the danger menacing the colony, and before his recall and disgrace before the French court, he published, in 1724, the famous Black Code.[12] This code followed the order of that of the West Indies but contains some provisions to meet local needs. The legal status of the slave was that of movable property of his master. Children born of Negro parents followed the condition of their mother. Slaves were forbidden to carry weapons. Slaves of different masters could not assemble in crowds by day or night. They were not permitted to sell "commodities, provisions, or produce" without permission from their masters, and had no property which did not belong to their masters. Neither free-born blacks nor slaves were allowed to receive gifts from whites. They could not exercise such public functions as arbitrator or expert, could not be partners to civil or criminal suits, could not give testimony except in default of white people, and could never testify against their masters. If a slave struck his master or one of the family so as to produce a bruise or shedding blood in the face, he had to be put to death. Any runaway slave who continued to be so from the day his master "denounced" him suffered the penalty of having his ears cut off and being branded on his shoulder with a fleur-de-lis. For a second offence the penalty was to hamstring the fugitive and brand him on the other shoulder. For the third such offence he suffered death. Freed or free-born Negroes who gave refuge to fugitive slaves had to pay 30 livres for each day of retention and other free persons 10 livres a day. If the freed or free-born Negroes were not able to pay the fine, they could be reduced to the condition of slaves and sold as such.

[12] Code Noir, 1724.

The slaves were socially ostracized. Marriage of whites with slaves was forbidden, as was also the concubinage of whites and manumitted or free-born blacks with slaves. The consent of the parents of a slave to his marriage was not required. That of the master was sufficient, but a slave could not be forced to marry against his will.

There were, however, somewhat favorable provisions which made this code seem a little less rigorous. The slaves had to be well fed and the masters could not force them to provide for themselves by working for their own account certain days of the week and slaves could give information against their owners, if not properly fed or clothed. Disabled slaves had to be sent to the hospital. Husbands, wives, and their children under the age of puberty could not be seized and sold separately when belonging to the same master. The code forbade the application of the rack to slaves, under any pretext, on private authority, or mutilation of a limb, under penalty of confiscation of the slave and criminal prosecution of the master. The master was allowed, however, to have his slave put in irons and whipped with rods or ropes. The code commanded officers or justices to prosecute masters and overseers who should kill or mutilate slaves, and to punish the murder according to the atrocity of the circumstance.

Other provisions were still more favorable. The slaves had to be instructed in the Catholic religion. Slaves appointed by their masters as tutors to their children were held set free. Moreover, manumitted slaves enjoyed the same rights, privileges and immunities that were enjoyed by those born free. "It is our pleasure," reads the document, "that their merit in having acquired their freedom shall produce in their favor, not only with regard to their persons, but also to their property, the same effects that our other subjects derive from the happy circumstance of their having been born free."[13]

From the first appearance of the *gens de couleur* in the colony of Louisiana dates the class, the *gens de couleur*

[13] Code Noir.

libres. The record of the legal tangles which resulted from the attempts to define this race in Louisiana is most interesting. Up to 1671, all Creoles, Mulattoes, free Negroes, etc., paid a capitation tax. In February 12 of that year, M. de Baas, Governor-General of Martinique, issued an order exempting the Creoles. Those Mulattoes who were also designated as Creoles claimed the same exemption and resisted paying the tax. M. Patoulet, Intendant, rendered a decision in 1683 and said: "The Mulattoes and free Negroes claimed to be exempt from the capitation tax: I have made them pay without difficulty. I decide that those Mulattoes born in vice should not receive the exemption, and that for the free Negro, the master could give him freedom but could not give him the exemption that attaches to the whites originally from France."[14] The next year, the Mulattoes refused to pay, and the successor of Minister Patoulet, M. Michel Begou, asked for a law to compel them.[15] In 1696, an agreement was reached exempting the Mulattoes and Creoles, leaving only the free black subject to the tax.[16] But in 1712, a M. Robert, in a decision on a subject, again included the Mulattoes, without, however, mentioning the Creoles, so that only the free Negroes and Mulattoes paid.[17] Thus they were held as a class apart. A free Negro woman, Magdelaine Debern, further contested the matter, and in 1724, in the colony of Louisiana, won a decision exempting free Negroes and Mulattoes, and again placing them on the same footing with the Creole. The Creoles had a decided advantage, however, because through the favor of those in authority, there was always a disposition to exalt them.[18]

It is in the definition of the word Creole that another

[14] Lebeau, De la condition des gens de couleur libres sous l'ancien régime, p. 49.

[15] *Ibid.*, 49.

[16] *Ibid.*, 50.

[17] *Ibid.*, 51.

[18] In the treaty of 1803 between the newly acquired territory of Louisiana and the government of the United States, they and all mixed bloods were granted full citizenship.

great difficulty arises. The native white Louisianian will tell you that a Creole is a white man, whose ancestors contain some French or Spanish blood in their veins. But he will be disputed by others, who will gravely tell you that Creoles are to be found only in the lower delta lands of the state, that there are no Creoles north of New Orleans; and will raise their hands in horror at the idea of being confused with the "Cajans," the descendants of those Nova Scotians whom Longfellow immortalized in Evangeline. Sifting down the mass of conflicting definitions, it appears that to a Caucasian, a Creole is a native of the lower parishes of Louisiana, in whose veins some traces of Spanish, West Indian or French blood runs.[19] The Caucasian will shudder with horror at the idea of including a person of color in the definition, and the person of color will retort with his definition that a Creole is a native of Louisiana, in whose blood runs mixed strains of everything un-American, with the African strain slightly apparent. The true Creole is like the famous gumbo of the state, a little bit of everything, making a whole, delightfully flavored, quite distinctive, and wholly unique.

From 1724 to the present time, frequent discussions as to the proper name by which to designate this very important portion of the population of Louisiana waged more or less acrimoniously.[20] It was this Creole element who in 1763 obtained a decision from Louis XV that all mixed bloods who could claim descent from an Indian ancestor in addition to a white outranked those mixed bloods who had only white and African ancestors.[21] In Jamaica, in 1733, there was passed a law that every person who could show that he was three degrees removed from a Negro ancestor should be regarded as belonging to the white race, and could sit as a member of the Ja-

[19] Most writers of our day adhere to this definition. See Grace King, "New Orleans, etc.," and Gayarré, "History of Louisiana."

[20] Lebeau, De la condition des gens de couleur libres sous l'ancien régime, passim.

[21] Ibid., 60.

maica Assembly.[22]   In Barbadoes, any person who had a
white ancestor could vote.   These laws were quoted in Louisiana and influenced legislation there.[23]

Gov. Perier succeeded Bienville as Governor of Louisiana.   His task was not a light one; the colony staggered
under "terror of attack from the Indians, sudden alarms,
false hopes, anxious suspense, militia levies, colonial paper,
instead of good money, industrial stagnation, the care of
homeless refugees, and worst of all, the restiveness of the
slaves.   The bad effects of slave-holding began to show themselves." Many of the slaves had been taken in war, and
were fierce and implacable.   Some were of that fiercest of
African tribes, the Banbaras.   A friendliness, born of common hatred and despair, began to show itself between the
colored people and the fierce Choctaw Indians surrounding
the colony, when Gov. Perier planned a master-stroke of
diplomacy.   Just above New Orleans lived a small tribe of
Indians, the Chouchas, who, not particularly harmful in
themselves, had succeeded in inspiring the nervous inhabitants of the city with abject fear.   Perier armed a band of
slaves in 1729 and sent them to the Chouchas with in-

[22] Laws of Jamaica.

[23] Litigation on the subject of the definition of the free person of color
reached its climax in the year of our Lord, 1909, when Judge Frank D. Chretien
defined the word Negro as differentiated from person of color as used in Louisiana.   The case, as it was argued in court, was briefly this.   It was charged that
one Treadway, a white man, was living in illegal relations with an octoroon,
Josephine Lightell.   The District Attorney claimed that any one having a trace
of African blood in his veins, however slight, should be classed as a Negro.
Counsel for the defence had taken the position that Josephine Lightell had so
little Negro blood in her veins that she could not be classed as one.   Judge
Chretien held in his ruling that local opinion, custom and sentiment had previously agreed in holding that the black, and not the white blood settled the
ethnological status of each person and that an octoroon, no less than a quad-
roon and a mulatto, had been considered a Negro.   But he held that if the
Caucasian wished to be considered the superior race, and that if his blood be
considered the superior element in the infusion, then the Caucasian and not the
Negro blood must determine the status of a person.   The case went to the
Supreme Court of Louisiana on an appeal from the decision of Judge Chretien
who held that a mulatto is not a Negro in legal parlance.   The Supreme Court
in a decision handed down April 25, 1910, sustained the view of Judge Chretien.
This decision was an interpretation of an act of 1908 which set forth a definition of the word Negro.—See State vs. Treadway, 126 Louisiana, 300.

structions to exterminate the tribe. They did their work with an ease and dispatch that should have been a warning to their white masters. In reporting the success of his plan Perier said: "The Negroes executed their mission with as much promptitude as secrecy. This lesson taught them by our Negroes, kept in check all the nations higher up the river."[24] Thus, by one stroke the wily Governor had intimidated the tribes of Indians, allayed the nervous fears of New Orleans, and effected a state of hostility between the Indians and the Africans, who were beginning to be entirely too friendly with each other. Then Perier used the slaves to make the entrenchments about the city. Thus we have the first instance of the arming of the Negro in Louisiana for the defense of the colony. On the 15th of January, 1730, Gov. Perier sent a boat containing twenty white men and six Africans to carry ammunition to the Illinois settlement up the Mississippi river whence tales of massacre and cruelty by the Indians filtered down.[25]

The arming of the slaves in defense of the whites gave impetus to the struggle for their own freedom. In the massacre of the French by the Natchez, at the village of that name, over three hundred women and slaves were kept as prisoners, and in January of the same year which witnessed the massacre of the Chouchas, the French surprised the Natchez Indians with the intention of recovering their women and slaves, and avenging the death of their comrades. Some of the Africans who had been promised their freedom if they allied themselves with the Natchez Indians, fought against their erstwhile masters, others were loyal, and helped the French. The battle became an issue, as it were, between the slaves. Over one hundred of them were recovered from the Indians.[26]

The first tribute we have paid to the black man as a soldier in Louisiana was paid by Gov. Perier in this war in his dispatch to the French government. "Fifteen negroes,"

[24] Gayarré, "History of Louisiana," I, 444, 448.
[25] Ibid., I, 365, 442, 454.
[26] Ibid., I, 448.

he wrote, "in whose hands we had put weapons, performed prodigies of valor. If the blacks did not cost so much, and if their labors were not so necessary to the colony, it would be better to turn them into soldiers, and to dismiss those we have, who are so bad and so cowardly that they seem to have been manufactured purposely for this colony."[27]

But the tiger had tasted blood. Perier's cruel logic was reactionary. Since he had used blacks to murder Indians in order to make bad blood between the races, the Indians retaliated by using blacks to murder white men. In August of that same fateful year, the Chickasaws, who had given asylum to the despoiled Natchez in order to curb the encroachments of the white men, stirred the black slaves to revolt. We have noted before the prevalence of the Banbara Negroes in the colony. It was they who planned the rebellion. Their plan was, after having butchered the whites, to establish a Banbara colony, keeping as slaves for themselves all blacks not of their nation. The conspiracy was discovered by the hints of a woman in the revolt before it had time to ripen, and the head of the revolt, a powerful black named Samba with eight of his confederates was broken on the wheel, and the woman hanged.[28]

Gov. Perier's administration did not lack interest. The next year, in 1731, we find him still struggling with his old enemies, the Natchez. His dispatches mention that a crew under one De Coulanges, with Indians and free blacks had been massacred by the Indians. One dispatch has the greatest interest for us, because of the expression "free blacks"[29] used. Here is one of the great mysteries of the person of color in Louisiana. Whence the free black? We are told explicitly that up to this time all Negroes imported into Louisiana were slaves from Africa, for the West Indian migration did not occur until a half century later. This dispatch from Gov. Perier recalls articles in the Black Code of 1724, where explicit directions are given for the disposition of the

---

[27] Gayarré, "History of Louisiana," I, 435.
[28] *Ibid.*, 440.
[29] *Ibid.*, I, 444.

children of free blacks. In the regulations of police under the governorship of the Marquis of Vandreuil, 1750, there is an article regulating the attitude of free Negroes and Negresses toward slaves. Here is the very beginning of that aristocracy of freedom so fiercely and jealously guarded until this day, a free person of color being set as far above his slave fellows as the white man sets himself above the person of color. Three explanations for this aristocracy seem highly probable: Some slaves might have been freed by their masters because of valor on the battlefield, others by buying their freedom in terms of money, and not a few slave women by their owners because of their personal attractions. It makes little difference in this story which of the three or whether all of the three were contributors to the rise of this new class. It existed as early as 1724, twelve years after the first recorded slave importation. It was in 1766 that some Acadians, complaining of their treatment to the Governor Ulloa, represented that Negroes were freemen while they were slaves.

Bienville returned to the colony as its governor in 1733, after an absence of eight years, and it is recorded that in 1735, when he reviewed his troops near Mobile while making preparations for an Indian war, he found that his army from New Orleans consisted of five hundred and forty-four white men, excluding the officers, and forty-five Negroes commanded by free blacks.[30] Here we note free black officers of Negro troops in 1735. If not actually the first regular Negro troops to appear in what is now the United States, they were certainly the first to be commanded by Negro officers.

The engagement with the Choctaw Indians was not altogether successful for the French. Disaster succeeded disaster, and the day closed with the French army deeply humiliated, and making a retreat as dignified as possible under the circumstances. A number of the French officers, as Gayarré tells us, stood under the shade of a gigantic oak discussing the defeat, and with them Simon, a free black, the

[30] Dumont, "Memoires Historiques sur la Louisiane," 225, 226.

commander of the troop of Negroes. He was deeply vexed because his troops had not stood fire, and expressed himself with so much freedom and disgust, that the French officers kept bantering him without mercy at the timidity of his soldiers, soothing their own wounded pride by laughing at his mortification. Stung to the heart, Simon finally exclaimed wrathfully, "A Negro is as brave as anybody and I will show it to you." Seizing a rope which was dangling from one of the tents, he rushed headlong toward one of the horses which were quietly slaking their thirst under the protection of the Indian muskets. To reach a white mare, to jump on her back with the agility of a tiger, and to twist around her head and mouth the rope with which to control her, was the affair of an instant. But that instant was enough for the apparently sleeping Indian village to show itself awake, and to flash forth into a hail of bullets. Away dashed Simon toward the Indian village, and back to the French camp where he arrived safe amid the cheering acclamations of the troops, and without having received a wound from the shots of the enemy.[31] This feat silenced at

[31] Another interesting story is related by Dumont, a historian of Louisiana, who published a work in 1753. The colony was then under the administration of Gov. Kerlerec, whose opinion of colonial courage was not very high. The colony was without an executioner, and no white man could be found who would be willing to accept the office. It was decided finally by the council to force it upon a Negro blacksmith belonging to the Company of the Indies, named Jeannot, renowned for his nerve and strength. He was summoned and told that he was to be appointed executioner and made a free man at the same time. The stalwart fellow started back in anguish and horror, "What! cut off the heads of people who have never done me any harm?". He prayed, he wept, but saw at last that there was no escape from the inflexible will of his masters. "Very well," he said, rising from his knees, "wait a moment." He ran to his cabin, seized a hatchet with his left hand, laid his right hand on a block of wood and cut it off. Returning, without a word he exhibited the bloody stump to the gentlemen of the council. With one cry, it is said, they sprang to his relief, and his freedom was given him.—Dumont, "Memoires Historiques sur la Louisiane," 244, 246.

The story is also told by Grace King of one slave, an excellent cook, who had once served a French governor. When, in one of her periodic transitions from one government to another, Louisiana became the property of Spain, the "Cruel" O'Reilly was made governor of the colony. He was execrated as were all things sent by Spain or pertaining to Spanish rule. However, having

once the jests of the French officers, of which Simon thought himself the victim.[32]

The beginning of the Revolutionary war in 1776 found Louisiana a Spanish province and the natives of the colony beginning to tolerate and even to like their erstwhile hated Spanish masters. Don Bernardo de Galvez was governor of the colony. His administration has a peculiar interest to us, because it was during his rule that the Court of Madrid, fully alive to the policy of extending the agriculture of Louisiana, issued a decree permitting the introduction of Negroes into Louisiana by French vessels, from whatever ports they might come.[33] This was the beginning of the rapid migration from the West Indian islands.

While Andrew Jackson was still a child, Louisiana had a deliverer from the British in the person of this brave Gov. Galvez. The strategical importance of the Mississippi River and of New Orleans was at once apparent to the British commanders, and Louisiana, being neutral territory, offered a most fascinating field of operation. Galvez, in July, 1777, had secured declaration of neutrality from the 25,000 or more Creeks, Choctaws and Chickasaws, but even this did not seem to satisfy the combatants. New Orleans was at the mercy of first the American troops and then the British. The mediation of Spain between France and England having been rejected in the courts of Europe, Spain decided to join France in the struggle against Great Britain. So on May 8, 1779, Spain formally declared war against Great Britain, and on July 8 authorized all Spanish subjects in America to take their share in the hostilities against the English. No news could be more welcome to the dashing young Galvez, to whom a policy of neutrality was decidedly distasteful. He decided to forestall the attack on New

heard of the fame of the Negro cook, he sent for him. ''You belong now,'' said he, ''to the king of Spain, and until you are sold, I shall take you into my service.'' ''Do not dare it;'' answered the slave, ''you killed my master, and I would poison you.'' O'Reilly dismissed him unpunished.—Gayarré, ''History of Louisiana,'' II, 344.

[32] Gayarré, ''History of Louisiana,'' I, 480.

[33] Ibid., III, 108.

Orleans, which he had learned was to be made by the British, by attacking first, and on August 26 gathered his little army together. From New Orleans, as Gayarré tells, were 170 veteran soldiers, 330 recruits, 20 carabiniers, 60 militiamen, and 80 free blacks and mulattoes. On the way up the river, they were reinforced by 600 men from the coast of "every condition and color," besides 160 Indians.[34]

On the march, the colored men and Indians were ordered to keep ahead of the main body of troops, at a distance of about three quarters of a mile, and closely to reconnoitre the woods. In capturing the two forts of Baton Rouge and Natchez, which were held by the British, Galvez found a considerable number of Negro slaves who had been armed by the British. Many of these he set free. In his dispatch to his government at Madrid, Galvez reports that the companies of free blacks and mulattoes, who had been employed in all the false attacks, and who, as scouts and skirmishers, had proved exceedingly useful, behaved on all occasions with as much valor and generosity as the white soldiers.[35] But not alone were the exploits of Galvez's little army celebrated in history. Poetry added her laurel wreath to its crown. Julien Poydras de Lalande, known to all Louisianians as Poydras, celebrated the victory in a poem, "The God of the Mississippi," wherein the brave deeds of the army, white and colored, are hailed in French verse, lame and halting, it may be in places, but impartial in its tribute.

The close of the Revolutionary war found the colony partially paralyzed as to industry. During the Spanish domination the indigo industry declined, tobacco was difficult to raise, and the production of cotton was not then profitable. Sugar raising was the only other industry to which they could turn. In 1751 the Jesuit fathers had received their first seed, or rather layers, from Santo Domingo and from that time sugar-cane had been grown with more or less success. But it was a strictly local industry. The Louisianians were poor sugar-makers. The stuff was badly

[34] Gayarré, "History of Louisiana," III, 108.
[35] Ibid., III, 126–132.

granulated and very moist, and when in 1765 an effort was made to export some of the sugar to France, it was so wet that half of the cargo leaked out of the ship before it could make port. It was just at this psychological moment, in 1791 to 1794, when the planters of the lower Delta saw ruin staring them in the face, that there came to the rescue of the colony a man of color, one of the refugees from Santo Domingo, where the blacks had risen in 1791. From the failure of this abortive attempt to emulate the spirit of the white man, refugees flew in every direction, and Louisiana welcomed them, if not exactly with open arms, at least with more indifference than other colonies. And these black refugees were her saviors. For they had been prosperous sugar-makers, and the efforts to make marketable sugar in Louisiana, which had ceased for nearly twenty-five years, were revived. Two Spaniards, Mendez and Solis, erected on the outskirts of New Orleans, the one a distillery, the other a battery of sugar-kettles, and manufactured rum and syrup. Still, the efforts were not entirely successful, until Etienne de Boré appeared. Face to face with ruin because of the failure of the indigo crop, he staked his all on the granulation of sugar. He enlisted the services of these successful Santo Dominicans, and went to work. In all American history there can be fewer scenes more dramatic than the one described by careful historians of Louisiana, the day when the final test was made and there was passed around the electrical word, "It granulates!"[36]

That year de Boré marketed $12,000 worth of super or sugar. The agriculture of the Delta was revolutionized; seven years afterwards New Orleans marketed 2,000,000 gallons of rum, 250,000 gallons of molasses, and 5,000,000 pounds of sugar. It was the beginning of the commercial importance of one of the most progressive cities in the country. Imagination refuses to picture what would have been the case but for the refugees from San Domingo.

But the same revolution which gave to Louisiana its prestige to the commercial world, almost starved the prov-

[36] Gayarré, "History of Louisiana," III, 348.

ince to death. In the year 1791, the trade, which had flourished briskly between Santo Domingo and New Orleans, was
closed because of the uprising, and but for Philadelphia,
famine would have decimated the city. 1,000 barrels of
flour were sent in haste to the starving city by the good
Quakers of Philadelphia. The members of the Cabildo, the
local council, prohibited the introduction of people of color
from Santo Domingo, fearing the dangerous ideas of the
brotherhood of man. But it was too late. The news of the success of the slaves in Santo Domingo, and the success of the
French Revolution, says Gayarré, had penetrated into the
most remote cabins of Louisiana, and in April, 1795, on the
plantation of the same Poydras who had sung the glory of
the army of Galvez, a conspiracy was formed for a general
uprising of the slaves throughout the parish of Pointe
Coupée. The leaders were three white men. The conspiracy failed because one of the leaders was incensed at his
advice not being heeded and through his wife the authorities
were notified. A struggle ensued, and the conspiracy was
strangled in its infancy by the trial and execution of the
slaves most concerned in the insurrection. The three white
men were exiled from the colony.[37] This finally ended the
importation of slaves from the West Indies.

                                        ALICE DUNBAR-NELSON

[37] Gayarré, ''History of Louisiana,'' III, 354.

THE DEFEAT OF THE SECESSIONISTS IN KENTUCKY IN 1861

The treatment of the Border States in the crisis of 1861 has received from historians the same attention as Saxony, the objective point between Prussia and Austria in the Seven Years' War. Directing special attention to Kentucky requires some explanation. The possession of this commonwealth was for several reasons more important than that of some other border States. The transportation facilities afforded by the Cumberland and Tennessee rivers furnished the key to carrying out the plan to divide the South. The possession of the State by the Confederates was of strategic importance for the invasion of the North too for the reason that the Ordinance of 1787 had been so interpreted as to fix the boundary of Kentucky on the north side of the Ohio River. It was, moreover, the native State of Abraham Lincoln and it was important to have that commonwealth support this untrained backwoodsman whom most statesmen considered incapable of administering the affairs of the nation.

In the beginning, the situation was not the least encouraging to the Unionists. The Breckenridge Democrats had carried the State in 1859 on a platform favoring Southern rights. Their chief spokesman had become such a defender of their faith that in 1860 he was chosen to lead the radically proslavery party which had come to the point of so doubting the orthodoxy of their Northern adherents as to deem it advisable to separate from them. Unalterably in favor of the rights of the slave States, the leaders of this persuasion had expressed themselves in terms that could not be misunderstood.[1] One of their spokesmen Humphrey Marshall contended that slavery is not a creature of municipal law. He believed that the institution followed the flag.

[1] See Debates in Congress.

He wanted Union but only with that equality which involved the recognition of the right of property in slaves everywhere.[2] Speaking in the House of Representatives on January 30, 1861, John W. Stephenson, another of this faction, said on the same topic: "Equality underlaid the whole Federal structure, and protection to persons and property within the Federal jurisdiction, was the price of allegiance of the States to such General Government, as delegated and prescribed in the constitution. Wherever the American banner floated upon the seas or land, all beneath it was entitled to the protection of the flag."[3]

On this question, their leader John C. Breckenridge, "a believer in the old Democratic creed and a supporter of the South and her institutions,"[4] took the same, if not higher ground. Referring to the Dred Scott decision in a speech delivered in Ashland, Kentucky, in 1859, Breckenridge said: "After this decision we had arrived at a point where we might reasonably expect tranquillity and peace. The equality of rights and property of all the states in the common Territory, having been stamped by the seal of judicial authority, all good citizens might well acquiesce."[5] When the Southern States seceded because of the threatened infringement of these rights, the President of the United States, according to Breckenridge, had no right to enlist men and no right to blockade the Southern ports, in short, no right to wage war on these commonwealths. Lincoln had thus overthrown constitutional government. If he was trying to preserve the Union, he must do it in a constitutional way. Breckenridge wanted the Union but contended that it would be no good without the constitution.[6] To sum up, as Southern Democrats they had helped to disrupt the Charleston Convention, and developing into a strict Southern rights

[2] Marshall, Speech in Washington on the Nomination of Breckenridge and Lane, p. 3.

[3] Speech of John Stephenson on the state of the Union in the House of Representatives, January 30, 1861.

[4] Bartlett, "Presidential Candidates in 1860," pp. 344–345.

[5] Speech of Hon. J. C. Breckenridge delivered at Ashland, Kentucky, p. 9.

[6] Speech of J. C. Breckenridge on Executive Usurpation, July 16, 1861.

party, they had through bolting made possible the election of Abraham Lincoln. They then finally joined the States' rights party, which, boldly declaring the election of Lincoln a just cause for the dissolution of the Union, undertook to secede.[7]

With such radical leaders in control it might seem strange that, in a State formed from an aristocratic commonwealth like Virginia and extending into the fertile region of the Mississippi, these protagonists of States' rights did not turn Kentucky over to the Confederacy. Exactly what part did the rich slaveholders play during this crisis when the State was called upon to decide the question between the North and South? What was the position of such influential men as James B. Clay, George B. Hodge, Cerro Gordo Williams, T. P. Porter, Roger W. Hansom, and S. B. Buckner?[8]

Other representative citizens, however, had been equally outspoken in favor of the Union. Voicing the sentiment of the Union party, which on the eighth of January met in Louisville to take steps to support the Federal Government, Bell said: "Let us offer everything we can to avert the torrent of evil, but let us always stand ready to support our rights in the Union: the State is deeply and devotedly attached to the Union."[9] Garrett Davis inquired: "Will you preserve the Union or rush into the vortex of revolution under the name of secession?"[10] J. T. Boyle said in the same convention that there could be no benefit or advantage, no civil or political rights, no interest of any kind whatever, secured by government in the Southern Confederacy which the people did not then enjoy in the "blessed Union formed by our fathers." In his opinion, it was the duty of Kentuckians "to stand by the Star Spangled Banner and cling to the Union."[11] Some of the most influential

[7] "The Frankfort Commonwealth," August 21, 1861.

[8] These were some of the most intellectual and aristocratic men of the State. Collins exaggerates, however, when he says that few leading men opposed secession. See Collins, "History of Kentucky," I, 82.

[9] Speed, "The Union Cause in Kentucky," 36.

[10] Ibid., 36.

[11] Ibid., 37.

newspapers were fearlessly advocating the Union cause. Among others were the Frankfort *Daily Commonwealth,* the Louisville *Courier* and the *Democrat.*

Exactly what support these leaders of the differing factions would obtain was determined by forces for centuries at work in that State. Southerners who thought that, because Kentucky was a slave State it should go with the South, had failed to take these causes into consideration. In the first place, not every slaveholder was an ardent proslavery agitator. There were masters who like Henry Clay considered slavery an evil and hoped to see it abolished, but while the majority of their fellow countrymen held on to it they did so too. Many Kentuckians, moreover, were like that restless class of Westerners who, dissatisfied with the society based on slavery, had taken up land beyond the mountains, where the poor man could toil up from poverty.[12] Kentucky was the first section west of the Allegheny mountains settled by these daring adevnturers because they were there cut off from the North by the French and from the South by the Spanish, and in Kentucky, a section hemmed in by these foreign possessions, the settlers were less liable to be disturbed. And even when the barrier of foreign claims had been removed, the movement of population from the East to the West took place along lines leading to the States later organized in the West rather than into Kentucky. The people of Kentucky, therefore, were not radically changed in a day by the influx of population. On the contrary, many of them, especially the mountaineers, have not changed since the days of Boone and Henderson. Some of them having left the uplands of the colonies because they were handicapped by slavery, were naturally opposed to the bold claims of that institution in 1861. They, like the Westerners, learned to look to the General Government for the establishment of commonwealths, the building of forts, and the maintenance of troops,[13] and, therefore, adhered to it when it was threatened with destruction.

[12] Hart, "Slavery and Abolition," 65, 178, 234; Turner, "Rise of the New West," 77.

[13] Report of the American Historical Association, 1893, pp. 219-221.

Another cause, moreover, was equally as potential. In Kentucky as in some other Southern States, there had grown up a considerable number of prosperous country towns, where resided lawyers, merchants, bankers, teachers, and mechanics, who had little property interest in slavery, who felt their own "intellectual superiority to the country squires and their fox-hunting, horse-racing, quarrelsome sons, and who consequently asserted social independence of them and social equality with them."[14]   They were hostile to the aristocratic masters, whom they generally denounced as "oligarchs," "slavocrats," "Lords of the Lash," and "Terror Engenders."[15]   This mercantile and professional class, inspired by such men as Hinton Rowan Helper, contemplated the removal of the Negroes and the bringing of white laborers into the South.[16]

In view of this cleavage, it was difficult in the beginning of the struggle to characterize the situation.   There were unconditional Secessionists and unconditional Union men. Judging from the condition then obtaining, no one could tell exactly which way the State would go.   "Sympathy, blood, and the community of social feeling growing out of slavery," says one, "inclined her to the South; her political faith which Clay more than any other man had inspired her with and which Crittenden now loyally represented held her fast to the Union."[17]   Many of the people, though believing in States' rights, did not think that the grievances of the South were such as to justify secession.   At the same time they opposed "coercion," and since a reconstructed Union was impossible they would have solved the difficulty by peaceful separation.   Writing to Gen. McClellan June 8, 1861, Garrett Davis said: "The sympathy for the South and the inclination to secession among our people is much stronger in the southwestern corner of the state than it is in any other part, and as you proceed toward the upper

---

[14] Burgess, "Civil War and the Constitution," I, 30.
[15] Ibid.
[16] McMaster, "History of the United States," VIII, 426–427.
[17] Rhodes, "History of the United States," III, 391.

section of the Ohio and our Virginia line, it gradually becomes weaker until it is almost wholly lost. . . . I doubt not
that two thirds of our people are unconditionally for the
Union. The timid are for it and they shrink from convul-
sion and civil war, while all the bold, the reckless, and the
bankrupt are for secession.''[18] This categorical distinction, however, is hardly right. There were Kentuckians of
representative families on both sides in all parts of the
State except in the extreme West.[19] A careful study of the
facts, however, leads one to the conclusion that even in the
beginning there were more Unionists than Secessionists.
The Unionists, unhappily, were not organized while the Secessionists were led by the State officials, chief among whom
was Governor Magoffin.

When the Southern States began to secede Governor
Magoffin called a special session of the State legislature,
thinking that he could have a secession convention called.
He said in part: "I therefore submit to your consideration
the propriety of providing for the election of delegates to a
convention to be assembled at an early day to which shall
be referred for full and final determination the future of the
Federal and interstate relations of Kentucky." He
further said: "Kentucky will not be an indifferent observer
of the force policy. The seceding States have not in their
haste and inconsiderate action our approval, but their cause
is our right and they have our sympathies. The people of
Kentucky will never stand by with folded arms while those
States are struggling for their constitutional rights and
resisting oppression and being subjugated to an anti-
slavery government.''[20] He believed that the idea of coercion, when applied to great political communities, is revolt-
ing to a free people, contrary to the spirit of our institutions,
and if successful would endanger the liberties of the
people.[21] But the legislature did not provide for such a

[18] Rhodes, ''History of the United States,'' VII, 392.
[19] Speed, ''The Union Cause in Kentucky,'' 158–179.
[20] *House Journal*, 1861, Governor's Message, p. 10.
[21] *Ibid.*, 11.

convention. On the eleventh of February this body adjourned. It reassembled on the twentieth of March and remained in session until the fourth of April, but still these important matters were not decided. Pursuant to another call of the Governor, it reassembled on the 6th of May and sat until the twenty-fourth of May when it adjourned. On the second of September the legislature elected in August came in, but still the important question as to what should be done hung in the balance. At first there came up the resolutions introduced by George W. Ewing on the twenty-first of January, expressing regret that certain States had furnished men and money for the coercion of the seceded States, and requesting the Governor of Kentucky to notify such States that should attempts be made to coerce these commonwealths, Kentucky would join the South.[22] This resolution passed the House but did not pass the whole legislature as so many have said. A resolution for calling a convention to amend the Constitution of the United States was passed.[23] Several distinguished men of Kentucky sat in this convention which was in session from the fourth to the twenty-second of February without accomplishing anything.

The majority of Kentuckians were then neutral. There were two classes of neturals, however. This was easily possible since neutrality meant one thing to one man and a different thing to another. Each faction looked forward to the adoption of this policy as a victory over the other. The Unionists accepted it as the best policy, not knowing that, taking such a position, they would aid the Confederacy. Even John J. Crittenden had this idea. He said: "If Kentucky and the other border States should assume this attitude, war between the two sections of the country would be averted and the Confederate states after a few years' trial of their experiment would return voluntarily to the Union."[24]

[22] House Journal, 1861, Governor's Message, p. 12.
[23] Ibid., 14.
[24] Letter of John J. Crittenden to Gen. McClellan.

Neutrality was considered a necessity for another reason; namely, the expected short duration of the war. No one believed at first that the war would last long. Even Lincoln thought that it would be over in ninety days. Some, therefore, felt that Kentucky would be foolish to cause blood to be shed on her soil when the war could easily be kept out of the State three months. This sentiment, however, must not be misunderstood as evincing a lack of interest in the Union, for in the address declaring for neutrality these same leaders said that the dismemberment of the Union was no remedy for existing evils but an aggravation of them all.[25] To many Unionists neutrality meant going slowly in the right direction. It was in keeping with Lincoln's plan not to go so rapidly toward "coercion" in Kentucky as he had in the other border States.

How then did the neutrality policy work out? On the twenty-ninth of January R. T. Jacob introduced in the lower house of the legislature a resolution declaring that the proper position of Kentucky was that of a mediator between the sections, and that as an umpire she would remain firm and impartial in that day of trial to their "beloved country that by counsel and mediation she might aid in restoring peace and harmony and brotherly love." Giving the reasons for adopting such a policy Jacob said:

"This leading sentiment of mediation was indorsed by the Union men of both Houses of the Legislature. . . . Some may say, why did not the Kentucky Legislature go for coercion? For two reasons: First, some States, it is true had seceded from the Union, but war had not actually commenced: second, the men at that time who would have undertaken to force coercion upon the Legislature would have been in the hopeless minority and would have immediately given a majority to the secessionists. It would have ended in total destruction to the cause of the Union in the State. Those resolutions were for two purposes. In good faith they were intended to compromise all difference between the States, and if possible to restore peace between sections. If that failed, they were intended to hold, if possible, our meagre majority until the people could act and we had no doubt that when they did speak it would be in unmistakable tones for the preservation of the Union."[26]

No action was taken on these resolutions, but on the eleventh of February there was passed a joint measure,

[25] Speed, "The Union Cause in Kentucky," 42.
[26] Speed, "The Union Cause in Kentucky," p. 45.

entitled "Resolutions Declaring action by the Legislature on political affairs unnecessary and inexpedient at this time."[27] These resolutions mentioned the great danger which environed the Union, asked the Confederates to stay the work of secession and protested against coercion. The last resolution favored the calling of a convention to amend the constitution of the United States. Significant too for the Unionists were the last words: "It is unnecessary and inexpedient for the Legislature to take any further action on the subject at the present time, and as an evidence of the sincerity and good faith of our propositions for an adjustment and our expression of devotion to the Union and the desire for its preservation Kentucky awaits with great solicitude the responses from her sister States."[28]

Neutrality, however, became the accepted policy of so many that it proved to be dangerous. The Union State Committee, in drawing up on the eighteenth of April a resolution to please all, seemingly pledged the State to join the South. These resolutions were severely criticised by the Unionists, especially that part which says: "What the future destiny of Kentucky may be we cannot with certainty foresee. But if the enterprise announced in the proclamation of the President should at any time hereafter assume the aspect of a war for overrunning and subjugation of the seceding States, then Kentucky ought to take her stand for the South."[29] Many thought that this obligated Kentucky to go with the South. Unionists of other States considered it a victory for the Confederacy. This committee, however, stipulated this proposition to satisfy those sympathizers with the South, who believed all the bad reports concerning the functionaries of the Federal Government, circulated by the leaders of the Confederacy. Hence, they said in this proposition not that Kentucky would go with the South, but if at any time thereafter the President's proclamation should assume the aspect of war, it would do so.

[27] *House Journal*, 1861, p. 33.
[28] *Ibid.*, 34.
[29] Speed, "The Union Cause in Kentucky," 57.

They evidently did not believe that it had or would assume such an aspect. They were also trying to pacify those who misunderstood the issues of "subjugation" and "coercion."[30] The relation of the States to the Union was yet a problem to many a statesman. Many thought that the colonists when in a state of nature came together and agreed to a compact, giving up some of their sovereignty and retaining the other, and, therefore, had the right to withdraw at pleasure, carrying a part of the national property with them. Such thinkers contended too that the Union had no right to "coerce" a seceded State. Calhoun had said that because the Union was a compact it could be broken; on the other hand, Jackson had said that because it was a compact it could not be broken. Now it was difficult for Kentuckians to decide who was right. That the committee had no intention of going with the Confederacy may be seen from the following declaration: "Seditious leaders in the midst of us now appeal to her (Kentucky) to furnish troops to uphold those combinations against the government of the Union. Will she comply with this appeal? Ought she to comply with it? We answer, no."[31]

While these things were going on, the great question of Fort Sumter was before the people. When the fort was finally bombarded and Lincoln called for seventy-five thousand troops Gov. Magoffin politely refused to comply. His reply was: "I say emphatically Kentucky will furnish no troops for the wicked purpose of subduing her sister Southern States."[32] He had already been much moved by the large vote given the delegates to the Border States Convention, indicating such a growth of Union sentiment that he called the legislature together, hoping to win the day for secession by changing the policy of the State from mediatorial to armed neutrality, resisting all forces, whether Confederate or Federal, which might bring war into the State. The body met on the sixteenth of May, passed a resolution

[30] Speed, "The Union Cause in Kentucky," 58–62.
[31] Ibid., 58.
[32] House Journal, 1861, p. 6.

of mediatorial neutrality and approved the Governor's refusal to furnish troops under the existing circumstances.[33]
This, however, did not mean that the legislature was in
sympathy with the efforts of the governor to support the
Southern cause. Writing to Gen. Scott John J. Crittenden
explained it thus:

"The position of Kentucky and the relation she occupies toward the government of the Union is not, I fear, understood at Washington. It ought to be
well understood. Very important consequences may depend upon it and upon
her proper treatment. Unfortunately for us our Governor does not sympathize
with Kentucky in respect to secession. His opinions and feelings incline him
strongly to the side of the South. His answer to the requisition for troops
was in terms hasty and unbecoming and does not correspond with the usual
and gentlemanly courtesy. But while she regretted the language of his answer,
Kentucky acquiesced in his declining to furnish the troops called for, and she
did so not because she loved the Union less but she feared that if she had parted
with those troops and sent them to serve in your ranks, she would have been
overwhelmed by secessionists at home, and severed from the Union. And it
was to preserve substantially and ultimately our connection with the Union that
induced us to acquiesce in the partial infraction of it by our governor's refusal
of the troops required. This was the most prevailing and general motive.
To this may be added the strong indisposition of our people to a civil war with
the South, and the apprehended consequences of a civil war within our state
and among our people. . . . I think Kentucky's excuse a good one and that
under all the circumstances of a complicated case she is rendering better service
in her present position than she could by becoming an active party in the
contest."[34]

The fact is that secession had little chance in Kentucky
after public opinion found expression. Neutrality early
became the order of the day. The elections of 1861 were
significant in that they gave the people a chance to express
their will. It should be borne in mind that the legislature
of 1859 was elected when the question of union or disunion
was not before the people. Now in 1861 they had to elect
members to the Border State Convention, a new legislature,
and congressmen to represent Kentucky at the special session called by President Lincoln. In all these elections,
Unionists won. Some historians like Smith and Shaler[35]

[33] Ibid., 94.
[34] Nicolay and Hay, "Life of Lincoln," IV, 233.
[35] Smith, "History of Kentucky," 610; Shaler, "History of Kentucky,"
243.

seem to think that the State had pledged itself to remain unconditionally neutral, that these elections had no particular
bearing on the situation and that if a "sovereignty convention" had been called, secession would have won. These
writers do not seem to see that the people of Kentucky, although nominally neutral, desired to remain with the Union.
Doubtless a better statement is that, although the election of
1861 showed that a large majority of the people were in favor
of the Union, the Union leaders did not show so in the early
part of the year and neutrality was adopted not as an end
but as a means that triumph over the enemies of the Union
might finally be assured.[36] We easily see now that there
was not much danger of secession, but the Unionists could
not see it so well at that time. Smith and Shaler doubtless
exaggerate the situation, for what danger of secession could
there have been when the people had elected the Union candidates for the Border State Convention to be convened at
Frankfort on May 27, when they sent nine Unionists out of
the ten congressmen to represent them in the special session
of Congress, and when on the 5th of the following August,
after the battle of Bull Run, they elected to the State Legislature 103 Unionists out of 141 members.[37] The calling of a
convention then would have made little difference, if the
people had chosen a majority of Unionists to represent

[36] Smith says in describing the period of 1861: "It were well nigh certain
that if a sovereignty convention could have been called at any time before the
formation of the Union sentiment and policy into action and life, the state
would have been carried off into the act of secession as Virginia and Tennessee
were by the sense of sympathy and kinship toward the South." Shaler thinks
the same. He says: "There is reason to believe that this course (neutrality)
was the only one that could have kept Kentucky from secession. If what had
been unhappily named a Sovereignty Convention had been called in 1861; if
the state had been compelled by the decision of a body of men who were acting
under the control of no constitutional enunciation, the sense of sympathy and
kinship with the Southern states, such as would easily grow up under popular
oratory in a mob, would probably have precipitated action." Speed, however,
is doubtless right in saying all this is mere assertion and that there was no
danger of secession after the people had a chance to transfer their will to the
government. Shaler, "Kentucky," p. 240; Smith, "History of Kentucky,"
p. 610.

[37] Speed, "The Union Cause in Kentucky," 93–98.

them in other bodies. How can one conclude then that they would have elected seceders to represent them in a ''sovereignty convention?'' Hodge states that the sympathizers with the Confederacy did not contest to any considerable extent the elections of August, 1861, and consequently the supporters of the Federal Government were in the ascendency in the next legislature. He seems to indicate that the Unionists used fraud, but the records show that the Secessionists, regarding it as a lost cause, in many cases withdrew their candidates. Evidently these elections showed not only that secession was impossible but that neutrality could not last.[38]

After this sentiment began to change. Men boldly took decisive positions. The unwieldy neutrality party then divided into three parts: those who went to the Confederate lines to aid the Southern cause; those who openly declared themselves in favor of the Union; and those sympathizers with the South, who although in favor of the seceding States, seeing that their cause was hopeless, advocated peaceful separation and finally, when that failed, a compromise peace between the two sections.[39] The Union party, though unalterably opposed to the abolitionists and not primarily attached to the Union because of antagonism to slavery, gradually acquiesced in the policy of the Federal Government with respect to that institution. This party first reached the position that Negroes taken from the Confederates could with propriety be disposed of as contraband of war and many of its adherents grew more favorable to the policy of general emancipation.

It was soon evident that war could not long be kept out of the State. As early as April, 1861, troops for service in the Confederacy were organized in Kentucky. This movement was somewhat accelerated by an act of the legislature providing that the arms supplied to the troops should not be used against either section and that the State companies as

[38] Collins, ''History of Kentucky,'' I, 243.

[39] *The Frankfort Commonwealth*, July 19; Aug. 19, 21, 23; Nov. 10, 20, 23; and Dec. 11, 1861; *The Yeoman Weekly*, May 10; June 21, 22; July 8, 1861; *Daily Louisville Democrat*, Sept. 7 and Oct. 8, 1861.

well as the Home Guards should take the same oath as the officers requiring fidelity to the constitution.[40]   At this point many Kentuckians of proslavery tendencies were forced out of their natural position and driven into the Confederate ranks.   Among these was S. B. Buckner, who went South to command about ten thousand secessionists, recruited, under the leadership of Colonels Roger W. Hanson, Lloyd Tilghman, and W. D. Lannon at Camp Boone.[41]

The Governor refused to furnish Lincoln troops but he was in touch with the Confederacy, doing all he could to equip soldiers for its service,[42] though not exactly openly, as that would have been sufficient excuse for the Unionists who desired to help the Union.   The Unionists who saw all of this going on desired to arm and organize their forces but they were handicapped in that the commander of the State guard was a Secessionist and care had been taken to hold the military forces for the South.   In consequence of this difficulty Lincoln was secretly appealed to for arms, which were shipped to cities on the Ohio River for secret distribution among the Unionists of Kentucky as the opportunity would permit.[43]   The Secessionists had referred to these guns as the first so-called violation of neutrality.   The Unionists defended themselves on the ground that since the Governor and his whole machine were about in the ranks of the Confederates they were justified in doing almost anything to defend the State.   Shaler says that the action on both sides was almost simultaneous and that the actual infringement of the neutrality proclamation issued by the Governor was due to the action of Polk and Zollicoffer and the simultaneous invasion of the State some hundreds of miles apart shows that the rupture of the neutrality of Kentucky was deliberately planned by the Confederate authorities.[44]

[40] *House Journal*, 1861, 240.

[41] Speed, ''The Union Cause in Kentucky,'' 192.

[42] War Records, Serial 108, p. 37; Serial 127, p. 234; Serial 110, pp. 44–64, and Serial 110, p. 71.

[43] Nicolay and Hay, ''Life of Lincoln,'' IV, 237.

[44] Shaler, ''History of Kentucky,'' 261.

The invasion by Polk in September produced great excitement. The legislature was then in session and passed a resolution that the invaders be expelled, and that the Governor call out the military force of the State and place the same under the command of Gen. Thomas L. Crittenden. The resolutions were vetoed by the Governor but passed by a vote of two thirds.[45] The desired proclamation was issued and soon sufficient men to form forty regiments answered the call.[46] Making further response to the invasion of the State by the Confederates, the legislature ordered that the United States flag be raised over the capitol at Frankfort, and by a resolution which "affirmed" distinctly. though not directly, the doctrine of States' rights placed Kentucky in political and military association with the North.[47]

WM. T. McKINNEY

[45] *House Journal*, 1861, p. 122.
[46] Speed, "The Union Cause in Kentucky," 300 *et seq*. See despatches and letters given in same.
[47] Rhodes, "History of the United States," III, 392.

NOTES ON NEGROES IN GUATEMALA DURING
THE SEVENTEENTH CENTURY

The introduction of Negroes into Guatemala commenced with the year of the conquest of that country by the Spaniards in 1524, when there came several Negro slaves with the *conquistadores* from Mexico. It seems that they soon increased in numbers, for among the decrees of the *conquistador,* Pedro de Alvarado, there is one which prohibits the selling of gunpowder to Indians and Negroes. The number of African slaves brought to Guatemala had, however, always remained relatively a very limited one, for as the Spaniards had plenty of cheap hands by means of a system of indentured labor forced upon the numerous Indian population, the importation of slaves evidently did not pay them well. It seems safe to say, that their total number never amounted to ten thousand.

The most copious, though still very sparse notices of them I have run across, are those given by Thomas Gage, an English Catholic educated in Spain, who, in the twenties and thirties of the seventeenth century, lived as a priest in the then city of Guatemala, nowadays called Antigua, and in some Indian villages not far from there.[1] One of the places where Thomas Gage observed a somewhat considerable population of Negroes was the so-called Costa del Sur, or Southern Coast, the hot land between the Andes and the Pacific, to the south of the capital. They were worked there on the indigo-plantations and large cattle *haciendas*. The Negroes impressed Thomas Gage as the only courageous people in Guatemala while the Spanish Mestizos and Indians seemed to him to be very cowardly.

This writer said that if Guatemala was powerful with

[1] Gage published in 1648 in London an account of his residence and voyages; I have only a French version of his work at hand, printed in Amsterdam, in 1721. The passages cited are re-translated from that language and, therefore, will not agree word for word with the original text.

respect to its people, for she was not in arms nor resources, then she was so merely by virtue of a class of desperate Negroes, who were slaves living on the indigo plantations. Though they had no arms but a machete, which was their small lance used for chasing the wild cattle (nowadays, that name is given to a long and broad, sword-like knife), they were so desperate that they often caused fear to the very city of Guatemala and had made their masters tremble. "There are among them," said he, "those who have no fear to brave a wild bull, furious though he be, and to attach themselves to the crocodiles in the rivers, until they have killed them and brought them to the bank."[2]

In reading these lines, one cannot help from remembering the classical description Alexander Von Humboldt gives of the Negro boatmen of the river Dagua, in the actual republic of Colombia. The inimitable skill and unsurpassable bravery Humboldt saw them display in the midst of the ferocious currents and loud-pouring rapids of that river caused him to exclaim: "Every movement of the paddle is a wonder, and every Negro a god!" A nice monument to the fame of indomitable bravery the Negroes manifested in past times in Guatemala exists still in a saying often heard by travelers: "*Esos son negros!*" "Those are Negroes," an exclamation which means: "Those are desperate men, who do not care for anything." One could also hear the saying: "*Esto es obra de negros,*" or "that is a work of Negroes," the meaning being that it was work for bold men with iron nerves.

Another expression brings out the fact that the Negroes were considered, or forced to be, very hard workers. "*Trabaja como un negro,*" or "he works like a Negro," signified doing "the most arduous labor." That the lot of the slaves was often a bitter one, though, because of the less greedy Spanish character, without doubt generally a less hard one than in North America, is shown by the fact that Guatemala had her "*Cimarrones*" just as Jamaica, and Guiana, had their Maroons.

[2] Gage's "Voyages," Part 3, Chapter II.

The Spanish word "*cimarron*" signifies indiscriminately a runaway head of cattle or horses, that had become wild, or a runaway slave. The fugitive Negroes of Guatemala had their chief stronghold in the inaccessible mountain woods of the Sierra de las Minas, which lies near the Atlantic coast between the Golfo Dulce and the valley of the river Motagua. The Golfo Dulce, which is now abandoned because of lack of sufficient depth for the big vessels of to-day, was at that time the port of entry for the whole of Guatemala. From it a bridle-path ran over the Sierra de las Minas to the valley of the Motagua and further on to the capital. In speaking of this path over the mountain, Gage remarks: "What the Spaniards fear most until they get out of these mountains, are two or three hundred Negroes, Cimarrones, who for the bad treatment they received have fled from Guatemala and from other places, running away from their masters in order to resort to these woods; there they live with their wives and children and increase in numbers every year, so that the entire force of Guatemala City and its environments is not capable to subdue them."

They very often came out of the woods to attack those who drove teams of mules, and took from them wine, salt, clothes and arms to the quantity they needed. They never did any harm to the mule drivers nor to their slaves. On the contrary, the slaves amused themselves with the Cimarrones, because they were of the same color and in the same condition of servitude, and not seldom availed themselves of the opportunity to follow their example, and united with them to obtain liberty, though obliged to live in the woods and mountains.

Their arms were arrows and bows, which they carried only for the purpose of defending themselves against attacks of the Spaniards; for they did not harm those who passed by peacefully and who let them have a part of the provisions they carried. They often declared that their principal reason for resorting to these mountains was to be ready to join the English or Dutch, if these some day appeared in the Gulf, for they well knew that these, unlike the Spaniards, would let them live in peace.

Among the most remarkable facts learned by Thomas Gage in Guatemala is the story of a Negro freedman who had accumulated great wealth. This Negro lived in Agua Caliente, an Indian village, on the road to Guatemala City, or Antigua, where the natives had obtained considerable quantities of gold from some spot in the mountains only known to them. The Spaniards, not content with an annual tribute paid them by the Indians, endeavored in vain to force the natives to show them the mine, and because they refused killed them, thus gaining no knowledge of the mine for which they were still searching in vain in the times of Thomas Gage. "In that place of Agua Caliente," continues Gage, "there is a Negro who lives and receives very well the travelers who call upon him. His wealth consists in cattle, sheep, and goats, and he furnishes the city of Guatemala and the environments with the best cheese to be found in the country. But it is believed that his wealth does not come so much from the produce of his farm and his cattle and cheese, but from that hidden treasure which is believed known to him. He, therefore, has been summoned to the Royal Audience in Guatemala, but he has always denied to have any knowledge of it."

He had been suspected because he had formerly been a slave and had secured his liberty by means of a considerable sum. After that, he had bought his farm and much of the surrounding land and had considerably increased his original holdings. To his inquisitors he replied that, "when young and still a slave he had a kind master who suffered him to do what he pleased, and that by economy he had accumulated where-with to buy his liberty and afterwards a little house to live in; and God had given His blessing to that and let him have the means for increasing his funds."

Another one of Gage's accounts discloses the abuses common among the slave-holders under Spanish rule, and the silliness of the belief that the masters for their own benefit would treat their human property well. This account refers to one Juan Palomeque, a rich landowner and promoter of mule-transports, who lived in Gage's parish of Mexico, near the actual capital of Guatemala. He was believed to be worth six hundred thousand ducats, about 1,400,000 dollars. He owned about a hundred Negroes, men, women, and children, but was so stingy that, to avoid the expense of decent house-keeping, he never lived in the city, though he had several houses there. Instead, he lived in a straw-hut and feasted on hard, black bread and on *tasajo,* or thin strips of salt beef dried in the sun.

He was so cruel to his Negroes, that, when one of them behaved badly, he would whip him almost to death. He had among others a slave named Macaco, "on behalf of whom," said Gage, "I often pleaded, but in vain. At times he hung him by the hands and beat him until he had his back entirely covered with blood, and in that state, the skin being entirely torn to pieces, in order to heal up the slave's sores the master poured hot fat over them. Moreover, he had marked him with a hot iron face, hands, arms, back, belly, and legs, so that this poor slave got tired to live and intended several times to suicide himself; but I prevented him from doing so every time by remonstrances I made him."

Juan Palomeque was so sensual and voluptuous that he constantly abused the wives of his slaves as he liked, and even when he saw in the city some girl or woman of that class whom he wanted, and she was not attracted to him, he would call upon her master or mistress and buy her, "giving much more than she had cost; afterwards he boasted that he would break down her pride in one year of slavery." "In my times," said Gage, "he killed two Indians on the road to the Gulf, but by means of his money he got so easily out of that affair as if he had killed but a dog." As Gage does not tell anything of a prosecution for the crimes against the Negro, no actual law seems to have been violated.[3]

The descendants of the ancient slaves have so completely

[3] It seems proper to add here, that three years after Guatemala had declared her independence of Spain, she abrogated slavery by decree of April 17, 1824. Thereby she got, by the way, into difficulties with Great Britain, which as late as in 1840 demanded the extradition of slaves run away from the adjacent British territory of Balize. Guatemala was by men-of-war sent to her coast forced to do so, though that was contrary to her constitution.

become mixed up with Spanish-Indian blood that, making exception of the valley of the Motagua River, they have practically disappeared as a race. In 1796, their number was considerably increased by the so-called Caribs, whom the English deported from the Island of St. Vincent and set ashore in Guatemala. They live now on the Atlantic coast, also on that of Honduras and Nicaragua, and are estimated to total about 20,000. They are Zambos, but the African blood seems to prevail.[4]

A Mulatto Corsair of the Sixteenth Century

When on his return voyage to England, sailing down the Atlantic coast of Costa Rica, Thomas Gage's ship was intercepted by two corsairs under the Dutch flag, one of them being a man-of-war. The struggle of the Netherlands for freedom against Spain had not then come to a close. The Dutch commander was a character, of whose strange experiences Gage gives an interesting account. Much to the surprise of the traveler the captain who had caught them was a mulatto named Diaguillo, who was born and brought up at Habana (Cuba), where his mother was still living. Having been maltreated by the Governor of Campeche in whose service he had been, this mulatto in a fit of utter desperation threw himself into a boat and ventured into the sea, where he met with some Dutch ships on watch for a prize. He swam to and went aboard one of these vessels, hoping to find better treatment than among his country-men. He offered himself to the Dutch and promised to serve them loyally against those of his nation who had maltreated him. Afterwards he proved himself so loyal and reliable to the Dutch, that he won much fame among them. He was married to a girl of their nation and later made captain of a vessel under that brave and noble Dutchman, whom the Spaniards dreaded much and whom they named Pie de Palo, or Wooden-leg.

[4] Within the last decades, some Negroes have been brought over, from the United States, to the banana-plantations of United Fruit Co., near the Atlantic coast, and occasionally, though very seldom, one meets with a black newcomer from Jamaica, Barbadoes, or other West Indian islands.

"That famous mulatto," said Gage, "was he who boarded our frigate with his soldiers. I lost four thousand pesos wealth in pearls and jewelry and about three thousand in ready money. I had still other things with me, viz., a bed, some books, pictures painted on copper, and clothes, and I asked that Mulatto captain to let me keep them. He donated me them liberally, out of consideration for my vocation, and said I must take patience, for he was not allowed to dispose in other way of my pearls and my money; moreover, he used the proverb: If fortune to-day is on my side, to-morrow it will be on yours, and what I have won to-day, that I may lose to-morrow. . . . He also ordered to give me back some single and double pistoles, out of generosity and respect to my garb. . . ."

"After having searched their prize," continued the traveler, "Captain and soldiers thought of refreshing themselves on the provisions we had on board; the generous captain had a luxurious dinner and invited me to be his guest, and knowing that I was going to Habana, he drank the health of his mother and asked me to go to see her and give her his kindest regards, saying that for her sake he had treated me as kindly as was in his power. He told us, moreover, when still at table, that for my sake he would give us back our ship, so that we could get back to land, and that I might find some other and safer way to continue my voyage to Spain. . . . Everything taken away from the ship save my belongings, which captain Diaguillo ordered to let me out of a generosity not often to be found with a corsair, he bade us fare-well thanking us for the good luck we had procured him."

Thomas Gage reached Habana in safety and called upon the mother of the Corsair, but does not say how he found her.

J. KUNST

DOCUMENTS

TRAVELERS' IMPRESSIONS OF SLAVERY IN AMERICA FROM 1750 TO 1800

From these writers, almost all of whom were foreigners, one would naturally expect such a portraiture of slavery as persons unaccustomed to the institution would give. Most Americans, of course, considered the institution as belonging to the natural order of things and, therefore, hardly ever referred to it except when they mentioned it unconsciously. Foreigners, however, as soon as they came into this new world began to compare the slaves with the lowest order of society in Europe. Finding the lot of the bondmen so much inferior to that of those of low estate in European countries, these travelers frequently made some interesting comparisons. We are indebted to them for valuable information which we can never hope to obtain from the literature of an essentially slaveholding people. Here we see how the American Revolution caused a change for the better in the condition of the Negroes in certain States, and how the rigorousness of slavery continued in the others. We learn too what enlightened Negroes thought about their state and what the white man believed should be done to prevent their reaching the point of self-assertion. That a large number of anti-slavery Americans were advocating and effecting the emancipation of slaves appears throughout these documents.

BURNABY'S VIEW OF THE SITUATION IN VIRGINIA

Speaking of Virginia, he said: "Their authority over their slaves renders them vain and imperious, and entire strangers to that elegance of sentiment, which is so peculiarly characteristic of refined and polished nations. Their ignorance of mankind and of learning, exposes them to many errors and prejudices, especially in regard to Indians and Negroes, whom they scarcely consider as of human species; so that it is almost impossible in cases of violence, or even murder, committed upon those unhappy people by any of the planters, to have delinquents brought to justice: for either the grand jury refuse to find the bill, or the petit jury bring in the verdict of not guilty."—*Andrew Burnaby, "Travels,"* 1759, p. 54.

GENERAL TREATMENT OF SLAVES AMONG THE ALBANIANS—CONSE-
QUENT ATTACHMENT OF DOMESTICS.—REFLECTIONS ON
SERVITUDE BY AN AMERICAN LADY

In the society I am describing, even the dark aspect of slavery was softened into a smile. And I must, in justice to the best possible masters, say, that a great deal of that tranquility and comfort, to call it by no higher name, which distinguished this society from all others, was owing to the relation between master and servant being better understood here than in any other place. Let me not be detested as an advocate for slavery when I say that I think I have never seen people so happy in servitude as the domestics of the Albanians. One reason was, (for I do not now speak of the virtues of their masters,) that each family had a few of them, and that there were no field negroes. They would remind one of Abraham's servants, who were all born in the house, which was exactly their case. They were baptized too, and shared the same religious instruction with the children of the family; and, for the first years, there was little or no difference with regard to food or clothing between their children and those of their masters.

When a negro-woman's child attained the age of three years, the first New Year's Day after, it was solemnly presented to a son or daughter, or other young relative of the family, who was of the same sex with the child so presented. The child to whom the young negro was given immediately presented it with some piece of money and a pair of shoes; and from that day the strongest attachment subsisted between the domestic and the destined owner. I have no where met with instances of friendship more tender and generous than that which here subsisted between the slaves and their masters and mistresses. Extraordinary proofs of them have been often given in the course of hunting or Indian trading, when a young man and his slave have gone to the trackless woods, together, in the case of fits of the ague, loss of a canoe, and other casualties happening near hostile Indians. The slave has been known, at the imminent risque of his life, to carry his disabled master through trackless woods with labour and fidelity scarce credible; and the master has been equally tender on similar occasions of the humble friend who stuck closer than a brother; who was baptized with the same baptism, nurtured under the same roof, and often rocked in the same cradle with himself. These gifts of domestics to the younger members of the family, were not irrevokable: yet they were very rarely withdrawn. If the kitchen family did not increase in proportion to that of the master, young children were purchased from some family where they abounded, to furnish those attached servants to the rising progeny. They were never sold without consulting their mothers, who if expert and sagacious, had a great deal to say in the family, and would not allow her child to go into any family with whose domestics she was not acquainted. These negro-women piqued themselves on teaching their children to be excellent servants, well knowing servitude to be their lot or life, and that it could only be sweetened by making themselves particularly useful, and excellent in their departments. If they did their work well, it is astonishing, when I recollect it, what liberty of speech was allowed to those active and prudent mothers. They would chide, reprove, and expostulate in a manner that we would not endure from our hired servants; and sometimes exert fully as much authority over the children of the family as the parents, conscious that they were entirely in their power. They did not crush freedom of speech and opinion in those by whom they knew they were beloved, and who watched with incessant care over their interest and comfort. Affectionate and faithful as these home-bred servants were in general, there were some instances (but very few) of those who, through levity of mind, or a love of liquor or finery, betrayed their trust, or habitually neglected their duty. In these cases, after every means had been used to reform them, no severe punishments were inflicted at home. But the terrible sentence, which they dreaded worse than death, was past—they were sold to Jamaica. The necessity of doing this was bewailed by the whole family as a most dreadful calamity, and the culprit was carefully watched on his way to New-York, lest he should evade the sentence by self-destruction.

One must have lived among those placid and humane people to be sensible that servitude, hopeless, endless servitude, could exist with so little servility and fear on the one side, and so little harshness or even sternness of authority on the other. In Europe, the footing on which service is placed in consequence of the corruptions of society, hardens the heart, destroys confidence, and embitters life. The deceit and venality of servants not absolutely dishonest, puts it out of one's power to love or trust them. And if, in hopes of having people attached to us, who will neither betray our confidence, nor corrupt our children, we are at pains to rear them from childhood, and give them a religious and moral education; after all our labour, others of their own class seduce them away to those who can afford to pay higher for their services. This is not the case in a few remote districts. Where surrounding mountains seem to exclude the contagion of the world, some traces of fidelity and affection among domestics still remain. But it must be remarked, that, in those very districts, it is usual to treat inferiors with courtesy and kindness, and to consider those domestics who marry out of the family as holding a kind of relation to it, and still claiming protection. In short, the corruption of that class of people is, doubtless, to be attributed to the example of their superiors. But how severely are those superiors punished? Why this general indifference about home; why are the household gods, why is the sacred hearth so wantonly abandoned? Alas! the charm of home is destroyed, since our children, educated in distant seminaries, are strangers in the paternal mansion; and our servants, like mere machines, move on their mercenary track without feeling or exciting one kind or generous sentiment. Home, thus despoiled of all its charms, is no longer the scene of any enjoyments but such as wealth can purchase. At the same time we feel there a nameless cold privation, and conscious that money can coin the same enjoyments with more variety elsewhere, we substitute these futile and evanescent pleasures for that perennial spring of calm satisfaction, "without o'erflowing full," which is fed by the exercise of the kindly affections, and soon indeed must those stagnate where there are not proper objects to excite them. I have been forced into this painful digression by unavoidable comparisons. To return:—

Amidst all this mild and really tender indulgence to their negroes, these colonists had not the smallest scruple of conscience with regard to the right by which they held them in subjection. Had that been the case, their singular humanity would have been incompatible with continued injustice. But the truth is, that of law the generality of those people knew little; and of philosophy, nothing at all. They sought their code of morality in the Bible, and there imagined they found this hapless race condemned to perpetual slavery; and thought nothing remained for them but to lighten the chains of their fellow Christians, after having made them such. This I neither "extenuate" nor "set down in malice," but merely record the fact. At the same time it is but justice to record also a singular instance of moral delicacy distinguishing this settlement from every other in the like circumstances: though, from their simple and kindly modes of life, they were from infancy in habits of familiarity with these humble friends, yet being early taught that nature had placed between them a barrier, which it was in a high degree criminal and disgraceful to pass, they considered a mixture of such distinct races with abhorrence, as a violation of her laws. This greatly conduced to the preservation of family happiness and concord. An ambiguous race, which the law does not acknowledge; and who (if they have any moral sense, must be as much ashamed of their parents as these last are of them) are certainly a dangerous, because degraded part of the community. How much more so must be those unfortunate beings who stand in the predicament of the bat in the fable, whom both birds and beasts disowned? I am sorry to say that the progress of the British army, when it arrived, might be traced by a spurious and ambiguous race of this kind. But of a mulatto born before their arrival I only remember a single instance; and from the regret and wonder it occasioned, considered it as singular. Colonel Schuyler, of whom I am to speak, had a relation so weak and defective in capacity, that he never was intrusted with any thing of his own, and lived an idle bachelor about the family. In process of time a favourite negro-woman, to the great offense and scandal of the family, bore a child to him, whose colour gave testimony to the relation. The boy was carefully educated; and when he grew up, a farm was allotted to him well stocked and fertile, but "in depth of woods embraced," about two miles back from the family seat. A destitute white woman, who had somehow wandered from the older colonies, was induced to marry him; and all the branches of the family thought it incumbent on them now and then to pay a quiet visit to Chalk (for so, for some unknown reason, they always called him). I have been in Chalk's house myself, and a most comfortable abode it was; but considered him as a mysterious and anomalous being.

I have dwelt the longer on this singular instance of slavery, existing devoid of its attendant horrors, because the fidelity and affection resulting from a bond of union so early formed between master and servant, contributed so very much to the safety of individuals, as well as the general comfort of society, as will hereafter appear.—"*Memoirs of An American Lady with Sketches of Manners and Customs In America as they existed previous to the Revolution,*" Chapter VII, pp. 26–32, by Mrs. Anne Grant.

IMPRESSIONS OF AN ENGLISH TRAVELER

"As I observed before, at least two thirds of the inhabitants are negroes. . . .

"It is fortunate for humanity that these poor creatures possess such a fund of contentment and resignation in their minds; for they indeed seem to be the happiest inhabitants in America, notwithstanding the hardness of their fare, the severity of their labour, and the unkindness, ignominy, and often barbarity of their treatment."—J. F. D., "*A Tour in the United States of America, containing an account of the present situation of that country*"; London, 1784, p. 39.

ABBÉ ROBIN ON CONDITIONS IN VIRGINIA

"The population of Virginia is computed at one hundred fifty thousand whites and five hundred thousand negroes. There is a still greater disproportion between the whites and blacks in Maryland, where there are not more than twenty thousand whites and at least two hundred thousand negroes. The English imported into these two provinces between seven and eight thousand yearly. Perhaps the lot of these slaves is not quite so hard as that of the negroes in the islands; their liberty, it is true, is irreparably lost in both places, but here they are treated with more mildness, and are supported upon the same kind of food with their masters; and if the earth which they cultivate, is moistened with their sweat, it has never been known to blush with their blood. The American, not at all industrious by nature, is considerate enough not to expect too much from his slave, who in such circumstances, has fewer motives to be laborious for himself."—Abbé Robin, "*New Travels through North America in a series of letters,*" Boston, 1784, p. 48.

OBSERVATIONS OF ST. JOHN DE CRÈVECOEUR

"There, arranged like horses at a fair, they are branded like cattle, and then driven to toil, to starve and to languish for a few years on the different plantations of those citizens.

"If negroes are permitted to become fathers, this fatal indulgence only tends to increase their misery. . . . How many have

I seen cursing the irresistible propensity, and regretting that by having tasted of those joys, they had become the authors of double misery to their wives. . . . Their paternal fondness is embittered by considering that if their children live, they must live to be slaves like themselves: no time is allowed them to exercise their pious offices, the mothers must fasten them on their backs, and, with the double load follow their husbands in the fields, where they too often hear no other sound than that of the voice or whip of the taskmaster, and the cries of their infants, broiling in the sun. . . . It is said, I know, that they are much happier here than in the West Indies; because land being cheaper upon this continent than in those Islands, the field allowed them to raise their subsistence from, are in general more extensive.

". . . We have slaves likewise in our northern provinces; I hope the time draws near when they will be all emancipated; but how different their lot, how different their situation, in every possible respect! They enjoy as much liberty as their masters, they are as well clad, and as well fed; in health and sickness they are tenderly taken care of; they live under the same roof, and are, truly speaking, a part of our families. Many of them are taught to read and write, and are well instructed in the principles of religion; they are the companions of our labours, and treated as such; they enjoy many perquisites, many established holidays, and are not obliged to work more than white people. They marry when their inclination leads them; visit their wives every week; are as decently clad as the common people; they are indulged in education, cherishing and chastising their children, who are taught subordination to them as to their lawful parents; in short, they participate in many of the benefits of our society without being obliged to bear any of its burdens. They are fat, healthy, and hearty, and far from repining at their fate; they think themselves happier than many of the lower class whites: they share with their master the wheat and meat provision, they help to raise; many of those whom the good Quakers have emancipated, have received that great benefit with tears of regret, and have never quitted, though free, their former masters and benefactors."—St. John de Crèvecoeur, "*Letters from an American Farmer, 1782*," pp. and 226 et seq.

Impressions of Johann D. Schoepf

"The condition of the Carolina negro slaves is in general harder and more troublous than that of their northern brethren. On the

rice plantations, with wretched food, they are allotted more work and more tedious work; and the treatment which they experience at the hands of the overseers and owners is capricious and often tyrannical. In Carolina (and in no other of the North American states) their severe handling has already caused several uprisings among them. There is less concern here as to their moral betterment, education, and instruction, and South Carolina appears little inclined to initiate the praiseworthy and benevolent ordinances of its sister states in regard to the negro. It is sufficient proof of the bad situation in which these creatures find themselves here that they do not multiply in the same proportions as the white inhabitants, although the climate is more natural to them and agrees with them better. Their numbers must be continually kept up by fresh importations; to be sure, the constant taking up of new land requires more and more working hands, and the pretended necessity of bringing in additional slaves is thus warranted in part; but close investigation makes it certain that the increase of the blacks in the northern states, where they are handled more gently, is vastly more considerable. The gentlemen in the country have among their negroes as the Russian nobility among the serfs, the most necessary handicrafts-men, cobblers, tailors,· carpenters, smiths, and the like, whose work they command at the smallest possible price or for nothing almost. There is hardly any trade or craft which has not been learned and is not carried on by negroes, partly free, partly slave; the latter are hired out by their owners for day's wages. Charleston swarms with blacks, mulattoes and mestizos; their number greatly exceeds that of the whites, but they are kept under strict order and discipline, and the police has a watchful eye upon them. These may nowhere assemble more than 7 male negro slaves; their dances and other assemblies must stop at 10 o'clock in the evening; without permission of their owners none of them may sell beer or wine or brandy. There are here many free negroes and mulattoes. They get their freedom if by their own industry they earn enough to buy themselves off, or their freedom is given them at the death of their masters or in other ways. Not all of them know how to use their freedom to their own advantage; many give themselves up to idleness and dissipation which bring them finally to crafty deceptions and thievery. They are besides extraordinarily given to vanity, and love to adorn themselves as much as they can and to conduct themselves importantly."
—Johann D. Schoepf, "*Travels in the Confederation,*" 1784, p. 220.

EXTRACTS FROM ANBUREY'S TRAVELS THROUGH NORTH AMERICA

"Thus the whole management of the plantation is left to the overseer, who as an encouragement to make the most of the crops, has a certain portion as his wages, but not having any interest in the negroes, any further than their labour, he drives and whips them about, and works them beyond their strength, and sometimes till they expire; he feels no loss in their death, he knows the plantation must be supplied, and his humanity is estimated by his interest, which rises always above freezing point.

"It is the poor negroes who alone work hard, and I am sorry to say, fare hard. Incredible is the fatigue which the poor wretches undergo, and that nature should be able to support it; there certainly must be something in their constitutions, as well as their color, different from us, that enables them to endure it.

"They are called up at day break, and seldom allowed to swallow a mouthful of homminy, or hoe cake, but are drawn out into the field immediately, where they continue at hard labour, without intermission, till noon, when they go to their dinners, and are seldom allowed an hour for that purpose; their meals consist of hominy and salt, and if their master is a man of humanity, touched by the finer feelings of love and sensibility, he allows them twice a week a little skimmed milk, fat rusty bacon, or salt herring, to relish this miserable and scanty fare. The man at this plantation, in lieu of these, grants his negroes an acre of ground, and all Saturday afternoon to raise grain and poultry for themselves. After they have dined, they return to labor in the field, until dusk in the evening; here one naturally imagines the daily labor of these poor creatures was over, not so, they repair to the tobacco houses, where each has a task of stripping allotted which takes them up some hours, or else they have such a quantity of Indian corn to husk, and if they neglect it, are tied up in the morning, and receive a number of lashes from those unfeeling monsters, the overseers, whose masters suffer them to exercise their brutal authority without constraint. Thus by their night task, it is late in the evening before these poor creatures return to their second scanty meal, and the time taken up at it encroaches upon their hours of sleep, which for refreshment of food and sleep together can never be reckoned to exceed eight.

"When they lay themselves down to rest, their comforts are equally miserable and limited, for they sleep on a bench, or on the ground, with an old scanty blanket, which serves them at once for bed and covering, their cloathing is not less wretched, consisting of a shirt and trowsers of coarse, thin, hard, hempen stuff, in the Summer, with an addition of a very coarse woolen jacket, breeches and shoes in Winter. But since the war, their masters, for they cannot get the cloathing as usual, suffer them to go in rags, and many in a state of nudity.

"The female slaves share labor and repose just in the same manner, except a few who are term'd house negroes, and are employed in household drugery.

"These poor creatures are all submission to injuries and insults, and are obliged to be passive, nor dare they resist or defend themselves if attacked, without the smallest provocation, by a white person, as the law directs the negroe's arm to be cut off who raises it against a white person, should it be only in defence against wanton barbarity and outrage.

"Notwithstanding this humiliating state and rigid treatment to which this wretched race are subject, they are devoid of care, and appear jovial, contented and happy. It is a fortunate circumstance that they possess, and are blessed with such an easy satisfied disposition, otherwise they must inevitably sink under such a complication of misery and wretchedness; what is singularly remarkable, they always carry out a piece of fire, and kindle one near their work, let the weather be so hot and sultry.

"As I have several times mentioned homminy and hoe-cake, it may not be amiss to explain them: the former is made of Indian corn, which is coarsely broke, and boiled with a few French beans, till it is almost a pulp. Hoe-cake is Indian corn ground into meal, kneaded into a dough, and baked before a fire, but as the negroes bake theirs on the hoes that they work with, they have the appellation of hoe-cakes. These are in common use among the inhabitants, I cannot say they are palateable, for as to flavor, one made of sawdust would be equally good, and not unlike it in appearance, but they are certainly a very strong and hearty food."—Anburey, *"Travels through America during the War,"* Vol. 2, pp. 330–5.

VINDICATION OF THE NEGROES: A CONTROVERSY

First let me repeat your longest section relative to that people.

'Below this class of inhabitants, (the whites of no property, in Virginia,) we must rank the Negroes, who would be still more to be

pitied, if their *natural insensibility did not in some measure alleviate the wretchedness inseparable from slavery*. Seeing them ill
lodged, ill clothed, and often overcome with labour, I concluded
that their treatment had been as rigorous as it is elsewhere. Notwithstanding I have been assured that it is very mild, compared to
what they suffer in the Sugar Colonies. And indeed one does not
hear habitually, as at Jamaica and St. Domingo, the sound of
whips, and the outcries of the wretched beings, whose bodies are
torn piece meal by their strokes. It is because the people of Virginia are commonly milder than those of the Sugar Colonies, which
consist chiefly of rapacious men, eager to amass fortunes, as soon as
possible, and return to Europe. The produce of their labours
being also less valuable, their tasks are not so rigorously exacted,
and in justice to both, it must be allowed that the Negroes themselves are less treacherous and thievish, than they are in the Islands:
for the propagation of the black species being very considerable
here, most of them are born in the country, and it is remarked that
these are in general less depraved than those imported from Africa.
Besides, we must do the Virginians the justice to remark, that many
of them treat their Negroes with a great deal of humanity, and
what is still more to their honor, they appear sorry there are any
among them, and are forever talking of abolishing slavery, and
falling upon some other mode of improving their land, &c.

'However this may be, it is fortunate that different motives
concur to deter mankind from exercising such tyranny, at least
upon their own species, if we cannot say, strictly speaking, *their
equals;* for the more we observe the Negroes, the more we are convinced that the differenc between us *does not lie in the colour
alone, &c.*

'Enough upon this subject, which has not escaped the attention
of the politicians and philosophers of the present age: I have only
to apologize for treating it without declamation; but I have always
thought, that eloquence can only influence the resolutions of the
moment, and that every thing which requires time, must be the
work of reason. And besides, it will be an easy matter to add ten
or twelve pages to these few reflections, which may be considered
as a concert composed only of principal parts, *con corni ad libertum.'*

Upon reading this passage attentively, I was surprised to find
it contain a singular mixture of contradictory principles, and in the
same breath, the sentiments of a philosopher and of a colonist; of
an advocate for the Negroes, and of their enemy.

It is evident that as a philosopher, and a friend to humanity, you are inclined to alleviate the lot of the Negroes, and commend those who do so, but this tenderness itself conceals a subtile venom that ought to be exposed. For you only bestow your pity upon the Negroes, while you owe them, if you are a philosopher, vindication and defense; you wish their masters to be humane; they ought to be just. Instead of praising such humanity, you ought to have blamed them for stopping there, in short, such a contempt for the Negroes pervades this whole article, as will necessarily encourage their tormentors to rivet their chains. Is not this contempt observable, for instance in the very first period?

"Below this class of inhabitants (the meanest whites of Virginia) we must rank the Negroes, who would be still more to be pitied, if their natural insensibility did not in some measure alleviate the wretchedness inseparable from slavery."

And who told you, Sir, that nature had created the Negroes with less feeling than other men? do you judge so because they have vegetated for three centuries in European fetters, and at this day have not altogether shaken off the horrid yoke? But do not their frequent risings, and the cruelties they from time to time retaliate upon their masters, give the lie to this natural insensibility? for an insensible being has no resentment. If he does not feel, how should he remember? Do you think the wretched Indians, who, since the discovery of the New world, are burried in the mines of Peru, are also naturally insensible, because they suffer patiently?

You calumniate nature in making her grant favours to particulars; in giving her a system of inequality among her offspring. All men are cast in the same mould.—The varieties which distinguish individuals, are the sports of chance, or the result of different circumstances; but the black comes into the world with as much sensibility as the white, the Peruvian, as the European.

What then degrades this natural and moral sensibility? The greater or less privation of liberty; in proportion as man loses it, he loses the powers of sensation; he loses the man; he sickens or becomes a brute. It is slavery alone which can reduce a man to a level with the brute creation, and sometimes deprives him of all sensibility; but you blame nature, that kind parent, who would have us all equal, free and happy, for the crime of social barbarity, and you pass by this crime, to extenuate another, to extenuate the horrid torments of slavery! Not satisfied with violating nature, by abusing her offspring, even in her name, you encourage slave-holders to torment them.

Do you not arm their tyrants, when you tell them, the insensibility of the Negroes alleviates their torments?

What! because greatness of soul raised Sidney above the terrors of death, the infernal Jefferies[1] who caused his execution, was less guilty! because the Quakers appeared insensible to insults, blows, or punishments, they are less to be pitied, and it was right to martyr them! A dangerous notion, whose consequences I am sure you would disapprove. If this insensibility with which you reproach the Negroes mitigated the cruelty of their masters, it were well: but their tormentors do not wish them not to feel; they would have them all feeling, for the pleasure of torturing them; and their punishments are increased in proportion to their insensibility.

Seeing the Negroes, say you, "Ill lodged, ill cloathed, and often overcome with labour, I concluded that their treatment had been as rigorous as it is elsewhere. Notwithstanding I have been assured that it is very mild, compared to what they suffer in the Sugar Colonies."

Why this comparison, which seems to insinuate a justification of the Virginians? does a misfortune cease to be such, because there is a greater elsewhere? Was Cartouche less detestable because Brinvilliers had existed before him? Let us not weaken by comparisons the idea of criminality, nor lessen the attention due to the miserable, this were to countenance the crime. The Negroes are ill lodged, ill cloathed, oppressed with labour in Virginia: this is the fact, this is the offence. It matters not whether they are worse treated elsewhere; in whatever degree they are so in Virginia, it is still outrage and injustice.

And again, why are the Negroes of Virginia less cruelly treated? Humanity is not the motive, it is because covetousness cannot obtain so much from their labours, as in the Sugar Islands. Was it otherwise, they would be sacrificed to it here, as well as there; how can we praise such forced humanity? how, on the contrary, not give vent to all the indignation, which must naturally arise in every feeling mind?

[1] This Jefferies was the most infamous Chief Justice that ever existed in England. Charles II. and James II. well acquainted with his talents for chicane his debauchery and blood-thirstiness, his baseness and his crimes, made use of him to exterminate, with the sword of law, all those worthy men who defended the constitution from their tyranny.

I often quote the History of England; unhappily for us it is too little known in France.

"And to do justice to both, you add, if the Virginians are not so severe, it is because the Negroes themselves are less treacherous and thievish than in the islands, because the propagation of the black species being very considerable here, most of the Negroes are born in the country, and it is remarked, that these are in general less depraved than those imported from Africa.''

Here is a strange confusion of causes and effects, and a strange abuse of words. First let us clear up the facts. Here are some valuable ones for the cause of the Negroes.

You say they are not so thievish in Virginia, propagate faster, and are less depraved: Why? Because they are less cruelly treated.—Here is the cause and the effect, you have mistaken one for the other.

We must conclude from this fact, that if the Virginians were no longer severe, and should treat the blacks like fellow-creatures, they would not be more vicious than their white servants.

The degree of oppression is the measure of what is improperly called the viciousness of the slaves.—The more cruel their tyrants, the more treacherous, villainous and cruel are the slaves in return —Can we wonder that Macronius should assassinate his master Tiberius? This viciousness is a punishment that heaven inflicts upon tyranny.

Can the efforts of a slave for the recovery of his liberty, be denominated vicious or criminal? From the moment you violate the laws of nature, in regard to them, why should not they shake them off in their relative duties to you? You rob them of liberty, and you would not have them steal your gold! You whip and cruelly torment them, and expect them not to struggle for deliverance! You assassinate them every day, and expect them not to assassinate you once! You call your outrages, rights, and the courage which repulses them, a crime! What a confusion of ideas! what horrid logic!

And you, sir, a humane philosopher! are accessory to this injustice, by describing the blacks in the style of a dealer in human flesh! You call what are no more than natural consequences of the compression of the spring of liberty—treachery, theft and depravation.[2] But can a natural consequence be criminal? Remove the cause or is it not the only crime?

[2] Most authors who have not studied the rights of men, fall into this error. I have remarked elsewhere (Vol. II of the *Journ. du Licee*, No. 4, page 222) that a writer, who, notwithstanding, deserves our esteem, for having written

For my part, sir, I firmly believe, that the barbarities committed by the Negroes, not merely against their masters, but even against others, will be attributed at the bar of eternal justice, to the slave-holders, and those infamous persons employed in the Guinea trade. I firmly believe, that no human justice has the right of putting a Negro slave to death for any crime whatever, because not being free, he is not sui juris, and should be regarded as a child or an idiot, being almost always under the lash. I believe that the real criminal, the cause of the crime, is the man who first seized him, sold him, or enslaved him.—And if ever I should fall under the knife of an unhappy runaway, I would not resent it upon him but upon those white men who keep blacks in slavery. I would tell them, your cruelty towards your Negroes, has endangered my life—they execrate you, they take me for a tyrant because I am white like you, and the vengeance due to your crimes has fallen upon me.

God forbid, however, that I should undertake to encourage the blacks to take up arms against their masters! God forbid, however, that I should undertake to justify the excesses to which their resentments have sometimes hurried them, and which have often fallen on persons who were not accessary to their wretchedness! The slavery under which they groan, must be abolished by peaceable means; and thanks to the active spirit of benevolence which animates the Quakers, the pious undertaking is already begun. In most of the United States of America, the yoke has been taken from their necks; in others the Guinea-trade has been prohibited. Societies have been formed both at Paris and London, to collect and circulate information upon this interesting subject, to induce the European governments to put a stop to the Negro trade, and provide for their gradual emancipation in the West-India islands: No doubt success will crown their views, and the friends of liberty will enjoy the satisfaction of communicating its blessings to the blacks.

But the blacks must wait for the happy moment that shall restore them to civil life, in silence and in peace; they must rely upon the unwearied diligence and zeal of the numerous writers who advocate their cause, and the efforts of the humane to second their endeavors; they must strive to justify and support the arguments

against the despotism of the Turkish government, has suffered himself to be drawn into it. M. le Baron de Tott says that the Moldavians are thievish, mean and faithless. To translate these words into the language of truth, we must say, the Turks, the masters of the Moldavians, are unjust, robbers, villains, and tyrants; and that the Moldavians revenge themselves by opposing deceit to oppression, etc. Thus, the people are almost everywhere wrongfully accused.

that are adduced in their favour, by displaying virtue in the very bosom of slavery; they must endeavour, in a word, to render themselves worthy of liberty, that they may know how to use it when it shall be restored to them; for liberty itself is sometimes a burden, when slavery has stupefied the soul.

Such blacks, therefore, as are so inconsiderate as to be concerned in insurrections, are guilty of retarding the execution of the general plan for their emancipation; for the question is not, at the present day, whether a million of slaves ought to be set at liberty, but whether they can when free, be put into a capacity of providing for the subsistence of themselves and their families. Insurrections, far from effecting this purpose, would destroy the means. Regard, therefore, to their own interests, if there were no other motive, should therefore engage the blacks to patient submission, and no doubt but they will yield it, if their masters and the ministers of the gospel in particular, to whom the task of comforting and instructing them, is committed, endeavour to prepare them for approaching freedom.

You sir, have adopted the vulgar notion, that the Negroes born in Virginia, are less depraved than those imported from Africa. You call the firmness which is common in the early stages of their slavery *greater degeneracy;* they are depraved, that is, in your language—they are wicked and treacherous to those who have purchased them, or brought them from their own country.—But in my mind, they are not depraved, because the acts of violence their genius inspires them to revenge themselves upon their tyrants, are justified by the rights of nature.

And why are those imported, more wicked in your opinion? In mine, more quick, more ardent in their resentments? because, not having forgotten their former situation, they feel their loss the more sensibly; and having strong ideas, their resolutions are more firm and their actions more violent, they not having yet contracted the habits of slavery.

They soon fall into that degree of apathy and insensibility, which you unjustly believe to be natural to them; that is, in your language, they become less depraved; but I would say that their depravity begins with this apathy and weakness.—For depravity is the loss of nature, and the want of those virtues inherent in man, courage and the love of liberty. Our readers may judge from this article, how strangely writers have wrested words to condemn these unhappy Negroes, and the unfortunate in general.

I do not, however, pretend to say, that the Negroes of Africa are all good, or even that many of them are not depraved. But is this fact to be imputed to them as a personal crime? Ought you not rather to have ascribed it to the foreign source by which they are corrupted. Alike in them and in the whites, the depravity of man is a consequence of his wretchedness, and the usurpation of his rights. Wherever he is free and at ease, he is good; wherever the contrary, he is wicked. Neither his nature nor the climate corrupt him, but the government of his country. Now that of the Negroes is almost universally despotic, such as must necessarily debase and corrupt the Negro.

How much is the depravity, occasioned by the government of his country, increased by his second slavery, far worse than the first— for he is no longer among friends in his native land—surrounded by the pleasing scenes of his childhood, he is among monsters who are going to live by, and trade in his blood, and has nothing before his eyes but death, or oppression equivalent to an endless punishment.

How is it possible such horrid prospects should not fire his soul? How, if chance should present him with arms and liberty, should he resist using them, to put an end to his own existence, or that of his tormentors? What white man would be less cruel in his situation? Truly I think myself of a humane disposition, that I love my fellow-creatures and detest the effusion of blood, but if ever a villain, white or black, should snatch me from my freedom, my family, and my friends, should overwhelm me with outrages and blows, to gratify his caprice, should extend his barbarities to my wife and children—my blood boils at the thought—perhaps in a transport of revenge. . . . If such vengeance would be lawful in me, what makes the Negro more guilty? Why should that be called wickedness and depravity in him, which would be stiled virtue in me, in you, in every white man? Are not my rights the same as his? Is not nature our common parent? God his father as well as mine? His conscience an infallible guide as well as mine? Let us then no longer make other laws for the blacks than those we are bound by ourselves, since Heaven has placed them on a level with us, has made them like us, since they are our brethren and our fellow-creatures.

Here you stop me, you say that *the Negro is not our fellow-creature, that he is below the white.*

How could so shocking an opinion escape the pen of a member

of the Royal Academy, a writer who would be thought a friend of mankind!

Do not you see the tormentors of St. Domingo, avail themselves of it already, redoubling their strokes, and regarding their slaves as mere machines, like the Cartesians do the brutes? They are not our fellow-creatures will they say: a philosopher of Paris has proved it?

What! the blacks our equals! Have not they eyes, ears, a shape, and organs like ours? Does nature follow another order, other laws for them?—Have not they speech, that peculiar characteristic of humanity? But then the colour! What of that? Are the pale white Albinos, the olive or copper coloured Indians also of different species! Who does not know that colour is accidental. They are not our equals! Have not they the same faculties—reason, memory, imagination? Yes, you reply, but they have written no books. Who told you so? Who told you there were no learned blacks? And supposing it were so, if none but authors are men, the whole human race is different from us.

Shall I tell you why there are no authors or men of learning among the Negroes? What has made you what you are? Education and circumstances!—Now where are the Negroes favoured by either? Consider them wherever they are to be found.—In Africa, wretchedly enslaved by domestic tyrants; in our islands perpetual martyrs; in the southern United States, the meanest of slaves; in the northern, domestics; in Europe, universally contemned, every where proscribed, like the Jews; in a word, every where in a state of debasement.

I have been told that there are blacks of property in the northern parts of America; but these, like the other settlers, are no more than sensible farmers or traders.—There are no authors[3] among them, because there are few rich and idle people in America.

What spring of action could raise a Negro from his debased condition? the road to glory and honor is impassible to him: What then should he write for? Besides, the blacks have reason to detest the sciences, for their oppressors cultivate them but they do not make them better.

Shall we say that the Indians or Arabs are not our equals, because they despise both our arts and our sciences? or the Quakers, because they neither respect academies nor wits?

[3] There was, however, a Negro author at London, whose productions are not without merit, and were lately published in two volumes. His name was Ignatius Sancho. He wrote in the manner of Sterne.

In short, if you will deny the Negroes souls, energy, sensibility, gratitude or beneficence, I oppose you to yourself, I might quote your own anecdote of Mr. Langdon's Negro, and abundance of other well known facts in favour of the blacks. You may find some striking ones in the Abbé Raynals' philosophical history. One of them would have been sufficient. The Negro who killed himself when his master who had injured him was in his power, was superior to Epictetus, and the existence of a single Negro of so sublime a character, ennobles all his kind.

But how could you judge whether the blacks were different from the whites, who saw them only in a state of slavery and wretchedness? Do we estimate beauty by the figure of a Laplander? magnanimity by the soul of a courtier? or intelligence by the stupidity of an Esquimaux?

If the traces of humanity were so much weakened and effaced in the Negroes, that you did not recognize them, I conclude not that they do not belong to our species, but that they must have been cruelly tormented to reduce them to this state of degeneracy. I do not conclude that they are not men, but that the Europeans who kidnap the blacks, are not worthy of the name.

You consider what precautions it may be necessary to take to avoid the danger which might attend a general emancipation of the Negroes.

I shall not now enter into a discussion of this nice question, but reserve it for another work: yet I must say in a word, that the Negroes will never be our friends, will never be men, until they are possessed of all our rights, until we are upon an equality. Civil liberty is the boundary between good and evil, order and disorder, happiness and misery, ignorance and knowledge. If we would make the Negroes worthy of us, we must raise them to our level by giving them this liberty.

Thus, the chief inconvenience you expect will follow the emancipation of the Negroes, may be avoided; that although free, they will remain a distinct species, a distinct and dangerous body.

This objection will vanish when we intermix with them, and boldly efface every distinction. Unless this is the case, I foresee torrents of blood spilt and the earth disputed between the whites and blacks, as America was between the Europeans and Savages.

Perhaps, and it is no extravagant idea—perhaps it might be more prudent, more humane, to send the blacks back again to their native country, settle them there, encourage their industry, and assist them to form connections with Europe and America. The celebrated doctor Fothergill conceived this plan, and the society for the abolition of slavery, at London, have carried it into execution at Sierra Leone. Time and perseverance, will discover the policy and utility of this settlement. If it should succeed, the blacks will quit America insensibly, and Sierra Leone become the centre from whence general civilization will spread over all Africa.

Perhaps, sir, you will place these thoughts upon the Negroes with those declamations you are pleased to ridicule: But what is the epithet of declaimer to me, if I am right, if I make an impression upon my readers, if I cause remorse into the breast of a single slave-holder; in a word, if I contribute to accelerate the general impulse toward liberty. '

You disapprove the application of eloquence to this subject; you think nothing can affect it but exertions of cool reason. What is eloquence but the language of reason and sensibility? When man is oppressed, he struggles, he complains, he moves our passions, and bears down all opposition. Such eloquence can perform wonders, and should be employed by those who undertake to plead the cause of the unfortunate who spend their days in continual agony, or he will make no impression.—I do not conceive how any man can display wit instead of feeling, upon this distracting subject, amuse with an antithesis, instead of forcible reasoning, and only dazzle where he ought to warm. I have no conception how a sensible and thinking being, can see a fellow-creature tortured and torn to pieces, perhaps his poor wife bathed in tears, with a wretched infant sucking her shriveled breast at his side; I say I have no conception how he can behold such a sight, with indifference; how, unagonized and convulsed with rage and indignation, he can have the barbarity to descend to jesting! Notwithstanding, your observations upon the Negroes, conclude with a jest.

It will be an easy matter, say you, to add ten or twelve pages to these few reflections, which may be considered as a concert, composed only of principal parts, "con corni ad Libertum."

I hope there is nothing cruel, because there is nothing studied in this connection, this inconsiderate manner: but how could such a comparison come into the head of a man of feeling? It is the sad effect of wit, as I said before; it contracts the soul. Ever glancing over agreeable objects, it is unfeeling when intruded upon by wretchedness—uneasy to obliterate the shocking idea, and elude the groans of nature, it rids itself of both by a jest. The humane

Benezet would never have connected this idea of harmony with the sound of a Negro driver's whip.

Having proved that you have wronged the Quakers and the Negroes, I shall proceed to shew that you have equally injured mankind and the people.—*Critical Examination of the Marquis de Chastellux's Travels in North-America, 1782. Translated from the French of Jean P. Verre Brissot de Warville, 1788*, pp. 51–63.

Sur l'état général, le genre d'industrie, les moeurs, le caractère, etc. des Noirs, dans les États-Unis

" Dans les quatre états du nord et dans ceux du midi, les noirs libres sont, ou domestiques, ou tiennent de petites boutiques, ou cultivent la terre. Vous en voyez quelques-unes sur les bâtimens destinés au cabotage. Peu osent se hasarder sur les vaisseau employés aux voyages de long cours, parce qu'ils craignent d'être transportés et vendus dans les îles.—Au physique, tous ces noirs sont généralement vigoureux,[1] d'une forte constitution, capables des travaux les plus pénibles; ils sont généralement actifs.—Domestiques, ils sont sobres et fidèles.—Ce portrait s'applique aux femmes de cette couleur.—Je n'ai vu faire aucune distinction entr'eux à cet égard et les domestiques blancs, quoique ces derniers les traitent toujours avec mépris, comme étant d'une espèce inférieure.—Ceux qui tiennent des boutiques, vivent médiocrement, n'augmentent jamais leurs affaires au-dela d'un certain point. La raison en est simple: quoique partout on traite les noirs avec humanité, les blancs qui ont l'argent, ne sont pas disposés à faire aux noirs des avances, telles qu'elles les missent en état d'entreprendre le commerce en grand; d'ailleurs, il faut pour ce commerce quelques connoissances préliminaires, il faut faire un noviciat dans un comptoir, et la raison n'a pas encore ouvert aux noirs la porte du comptoir. On ne leur permet pas de s'y asseoir à côté des blancs.—Si donc les noirs sont bornés ici à un petit commerce de détail, n'en accusons pas leur impuissance, mais le préjugé des blancs, qui leur donnent des entraves. Les mêmes causes empêchent les moirs qui vivent à la compagne d'avoir des plantations étendues; celles qu'ils cultivent sont bornées, mais généralement assez bien cultivées: de bons habits, *une log house,* ou maison de bois en bon état, des enfans plus

[1] Les noirs maries font certainement autant d'enfans que les blancs; mais on a remarqué que dans les villes, il perissoit plus d'enfans noirs. Cette difference tient moins a leur nature qu'au défaut d'aisance et de soins, sur-tout des médecins et des chirurgiens.

nombreux les font remarquer des Européens voyageurs, et l'oeil
du philosophe se plaît à considérer ces habitations, où la tyrannie
ne fait point verser de pleurs. Dans cette partie de l'Amerique,
les noirs sont certainement heureux; mais ayons le courage de
l'avouer, leur bonheur et leurs talens ne sont pas encore au degré
où ils pourroient atteindre.—Il existe encoure un trop grand inter-
valle entre eux et les blancs, sur-tout dans l'opinion publique, et
cette difference humiliante arrête tous les efforts qu'ils feroient
pour s'élever. Cette difference se montre par-tout. Par exemple,
on admet les noirs aux écoles publiques; mais ils ne peuvent franchir
le seuil d'un collège. Quoique libres, quoique indépendans, ils
sont toujours eux-mêmes accoutumés à se regarder comme au-des-
sous du blanc; il y a des droits qu'ils n'ont pas.[2] Concluons de là
qu'on jugeroit mal de l'étendue, de la capacité des noirs, en prenant
pour base celle des noirs libres dans les états du nord.

Mais quand on les compare aux noirs, esclaves des états du midi,
quelle prodigieuse différence les sépare! Dans le midi, les noirs
sont dans un état d'abjection et d'abrutissement difficile à peindre.
Beaucoup sont nuds, mal nourris, logés dans de miserables huttes,
couchés sur la paille.[3] On ne leur donne aucune éducation; on ne

[2] N'y eut-il que l'aversion des blancs pour le mariage de leurs filles avec
les noirs, ce seul sentiment suffiroit pour avilir ces deniers. Cependant il y a
quelques exemples de ces mariages.

Il existe a Pittsbourg sur l'Ohio une blanche d'origine françoise, menée a
Londres, et enlevée, à l'âge de douze ans, par des corsaires qui faisoient métier
d'enlever des enfans, et de les vendre en Amerique pour un temps fixé de leur
travail.—Des circonstances singulieres l'engagèrent à épouser un nègre qui lui
acheta sa liberté, et qui la tira des mains d'un blanc, maître barbare et libi-
dineux, qui avoit tout employé pour la desuire.—Une mulâtresse, sortie de cette
union, a épousé un chirurgien de Nantes, établi à Pittsburg.—Cette famille est
une des plus respectables de cette ville; le nègre fait un très bon commerce, et
la maîtresse se fait un devoir d'accueillir et de bien traiter les étrangers, et
sur tout les François que le hasard amène de ce côté.

Mais on n'a point d'idée d'une pareille union dans le nord; elle revol-
teroit.—Dans les etablissemens, le long de l'Ohio il y a bien des négresses qui
vivent avec des blancs non mariés.—Cependant on m'assura que cette union
est regardée de mauvais oeil par les nègres mêmes. Si une négresse a une-
querelle avec une mulâtresse, elle lui reproche d'être d'un sang mêlé.

[3] Le docteur Rush, qui a été portée de traiter ces noirs, m'a communiqué
une observation bien importante, et qui prouve combien l'énergie morale et
intellectuelle d'un individu influe sur sa santé et son état physique. Il m'a dit
qu'il étoit bien plus difficile de traiter et de guérir ces noirs esclaves que les
blancs; qu'ils résistoient bien moins aux maladies violentes ou longues. C'est
qu'ils tiennent peu par l'âme à la vie: la vitalité ou le ressort de la vie est
presque nul dans eux.

les instruit dans aucune religion; on ne les marie pas, on les accouple; aussi sont ils avilis, paresseux, sans idées, sans énergie.—
Ills ne se donneroient aucune peine pour avoir des habits, ou de
meilleures provisions; ils aiment mieux porter des haillons que de
les raccommoder. Ills passent le dimanche, qui est le jour du repos,
entièrement dans l'inaction.—L'inaction est leur souverain bonheur; aussi travaillent-ils peu et nonchalamment.

Il faut rendre justice à la vérité; les Américains du midi traitent doucement les esclaves, et c'est un des effets produits par l'extension générale des idées sur la liberté; l'esclave travaille moins
par-tout; mais on s'est borné là. Il n'en est pas mieux, ni pour la
mourriture, ni pour son habillement, ni pour ses moeurs, ni pour
ses idées; ainsi le maître perd, sans que l'esclaves acquière; et s'il
suivoit l'exemple des Americains du nord, tous deux gagneroient
au changement.

On a cru généralment jusqu'à ces derniers temps, que les nègres
avoient moins de capacité morale que les blancs; des auteurs même
estimables l'ont imprimé.[4] Ce préjugé commence à disparoitre; les
états du nord pourroient fournir des exemples du contraire. Je
n'en citerai que deux frappans; le premier, prouvera, qu'avec l'instruction, on peut rendre les noirs propres à toutes les professions;
le second, que la tête d'un nègre est organsée pour les calculs les
plus étonaus, et par conséquent pour toutes les sciences.

J'ai vu, dans mon séjour à Philadelphie, un noir, appelé Jacques
Derham, médecin, qui exerce dans la Nouvelle-Orléans, sur le Mississippi; et voici son histoire, telle qu'elle m'a été attestée par plusieurs médecins.—Ce noir a été élevé dans une famille de Philadelphie, où il a appris à lire, à écrire, et où on l'a instruit dans les
principes du christianisme. Dans sa jeunesse, il fut vendu au feu
docteur Jean Kearsley le jeune, de cette ville, qui l'employoit pour
composer des médecines, et les administrer á ses malades.

A la mort du docteur Kearsley, il passa dans différentes mains,
et il devint enfin l'esclave du docteur George West, chirurgien du
seizième régiment d'Angleterre, sous lequel, pendant la dernière
guerre en Amérique, il remplit les fonctions les moins importantes
de la médecine.

A la fin de la guerre, le docteur West le vendit au Docteur
Robert Dove, de la Nouvelle-Orleans, qui l'employa comme son

[4] J'ai deja plusieurs fois refuté cette opinion et sur-tout dans mon Examen
critique des voyages de M. Chatellux. Elle a d'alleurs été détruite dans une
foule d'excellens ouvrages.

second. Dans cette condition, il gagna si bien la confiance et l'-
amité de son maître, que celui-ci consentit à l'affranchir deux ou
trois ans après, et à des conditions modérées.—Derham s'étoit tel-
lement perfectionné dans la medecine, qu'à l'époque de sa liberté,
il fut en état de la pratiquer avec succès à la Nouvelle-Orleans.—Il
a environ 26 ans; il est marié, mais il n'a point d'enfans; la medecine lui rapporte 3000 dollars, ou 16000 l. environ par an.

J'ai causé, m'a dit le docteur Wistar, avec lui sur les maladies
aiguës et épidémiques du pays où il vit, et je l'ai trouve bien versé
dans la méthode simple, usitée par les modernes pour le traitement
de ces maladies.—Je croyois pouvoir lui indiquer de nouveaux
remèdes; mais ce fut lui qui me les indiqua.—Il est modeste, et a
des manières très-engageantes; il parle francois avec facilité, et a
quelques connoisances de l'espagnol.—Qoique né dans une famille
religieuse, on avoit, par accident, oublié de le faire baptiser. En
conséquence, il s'est adressé au docteur Withe pour recevoir le
baptême; il le lui a conféré, apres l'en avoir jugé digne, non-seule-
ment par ses connoisances, mais par son excellente conduite.

Voice l'autre fait, tel qu'il m'a été attesté, et imprimé par le
docteur Rush,[5] célèbre médecin et auteur, établi à Philadelphia; et
plusieurs détails m'en ont été confirmés par l'épouse de l'immortel
Washington, dans le voisinage duquel ce nègre est depuis longtemps.

Son nom est Thomas Fuller; il est né en Afrique, et ne sait ni
lire ni écrire; il a maintenant soixante-dix ans, et a vécu toute sa
vie sur la plantation de Mme Cox, a quatre milles d'Alexandrie.
Deux habitans respectables de Pensylvanie, MM. Hartshom et Samuel Coates, qui voyageoient en Virginie, ayant appris la facilité
singuliere que ce noir avoit pour les calculus les plus compliques,
l'envoyèrent chercher, et lui firent differentes questions.

Première.   Etant interrogé, combien de secondes il y avoit dans
une année et demie, il repondit en deux minutes, 47,304,000, en
comptant 365 jours dans l'année.

Deuxième.   Combien de secondes auroit vécu un homme âgé de
soix-ante-dix ans dix-sept jours et douze heures? Il répondit dans
une minute et demie, 2,210,500,800.

Un des Americains qui l'interrogeoit et qui vérifioit ses calculs
avec la plume, lui dit qu'il se trompoit, que la somme n'étoit pas si
considerable; et cela étoit vrai: c'est qu'il n'avoit pas fait attention aux années bissextiles; il corrigea le calcul avec la plus grande
célérité.

---

[5] Ce médecin est aussi célèbre en Amerique, par de bons écrits politiques.
C'est un apôtre infatigable de la liberté.

Autre question. Supposez un laboureur qui a six truies, et que chaque truie en met bas six autres la première année, et qu'elles multiplient dans la même proportion jusqu'à 1 fin de la huitème année: combien alors de truies aura le laboureur, s'il n'en perd aucune? Le vieillard répondit en dix minutes, 34,588,806.

La longueur du temps ne fut occasionée que parce qu'il n'avoit pas d'abord compris la question.

Après avoir satisfait à toutes les questions, il raconta l'origine et les progrès de son talent en arithmétique.—Il compta a'abord jusqu'a 10, puis 100; et s'imaginoit alors, disoit-il, être un habile homme. Ensuite il s'amusa à compter tous les grains d'un boisseau de ble, et successivement il sut compter le nombre de rails ou morceaux de bois necessaires pour enclore un champ d'une telle étendue, ou de grains nécessaires pour le semer.—Sa maîtresse avoit tiré beaucoup d'advantages de son talon; il ne parloit d'elle qu'avec la plus grande reconnoissance, parce qu'elle ne l'avoit jamais voulu vendre, malgre les offres considerables qu'on lui avoit faites pour l'acheter.—Sa tête commençoit à foiblir.—Un des Americains lui ayant dit que c'étoit dommage qu'il n'eut pas recu de l'éducation: Non, maître, dit-il; il vaut mieux que je n'aie rien appris, car bien des savans ne sont que des sots.

Ces exemples prouveront, sans doute, que la capacité des nègres peut s'étendre a tout; ils n'ont besoin que d'instruction et de liberté.—La différence qui se remarque entre ceux qui sont libres et instruits et les autres, se montre encore dans leurs travaux.—Les terres qu'habitent et les blancs et les noirs, soumis à ce régime, sont infiniment mieux cultivées, produisent plus abondamment, offrent par-tout l'image de l'aisance et du bonheur; et tel est, par exemple, l'aspect du Connecticut et de la Pensylvanie.—Passez dans le Maryland ou la Virginie, encore une fois, vous croyez être dans un autre monde. Ce ne sont plus des plaines bien cultivées, des maisons de campagne, propres et meme élégantes, des vastes granges bien distribuées; ce ne sont plus des troupeaux nombreux de bestiaux gras et vigoureux: non, tout dans le Maryland et la Virginia, porte l'empreinte de l'esclavage; sol brulé, culture mal entendue, maisons délabrées, bestiaux petits et peu nombreux, cadavres noirs ambulans; en un mot, vous y voyez une misère réelle a côté de l'apparence du luxe.

On commence à s'appercevoir, même dans les états méridionaux, que nourrir mal un exclave est une chétive économie, et que le fonds placé dans l'esclavage ne rend pas son interêt. C'est peut-être plus à cette considération, plus encore à l'impossibilité pécuniaire de recruter; c'est plus, dis-je, à ces considérations qu'à l'humanité, qu'on doit l'introduction du travail libre dans une partie de la Virginie, dans celle qui avoisine la belle rivière de la Shenadore. Aussi croiroit-on, en la voyant, voir encore la Pensylvanie.

Osons l'espérer, tel sera un jour le sort de la Virginie, quand elle ne sera plus souillée par l'esclavage; et ce terme n'est peut-être pas eloigné.   Il n'y a des esclaves que parce qu'on les croit nécessaires à la culture du tabac, et cette culture décline tous les jours et doit décliner.   Le tabac, qui se cultive près de l'Ohio et du Mississippi, est infiniment plus abondant, de meilleure qualité, exige moins de travaux.   Quand ce tabac se sera ouvert le chemin de l'Europe, les Virginiens seront obligés de cesser sa culture, et de demander à la terre du blé, des pommes de terre, de faire des prairies et d'élever des bestiaùx.   Les Virginiens judicieux pré-voient cette revolution, l'anticipent, et se livrent à la culture du blé.—A leur tête, on doit mettre cet homme étonnant, qui, général adoré, eut le courage d'être republican sincère; qui, couvert de gloire, seul, ne s'en souvient plus; héros dont la destinée unique sera d'avoir sauvé deux fois sa patrie, de lui ouvrir le chemin de la prospérité, apres avoir ouvert celui de la liberté.   Maintenant *entièrement* occupé[6] du soin d'améliorer ses terres, d'en varier le produit, d'ouvrir des routes, des communications, il donne à ses compatriotes un exemple utile, et qui sans doute sera suivi.   Il a cependant, dois-je, le dire? une foule nombreuse d'esclaves noirs.— Mais ils sont traites avec la plus grande humanité.   Bien nourris, bien vêtus, n'ayant qu'un travail modéré à faire, ils bénissent sans cesse le maître que le Ciel leur a donné.—Il est digne sans doute d'une âme aussi élevée, aussi pure, aussi désinteressé, de com-mencer la révolution en Virginie, d'y preparer l'affranchissement des nègres.—Ce grand homme, lorsque j'eus le bonheur de l'en-tretenir, m'avoua qu'il admiroit tout ce qui se faissoit dans les autres états, qu'il en desiroit l'extension dans son propre pays; mais il ne me cacha pas que de nombreux obstacles s'y opposoient encore, qu'il seroit dangereux de heurter de front un préjugé qui com-mencoit à diminuer.—Du temps, de la patience, des lumières, et on le convaincra, me dit-il.   Presque tous les Virginiens, ajoutoit-il, ne croyent pas que la liberté des noirs puisse sitôt devenir générale.

[6] Il n'étoit pas alors président des Etats-Unis. J'anticipe ici sur plusieurs conversations que j'ai eues avec ce grand homme, et dont je parlerai par la suite.

Voilà pourquoi ils ne veulent point former de société qui puisse donner des idées dangereuses à leurs esclaves. Un autre obstacle s'y oppose. Les grandes propriétés éloignent les hommes, rendent difficiles les assemblées, et vous ne trouverez ici que de grands propriétaires.

Les Virginiens se trompent, lui disois-je; il est evident que tôt ou tard les nègres obtiendront par-tout leur liberté, que cette révolution s'étendra en Virginie. Il est donc de l'intérêt de vos compatriotes de s'y préparer, de tacher de concilier la restitution des droits des nègres avec leur propriété. Les Moyens à prendre, pour cet effet, ne peuvent être l'ouvrage que d'une société, et il est digne du sauveur de l'Amerique d'en être le chef, et de rendre la liberté à 300,000 hommes malheureux dans son pays. Ce grand homme me dit qu'il en desiroit la formation, qu'il la seconderoit; mail il ne croyoit pas le moment favorable. Sans doute des vues plus élévees absorboient alors son attention et remplissoient son âme; le destin de l'amerique étoit prêt à être remis une seconde fois dans ses mains.

C'est un malheur, n'en doutons pas, semblable société n'existe pas dans le Maryland et dans la Virginie; car c'est au zèle constant de celles de Philadelphie et de New-Yorck qu'on doit tous les progrès de cette révolution en Amerique, et la naissance de la société de Londres.

Que ne puis-je ici vous peindre l'impression dont j'ai été frappé en assistant aux séances de ces trois sociétés!—Quelle gravité dans la contenance des membres! quelle simplicité dans leurs discours! quelle candeur dans leurs discussions! quelle bienfaisance! quelle énergie dans leur résolution! Chacun s'empressoit d'y prendre part, non pour briller, mais pour être utile.—Avec quelle joie ils apprirent qu'il s'élevoit une société semblable à la leur dans Paris, dans cette capitale immense, si célèbre en Amerique par l'opulence, le faste, l'influence sur un vaste royaume, et sur presque tous les états de l'Europe! Avec quel empressement ils publièrent cette nouvelle dans toutes leurs gazettes, et répandirent partout la traduction du premier discours lu dans cette société! Avec quelle joie ils virent dans la liste des membres de cette société, un nom cher à leurs coeurs, et qu'ils ne prononcent qu'aves attendrissement, et les noms d'autres personness connues par leur énergie et leur patriotisme! Ils ne doutoient point que si cette société s'étendoit, bravoit les obstacles, s'unissoit avec celle de Londres, les lumières repandues par elles sur le trafic des nègres et sur son infamie inutile, n'éclairassent les gouvernmens, et n'en determinassent la suppression.

Ce fut, sans doute, à cet élan de joie et d'espoir, et aux recommendations flatteuses que j'avois emportées d'Europe, plus qu'à
mes foibles travaux, que je dus l'honneur qu'ils me firent de m'-
associer à leur rang.

Ces sociétés ne se bornèrent pas à ces démonstrations; elles nom-
mèrent dés comités pour m'assister dans mes travaux; leurs archives me furent ouvertes.

Ces sociétés bienfaisantes s'occupent maintenant de nouveaux
prospects pour consommer leur oeuvre de justice et d'humanité; elles
s'occupent à creer de nouvelles sociétés dans les états qui n'en ont
point; c'est ainsi qu'il vient de s'en élever une dans l'état de
Delaware.—Elles forment de nouveaux projets pour décourager
l'esclavage et le commerce des esclaves.—C'est ainsi que, pour ar-
rêter les ventes scandaleuses qui s'en font encore dans New Yorck,[7]
à des enchères publiques, tous les membres se sont engagés à ne
jamais employer l'officier public, l'huissier-priseur qui présideroit à
de pareilles ventes.   Mais c'est sur-tout à sauver des mains de la
cupidité des esclaves, qu'elle voudroit et ne doit pas retenir, que la
société de Philadelphie est ingénieuse.—Un esclave est-il maltraité,
il trouve dans elle une protection assurée et gratuite.—Un autre
a fini son temps, et est toujours détenu; elle reclame ses droits.—
Des étrangers amènent des noirs, et ne satisfont pas à la loi; la
société en procure le benefice à ces malheureux nègres.—Un des plus
célèbres avocats de Philadelphie, dont j'aime à vanter les talents
et l'amitié qui nous unit, M. *Myers Fisher*, lui prête son ministère,
presque toujours avec succès, et tojours avec désintéressement.
Cette société s'est apperçue que de nombreuses assemblées, n'avoient
pas d'action, parce que le mouvement se perdoit en se divisant en
trop de membres; elle a créé plusiers comités, toujours en activite;
elle sollicite des créations semblables dans tous les états; afin que
par-tout les loix sur l'abolition de la traite et sur l'affranchissement
soient executées; afin que par-tout on presente des pétitions aux
legislatures, pour obtenir de nouvelles loix pour les cas non prévus.
—Enfin, c'est a cette société, sand doute, que l'on devra un jour de
semblables établissemens dans le midi.   J. P. Brissot, (Warville).
—"*Nouveau Vouage dans les États-Unis de l'Amerique Septentri-
onale, 1788,*" Tome Second, 31–49.

[7] A l'assemblée de la société de New-Yorck, du 9 nobembre 1787, il a été
arrêté qu'on donneroit une medaille d'or pour le meilleur discours qui seroit
prononcé à l'ouverture du college de New-Yorck sur l'injustice et la cruaute
de la traite des nègres, et sur les funestes effets de l'esclavage.

Slavery as seen by Henry Wansey

"In this state (He was then at Worcester) the Negroes are free and happy, are electors, but not elected to offices of state; their education, however, is the same as the whites. . . . No negro child is suffered to be endentured beyond twenty-four years of age.

"We observe a school by the road-side in almost every parish, and out of it run negro boys and girls as well as white children, without any distinction. . . . A road branched off here to our right hand, leading to Albany about 60 miles distant. I now observe six or eight negroes working together in a field, well dressed as other people. Notwithstanding, they are here free, and admitted to equal privileges with the white people, yet they love to associate with each other. It is observed that they are naturally lazier, and will not work so hard as a white servant.—Perhaps, the remembrance of former compulsory service, may make them place a luxury in idleness. Nor do they yet seem to feel their importance in society; this is a portion of inheritance reserved to the next generation of them. . . .

"Came on to Hartford. . . .

Here I staid two days that I might have time to inspect the woolen manufactory of this place, and attend the debates of the House of Representatives of this state. . . . Two very interesting subjects were in debate:—a bill brought in to repeal a law, passed in October last to order 'That the money arising from the sale of their lands, between the Ohio and Lake Erie, should be appropriated to increase the salaries of the ministers of the gospel and the masters of schools;' and another bill (for its second reading) 'To provide for those poor and sick negroes, who having been freed from slavery might be unprovided for; and that till the master was exculpated, by receiving a certificate from the state, that negro was discharged in perfect health, it should be incumbent on the master to continue to take care of him during sickness, or, at least, pay the expenses of his cure.' I was much pleased to see a legislature extend its humanity and care so far.

After our breakfast, which was not a very good one, we set off for Elizabeth Town, near which, on the right, is Governor Livingstone's handsome house. This is six miles from Newark. . . .

I observed several negro houses, (low buildings of one story) detached from the family house; for the slaves (from their pilfering disposition) are not allowed to sleep in the same houses with

their masters.　Slavery, although many regulations have been made
to moderate its severity, is not yet abolished in the New Jerseys. . . .

"Most of the families of New York have black servants.　I should
suppose that nearly one fifth of the inhabitants are negroes, most of
whom are free, and many in good circumstances."—Henry Wansey,
F.A.S., "*The Journal of an excursion to the United States of America in the summer of 1794 (Journey from New York to Boston),*"
pp. 53, 57, 58, 67, and 227.

ESCLAVAGE PAR LA ROCHEFOUCAULD-LIANCOURT

Quant à l'esclavage, l'État de New-Yorck est un de ceux où les
idées m'ont paru le moins liberales.　Il est donc naturel que les
loix qui dans tous les pays suivent plus ou moins l'opinion générale, manquent aussi de libéralité à cet égard.

On peut concevoir comment dans les États du Sud le grand
nombre des esclaves rend leur émancipation difficile, et comment
cette difficulté d'émancipation donne pretexte à l'opinion de la
necessité de loix extrêmement sévères contre eux.　Mais dans l'État
de New-Yorck, où sur une population de plus de quatre cent mille
âmes on ne compte pas vingt mille nègres; il est impossible de com-
prendre quels si grands obstacles l'émancipation peut rencontrer, et
sur quoi l'on peut fonder l'opinion qui'il faut pour ce petit nombre
de nègres des loix plus sévères que pour les hommes d'une autre
couleur.

Quoiqu'il en soit, une loi qui n'est pas plus ancienne que 1788,
confirme l'état d'esclavage pour tout nègre, mulâtre our mêtif esclave à l'époque où elle a été rendue; déclare esclave tout enfant
né ou à naître d'une femme esclave; autorise la vente des esclaves
et les soumet pour les petits crimes, à un jugement, que l'on peut
appeler prévotal, des juges de paix, qui peuvent les condamner à
l'emprisonnement ou aux coups de fouet.　Un article de cette loi
les assuejétit à ce genre de jugement et à cette espèce de sentence
pour avoir frappé un blanc, sans faire exception du cas où le blanc
serait l'aggresseur.　La faveur du jury est cependant accordée à
l'esclave, si le crime dont il est accusé peut emporter peine de mort.
Il est aussi admis en témoignage dans les affaires criminelles où
d'autres nègres sont impliqués.

La nouvelle jurisprudence criminelle, fondée sur les principes
d'humanité et de justice, ne détruit aucune des dispositions réel-
lement injustes et barbares, contenues dans cette loi.　Cependant,
les esclaves sont généralement traités avec plus de douceur par leurs

maîtres dans l'État de New Yorck, et moins surchargés de travail
que dans les États du Midi. Les moeurs prévalent à cet égard sur
la rigidité des loix; mais les moeurs y sont aussi, comme dans beaucoup d'autres États de l'Amerique, imprégnées d'avidité et d'-
avarice. Cette disposition seule y empêche l'abolition de l'esclavage.
Elle est fréquemment proposée dans la législature, et jusqu'ici tout
moyen, même préparatoire, y a été rejetté. Quoique la proportion
des hommes libres aux esclaves soit telle que le plus grand nombre
des habitans de l'État de New-Yorck ne possède pas d'esclaves, le
petit nombre de ceux qui en possèdent sont les plus riches, les plus
grands propriétaires; et, dans l'État de New-Yorck comme ailleurs,
ils ont la principale influence.

Le respect dû à *la propriété*, est l'arme avec laquelle on combat
toute proposition que tient à l'affranchissement. J'ai entendu un
des hommes de loi les plus éclairés, et dont à tout autre égard les
opinions sont libérales, soutenir que "ce serait attenter à *la propriété* que de déclarer libres même les enfans à naître des femmes
esclaves, parce que, disait-il, les maîtres qui ont acheté ou hérité
des esclaves, les possèdent dans la confiance que leur *issue* sera leur
propriété utile et disponible."

Ainsi, quand on dit en Virginie "qu'on ne peut y changer le
sort de l'esclavage qu'en exportant a-la-fois tous les nègres de
l'État; on dit à New-Yorck "qu'on ne peut y penser à abolir l'es-
clage, ni rien faire de préparatoire à cette intention, sans payer
à chaque possesseur d'esclaves le prix actuel de la valeur de ses
nègres jeunes et vieux, et le prix estimé de leur descendance sup-
posée." C'est sans doute opposer à l'abolition de l'esclavage tous
les obstacles imaginables, c'est se montrer bien ennemi de cette
abolition.

Cependant l'obstacle présenté par les citoyens de New-Yorck,
est moins difficile à vaincre. En admenttant le principe de la
nécessité d'un dédommagement donné aux maîtres pour les nègres à
affranchir, et en évaluant chaque nègre à cent trente dollars, la
somme totale ne serait que de trois millions de dollars.

Ce prix serait encore susceptible de reduction, par le puissant
motif d'intérêt et d'honneur public auquel chaque membre de la
société doit faire des sacrifices.

La question de la propriété des enfans à naître ne tiendrait
pas à un quart-d'heure de discussion, si elle était agitée devant la
legislature; enfin cet affranchissement qui ne devrait être fait que
par degrés, coûterait à l'État des sacrifices moins grands encore, et

dont la succession les rendrait presqu'imperceptibles aux finances de l'État, qui ne pourraient d'ailleurs avoir un plus saint emploi.

A New-Yorck comme ailleurs, l'affranchissement des nègres doit avoir pour but le bonheur de l'État, son bon ordre, le bonheur même des nègres qu'on veut affranchir. Un affranchissement trop prompt, trop subitement général, manquerait ces differens buts de première nécessité. Je ne répéterai pas ici ce que j'ai dit ailleurs à cet égard, et ce que tant d'autres ont dit avant moi. La dépense pour l'État serait donc réduite à de bien petites sommes, en les comparant avec l'utilité et le devoir de cette opération. Mais tant que l'État de New-Yorck, entouré des exemples du Connecticut, du Massachusetts et de Pensylvanie, ne fait rien qui conduise à cette libération, tant qu'il semble approuver par le silence ou les refus de sa legislature, la permanence de l'esclavage, il laisse sa constitution et ses loix flétries d'une tâche que l'on peut, sans exageration, dire deshonorante, puisqu'elle ne peut être excusée, ni palliée, par aucune des circonstances où se trouve cet État.

L'importation dans l'État de New-Yorck d'esclaves étrangers est prohibée par la même loi qui confirme l'esclavage de ceux qui y existaient à l'éopque où elle a été rendue; ainsi cette disposition de la loi, et la manière douce dont sont traités les esclaves en général, confirment dans l'opinion que l'intérêt pécuniaire, plus qu'une véritable approbation de l'esclavage empêche la legislature de New-Yorck, de procéder à cet égard avec la justice et les lumières qui dirigent généralement ses délibérations.—"*Voyage dans Les États-Unis D'Amerique.*" *Fait en 1795, 1796 et 1797.* Par La Rochefoucauld-Liancourt. Tome Septième, 114–119.

OBSERVATIONS SUR L'ESCLAVAGE PAR LA ROCHEFOUCAULD-LIANCOURT

Il est natural de supposer qu'un nègre esclave, fatigué de travail depuis le commencement de l'année jusqu'à la fin, obligé, sous peine du fouet, d'aller aux champs, qu'il soit où non en état de santé, ne voye dans la liberté que la faculté de ne plus travailler. Tant qu'il était esclave, il était plus ou moins mal nourri, mais il l'était sans aucun soin de sa part, et sans qu'un travail plus assidu, plus actif, lui valut une meilleure nourriture ou un meilleur nourriture ou un meilleur vêtement. Le travail n'était donc pour lui qu'une peine, sans être jamais un moyen de bien être, il est donc, il doit donc être paresseux et imprévoyant. Il jouit des premiers momens de sa liberté, en ne travaillant point, car le fouet ne claque plus à ses oreilles; les besoins se font sentir; aucune éducation ne lui a été donnée que celle de l'esclavage, qui enseigne à tromper, à voler, comme à mentir; il cherche à satisfaire ses besoins, auxquels son travail n'a pas pourvu, en dérobant quelques bleds, quelques provisions à ses voisins; il devient recéleur des nègres esclaves.

Tout cela peut et doit être, mais ne doit dégouter de l'affranchissement progressif des nègres que ceux ne veulent pas penser qu'avec des soins préparatoires, et sur-tout des soins généreux qui auraient pour objet une émancipation générale successive, appropriée au nombre des nègres dans le pays, et à plusieurs autres circonstances, la plus grande quantité de ces inconvéniens serait evitée, et le serait totalement pour la génération future si elle ne pouvait l'être pour la présente. Mais comment espérer une philanthropie si prévoyante de ceux qui ne voyent que leur intérêt du moment, et qui le croyent blessé.

Dans l'État de Maryland les esclaves sont jugés par les mêmes tribunaux que les blancs, et comme eux par l'arbitrage des juris. Les punitions pour les noirs sont plus sévères; mais les moeurs sont douces au moins dans la partie du Maryland où je suis a présent, et elles prévalent sur la rigueur des loix. J'ai été témoin d'un fait qui prouve que l'humanité des juges et le désir de rendre une exacte justice les occupent pour les accusés esclaves, comme pour les blancs. Une négresse est en prison, accusée d'avoir voulu empoisonner sa maîtresse et d'avoir empoisonné un enfant. Sa maîtresse est son accusatrice. C'est une femme d'une bonne reputation dans le pays, appartenant à une famille très-etendue dans le comté, et y ayant d'ailleurs beaucoup d'influence; les juges craignant l'effet de cette influence sur les juris, ont profité de la faculté qu'ils ont de renvoyer le jugement à la cour générale du district qui se tient à soixante milles de Chester, pour donner à l'accusée toute la chance possible d'un jugement sain et impartial.

Il n'y a encore aucune mesure prise en Maryland pour l'affranchissement progressif des esclaves. Quelques hommes bien intentionnées espèrent amener la legislature dans peu de temps à une démarche à cet égard, mais l'opinion du pays n'y semble pas dispossée.—*"Voyage dans Les États-Unis D'Amerique." Par La Rochefoucauld-Liancourt. Tome Sixième, 69-71.*

Les nègres libres se trouvent assez facilement pour le travail des champs. Ils coûtent quatre-vingt dollars par an. Les nègres esclaves se louent à cinquante. Quelques planteurs préfèrent des ouvriers blancs et des nègres libres aux esclaves; ils ont moins d'embarras et plus de profit. Les vaches se vendent ici de quinze à vingt dollars, les boeufs quarante, les chevaux pour le labour cent; ceux

pour la voiture coutent souvent six cents dollars la paire. Le comté
de Kent, dont Chester est le cheflieu, contient treize mille habitans,
dont cinq mille six cents sont nègres esclaves; il fournit peu de betail
aux marchés de Baltimore et de Philadelphie. Presque tout ce
qu'il produit dans ce genre est consommé dans son enciente.—"*Voyage dans Les États-Unis D'Amerique.*" Par La Rouchefoucauld-
Liancourt. Tome Sixieme, 79–80.

WHAT ISAAC WELD OBSERVED IN SLAVE STATES

"The principal planters in Virginia have nearly every thing
they can want on their estates. Amongst the slaves are found
tailors, shoe-makers, carpenters, smiths, turners, wheelwrights,
weavers, tanners, etc. I have seen patterns of excellent coarse woollen cloth made in the country by slaves, and a variety of cotton
manufacturers, amongst the rest good nankeen. Cotton grows here
extremely well; the plants are often killed by frost in winter, but
they always produce abundantly the first year in which they are
sown. The cotton from which nankeen is made is of a particular
kind, naturally of a yellowish color.

"The large estates are managed by stewards and overseers, the
proprietors just amusing themselves with seeing what is going forward. The work is done wholly by slaves, whose numbers are in
this part of the country more than double that of white persons.
The slaves on the large plantations are in general very well provided for, and treated with mildness. During three months nearly,
that I was in Virginia, but two or three instances of ill treatment
towards them came under my observation. Their quarters, the
name whereby their habitations are called, are usually situated one
or two hundred yards from the dwelling house, which gives appearance of a village to the residence of every plantation in Virginia;
when the estate, however, is so large as to be divided into several
farms, then separate quarters are attached to the house of the overseer on each farm. Adjoining their little habitations, the slaves
commonly have small gardens and yards of poultry, which are all
of their property; they have ample time to attend to their own
concerns, and their gardens are generally found well stocked, and
their flocks of poultry numerous. Besides the food they raise for
themselves, they are allowed liberal rations of salted pork and
Indian corn. Many of their little huts are comfortably furnished,
and they are themselves, in general, extremely well clothed. In
short their condition is by no means so wretched as might be imagined. They are forced to work certain hours in the day; but in

return they are clothed, dieted, and lodged comfortably, and saved all anxiety about provision for their offspring. Still, however, let the condition of the slave be made ever so comfortable, as long as he is conscious of being the property of another man, who has it in his power to dispose of him according to the dictates of caprice; as long as he hears people around him talking about the blessings of liberty, and considers that he is in a state of bondage, it is not to be supposed that he can feel equally happy with the freeman. It is immaterial under what form slavery presents itself, whenever it appears there is ample cause for humanity to weep at the sight, and to lament that men can be found so forgetful of their own situations, as to live regardless of the blessings of their fellow creatures.

"With respect to the policy of holding slaves in any country, on account of the depravity of morals which it necessarily occasions, besides the many other evil consequences attendant upon it, so much has already been said by others, that it is needless here to make comments on the subject.

"The number of the slaves increases most rapidly, so that there is scarcely any state but what is overstocked. This is a circumstance complained of by every planter as the maintenance of more than are requisite for the culture of the estate is attended with great expense. Motives . . . of humanity deter them from selling the poor creatures, or turning them adrift from the spot where they have been born and brought up, in the midst of friends and relations.

"What I have here said, respecting the condition and treatment of slaves, appertains, it must be remembered, to those only who are upon the larger plantations in Virginia; the lot of such as are unfortunate enough to fall into the hands of the lower class of white people, and of hard task-masters in towns, is very different. In the Carolinas and Georgia again, slavery presents itself in very different colors from what it does even in its worst form in Virginia. I am told that it is no uncommon thing there, to see gangs of negroes staked at a horse race, and to see these unfortunate beings bandied about from one set of drunken gamblers to another for days together. How much to be deprecated are the laws which suffer such abuses to exist! Yet these are the laws enacted by the people who boast of their love of liberty and independence, and who presume to say, that it is in the breasts of Americans alone that the blessings of freedom are held in just estimation."—*Isaac Weld, Jr., "Travels through the States of North America and the provinces of Upper & Lower Canada, 1795, 96, 97*

provinces of Upper and Lower Canada," 1795, 1796, and 1797.
(London, 1799.)

JOHN DAVIS'S THOUGHTS ON SLAVERY

"The negroes on the plantation, including house-servants and children, amounted to a hundred; of whom the average price being respectively seventy pounds, made them aggregately worth seven thousand to their possessor.

"Two families lived in one hut, and such was their unconquerable propensity to steal, that they pilfered from each other. I have heard masters lament this defect in their negroes. But what else can be expected from man in so degraded a condition, that among the ancients the same word implied both a slave and a thief.

"Since the introduction of the culture of cotton in the State of South Carolina, the race of negroes has increased. Both men and women work in the field, and the labour of the rice plantation formerly prevented the pregnant negroes from bringing forth a long-lived offspring. It may be established as a maxim that on a plantation where there are many children, the work has been moderate. . . .

"Of genius in negroes many instances may be recorded. It is true that Mr. Jefferson has pronounced the Poems of Phillis Wheatley, below the dignity of criticism, and it is seldom safe to differ in judgment from the author of Notes on Virginia. But her conceptions are often lofty, and her versification often surpasses with unexpected refinement. Ladd, the Carolina poet, in enumerating the bards of his country, dwells with encomium on "Wheatley's polished verse"; nor is his praise undeserved, for often it will be found to glide in the stream of melody. Her lines on Imagination have been quoted with rapture by Imley of Kentucky, and Steadman the Guinea Traveler; but I have ever thought her happiest production the Goliath of Gath.

"Of Ignatius Sancho, Mr. Jefferson also speaks neglectingly; and remarks, that he substitutes sentiment for argumentation. But I know not that argumentation is required in a familiar epistle; and Sancho, I believe, has only published his correspondence."—John Davis, *"Travels of four years and a half in the United States of America during 1798, 1799, 1800, 1801, 1802,"* p. 86.

OBSERVATIONS OF ROBERT SUTCLIFF

"I had the curiosity to look into some of their little habitations; but all that I examined were wretched in the extreme and far inferior to many Indian cottages I have seen.

"I slept at C. A.'s and this morning set out for Fredericksburg, being accompanied by his young man, our road lying through the woods the greater part of the way. At the place where we dined, we were waited on by two mulatto girls, whose only clothing appeared to be loose garments of cotton and woollen cloth, girt round the waist with a small cord. I had observed that this was the common dress of the working female negroes in the fields; but when engaged in business in the house it seemed hardly sufficient to cover them. In the yard, I observed a number of slaves engaged in the management of a still, employed in making spirits from cider. Here again I had the curiosity to look into some of the negro huts, which like those I had seen, presented little else but dirt and rags.

"We came to Fredericksburg and lodged at Fisher's Tavern. The next morning I was waked early by the cries of a poor negro, who was undergoing a severe correction, previously to his going to work. On taking a walk on the banks of the Rappahannock, the river on which the town is seated, I stepped into one of the large tobacco warehouses which are built here, for the reception and inspection of that plant before it is permitted to be exported. On entering into conversation with an inspector, as he was employed in looking over a parcel of tobacco, he lamented the licentiousness which he remarked so generally prevailed in this town. He said, that in his remembrance, the principal part of the inhabitants were emigrants from Scotland, and that it was considered so reproachful to the white inhabitants, if they were found to have illicit connection with their female slaves, that their neighbors would shun the company of such, as of persons whom it was a reproach to be acquainted. The case was now so much altered that, he believed, there were but few slave holders in the place who were free from guilt in this respect: and that it was now thought but little of. Such was the brutality and hardness of heart which this evil produced, that many amongst them paid no more regard to selling their own children, by their females slaves, or even their brothers and sisters, in the same line, than they would do to the disposal of a cow or a horse, or any other property in the brute creation. To so low a degree of degradation does the system of negro slavery sink the white inhabitants, who are unhappily engaged in it."—Robert Sutcliff, *Travels in some parts of North America in Years 1804, 1805, 1806*, pp. 37–52.

SOME LETTERS OF RICHARD ALLEN AND ABSALOM JONES TO DOROTHY RIPLEY

Philadelphia, 1st, 5th month, 1803.—Naming my concern to some of my solid friends to have a meeting with the Africans, I influenced them to send for Absalom Jones, the Black Bishop, and Richard Allen, the Methodist Episcopal Preacher, who also was a coloured man, and the principal person of that congregation. A. Jones complied with my request, and appointed a meeting for me on first day evening, which was a solid time where many were deeply affected with the softening power of the Lord, who unloosed my tongue to proclaim of his love and goodness to the children of men, without respect to person or nation. There was a respectable number of coloured people, well dressed and very orderly, who conducted themselves as if they were desirous of knowing the mind of the Lord concerning them. The first and greatest commandment of Jesus Christ, the Law-giver, came before me: "Thou shalt love the Lord thy God with all thy heart, and with all thy soul and with all thy mind," which I endeavoured to enforce as their duty to their Creator who alone could make them happy by his blessing through their obedience to his lawful command. My own experience of thus loving him, I thought would illustrate it, therefore, added it to shew the possibility of pleasing him, and obtaining his divine favor, which was our interest and duty, as soon as we were able to distinguish right from wrong. To see them have this good house for worship, I told them rejoiced me much, and encouraged such as were servants present to be faithful in their situation, and seek the blessing of God, that at the last they might be happy in the enjoyment of his love forever. Supplicating the Throne of mercy in their behalf, my spirit was deeply humbled, and I felt power to plead with the Father on the account of the Africans every where, who were captivated by the oppressive power of men. When we had separated, my mind was much relieved from the weight which pressed my spirit while I had contemplated the matter, desiring to move by special direction of God.

A Letter which I received from Bethel Church.

"Madam,

"I have proposed to the Board of Trustees of Bethel Church your request respecting your speaking in our Church; they have candidly considered the same, and after due investigation, the board unanimously concludes, that as it is diametrically opposite to the letter and spirit of the rules of society in particular, and the discipline in general of the Methodist Episcopalian Church, They therefore are sorry to inform you, that it is not in their power to comply with your request.

"I am, madam,
"With much respect,
"Yours, &c.
"Richd. Allen."

"May 11, 1803."

After R. Allen had sent me this letter by way of denial, the Lord commanded me to "Stand still for I should most assuredly have his place to testify his goodness there." Putting the letter into my pocket, I silently waited for the answer of promise; and while I was thus watching the fulfilment of God's word, there came into my friend's house J. & P. P. two men who enquired if I could not be satisfied without an appointment with R. Allen's people, I said No: for that I believed it was required of me by God. They enquired if I had not received a letter as a denial, which I marvelled at, having shewn it to no person living. I answered their question by handing the letter to them which when they had read it they returned, and signified they would go themselves to see after an opportunity, and obtained permission after the minister had finished his sermon, he being desired to be concise to accomodate a stranger who was then concerned for them. I went to the meeting, or their church, and heard a short methodist sermon, which I thought very instructive, and added thereunto, respecting the conversion of "A man of Ethiopia, an eunuch of great authority under Candace, Queen of the Ethiopians, who had the charge of all her treasure, and had come to Jerusalem for to worship." This pleased them so much when it was opened, that they were willing that I should have another meeting on the second day evening at seven, which I attended, and was brought into great difficulty through an intoxicated soldier pressing by the crowd which stood without. A number of friends being there, were unsettled, fearing lest the house would come down upon us, and for my part, I was actually afraid of satan's malice, lest we should perish in this storm which he raised in a moment. The disquietude of the people made me tremble and shake every limb, not knowing what course to betake myself to for the preservation of us each. I therefore gave up speaking: but this only encouraged the accuser of the brethren, who had come there in the hearts of many, as well as in the poor drunkard, who was taken away and confined. Pouring out my soul to God, I vowed to serve him yet more faithfully, if he would quell the rage of the adversary, and cause us to depart in peace; and I was instantly directed to prostrate myself before him, in faith believing that no harm should befall any of us at that time, which doing commanded the care of Almighty God over us, and the blessing of the Most High to rest upon us, continuing wrestling for some time, knowing this was a powerful weapon against satan, for thus interrupting us in our solemn engagement with God. When I had prayed by the aid of his Holy Spirit, which calmed the minds of the people, I thought I would leave the subject until I came back again,[1] and so come suddenly upon the monster, if it was the will of God: but he pretended that he would do terrible things if I came thither again, so I suppose King Apollyon and I shall have a strong battle to combat, before I enter the house of God: for I mean to war with him on his own ground, and gain the victory before I enter there again. Concluding the meeting sooner than was expected, R. Allen stopped the congregation and told them, "It was no new thing which had happened to us then: for in the days of old, when the sons and daughters of God met together, satan presented himself also, to interrupt their peace." I was much pleased to hear what was advanced, as it shewed the preacher (although a coloured man) to have a knowledge of divine things, and able to attack the enemy of our souls in a suitable degree.

Feeling desirous to follow the Shepherd of my soul, and seeing no further work at this time for me, I leave this city in peace, requesting the Lord to bless the seed sown in great weakness, and to water it with the descending showers of his spiritual rain, that the glory may arise to him alone who is worthy to be praised by every creature, but especially by a worm whom he has preserved thus far from the destructive power of sin, and satan. I trust the Lord will repay each here who have contributed to comfort my soul in the day of distress and heavy travail, and I beseech him of his

[1] From England.

infinite mercy to forgive such as have blindly persecuted me, by saying unjust things of me, which they have reported merely to gratify the curiosity of others, without considering the waste of their precious moments, or that they will be accountable at the last for "Every idle word" that they may speak while on earth, if not repented of, by a gracious visitation of God's humbling power, which they will find painful, when his judgment, takes place in them to weigh all their words, thoughts, and actions.—Philadelphia, 5th month, 1803.

I have been five weeks and four days in New York, and the neighbouring plains, and have met with sympathizing friends to relieve my mind when full of anxious care concerning the vineyard of the Lord.—Several have told me that I was one of those strangers who should feed the flock of Israel by the appointment of God, which revives me when I consider how significant a creature I am in my own eyes.

The yearly meeting was large, and attended by some precious ministers, whose testimonies will cause them to be written on my heart as living epistles. How do I feel myself united with spiritual worshippers, who desire to ascribe all glory to the Father, through the Son's reigning power in them, by the sanctifying influence of the Holy Ghost which leads them into the depth of self-abasement, and gathers all their powers to centre them in the God of all grace and glory. I rejoice that ever I met with this people, whom I often lament for, because so many live not in the pure principle of Truth, which if they as a body did, the whole earth would soon be filled with the knowledge of the Lord. O that my advantages which I have had up and down among this people, may lead me to honor their God, whom the pure in heart are concerned to worship continually! I have had three large meetings with the Africans in this city, and have great reason to be thankful that the Lord aided me with his Spirit, helping my infirmities in the hour of necessity, when I stood in need of his assistance, standing up to exalt the great Redeemer who died for all nations. O that the Lord would bless my little labour of love among this people whom I have secretly mourned for!

I cannot avoid commending the citizens of New York and Philadelphia, for their help to those that have been greatly oppressed, driving slavery out of their States, that they may have the peace of God, and his belssing upon the heads of their children, and children's children. I trust also to see the efforts of individuals crowned with a blessing in the Southern States, where barrenness of the land bespeaks the poverty and wretchedness of thousands of its inhabitants who might enjoy the smile of Heaven, if they would learn to fear God and love their neighbor.

When comparing those States one with the other, what a vast difference there is between them in the outward appearance of things: but I trust the minds of the people to the southward, are not like the barren appearance of many parts I have already travelled, or may yet have to do: for I perceive the Lord intends me to return back to discharge my duty to him, and the people up and down.

I have received the following letters from Philadelphia and think them worthy to make up a page or two in my life.

Letter from Absalom Jones, Black Bishop of the Episcopal Church, in Philadelphia, addressed to Dorothy Ripley, at New York, dated Philadelphia, June 3, 1803.

Dear Friend,

It is with pleasure that I now sit down to inform you, that your kind and very affectionate letter came safe to hand; and am happy to hear that kind Providence has conducted you so far on your journey in health of body as well as of mind; and I trust that the Lord will continue to be your Guide, and that your labours may prove as great a blessing to the inhabitants of New-York, as they have been to numbers in this city.

Your letter I read with care and attention, as well as many others of my congregation, and I heartily thank you for your friendly advice and godly admonitions; believing them to have been given in that love which purifies the heart. I am very sensible that the charge committed to my care is very great; and am also fully convinced of my own inability for so great an undertaking. And I do assure you, that when I was called to the task, I trembled at the idea, and was ready to say, "Who am I." But when I consider that God can send by whom he will, and as you very justly have observed, he sometimes makes use of the feeblest instruments for the promotion of Truth; I say under these considerations, I was led to believe that the Lord would perfect strength in my weakness; and glory be to his ever-adorable Name for it. I have cause to believe, my labour has not been altogether in vain.

You wish to know the number I consider to be under my care. Our list of members contains about five hundred, although we have a great many more who constantly attend worship in our church, of whom I have a comfortable hope that they will be brought unto the knowledge of the Truth.

My wife joins me in love. I remain, with sentiments of high esteem and respect,

Your esteemed Friend,

ABSALOM JONES

LETTER FROM AN AFRICAN MINISTER, RESIDENT IN PHILADELPHIA ADDRESSED TO DOROTHY RIPLEY

PHILADELPHIA, 24th, of 6th mo. 1803.

Friend Ripley,

I Received thy epistle, dated New-York, 26th of 5th month, with much joy, thanks and satisfaction; and am thankful for thy kind spiritual advice, and grateful for thy concern for me and my people.

With the assistance of the good Spirit, I will attend to thy serious admonitions in the Lord, and listen to the small still voice of Christ within, as thou dost observe in thy epistle, for it is He that must enable me to observe his holy law written on the heart by his Spirit.

I wish to take thy sisterly counsel; but O! my abounding weakness. I wish to be more sensible of it, so that I alone may feel it. I would hide it from my friends, but they are too eagle-eyed not to discover it; yet they have the charity to bear with me.—I often bow at the foot-stool of divine mercy, that I may obtain strength to overcome corrupt nature.—None knows but myself my strivings to walk in the narrow way, in which the poor worm has no desire to rob God of his honor. I see the beauty of nakedness to be far superior than to be clothed with rags of self-righteousness.

Thou enquirest how many communicants there are in our church. The precise number of my communicants is 457. All our members are communicants. There is a communion of saints which exceeds all formality, and which even the Apostles were ignorant of, when they gave an account to their Master, on their return from their mission, and told him, "We saw men casting out devils in thy name, and we forbade them, because they followed not us." Yet I still continue of the same mind, that it would be best for thee to be a member of some religious society.—The teachings of Priscilla and Aquila have been found profitable to the eloquent and wise.

The members of the African Methodist Episcopal church (called Bethel) live in love and harmony with each other.

My fellow laborer, Absalom Jones, joins me in a salutation of love to thee, with desires for thy growth and increase in the favor of God: He says he would have written to thee, had he known of thy continuance at New-York.

Praying God to bless and make thee instrumental in promoting his glory and the good of souls, I remain, thine, &c.

RICHARD ALLEN

LETTER FROM AN AFRICAN, RESIDENT IN PHILADELPHIA, TO DOROTHY RIPLEY

May 17, 1803.

Respected Friend,

I am perhaps presumptuous in troubling you to read this. But cannot let slip an opportunity of addressing you with what I wish you to know even when you have arrived at your native country, and may contemplate on a subject which I hope will not displease you, and I will thank Heaven I have it in my power to let one amongst the people called Quakers[2] see, written by the hand of an African, the sentiments of his soul. I mean only to trouble you with the obligations that race of people, myself amongst that great multitude, are to you indebted; and may the unremitting pains which have been taken not fall to the ground. We have been oppressed with cruelty and the heavy task-masters in the West Indies and the southern States of America for many centuries back, with not only the horrible weight of bondage, but have been subject to heavy iron chains, too heavy to bear, had not the Creator of all things framed our constitutions to bear them, and all the deep cuts and lashes the inhuman-hearted drivers please to mangle us with. Had not the all-directing hand of Providence made us come under the notice of the Friends, who formed an abolition society for our relief, many thousands of us would be dragging out our lives in wretchedness, like those of our brethren who have never yet tasted the sweet cup of liberty. Yet while the nations of Europe are contending to catch the draught, the African is forbidden to lift up his head towards it. Every man has a right to his liberty, and we

---

[2] He expected I was a member of that society, which I never yet have been.

must by the ties of nature come under the title of men: but are dragged from our native land, in our old age or in our infancy, and sold as the brute, to the planters; the infant dragged from its parents, and the husband from wife and children, and hurried into the cane field, to give independence to their owners, and annex abundance to their riches. And how is this, that God created us amongst the rest of human beings, and yet man would level us with the brute? We were not all born Christians, but many have become so; and I pray Heaven many thousands of us may be received at the bar of God amongst the righteous at his right hand, and with you glorify him in Heaven for ever. I pray that the Africans may enjoy his holy privileges, and let their light shine before men.

The cross[3] you met with in your sermon at Bethel African church grieved me much, but it originated with white men. Had it been one of my complexion, it would prey on my feelings to the very heart. But I hope you will forget it. If I was a converted soul in the Lord, I could address you on a more spiritual subject. But alas! I am an unfortunate being not born a second time. Yet weak as I am, the prayers of an unconverted African shall be offered to Heaven for your happiness on earth, and in the world to come life everlasting. And may the vessel in which you may embark for England be attended with a fair and pleasant passage, and land you safe on its shores. And when you shall lay your head on a dying pillow, to leave this troublesome world, may you be surrounded with a blessed convoy of angels to attend you to the Throne of God.

I am, Yours,

OF THE AFRICAN RACE

—"*The Extraordinary Conversion and Religious Experience of Dorothy Ripley with her First Voyage in America,*" 132–144.

[3] The cross here mentioned has an allusion to an attempt made by an intoxicated soldier, to disturb our peace, who caused great confusion for a few moments; but kneeling in the midst of this tempestuous storm, God instantly caused a calm, so that no one received harm.

BOOK REVIEWS

The Aftermath of the Civil War, in Arkansas. By POWELL CLAY-
TON, Governor of Arkansas, 1868 to 1871. Neale Publishing
Company, New York, 1915. Pp. 378.

Looking at the title of this work the student of history would
expect that same scientific treatment which is observed in so many
of the Reconstruction studies. On the contrary, he finds in this a
mere volume of memoirs of a political leader completed in his
eighty-second year. The work gives an account of the author's own
administration as governor of Arkansas ''also of those events that
commenced before and extended into it, and those that occurred
during that period and continued beyond it.''

In view of the fact that he, a man of well-known partisan pro-
clivities, may be charged with criticising his defenseless and dead
contemporaries the author says that he endeavored to substantiate
''every controvertible and important conclusion.'' To do this he
collected ''an immense amount of documentary evidence'' from
which he selected the most appropriate for that purpose. The
writer made use of certain documents in the Library of Congress
and had frequent recourse to the *Arkansas Gazette.*

The book as a whole is essentially political history. It is chiefly
concerned with ''the Murphy Government,'' the ''Organization and
Operations of the Klu Klux Klan,'' ''Martial Law,'' and the peculiar situation in the counties of Crittenden and Conway. The
subjects of immigration, education, State aid to railroads, and the
funding of the State debt are all mentioned but they suffer because
of the preference given to the discussion of political questions.
When one has read the book he is still uninformed as to what was
the actual working of the economic and social forces in Arkansas
during this period.

This work, however, is valuable for several reasons. In the first
place, whether the reader agrees with the author or not, he gathers
from page to page facts which throw light on other conditions.
Moreover, consisting mainly of a discussion of extracts from various
records it is a good source book for students who have not access
to the documents the author has used. It is also important to
get the viewpoint of the distinguished author who lived through

what he writes of and is now sufficiently far removed from the struggle to study it somewhat sympathetically.

C. R. WILSON

Black and White in the Southern States. By MAURICE S. EVANS, C.M.G. Longmans, Green and Company, London, 1915. Pp. 209.

This book cannot be considered an historical work. Yet when the author makes a survey of the slavery and Reconstruction periods with a view to estimating what the Negro has been, what has been done for him, and what he himself has accomplished, it claims the attention of historians. From this historic retrospect the author approaches such questions as the Negroes' grievances, their political rights and wrongs, blood admixture, race hostility and grounds for hope and the like.

The author has had experiences in South Africa and traveled in the United States with a view to studying the condition of the descendants of the African race in this country. His effort seems to be to write such a work as some of those of Sir H. H. Johnson or W. P. Livingstone. He justifies the writing of this work on the ground that "the partisan spirit, partial to one race or other, permeates most of the writings on this subject." Feeling that the issues involved are too great, he hoped to avoid this "that no preconceived ideas or partiality should be allowed to cloud clarity of view, or warp the judgment."

Yet although the author speaks well of his good intentions, it is apparent that he did not live up to this profession. In the first place, the work is not scientific, facts are not "observed and noted with scrupulous care," and conclusions are drawn without warranted data to support them. On the whole then, one must say that this work fails to unravel some "knots in this tangled skein of human endeavor and error." When after a survey of the history of the Negro during the last fifty years an investigator concludes that the Negro has shown an incapacity for commerce and finance, and that he must not struggle to equip himself in the same way that the white man has, one must believe that the writer has not the situation thoroughly in hand. The great difficulty of the author seems to be that he did not remain in the country long enough to know it, did not give sufficient time to the study of conditions, and based his conclusions largely on information obtained from persons who were either too prejudiced or had neither the scientific point of view nor adequate mental development to describe social conditions.

It is not surprising, therefore, that the author asserts that the record of the Negro during the last fifty years shows that they are chiefly valuable as laborers in drudgery, or weak in foresight and thrift, and unfit for city life. Yet he believes that there is some hope for the blacks, since they can get work and buy land and thereby become economically independent. He calls attention to such injustices as miscegenation, lynching, unfairness of the courts, and discrimination in traveling.   W. R. WARD

Samuel Coleridge-Taylor—Musician. His Life and Letters. By W. C. BERWICK SAYERS. Cassell and Company, London, 1915. Pp. 328.

In this work we have the first extensive account of Samuel Coleridge-Taylor. The author of this volume has succeeded in producing a sympathetic and interesting narrative of the life of one of the greatest musicians of his time. Taking up his birth and childhood and then his college days, ending in the romance which attached him to a young Croydon girl, the author does not delay in bringing the reader to a consideration of those fundamentals which made Samuel Coleridge-Taylor famous. . . .

Much space is devoted to Coleridge-Taylor's achievement of success with his "Ballade in A Minor." How Sir Edward Elgar extended the promising composer a welcoming hand and arranged for him to write for a concert a short orchestral piece which turned out to be the artist's first great success is well described. The author emphasizes the barbaric strain and orchestral coloring, the prominently marked features which made the composer great.

The next task of the author is to show how the "essential beauty, naïve simplicity, unaffected expression and unforced idealism," of Longfellow's "Hiawatha" stirred the artist and set him composing an unambitious cantata which resulted in "Hiawatha's Wedding Feast," and the "Song of Hiawatha." The expressions of enthusiasm and the eulogies which crowned the musician as one of the greatest artists that Great Britain has produced justly constitute a large portion of the work.

His "Visit to America" is an important chapter of the volume. The manner in which the oppressed of his race received him in their troubled land is treated in detail, and the names of the per-

---

sons and organizations that arose to welcome him are given honorable mention. The author brings out too that so impressed was Coleridge-Taylor with the frank recognition of pure music in America that he once "contemplated the desirability of emigrating to this land."

The book abounds with letters and extracts from publications, which enable the reader to learn for himself how the artist's work was appreciated. The volume is well illustrated. In it appear the early portraits of Coleridge-Taylor's mother, of himself, and family, and home, and of the Coleridge-Taylor Society in Washington, D. C. Not only persons who appreciate music but all who have an intelligent interest in the achievements of the Negro should read this work.　　　　　　　　　　　　　　　　　　　J. R. Davis

Race Orthodoxy in the South and other Aspects of the Negro Problem. By Thomas Pearce Bailey, Ph.D. The Neale Publishing Company, New York, 1914.

The author of this volume has a long intellectual pedigree. Pedigrees are important in authors who write on the race problem. This is particularly true when they attempt to tell us what the orthodox opinion of the South is regarding the Nego. Much that passes for Southern opinion on the Negro is too violent to be taken at its face value. Other interpretations of the South have too frequently been the individual views of eminent men of Southern origin who no longer hold orthodox views.

The author discusses some of these interpretations and criticises them. There are four principal types. There is the philosophical view, represented by Edgar Gardiner Murphy's "*The Basis of Ascendancy.*" Mr. Murphy "is one of the choicest specimens of noble character that the South has produced," but he came under Northern influences and his book represents a struggle between Northern and Southern points of view. "The first part of his book seems to be, in the main, pro-Southern and defensive of the South, while the latter part becomes largely Northern and critical of the South." He does not succeed, in the opinion of the author, in synthesizing these two divergent views.

The second type is sociological, represented by "*The Southerner,*" a novel written in the form of an autobiography or, perhaps, rather an autobiography written in the form of a novel. The author is supposed to be Walter Hines Page, at present American ambassador to Great Britain. Of this book Mr. Bailey says: "The author is not a Southerner of the spirit, whatever he may be of the flesh. There is something of North Carolina and something of Massachusetts in his attitude, but none of the all-inclusive Americanism that alone is able to write about the South with sympathy of the heart yet with balanced discrimination."

To understand the South one must have lived in South Carolina, and understand the "apparent violence" of Ben Tilman, or in Mississippi, the home of Senator Vardaman. The South, the orthodox South, is today as it was before the war, the "far South"; but the sentiments which dominate it are not now, as in slavery days, the sentiments of the "master class" but rather those of the "poor white man."

The third type of interpretation is represented here by "Uncle Tom's Cabin." The criticism of this book is so subtle that it is difficult to indicate the outlines of it in a single paragraph. The difficulty with Mrs. Stowe's interpretation of the South and the Negro is that she, just as certain Southern humanitarians of the present day, is inclined to treat the Negroes as a class. She does not regard them as a race, a different breed, whose blood is a contamination. "No one," says the writer, "has come within shouting distance of the real Negro problem who does not appreciate this distinction. Indeed, almost everything critical that can be alleged against Uncle Tom's Cabin springs from the failure of its humanitarian author to sympathize with race consciousness as such."

Finally there is the scientific interpretation of Southern sentiment, and the "race instinct" which is back of most Southern opinion in regard to the Negro. This scientific interpretation is represented by Boas, "The Mind of Primitive Man." "Ultimately," according to Professor Boas, "this phenomenon (race instinct) is a repetition of the old instinct and fear of the connubium of the patricians and the plebeians, of the European nobility and the common people, or of the castes of India. The emotions and reasoning are the same in every respect."

To this scientific exposition of the Southern attitude Mr. Bailey replies: "Even if it could be scientifically proved that an infusion of Negro blood would help the white race, the prejudice against a really great branch of the white race like the Jews is sufficient warning to us not to confine our discussion of race problems to the question of equality or inequality of physical and mental endowment."

What then is race orthodoxy? Where shall we look for a true

statement of the attitude of the South on the subject of the Negro since none of these attempts at interpretation have done justice to it? The racial creed has been expressed at different times in a number of pithy expressions current in the Southern states. Here they are in order as the author gives them: "Blood will tell; the white race must dominate; the Teutonic peoples stand for race purity; the Negro is inferior and will remain so; this is a white man's country." Let there be no social equality; no political equality. In matters of civil rights and legal adjustments give the white man as opposed to the colored man the benefit of the doubt. In educational policy let the Negro have the crumbs that fall from the white man's table. Let there be such industrial education of the Negro as will fit him to serve the white man. Only Southerners understand the Negro question. Let the South settle the Negro question. The status of peasantry is all the Negro may hope for, if the races are to live together in peace. Let the lowest white man count for more than the highest Negro. The above statements indicate the leadings of Providence.

This statement of the Southern creed is practically the common opinion of the South. It is not the only opinion. It is not, perhaps, the "best" opinion. But is it right opinion? Mr. Bailey thinks it is, in its underlying meaning at any rate, but not in its "present shape." His book may be said, on the whole, to be an interpretation and a justification of this "underlying meaning."

Race orthodoxy in the South is, take it all in all, the most candid statement of the race problem; the most searching, suggestive and revealing interpretation of the attitude of the Southern white man that has ever been written. The book is, however, merely a statement of the problem and not a solution. Rather it is intended, as the author suggests again and again, to provoke and stimulate—not discussion, heaven forbid,—but inquiry, investigation. In spite of the fact that the author professes his personal loyalty to the dogma upon which race orthodoxy is founded, still, by stating it in the clear and candid way in which he has, in pointing out with unflinching directness the moral cul-de-sac into which it has forced the Southern people, he has at once enabled and compelled them to put their faith on rational grounds. His is the higher criticism in race creeds, and it is hard to tell where criticism once started will lead.   ROBERT E. PARK

NOTES

Mr. Monroe N. Work has brought out the *Negro Year Book for 1916–1917*. In keeping with the progress hitherto shown this edition surpasses that of last year. Here one finds an unusually large collection of statistical material as to the economic, social and religious progress of the black race; and a brief account of what exceptional Negroes have done to distinguish themselves in various fields. It contains also a brief history of the Negro given in such succinct statements as will please the hurried reader and meet the requirements of those who have not access to reference libraries.

The striking new feature of the work, however, is a brief account of what leading thinkers and the press have said about such perplexing problems as the "Birth of a Nation," "Miscegenation," and "Segregation." The editor has endeavored to present in popular style a brief account of everything of importance with which the Negro has been concerned during the year. He has done his task well. Sold at such a reasonable price as thirty-five cents a copy, this valuable book should find its way to the home of every one who desires to keep himself informed on what the Negro is actually achieving.

The United Brethren Publishing Co., Huntington, Ind., has published M. B. Butler's *My Story of the Civil War and the Underground Railroad*. A native of Vermont, where he had an opportunity to see many a fugitive on his way to freedom, the author naturally makes his narrative interesting and straightforward. He recounts his unusual experiences as a soldier in detail but does not grow tiresome.

In the Mississippi Valley, Historical Review, II, March, 1916, appeared Doctor H. N. Sherwood's *Early Negro Deportation Projects*. This is a selected part of the author's doctorate thesis. It treats of the endeavors to ameliorate the condition of emancipated slaves and the colonization plans which finally led to the establishment of the republic of Liberia.

The *Tennessee Historical Magazine* for June contains a dissertation by Asa Earl Martin, entitled *Anti-Slavery Activities of the*

Methodist Episcopal Church in Tennessee. The article covers the period from 1784 to the time of the great schism of 1844.

Professor Tenny Frank has contributed to the July number of the *American Historical Review* a valuable article entitled *Race Mixture in the Roman Empire.*

In the same number of this publication appear also twenty-three pages of documents on the *Cane Sugar Industry* collected by Irene A. Wright. As the Negroes proved to be a great factor in the development of this industry, these documents will be helpful to those who desire to study the bearing of the Negro on its origin and early growth.

Miss Helen Nicolay has turned over to the Library of Congress some important Lincoln Manuscripts, among which are the first and second autograph copies of the Gettysburg Address, the autograph of the Second Inaugural Address, and the President's memorandum of August 23, 1864, pledging support to the next administration.

In *The Case for the Filipino,* Maximo M. Kalaw gives an account of the American occupation of the Archipelago, and in presetning his claims for independence he puts his countrymen in the attitude of an oppressed people.

Dr. C. G. Woodson delivered at the University of Chicago in July a lecture on *The varying Attitude of the White Man toward the Negro in the United States.*

A HAPPY SUGGESTION

My dear Dr. Woodson: I am in receipt of the current number of THE JOURNAL OF NEGRO HISTORY and am more and more delighted with it. I think it furnishes the richest source for available information on the Negro that I have yet found. The leading article in this number is inspiring as well as illuminating and the idea has come to me that it would be an excellent thing to have history reading circles organized in all our schools for the purpose of systematically reading the JOURNAL. A hundred or more such organizations with the JOURNAL as a text would accomplish two or three very valuable things, viz., promote the circulation of the JOURNAL and disseminate historical knowledge of the race so necessary to give it self-respect and pride. These historical clubs might meet monthly and include others than teachers. By all means your work should not lack for funds for keeping it going.

I hope to interest the colored High School Alumni here at its annual meeting next week. I shall also call the attention of my teachers here to your publication. It is great.

Very truly yours,

J. W. SCOTT,

Principal, Douglass High School,

Huntington, W. Va.

INDEX TO VOLUME I.

www.ingramcontent.com/pod-product-compliance
Lightning Source LLC
Chambersburg PA
CBHW041929260326
41914CB00009B/1230